Direct Democracy and the Courts

Who should have the last word on fundamental policy issues? This book analyzes the rise of two contenders – the people, through direct democracy, and the courts. Introduced in the United States during the Progressive Era and now available in nearly half the states, direct democracy has surged in recent decades. Through an outpouring of ballot measures, voters have slashed taxes, mandated government spending, imposed term limits on elected officials, enacted campaign finance reform, barred affirmative action, banned same-sex marriage, and adopted many other controversial laws. In several states, citizens now bypass legislatures to make the most important policy decision
This book demonstrates tl   _ _s nave used _n _x___ _ _ p ___ _ _li-
cial review to invalidate citizen-enacted laws at remarkably high rates. The resulting conflict between the people and the courts threatens to produce a popular backlash against judges and raises profound questions about the proper scope of popular sovereignty and judicial power in a constitutional system.

Kenneth P. Miller is an associate professor of Government at Claremont McKenna College in California. He holds a BA from Pomona College, a JD from Harvard Law School, and a PhD from the University of California at Berkeley. His most recent publication is a volume coedited with Frédérick Douzet and Thad Kousser titled *The New Political Geography of California* (2008). He has published articles on topics including the initiative process, the recall of California governor Gray Davis, and the federal Voting Rights Act. He has also served as a political analyst in various media outlets, including National Public Radio, BBC World Service Radio, and the *Los Angeles Times*.

Direct Democracy and the Courts

KENNETH P. MILLER
Claremont McKenna College

CAMBRIDGE
UNIVERSITY PRESS

CAMBRIDGE UNIVERSITY PRESS
Cambridge, New York, Melbourne, Madrid, Cape Town, Singapore,
São Paulo, Delhi, Dubai, Tokyo

Cambridge University Press
32 Avenue of the Americas, New York, NY 10013-2473, USA

www.cambridge.org
Information on this title: www.cambridge.org/9780521747714

First published 2009

Printed in the United States of America

A catalog record for this publication is available from the British Library.

Library of Congress Cataloging in Publication data

Miller, Kenneth P.
Direct democracy and the courts / Kenneth P. Miller.
    p.   cm.
Includes bibliographical references and index.
ISBN 978-0-521-76564-0 (hardback) – ISBN 978-0-521-74771-4 (pbk.)
1. Direct democracy – United States.   2. Judicial review – United States.   I.   Title.
JF494.M55   2009
328.273–dc22   2009010900

ISBN 978-0-521-76564-0 Hardback
ISBN 978-0-521-74771-4 Paperback

Contents

List of Tables and Figures

Preface

As a native of California, I grew up in a state where citizens expect, as a birthright, to vote directly on questions of public policy. Multitudes in my state (and in several other states that have adopted the initiative process), regularly exercise this power. Sometimes dutifully, other times enthusiastically, we cast votes for or against citizen-initiated laws. Having participated in this process, I easily understand the appeal of a system that allows citizens to weigh the pros and cons of a policy proposal and vote "yes" or "no."

I never considered the potential disadvantages of direct democracy until the late 1980s, when I worked for a year as a legislative assistant in the California state senate. As part of my orientation, I met with several legislative leaders. One of them said, "The initiative process has become more powerful than the legislature in this state. A big part of what we do here is clean up after ballot initiatives. You begin to feel like the guy who follows the parade and sweeps up after the elephants!"

That provocative remark made a lasting impression. It caused me to think more seriously about the quality of laws enacted through the initiative process, the institutional conflict between direct democracy and representative government, and the place of direct democracy in a constitutional system.

Several years later, as I began a graduate program at the University of California at Berkeley, my interest turned to the conflict between the initiative process and the courts. At the time, many controversial California initiatives (addressing affirmative action, term limits, campaign finance reform, open primaries, immigrant social services, bilingual education, tribal gaming, and criminal punishment, among other issues) were tied up in litigation. I found it striking that judges had somehow assumed a central role in the California initiative process. I wanted to learn how and why that had happened and to see whether other states had similar experiences.

Eventually, my attempts to answer those questions produced a dissertation, several articles, and this book. During the time I worked on the project, new controversies emerged, including the fight between popular majorities and courts over same-sex marriage. These developments confirmed the theoretical and practical importance of this conflict and renewed my hope that the book will help readers understand its dynamics.

Many people generously contributed to the book. At U.C. Berkeley, Bruce Cain, Sandy Muir, and Bob Kagan were outstanding mentors. They helped me develop a theoretical framework for analyzing the conflict between direct democracy and judicial review and an empirical approach that combined my interests in history and law. As I learned more about the initiative process, I drew on the work of many fine scholars who are listed in the notes and references. At various times, I also received specific help and encouragement from Richard Ellis, Hans Linde, Dan Lowenstein, Shaun Bowler, Dane Waters, Gerald Uelmen, Dan Smith, Liz Gerber, Thad Kousser, Todd Donovan, John Dinan, and Peter Schrag.

A small legion of current and former students also provided valuable assistance. They tracked down obscure information on initiatives, summarized numerous legal cases, and confirmed other facts and citations. Morgan Rice and Laura Sucheski deserve special mention. They both made long-term commitments to this book, and their contributions were indispensable. Deonne Contine, Taryn Benarroch, Justin Levitt, Carl Vos, and Brendan Sasso also ably completed various research tasks. Finally, Andrew Lee, Josh Schneider, Abhi Nemani, and Jacinth Sohi, with their student research teams at the Rose Institute of State and Local Government, helped me build a 24-state initiative database. This resource, which provides searchable information on the initiatives and challenges summarized in these pages, is hosted at the Rose Institute's Web site, www.cmc.edu/rose.

The project was sustained by generous institutional support. At Berkeley, the Institute of Governmental Studies, under the leadership of Bruce Cain and Jack Citrin, provided a congenial research environment, an outstanding library, and expert assistance from research librarians Terry Dean and Ben Burch. At Claremont McKenna College, the Rose Institute, under the leadership of Ralph Rossum and Florence Adams, supplied research teams and other resources to support the book's empirical elements; the late Ruth Schooley at Honnold Library offered crucial research assistance; and the Dean of Faculty Greg Hess provided a junior research leave and funding for summer research.

I am greatly indebted to Eric Crahan at Cambridge University Press, who clearly understood my vision for the book and expertly shepherded it to publication. At various stages, the manuscript also benefited from careful reading by Sandy Muir, Joe Bessette, Eric Helland, and Kathy Uradnik, as well as the anonymous reviewers and the production staff at Cambridge University Press.

Finally, I wish to thank my parents and other members of my family. Over the years, they have given me abundant encouragement and support. With gratitude, I dedicate the book to them.

Introduction: A Clash of Rising Powers

A century ago, the Progressive Era's enthusiasm for "experiments in government" led many states to embrace new forms of direct democracy.[1] The experiments included recall of public officials, popular referendum over acts of the legislature, and, most consequentially, the citizen's initiative process.[2] The initiative device allowed citizens to propose laws, place them on the ballot, and enact them at the polls by simple majority vote.[3] For the first time, popular majorities could bypass their representatives and directly dictate policy – an innovation that challenged long-established principles of American constitutional design. But, radical though they were, the reforms did not abolish representative institutions nor create what James Madison would call a "pure democracy."[4] Instead, the initiative, referendum, and recall were grafted into state constitutions alongside the legislature, executive, and courts to create a new, hybrid constitutional system, part representative, part direct.[5] With these

---

[1] See Elihu Root, "Experiments in Government and the Essentials of the Constitution," in Robert Bacon and James Brown Scott, eds. *Addresses on Government and Citizenship* (Cambridge: Harvard University Press, 1916), 77–97.

[2] The recall allows citizens to circulate a petition to force an election to remove an official from office before the normal expiration of his or her term. The popular referendum allows citizens to challenge laws recently enacted by the government. After the law is enacted, citizens have a limited amount of time to circulate petitions to place it on the ballot. If voters defeat the law, it is void. For further descriptions of direct democracy devices such as referendum and recall, see e.g., David Butler and Austin Ranney, eds., *Referendums: A Comparative Study of Practice and Theory* (Washington, D.C.: American Enterprise Institute for Public Policy Research, 1978); Thomas E. Cronin, *Direct Democracy: The Politics of Initiative, Referendum and Recall* (Cambridge: Harvard University Press, 1989), 125–56.

[3] Specific rules for qualifying and adopting initiatives vary from state to state. For a discussion, see Chapter 1.

[4] James Madison, *Federalist* 10 in Alexander Hamilton, James Madison, and John Jay, *The Federalist Papers*, Clinton Rossiter, ed. (New York: Signet Classic, 2003), 76.

[5] For other discussions of this system as a "hybrid," see, e.g., Elizabeth Garrett, "Hybrid Democracy," 73 GEO. WASH. L. REV. 1096 (2005); Shaun Bowler and Amihai Glazer, "Hybrid

experiments in place, it remained to be seen how they would work – how direct democracy and representative institutions would interact in different states, under various circumstances, and over time.

This book analyzes the relationship between two of these powers – the initiative process and the courts – over the past century. This relationship is compelling because the two forces are near opposites. Whereas the initiative process is designed to translate the majority's preferences into law, judicial review is designed in part to counter majorities. Of course, judicial review is not a general power of *veto*; courts can strike down the will of the people only if it is unconstitutional, not if it is merely unwise. But, if they choose, courts can exercise the power expansively, in ways that aggressively counter the majority will.

Moreover, courts are often the only effective institutional check on citizen-initiated laws. The reformers designed the initiative process to bypass the legislature and the executive, but they could not make it bypass the courts. From the earliest days of the Republic, courts have asserted the power to strike down any state law that conflicts with state constitutions or the Constitution of the United States. Because this power extends to laws enacted directly by the people, courts provide a broad institutional limitation on the people's rule.

Although judicial oversight of initiatives guards against the dangers of pure majority rule, it also creates an extreme form of what legal scholar Alexander Bickel called the "counter-majoritarian difficulty."[6] Normally, a court exercising judicial review overturns the decisions of another branch of the government, but, when it strikes down an initiative, it overrides the people themselves. With the stroke of a pen, a few judges can thwart the will of thousands or even millions of voters. To cite one example, in the late 1990s, citizens in Washington State, tiring of high taxes, used the initiative process to impose limits on state taxes and fees. The measure won a decisive victory, with nearly one million citizens voting to enact it. But, shortly after the election, a Washington state judge struck down the initiative on state constitutional grounds.[7] Emerging from the courthouse, the measure's sponsor exclaimed: "One guy with a robe on, but he might as well wear a crown if he is going to act like a king!"[8] And,

---

Democracy and Its Consequences," in Shaun Bowler and Amihai Glazer, eds., *Direct Democracy's Impact on American Political Institutions* (New York: Palgrave Macmillan, 2008), 1–19.

[6] Alexander M. Bickel, *The Least Dangerous Branch: The Supreme Court at the Bar of Politics* (New York: Bobbs-Merrill, 1962), 16.

[7] On November 2, 1999, Washington voters adopted Initiative 695, a measure to reduce vehicle license fees and require voter approval for future tax and fee increases. The vote on the measure was 992,715 Yes to 775,054 No, a 58-to-42 percent margin. On March 14, 2000, on cross motions for summary judgment, Washington Superior Court Judge Robert Alsdorf issued a written decision striking down the initiative in its entirety. On appeal, the Washington Supreme Court affirmed, holding that the initiative conflicted with several state constitutional provisions. See *Amalgamated Transit Union Local 587 v. State of Washington*, 142 Wash.2d 183 (2000).

[8] The initiative's sponsor, Tim Eyman, is quoted in David Postman, "I-695 Ruling Fuels Debate over Role of Courts," *The Seattle Times*, April 11, 2000, B-1.

indeed, conflicts of this type raise the question: Who is sovereign in this system – the people or the judges?

American judges have long subscribed to John Marshall's maxim that "it is emphatically the province and duty of the judicial department to say what the law is."[9] In practice, this means that if a court and the people disagree about a constitutional issue, the court's view must prevail. But, Progressive Era reformers, frustrated by opposition from the courts, sought to reverse this hierarchy by giving the people, not courts, the last word on contested state constitutional questions. Notably, Theodore Roosevelt promoted a plan for "recall" of judicial decisions, which would have allowed citizens of a state to approve or reject a court's ruling that a law violated the state's constitution. Roosevelt's plan failed, but in some states a different form of direct democracy, the initiative constitutional amendment (ICA), achieved similar ends. Armed with the ICA, citizens could override an unpopular judicial interpretation of a state constitution by directly amending the constitution. This form of direct democracy would not constrain judicial interpretation of the *federal* Constitution, but it gave the people in several states a counterweight to the judicial power.

The conflict between direct democracy and courts has become more intense as the two powers have gained strength. Twenty-four states now allow citizens to enact laws directly, and the use of the initiative process in the United States has grown several-fold since the 1970s. In several states, especially in the West, citizens have increasingly sought to use the initiative process to dictate outcomes in the most important areas of state responsibility, including taxing and spending, education, environmental regulation, election law, and criminal justice policy. At the same time, the judicial power has greatly expanded as courts have used judicial review to enforce a growing sphere of minority and individual rights, especially in the areas of equal protection, due process, privacy, free speech, and criminal procedure and punishment. By redefining many political controversies in rights terms, courts have shifted much policy making from majoritarian political processes to the judicial arena.

A recent controversy in California shows how a constitutional system that combines a strong form of direct democracy and an expansive judicial power can produce dramatic conflict.

IN RE MARRIAGE CASES

When California voters went to the polls on March 7, 2000, they faced a long list of decisions. The ballot included primary elections for U.S. president and various federal, state, and local legislative offices as well as 20 statewide ballot propositions, some placed on the ballot by the legislature, others by citizens through initiative petition. In all, the twenty propositions, including text, summaries, and arguments, filled 164 pages in the state ballot pamphlet. The shortest measure, Proposition 22, was a citizen initiative. Just 14 words

---

[9] *Marbury v. Madison*, 5 U.S. 137, 177 (1803).

long, it sought to add Section 308.5 to the state Family Code to read, "Only marriage between a man and a woman is valid or recognized in California."[10]

Proposition 22 was sponsored by Republican state legislator (and former Air Force test pilot) Pete Knight. Knight believed that the emerging movement for same-sex marriage threatened the marriage institution. He wanted to resist this movement in California, but was unable to convince his legislative colleagues to ban the recognition of same-sex marriages. Although polls showed that a majority of California voters wanted to preserve marriage as a union between a man and a woman, the legislature killed several of Knight's bills designed to set these limits.[11] Knight thus turned to the initiative process.

Beginning in 1997, Knight and a coalition of religious groups pursued an effort to place the nation's first citizen-initiated defense of marriage law on the California ballot.[12] At the outset, the proponents had to reach agreement on the measure's language. Based on research indicating that the proposal had the best chance of success if drafted in concise, easy-to-understand language, the proponents settled on the simple one-sentence text. Next, the proponents had to make the crucial decision whether to qualify the measure as an initiative statute or a state constitutional amendment. In California, as in many other initiative states, the signature requirements for initiative constitutional amendments are higher than for initiative statutes. To reach the ballot, California statutory initiatives must receive signatures equaling five percent of the vote for governor in the last election, whereas initiative constitutional amendments need eight percent – both within a 150-day window.[13] At the time, this meant that a constitutional amendment would need more than 693,000 valid signatures, compared with slightly more than 433,000 valid signatures for an initiative statute – a difference of nearly 260,000 signatures.[14] Many considered the higher figure to be prohibitive, and the proponents decided to draft the measure as an initiative statute rather than a constitutional amendment. Using a combination of for-profit petition gathering firms, direct mail, and a large volunteer effort, the proponents were able to gather the necessary signatures. Proposition 22 qualified for the March 2000 ballot.[15]

---

[10] California Secretary of State, *California Voter Information Guide, Primary Election, March 7, 2000*, 132, http://traynor.uchastings.edu/ballot_pdf/2000.pdf.

[11] During the 1995–1996 session, Knight introduced AB 1982, which would have amended the California Family Code to prevent recognition of out-of-state, same-sex marriages. The bill won approval in the state assembly, but was defeated in the state senate. Knight later introduced similar bills, but none were passed out of the house of origin.

[12] In 1998, voters in Hawaii and Alaska approved defense-of-marriage amendments that had been approved by the legislatures of those states. The California measure was the first to be put on the ballot by citizen petition. For further discussion, see Chapter 7.

[13] See CAL. CONST. art. II, sec. 8(b); *California Elections Code* sec. 336. Other states have different signature requirements.

[14] These figures were based on the vote for all candidates for governor in the 1994 general election, which totaled 8,665,375. Because some signatures are invalid for one reason or another, proponents have to submit a larger number than the thresholds to qualify a measure for the ballot.

[15] Andrew Pugno, (attorney, Proposition 22 Legal Defense and Education Fund), interview with the author, August 22, 2008.

Weeks before the election, the California secretary of state mailed a ballot pamphlet to all voters in the state. The pamphlet contained the text of the measures, summaries prepared by the attorney general and legislative analyst, and arguments by proponents and opponents of each measure. In their ballot argument, proponents warned voters that "judges in some... states want to define marriage differently than we do. If they succeed, California may have to recognize new kinds of marriages, even though most people believe marriage should be between a man and a woman."[16] In response, the opponents did not try to persuade voters to embrace same-sex marriage, but urged them to view the measure as an unnecessary and mean-spirited effort to "pick on specific groups of people and single them out for discrimination."[17]

In the March 2000 election, California voters approved Proposition 22 by a 61 to 39 percent margin. The statewide vote was 4,618,673 to 2,909,370, with majorities in all regions of the state, except the San Francisco Bay Area, supporting its adoption.[18] But, this vote of the people did not settle the issue. Proposition 22's opponents vowed to resist the outcome by various means. Their options were limited, however, by the unique nature of California's constitutional design. Most importantly, the California Constitution prohibits the legislature from amending or repealing statutes enacted through the initiative process, unless the initiative itself so allows. As a result, the legislature was powerless to repeal Proposition 22 or to enact a statute recognizing same-sex marriage in the state. Any repeal of Proposition 22 would require a new vote of the people.[19]

Although Proposition 22's opponents could not repeal the measure in the legislature, they could challenge it in the courts. At the time, gay rights groups were reluctant to challenge state marriage laws on federal constitutional grounds.[20] From their perspective, the worst outcome would be to raise these

---

[16] Gary Beckner, Thomas Fong, and Jeanne Murray, "Argument in Favor of Proposition 22" in California Secretary of State, *California Voter Information Guide, Primary Election, March 7, 2000*, 52.

[17] Antonio R. Villaraigosa, the Right Reverend William E. Swing, and Krys Wulff, "Argument Against Proposition 22," in ibid., 53.

[18] California Secretary of State, *Statement of Vote, March 7, 2000 Primary Election.*

[19] CAL. CONST. art. II, sec. 10(c) states that "[t]he Legislature . . . may amend or repeal an initiative statute by another statute that becomes effective only when approved by the electors unless the initiative statute permits amendment or repeal without their approval." Many other initiative states place some restrictions on future legislative amendment to or repeal of voter-approved initiatives, but no other state has an absolute prohibition. In 2005, the California legislature approved AB 849 (Leno), a bill that would have allowed same-sex couples to marry in the state. Governor Schwarzenegger vetoed the bill on the grounds that the legislature could not override Proposition 22. The California Supreme Court confirmed this view in *In re Marriage Cases*, 43 Cal.4th 757 (2008).

[20] An exception was *Citizens for Equal Protection, Inc. v. Bruning*, the federal constitutional challenge to Nebraska's defense-of-marriage amendment, I-416 of 2000. In this case, advocates of same-sex marriage sought to invalidate I-416, but notably did not seek a federal constitutional right to marry, nor any remedies related to marriage, civil unions, or domestic partnerships. Instead, they made the more limited argument that I-416 violated the equal protection clause of the Fourteenth Amendment by preventing petitioners from lobbying their elected representatives

claims prematurely and receive an adverse ruling by the U.S. Supreme Court. However, these groups were prepared to attack marriage statutes in state courts on state constitutional grounds. This strategy would limit the number of states where challenges were possible. Wherever marriage limitations were embedded in a state constitution – as "Defense of Marriage Amendments" soon were in many states – they were largely insulated against state constitutional challenge.[21] Indeed, had the proponents of Proposition 22 qualified the measure as a state constitutional amendment, they would have effectively protected it from the charge that it violated state constitutional rights. But, Proposition 22 was a statute, and thus vulnerable to this form of attack.

The opponents of Proposition 22 did not immediately challenge the measure in court. Instead, they offered resistance by other means. In early 2004, San Francisco Mayor Gavin Newsom defied the marriage restriction by ordering San Francisco officials to issue marriage licenses to same-sex couples. Approximately 4,000 same-sex couples participated in marriage ceremonies in the city before the California Supreme Court stepped in and declared these marriages void. At the time, the court expressly noted that it was reserving judgment on the substantive question of Proposition 22's constitutional validity.[22] Soon, same-sex couples filed challenges in state trial courts, and these and related cases were joined in a coordinated action titled *In re Marriage Cases*.[23]

The plaintiffs in these actions asserted that the limitation of marriage to "a man and a woman" violated their rights under the state constitution. In particular, they argued that the restriction violated their fundamental right to marry as protected by the California Constitution's privacy, free speech, and due process clauses, as well as the state constitution's equal protection guarantee.[24] After skirmishes in the lower courts, the California Supreme Court granted review.

---

for legal protection for same-sex relationships. A federal district judge embraced this theory, but the Eighth Circuit reversed. See *Citizens for Equal Protection, Inc. v. Bruning*, 455 F.3d 859 (8th Cir. 2006), reversing 290 F.Supp.2d 1004 (D. Neb. 2003).

[21] The only basis for a *state* constitutional challenge to a state constitutional amendment is that the amendment violates the state's rules for constitutional amendment – for example, it contains multiple subjects or constitutes a "revision" rather than an amendment. Of course, state constitutional amendments may also be vulnerable to a range of *federal* constitutional challenges.

[22] *Lockyer v. City and County of San Francisco*, 33 Cal.4th 1055, 1073–4 (2004).

[23] *In re Marriage Cases*, JJCP No. 4365, consolidating *Woo v. Lockyer* (Super. Ct. S.F. City & County, No. CPF-04-504038); *Tyler v. County of Los Angeles* (Super. Ct. L.A. County, No. BS-088506); *City and County of San Francisco v. State of California* (Super. Ct. S.F. City & County, No. CGC-04-429539); as well as litigation seeking enforcement of Proposition 22, *Proposition 22 Legal Defense and Education Fund v. City and County of San Francisco* (Super. Ct. S.F. City & County, No. CPF-04-503943); *Campaign for California Families v. Newsom*, Super. Ct. S.F. City & County, No. CGC-04-428794). An additional action filed by same-sex couples was also later added to the coordination proceeding. *Clinton v. State of California* (Super. Ct. S.F. City & County, No. CGC-04-429548).

[24] See *In re Marriage Cases*, 143 Cal. App. 4th 873 (Cal. App. 1st Dist., 2006); CAL. CONST. art. I, sections 1, 2, 7.

Both sides understood that the stakes were high. After the Massachusetts Supreme Judicial Court had declared in 2003 that same-sex couples had a right to marry that was protected by that state's constitution, no other state had followed its lead.[25] Indeed, courts in New York (2006), Washington (2006), New Jersey (2006), and Maryland (2007) had ruled the other way, and similar challenges were still pending in Connecticut and Iowa.[26] The outcome of the litigation in California, the nation's most populous state, would either strengthen the consensus against same-sex marriage or, conversely, revive the movement for widespread recognition of this right. The parties and a multitude of *amici curiae* briefed the issues at length, the lawyers engaged in an extended oral argument, and the court took the case under submission.

The Court's Decision: A Declaration of Rights

On May 15, 2008, a divided court issued its decision in *In re Marriage Cases*.[27] By a 4-to-3 vote, the court struck down Proposition 22 and other state marriage laws on state constitutional grounds. The decision, authored by Chief Justice Ronald George, framed the case in the language of rights and cast a broad vision of the state constitutional rights of gay persons and same-sex couples.

The court began by acknowledging that the California Constitution does not include an explicit "right to marry," but observed that past cases had located this right elsewhere in the text, including Article I's due process and privacy clauses.[28] Then, crucially, the court held that this fundamental right is an individual freedom "to join in marriage with the person of one's choice" and that "the California Constitution properly must be interpreted to guarantee this basic civil right to all individuals and couples, without regard to their sexual orientation."[29] The court denied that it was creating a new right of same-sex marriage; instead, it was declaring that the right to marry could not be denied to same-sex couples. Proposition 22 and the state's other marriage

---

[25] The Massachusetts case was *Goodridge v. Department of Public Health*, 440 Mass. 309 (2003). See also *Opinions of the Justices to the Senate*, 440 Mass. 1201 (2004).

[26] *Hernandez v. Robles*, 7 N.Y.3d 338 (2006), upholding New York's marriage laws; *Andersen v. King County*, 158 Wn.2d 1 (2006), upholding Washington marriage laws; *Lewis v. Harris*, 188 N.J. 415 (2006), declaring a right to same-sex civil unions with benefits of marriage, but not requiring those unions be labeled "marriages"; and *Conaway v. Deane*, 401 Md. 219 (2007), upholding Maryland marriage laws. In October 2008, five months after the California Supreme Court's decision in *In re Marriage Cases*, the Connecticut Supreme Court issued its decision in *Kerrigan v. Commissioner of Public Health*, 289 Conn. 135 (2008) striking down Connecticut's marriage laws and establishing the state constitutional right of same-sex couples to marry. In April 2009, the Iowa Supreme Court issued a similar ruling in *Varnum v. Brien*, 763 N.W.2d 862 (Iowa 2009).

[27] *In re Marriage Cases*, 43 Cal.4th 757 (2008).

[28] Ibid., 809–10.

[29] Ibid., 811, 820, citing *Perez v. Sharp*, 32 Cal.2d 711, 715, 717 (1948), a case invalidating California's anti-miscegenation law on state constitutional grounds.

laws denied same-sex couples this fundamental right, and thus violated the state constitution.

This holding would have been sufficient to resolve the case, but, the court further held that the marriage restriction violated the state constitution's equal protection clause. For the first time, the court announced that, under this clause, all classifications based on sexual orientation are constitutionally suspect and subject to strict judicial scrutiny. This move was groundbreaking because American courts, including the U.S. Supreme Court, had previously declined to declare sexual orientation a suspect classification. But, the California Supreme Court asserted that there was no persuasive reason for applying a more lenient standard to classifications based on sexual orientation than to those based on gender, race, or religion. According to the court, the California marriage restriction discriminated against persons based on their sexual orientation and could not survive this strict level of judicial scrutiny.[30]

The court thus used an expansive interpretation of two state constitutional rights – the implied right to marry and the equal protection guarantee – to strike down Proposition 22.[31]

The Court vs. the Voters

In an important passage in his opinion, Chief Justice George rejected the view that the court should give greater deference to the marriage restriction because it had been directly enacted by the voters. "[T]he circumstance that the limitation of marriage to a union between a man and a woman...was enacted as an initiative measure by a vote of the electorate...neither exempts the statutory provision from constitutional scrutiny nor justifies a more deferential standard of review," the Chief Justice wrote. "[I]nitiative measures adopted by the electorate are subject to the same constitutional limitations that apply to statutes adopted by the Legislature, and our courts have not hesitated to invalidate measures enacted through the initiative process when they run afoul of constitutional guarantees provided by either the federal or California Constitution."[32]

Associate Justice Joyce Kennard, in a concurring opinion, even more pointedly asserted the court's authority to override the will of the people. "The architects of our federal and state Constitutions understood that widespread and deeply rooted prejudices may lead majoritarian institutions to deny fundamental freedoms to unpopular minority groups," she wrote. "[T]he most effective remedy for this form of oppression is an independent judiciary charged with the solemn responsibility to interpret and enforce the constitutional provisions guaranteeing fundamental freedoms and equal protection."[33]

---

[30] Ibid., 840, 854.
[31] Ibid., 855–7.
[32] Ibid., 851.
[33] Ibid., 859–60, Kennard, J., concurring.

A Dissenting View

Three of the court's seven justices dissented. In the lead dissent, Justice Marvin Baxter rejected the view that the marriage controversy was a question of constitutional rights to be determined by courts. Instead, he argued, it was a question of social policy best resolved by the people, acting either directly or through their elected representatives. "Nothing in our Constitution, express or implicit, compels the majority's startling conclusion that the age-old understanding of marriage – an understanding recently confirmed by an initiative law – is no longer valid," Baxter wrote. The people could legitimately choose, if they wished, to change that definition. And, indeed, it was quite possible that "left to its own devices," a democratic consensus would form to give legal recognition to same-sex marriage. "But a bare majority of this court, not satisfied with the pace of democratic change, now abruptly forestalls that process and substitutes, by judicial fiat, its own social policy views for those expressed by the People themselves."[34] The court had improperly "invent[ed] a new constitutional right," Baxter argued, and had found that "our Constitution suddenly demands no less than a permanent redefinition of marriage, regardless of the popular will."[35]

Popular Constitutionalism and the Last Word

Near the end of *In re Marriage Cases*, Chief Justice George quoted from the U.S. Supreme Court's famous decision in *West Virginia State Board of Education v. Barnette* (1943).[36] In that case, the Supreme Court invoked the First Amendment to strike down a West Virginia statute requiring public school students to salute the American flag. Writing for the Court, Justice Robert Jackson argued that "[t]he very purpose of a Bill of Rights was to withdraw certain subjects from the vicissitudes of political controversy, to place them beyond the reach of majorities and officials and to establish them as legal principles to be applied by the courts. One's right to life, liberty, and property, to free speech, a free press, freedom of worship and assembly, and other fundamental rights may not be submitted to vote; they depend on the outcome of no elections."[37]

In this passage, Justice Jackson was enunciating the principle of "higher constitutionalism" – the idea that constitutional rights rise above normal democratic politics and that courts, not the people, are the final interpreters and guardians of these rights.

In *Marriage Cases*, Chief Justice George sought to portray the state constitutional marriage rights of same-sex couples in the same higher constitutional

---

[34] Ibid., 861, Baxter, J., dissenting.
[35] Ibid., 863–4.
[36] *In re Marriage Cases*, 43 Cal.4th at 852, citing *West Virginia State Board of Education v. Barnette*, 319 U.S. 624, 638 (1943).
[37] Ibid.

terms – *beyond the reach of majorities*. But, the analogy was flawed. Federal constitutional rights are elevated above normal democratic politics only because the supermajority requirements for federal constitutional amendments are so exacting. But, the constitutional dynamics are quite different in the states, especially in states that allow for direct initiative constitutional amendment. If the people can amend their constitution by petition and simple majority vote, constitutional rights are up for grabs. Courts may seek to define the scope of these rights, but, their decisions are always subject to popular override. Unlike the federal constitutional rights Justice Jackson described in *Barnette*, state constitutional rights *may* be submitted to a vote and *do* depend on the outcome of elections.

Opponents of same-sex marriage understood this dynamic. As *In re Marriage Cases* was pending in the California Supreme Court, they gathered signatures for a new initiative with the exact same fourteen words as Proposition 22 – but, this time, they were able to qualify the measure as a state constitutional amendment. The new initiative, Proposition 8, would amend the California Constitution to include the same 14 words as in Proposition 22: "Only marriage between a man and a woman is valid or recognized in California." The measure appeared on the November 4, 2008, ballot and gave the people the opportunity to override the state Supreme Court on this controversial question.

The pre-election fight over Proposition 8 was intense. One early skirmish involved the wording of the ballot title – a factor that can greatly influence voter attitudes toward a ballot measure. In 2000, Proposition 22 had been titled: "Limit on Marriages: Initiative Statute." But, in 2008, Attorney General Jerry Brown revised the title for Proposition 8 to read: "Eliminates Right of Same-Sex Couples to Marry."[38] Polls indicated that this reframing of the issue as an elimination of a right undermined support for the measure.[39]

The Yes-on-8 side fought back by emphasizing that the California Supreme Court had thwarted the will of the voters when it overturned Proposition 22, and that the new measure restored the people's preferred definition of marriage. In the official ballot pamphlet, the sponsors of Proposition 8 argued that

Proposition 8 is simple and straightforward. It contains the same 14 words that were previously approved in 2000 by over 61% of California voters: "Only marriage between a man and a woman is valid or recognized in California."

---

[38] Proponents of Proposition 8 unsuccessfully challenged this change to the ballot title. Aurelio Rojas, "Ruling on Ballot Title is Setback for Proposition 8 Backers," *The Sacramento Bee*, August 9, 2008, 3A.

[39] Mark DiCamillo and Mervin Field, "55% of Voters Oppose Proposition 8, the Initiative to Ban Same-Sex Marriages in California," The Field Poll, Release #2287, September 18, 2008. Surveying respondents between September 5 and September 14, 2008, the poll found that opposition to Proposition 8 increased when respondents were read the new ballot summary that Proposition 8 "eliminates right." According to DiCamillo and Field, "These findings indicate that similar to past initiative campaigns the wording of a ballot summary can have a pronounced impact on how voters make judgments about a proposition."

Because four activist judges in San Francisco wrongly overturned the people's vote, we need to pass this measure as a constitutional amendment to RESTORE THE DEFINI-TION OF MARRIAGE as a man and a woman. . . .

CALIFORNIANS HAVE NEVER VOTED FOR SAME-SEX MARRIAGE. If gay activists want to legalize gay marriage, they should put it on the ballot. Instead, they have gone behind the backs of voters and convinced four activist judges in San Francisco to redefine marriage for the rest of society. That is the wrong approach.

Voting YES on Proposition 8 RESTORES the definition of marriage that was approved by over 61% of voters. Voting YES overturns the decision of four activist judges. . . .

Please vote YES on Proposition 8 to RESTORE the meaning of marriage.[40]

Meanwhile, opponents of Proposition 8 sought to frame the debate in the language of rights and equality. They relied heavily on the argument that same-sex couples had a fundamental right to marry and that Proposition 8 would deny them that right. In the ballot pamphlet, they argued:

OUR CALIFORNIA CONSTITUTION – the law of our land – SHOULD GUARAN-TEE THE SAME FREEDOMS AND RIGHTS TO EVERYONE – NO ONE group SHOULD be singled out to BE TREATED DIFFERENTLY.

In fact, our nation was founded on the principle that all people should be treated equally. EQUAL PROTECTION UNDER THE LAW IS THE FOUNDATION OF AMERICAN SOCIETY.

That's what this election is about – equality, freedom, and fairness, for all.

Marriage is the institution that conveys dignity and respect to the lifetime commitment of any couple. PROPOSITION 8 WOULD DENY LESBIAN AND GAY COUPLES that same DIGNITY AND RESPECT.

That's why Proposition 8 is wrong for California.

Regardless of how you feel about this issue, the freedom to marry is fundamental to our society, just like the freedoms of religion and speech.

PROPOSITION 8 MANDATES ONE SET OF RULES FOR GAY AND LESBIAN COUPLES AND ANOTHER SET FOR EVERYONE ELSE. That's just not fair. OUR LAWS SHOULD TREAT EVERYONE EQUALLY.[41]

In the weeks leading up to the election, both sides organized extensive grass-roots campaigns and flooded the airwaves with paid commercial advertise-ments. The campaign for and against Proposition 8 was the most expensive ever for a social issue. Reports indicated that the Yes-on-8 campaign raised nearly

---

[40] Ron Prentice, Rosemary "Rosie" Avila, and Bishop George McKinney, "Argument in Favor of Proposition 8" in California Secretary of State, *California General Election, Tuesday, Novem-ber 4, 2008 Official Voter Information Guide*, 56. http://traynor.uchastings.edu/ballot_pdf/2008g.pdf.

[41] Samuel Thoron and Julia Miller Thoron, "Argument Against Proposition 8," in ibid., 57.

$40 million; No on 8, more than $43 million.[42] In the final days of the campaign, Yes-on-8 gained ground and narrowly won the election. Voters approved Proposition 8 by a 52.3-to-47.7 percent margin, with more than 7 million Californians voting in favor of the proposition, even as the highly diverse and Democratic state was voting overwhelmingly for Barack Obama for president.[43] A crucial reason for Proposition 8's success was that many Democrats, including religiously observant blacks and Latinos, supported the measure.[44]

The day after the election, opponents of Proposition 8 filed several challenges to the measure in the California Supreme Court.[45] Again, the litigants were unwilling to raise federal constitutional claims. Instead, they relied on a state constitutional argument regarding the permissible scope of the California initiative process. The suits argued that by eliminating a fundamental right, Proposition 8 changed the California Constitution so significantly that it constituted a "revision" rather than an "amendment" – and thus exceeded the people's power to amend the state constitution through the initiative process. But in *Strauss v. Horton* (2009), the California Supreme Court, by a 6-to-1 vote, rejected this argument. In a lengthy decision authored by Chief Justice George, the court was forced to acknowledge that California's strong form of direct democracy gave the people, not the court, the last word on this contested issue. As a consequence, Proposition 8 was now embedded in the California Constitution and could be overturned only by a new vote of the people – or by a ruling that the state's marriage restriction violated a higher law, the Constitution of the United States.[46]

---

[42] Jesse McKinley, "California Releasing Donor List for $83 Marriage Vote," *New York Times*, February 2, 2009, A-13.

[43] The vote for Proposition 8 was 7,001,084 Yes; 6,401,482 No, 52.2-to-47.8 percent margin. The same electorate supported Barack Obama for president over John McCain, 61.1-to-37.0 percent. California Secretary of State, *Statement of Vote: November 4, 2008 General Election*, 7–8.

[44] The National Election Poll Exit Poll reported that 36 percent of Democrats (and 30 percent of Obama voters) supported Proposition 8. The same NEP poll reported that 70 percent of African American voters supported Proposition 8, as did 53 percent of the Latinos. See "National and California Exit Poll Results," *The Los Angeles Times*, November 6, 2008, A1. Later survey research by Patrick Egan of New York University and Kenneth Sherrill of Hunter College challenged some of the NEP results, finding instead that 58 percent of African Americans and 59 percent of Latinos voted for Proposition 8. Egan and Sherrill also found that, across racial groups, religious commitment (as measured by frequency of church attendance) was a crucial factor in determining attitudes toward the initiative. Patrick J. Egan and Kenneth Sherrill. "California's Proposition 8: What Happened, and What Does the Future Hold?" National Gay and Lesbian Task Force: January 2009, http://www.thetaskforce .org/downloads/issues/egan_sherrill_prop8_1_6_09.pdf. See also Cara Mia DiMassa and Jessica Garrison, "Why Gays, Blacks are Divided on Proposition 8: For Many African Americans, it's not a Civil Rights Issue," *The Los Angeles Times*, November 8, 2008, A-1.

[45] *Strauss, v. Horton*, California Supreme Court Case No.Case No. S168047; *Robin Tyler, et al. v. State of California, et al.*, Case No. S168066; *City and County of San Francisco et al. v. Horton, et al.*, Case No. S168078.

[46] *Strauss v. Horton*, California Supreme Court Case No. S168047 (May 26, 2009).

Legal scholar Douglas S. Reed has described this type of state-level conflict between the people and the courts as a unique form of "popular constitutionalism" – "a dialectical exchange between judicial rulings based on state constitutional provisions and popular initiative politics that seek to redefine or reinterpret those same or other provisions."[47] In this dialectic, advocates of minority rights mobilize in the courts, whereas those who seek to limit rights claims and reassert the majority will invoke the tools of direct democracy and mobilize the electorate. The specific patterns of popular constitutionalism can vary, but the marriage controversy played out as follows:

Legal mobilization
(litigation to establish state constitutional right)
(various states, 1990s)

↓

Democratic counter-mobilization
(initiative to prevent recognition of right)
(California Proposition. 22, 2000)

↓

Legal counter-mobilization
(court decision striking down initiative and recognizing right)
(In re Marriage Cases, May 2008)

↓

Democratic counter-mobilization
(ICA to override court and disestablish right)
(California Proposition 8, November 2008)

↓

Further rounds of legal and democratic
counter-mobilizations

This interplay shows how the introduction of direct democracy and the rise of a strong, rights-generating judicial power have created high-stakes, state-level constitutional conflicts between the people and the courts.

Other Conflicts and Landmark Cases

But conflicts between direct democracy and the courts follow different patterns when initiatives raise *federal* constitutional questions. As noted, the provisions of the U.S. Constitution have the status of higher law, and the courts almost always have the final authority to interpret and enforce them. If an initiative is

---

[47] Douglas S. Reed, "Popular Constitutionalism: Toward a Theory of State Constitutional Meanings," 30 RUTGERS L. J. 871 (1999).

challenged on federal constitutional grounds, the judges, not the people, will determine its fate.

Consequently, a judicial ruling that an initiative violates the federal Constitution is the most powerful institutional limitation on direct democracy. And, throughout the initiative era, courts have not been reluctant to exercise this check. Both state and federal courts have frequently invoked the First Amendment, the Fourteenth Amendment equal protection and due process clauses, the commerce clause, the Article VI supremacy clause, and other federal constitutional provisions to strike down voter-approved initiatives. A number of these controversies have found their way to the U.S. Supreme Court and have contributed to the Court's interpretation of minority and individual rights and the institutional powers of government.

Most notably, the Supreme Court has struck down numerous initiatives that conflicted with its expanding interpretation of federal constitutional rights. In an early initiative challenge, *Guinn & Beal v. United States* (1915), the Court invoked the Fifteenth Amendment to strike down an Oklahoma initiative designed to disenfranchise blacks through literacy tests and grandfather clauses. In *Pierce v. Society of Sisters* (1925), the Court applied an expansive interpretation of substantive due process to invalidate an anti-Catholic Oregon initiative that barred children from attending private schools. In *Griffin v. California* (1965), the Court used the Fifth Amendment to invalidate a California initiative that allowed judges and prosecutors to comment on a defendant's refusal to testify. In *Lucas v. Forty-Fourth General Assembly of Colorado* (1964), the Court strengthened its "one-person-one-vote" doctrine by striking down a Colorado initiative establishing a "federal model" redistricting plan for the state legislature. In *Reitman v. Mulkey* (1967), the Court invoked the Fourteenth Amendment's equal protection clause to strike down a California initiative banning fair housing laws. In *Washington v. Seattle School Dist. No. 1* (1982), the Court invalidated a Washington initiative restricting school busing on Fourteenth Amendment grounds. And, in *Romer v. Evans* (1996), the Court invoked the Fourteenth Amendment to invalidate a Colorado initiative that banned efforts by state and local governments to prevent discrimination based on sexual orientation.[48]

Similarly, the Court has struck down initiatives that tested the boundaries of federalism, or otherwise conflicted with the institutional powers of government set forth in the Constitution. Most importantly, in *U.S. Term Limits, Inc. v. Thornton* (1995), the Court invalidated an Arkansas initiative imposing

---

[48] *Guinn & Beal v. United States*, 238 U.S. 347 (1915); *Pierce v. Society of Sisters*, 268 U.S. 510 (1925); *Lucas v. Forty-Fourth General Assembly of Colorado*, 377 U.S. 713 (1964); *Griffin v. California*, 380 U.S. 609 (1965), reversing *Adamson v. California*, 332 U.S. 46 (1947); *Reitman v. Mulkey*, 387 U.S. 369 (1967); *Washington v. Seattle School Dist. No. 1*, 458 U.S. 457 (1982); *U.S. Term Limits, Inc. v. Thornton*, 514 U.S. 779 (1995); *Romer v. Evans*, 517 U.S. 620 (1996).

term limits on members of Congress, as well as similar initiatives adopted by voters in 19 other states, on the grounds that individual states could not add new qualifications for members of Congress.[49] In this one decision, the Court overturned the will of tens of millions of voters on a highly consequential issue – one of the largest single acts of counter-majoritarian power in U.S. history.

These landmark Supreme Court invalidations of initiatives are surely important, but, they are just part of a much larger body of conflicts between direct democracy and courts over the past century. In every initiative state, the two forces have engaged in battle through petitions, ballots, and litigation in state and federal courts.

A Comprehensive View

The dynamics described in this book raise profound questions about the scope of popular sovereignty in a constitutional system. By their very nature, constitutions regulate, and thereby limit, direct popular rule. Yet, in the modern liberal tradition, constitutions are authoritative only because they are chosen, or ratified, by popular majorities. If majorities can easily override constitutional powers and rights, then constitutionalism collapses into direct democracy. But, conversely, if constitutions are impervious to popular control, then, as Abraham Lincoln said about the Supreme Court's decision in *Dred Scott*, "the people will have ceased to be their own rulers."[50] Nowhere in American politics is this practical tension more fully revealed than in the conflict between direct democracy and the courts.

The book aims to provide a comprehensive account of this conflict. To explain why direct democracy and the courts interact in the ways that they do, it traces the respective origins and development of the two powers from the founding period through the Progressive Era and the century that followed. The account shows how the Progressive Era's most consequential "experiment in government" has combined with a rising judicial power to produce a unique constitutional system, and, how, in turn, that system has generated remarkable controversies like *U.S. Term Limits* and *In re Marriage Cases*.

---

[49] *U.S. Term Limits* also invalidated a congressional term limits initiative in a twentieth state, Nevada. In 1994, Nevada citizens had approved an initiative constitutional amendment to impose congressional term limits by a 70% vote, but the Nevada rules required the measure to receive a second affirmative vote for enactment. The Court handed down its decision in *U.S. Term Limits* prior to Nevada's second vote. *U.S. Term Limits* also invalidated congressional term limits adopted by state legislatures in New Hampshire and Utah. For a discussion, see Chapter 6.

[50] Abraham Lincoln, *First Inaugural Address*, March 4, 1861, critiquing *Scott v. Sandford*, 60 U.S. 393 (1857).

In exploring these themes, readers should consider the following questions:

- What has direct democracy accomplished? Has it improved or weakened the constitutional design in the states where it is used? Is it out of control?
- Have courts appropriately countered direct democracy? Is the judicial check on direct democracy adequate? Is it excessive?
- Is a popular check on courts beneficial or dangerous?
- And, what are the prospects for a constitutional system that combines strong forms of direct democracy and judicial review?

PART I

THE QUEST FOR MAJORITY RULE

I

The Epic Debate

In lectures at Princeton in 1913, U.S. Senator Elihu Root warned that the Progressive Era's fast-spreading direct democracy movement was threatening major premises of American constitutional design. "[E]ssential principles embodied in the Federal Constitution of 1787, and long followed in the constitutions of all the States, are questioned and denied," Root said. "The wisdom of the founders of the Republic is disputed and the political ideas which they repudiated are urged for approval."[1] Although lamenting these developments, Root understood that "[q]uestions of general and permanent importance are seldom finally settled" and that "[p]ostulates... cease to be accepted without proof and the whole controversy in which they were originally established is fought all over again."[2]

What foundational issues of the 1780s were reformers revisiting at the turn of the twentieth century? What essential principles of American constitutional tradition did they deny? And, which political ideas rejected by the Founders did the reformers now promote? In Senator Root's view, the fundamental issue in both eras was how much power the people should exercise *directly*. A closer look at the founding era reveals that the Progressive Era advocates of direct democracy were, in fact, reopening an old debate.

THE FOUNDERS' REJECTION OF DIRECT DEMOCRACY

James Madison and the other framers of the federal Constitution flatly rejected direct democracy. Having fought a revolution against monarchy, they were committed to the principle that all legitimate power flows from the people, yet,

---

[1] Elihu Root, "Experiments in Government and the Essentials of the Constitution" in Robert Bacon and James Brown Scott, eds., *Addresses on Government and Citizenship* (Cambridge, MA: Harvard University Press, 1916), 78.

[2] Ibid.

they feared unchecked popular rule.[3] Their fears were rooted in their assessment of human nature, their historical analyses of failed popular governments, and their close observation of a post-revolutionary period marked, in their view, by democratic excess.

Madison's reading of human nature can be summed up in four words: *men are not angels*.[4] To the contrary, human beings are often driven by selfish interest or passion, prone to mutual animosities, and "much more disposed to vex and oppress each other than to co-operate for their common good."[5] A constitution, Madison insisted, must account for these human propensities and place checks on anyone who exercises authority – including the people themselves.

Alexander Hamilton shared this view. "Give all power to the many, and they will oppress the few," he wrote. "Give all power to the few, they will oppress the many."[6] Madison argued that, in the American context, majority tyranny was the greater threat. As he wrote to Thomas Jefferson, "Wherever the real power in a government lies, there is the danger of oppression. In our Governments, the real power lies in the majority of the community, and the invasion of private rights is to be chiefly apprehended, not from acts of Government contrary to the sense of its constituents, but from acts in which the Government is the mere instrument of the major number of the constituents."[7]

The challenge was to harmonize popular sovereignty with limitations on majority rule.[8] Madison's solution was "republican government." Far from a "pure democracy," this system was defined by the *"total exclusion of the people in their collective capacity* from any share" in the administration of government.[9] Republican government was emphatically representative,

---

[3] James Madison, *Federalist* 49 in Alexander Hamilton, James Madison, and John Jay, *The Federalist Papers*, Clinton Rossiter, ed. (New York: Signet Classic, 2003), 310. Bernard Bailyn stresses that American political thought was transformed in the revolutionary period to embrace the idea that the people were "[n]o longer merely an ultimate check on the government, they *were* in some sense the government. Government had no separate existence apart from them; it was *by* the people as well as *for* the people; it gained its authority from their continuous consent." Bernard Bailyn, *The Ideological Origins of the American Revolution* (Cambridge, MA: Harvard University Press, 1967), 173.

[4] Madison, *Federalist* 51, 319.

[5] Madison, *Federalist* 10, 73.

[6] Alexander Hamilton (June 18, 1787), quoted in Jonathan Elliot, ed., *Debates on the Federal Constitution in the Convention Held at Philadelphia in 1787*, Vol. V (New York: Burt Franklin, 1888), 203.

[7] Letter from James Madison to Thomas Jefferson, 1788, cited in Gordon Wood, *The Creation of the American Republic, 1776–1787* (Chapel Hill: University of North Carolina Press, 1969), 410. Wood observed that the danger of majority tyranny in a democratic form of government is all the more acute because a majority can impose its tyranny as of right.

[8] Robert A. Dahl, A *Preface to Democratic Theory*, expanded edition. (Chicago: University of Chicago Press, 2006), 4.

[9] Madison, *Federalist* 63, 385 (emphasis in original). See Charles Kesler, "The Founders' Views of Direct Democracy and Representation," in Elliott Abrams, ed. *Democracy: How Direct? Views from the Founding Era and the Polling Era* (Lanham, MD: Rowman and Littlefield, 2002), 1.

characterized by delegation, deliberation, separated powers, and multiple layers of checks and balances.[10] The people exercised power, but indirectly, through the mediation of representatives. As an additional precaution, each delegation of power was carefully matched with a counter-power. The Constitution set the government in opposition to itself, in an almost isometric way. Different elements were paired off so that "ambition [was] made to counteract ambition."[11]

Scholars dating back to Woodrow Wilson have argued that Madison's design owed much to Isaac Newton. In *Constitutional Government of the United States* (1908), Wilson wrote that

[t]he government of the United States was constructed upon the Whig theory of political dynamics, which was sort of an unconscious copy of the Newtonian theory of the universe.... Every sun, every planet, every free body in the spaces of the heavens, the world itself, is kept in its place and reined to its course by the attraction of bodies that swing with equal order and precision about it, themselves governed by the nice poise and balance of forces which give the whole system of the universe its symmetry and perfect adjustment.... [The framers] sought to balance executive, legislative, and judiciary off against one another by a series of checks and counterpoises, which Newton might readily have recognized as suggestive of the mechanism of the heavens.[12]

For Madison, the purpose of this careful equilibrium – this balance of the people against the government and different elements of the government against one another – was to protect liberty by preventing excessive concentrations of power, and thus of tyranny, by the few or by the many.

THE ANTI-FEDERALIST CRITIQUE AND CONSTITUTIONAL VISION

The Anti-Federalists were the first to attack this constitutional design. In their view, the Federalists had misjudged the most likely source of tyranny. Liberty was threatened by *rulers*, not by the people. Patrick Henry famously argued that instead of placing so many limits on majorities, the Constitution should have set more restraints on representatives.[13] The Anti-Federalist writer Centinel agreed, arguing that the new Constitution's system of internal checks and

---

[10] See, e.g., Madison, *Federalist* 10, 76–7; *Federalist* 51, 317–22; *Federalist* 53, 329–30. For a discussion of the Founders' views on the importance of informed deliberation by knowledgeable representatives, see Joseph M. Bessette, *The Mild Voice of Reason: Deliberative Democracy and American National Government* (Chicago: University of Chicago Press, 1994), 1–66.

[11] Madison, *Federalist* 51, 319.

[12] Woodrow Wilson, *Constitutional Government in the United States* (New York: Columbia University Press, 1908), 54–6.

[13] "Speeches of Patrick Henry in the Virginia State Ratifying Convention" in Herbert J. Storing, ed. *The Anti-Federalist: Writings by the Opponents of the Constitution* (Chicago: The University of Chicago Press, 1985), 300. Henry: "I am not well-versed in history, but I will submit to your recollection, whether liberty has been destroyed most often by the licentiousness of the people, or by the tyranny of the rulers? I imagine, Sir, you will find the balance on the side of tyranny." Massachusetts' Elbridge Gerry agreed that the plan placed too much confidence

balances would not prevent government tyranny and that "the only operative
and effective check, upon the conduct of administration, is the sense of the people at large."[14] Anti-Federalists thus attacked elements of the new Constitution,
which limited the people's power.

Throughout this debate, the Anti-Federalists advanced an alternative constitutional vision embodied in the existing state constitutions.[15] Whereas these
constitutions were representative in form, several of them contained provisions
that resembled direct democracy as closely as possible.[16] The Pennsylvania
Constitution of 1776 was the most notable model. That constitution created a
unicameral legislature consisting of numerous representatives who served one-
year terms and were soon rotated out of office by mandatory term limits. These
arrangements were designed to approximate direct democracy by making representatives highly responsive to the popular will.[17] But, Madison's plan, the
Anti-Federalists argued, led in the opposite direction. It would separate representatives from the people they were supposed to serve and undermine the
sovereignty of the people.[18]

The Anti-Federalists eventually succumbed as, one-by-one, states voted to
ratify the new federal Constitution. This outcome made many of the Constitution's provisions – including its rejection of direct democracy – essential
principles of American constitutional thought. Yet, the debate was neither fully
nor finally settled. Objections to the Madisonian design persisted, and a constitutional tradition more receptive to direct popular control survived at the state
level.

NINETEENTH-CENTURY DEMOCRATIC ASPIRATIONS

In the century between 1790 and 1890, Americans continued in their quest
for popular rule. The eminent British historian James Bryce observed: "As
the Republic went on working out both in theory and in practice those conceptions of democracy and popular sovereignty which had been only vaguely
apprehended when enunciated at the Revolution, the faith of the average man
in himself became stronger, his love of equality greater, his desire, not only to
rule, but to rule directly in his own proper person, more constant."[19] Bryce

---

in representatives and "confidence is the road to tyranny." Herbert J. Storing, *What the Anti-
Federalists Were* For (Chicago: University of Chicago Press, 1981), 51.

[14] Centinel, "Letter I" in Storing, ed., *The Anti-Federalist*, 14–15.

[15] Storing, *What the Anti-Federalists Were* For, 17.

[16] Charles R. Kesler, "Introduction" in *The Federalist*, xxiv.

[17] Centinel, "Letter I," in Storing, ed., *The Anti-Federalist*, 15. See G. Alan Tarr, "For the People:
Direct Democracy in the State Constitutional Tradition," in Abrams, ed. *Democracy: How
Direct?*, 91.

[18] Christopher M. Duncan, *The Anti-Federalists and Early American Political Thought* (DeKalb,
IL: Northern Illinois University Press, 1995), 160.

[19] James Bryce, *The American Commonwealth*, Volume I (Indianapolis: Liberty Fund 1995) (first
published 1914), 416.

noted that these rising democratic aspirations were mostly satisfied in local communities, where citizens could participate more directly in government, but the democratic impulse also extended to the state and national sphere.

Throughout the nineteenth century, states adopted various democratizing reforms.[20] Notably, many states began to use popular referenda to ratify and amend state constitutions and to determine certain questions such as the siting of new state capitals.[21] Bryce observed that in the northern states after the mid-nineteenth century, it was "an article of faith that no constitution could be enacted save by the direct vote of the citizens."[22] One can see these referrals as a form of direct democracy germinating in representative structures. Yet, crucially, legislatures still controlled the framing of these options, and citizens could not bypass representatives to enact law directly. Representative government remained the dominant constitutional orthodoxy.

During the 1890s, however, Americans increasingly lost faith in the Madisonian way. The economic abuses of the era caused distressed farmers and laborers to appeal to the government for relief, but government was often unresponsive or even hostile. Many believed that the government had been captured by powerful economic interests and, worse, that the constitutional design prevented majorities from breaking the corrupt axis of economic and political power. In their frustration, many Americans joined new political movements. A significant number identified with a new national party called the "People's Party," also known as the "Populists."[23] It was the Populists who organized the first efforts to introduce the devices of direct democracy – the initiative, referendum, and recall – into the American constitutional system.

THE POPULISTS

The Populists were aptly named because the quest for popular sovereignty formed the core of their beliefs. Their deep commitment to the people's rule drew explicitly on Anti-Federalist as well as Jacksonian ideology. John D. Hicks, the leading historian of the movement, wrote that "[t]he Populist philosophy . . . boiled down finally to two fundamental propositions; one, that the government must restrain the selfish tendencies of those who profited at the

---

[20] For a discussion, see Tarr, "For the People," 93–7.
[21] E.g., Texas (1850), Oregon (1857), Kansas (1859), Colorado (1881), South Dakota (1889), Montana (1892). Ellis Paxson Oberholtzer, *The Referendum in America, Together with some Chapters on the History of the Initiative and Other Phases of Popular Government in the United States* (New York: Charles Scribner's Sons, 1900), 176–8.
[22] Bryce, *The American Commonwealth*, 416; See also, Charles A. Beard and Birl E. Shultz, *Documents on the Statewide Initiative, Referendum, and Recall* (New York: The Macmillan Company, 1912), 16.
[23] The term "Populist" was first used in the early 1890s as an epithet against the People's Party and its members, but party adherents gradually came to accept it. John D. Hicks, *The Populist Revolt: A History of the Farmers' Alliance and the People's Party* (Minneapolis: University of Minnesota Press, 1931), 238. I capitalize the term "Populist" only when referring to the People's Party of the 1890s.

expense of the poor and needy; the other, that the people, not the plutocrats, must control the government."[24]

The latter proposition led Populists to advocate a range of reforms designed to restrict the power of representatives and party machines and empower the people to rule more directly. At their first national convention in 1892, the People's Party ratified a platform that called for political reforms including the secret ballot, the direct election of senators, and "the legislative system known as the initiative and referendum."[25]

At that point, the initiative and referendum were still largely unknown in the United States. An American reformer named James W. Sullivan had recently studied the use of these devices in Swiss cantons and had returned to the United States eager to advocate for their adoption. He wrote a book explaining how the devices work, formed the People's Power League, sent emissaries to the 1892 national party conventions, and convinced the People's Party, as well as the Socialist Labor Party, to join the movement for direct democracy.[26]

Advocacy of the initiative and referendum quickly became a centerpiece of the Populist agenda.[27] Populist candidates enjoyed a surge of success in the elections of 1892 and 1894, especially in the West and Midwest.[28] In 1896, the People's Party platform again called for "a system of direct legislation through the initiative and referendum," and the party joined the Democrats in nominating for president the Great Commoner, William Jennings Bryan, who became one of the nation's leading advocates of direct democracy.[29]

Direct legislation by the people became an obsession for many Populists, and during the last years of the nineteenth century, activists such as William

---

[24] Hicks, *The Populist Revolt*, 405; Thomas E. Cronin, *Direct Democracy: The Politics of Initiative, Referendum, and Recall* (Cambridge, MA: Harvard University Press, 1989), 406.

[25] James W. Sullivan, *Direct Legislation by the Citizenship through the Initiative and Referendum* (New York: Twentieth Century Publishing Co. 1892); "People's Platform of 1892" in Donald Bruce Johnson and Kirk H. Porter, eds., *National Party Platforms, 1840–1972* (Urbana: University of Illinois Press, 1973), 89–91. For a discussion of the relationship between the Populist Party movement and the origins of direct democracy in the United States, see Steven L. Piott, *Giving Voters a Voice: The Origins of the Initiative and Referendum in America.* (Columbia, MO: University of Missouri Press, 2003), 1–15.

[26] David D. Schmidt, *Citizen Lawmakers: The Ballot Initiative Revolution* (Philadelphia: Temple University Press, 1989), 6.

[27] Ibid., 7–8.

[28] For example, in 1892, Populist presidential candidate James Weaver won the states of Colorado, Idaho, Kansas, Nevada, and North Dakota, for a total of 22 electoral votes. Dave Leip, "1892 Presidential General Election Results." *Dave Leip's Atlas of U.S. Presidential Elections.* http://www.uselectionatlas.org/RESULTS/national.php?f=0&year=1892. In the early 1890s, Populist Party candidates also won many state and local offices and a number of congressional seats.

[29] "People's Platform of 1896" in Johnson and Porter, eds., *National Party Platforms*, 104–6. In 1896, Bryan became an active supporter of the Direct Legislation League. Schmidt, *Citizen Lawmakers*, 7. He unsuccessfully attempted to include an endorsement of initiative and referendum in the 1896 Democratic Party platform; the Democrats did include a qualified endorsement of initiative and referendum in their platform of 1900. *Direct Legislation Record*, September 1896, 25–6; Joseph G. LaPalombara, *The Initiative and Referendum in Oregon: 1938–1948* (Corvallis: Oregon State College Press, 1950), 6.

U'Ren in Oregon and Dr. John Randolph Haynes in California worked at the state and local levels for adoption of the initiative, referendum, and recall.[30] The direct democracy movement thus had its first breakthroughs in states where the Populists were strong. In 1897, Bryan's home state of Nebraska passed a statute allowing cities to include initiative and referendum in their charters; in 1898, South Dakota became the first state to adopt initiative and referendum statewide; and, in 1899, the Oregon legislature, under pressure from U'Ren, approved amendments for initiative and referendum, which Oregon voters adopted by an overwhelming margin in 1902.[31]

Like most third-party movements in the United States, the Populists did not survive long as an organized body, not even long enough to celebrate these early adoptions of direct democracy. But Hicks's epitaph for the Populist Party was apt: "The party itself did not survive, nor did many of its leaders ... but Populistic doctrines showed an amazing vitality."[32] Historian Richard Hofstadter agreed: "In the short run, the Populists did not get what they wanted, but they released the flow of protest and criticism that swept through American political affairs from the 1890's to the beginning of the first World War."[33]

THE PROGRESSIVE ERA DEBATE

At the dawn of the twentieth century, protest and criticism developed an increasingly earnest and moralistic quality, animated by a belief in the rapid advance of human civilization if not the perfection of man himself. The language of "improvement" and "progress" permeated all spheres of life and was conducive to new experiments in government.

Proposals for direct democracy soon moved from the margins to the center of state and national politics. Between 1898 and 1910, ten states and many more local jurisdictions adopted either the initiative or referendum, or both.[34] In 1911, momentum for the initiative and referendum continued to build. That year, Hiram Johnson, California's new governor, called a special election and urged voters to adopt the statewide initiative, referendum, and recall as part of a slate of twenty-three separate reforms. Voters endorsed the initiative, referendum, and recall amendments by overwhelming 3-to-1 margins. The same

---

[30] Piott, *Giving Voters a Voice*, 32–50, 110–11, 153–69.

[31] Ibid., 30–1, 40. The Oregon vote was 62,024 to 5,668. Utah voters approved an initiative and referendum amendment in 1900, but the amendment was not self-executing and the legislature failed to adopt enabling legislation until 1917. Ibid., 51.

[32] The party's fateful decision in 1896 to fuse with the Democrats in endorsing Bryan, and Bryan's landslide defeat to McKinley, contributed to the party's demise. Hicks, *The Populist Revolt*, 378–9, 404.

[33] Richard Hofstadter, *The Age of Reform: From Bryan to F.D.R.* (New York: Vintage Books, 1955), 60.

[34] States that adopted the initiative and referendum between 1898 and 1910 were: South Dakota (1898); Utah (1900); Oregon (1902); Nevada (1904) (referendum only); Montana (1906); Oklahoma (1907); Maine (1908); Michigan (1908); Missouri (1908); Arkansas (1910); Colorado (1910). See Table 1.1.

year, voters in the territory of Arizona adopted initiative, referendum, and recall as part of their new state constitution.[35]

By 1912, direct democracy had become a major issue of national politics. The leading candidates in that year's presidential election – William Howard Taft, Theodore Roosevelt, Woodrow Wilson, and Eugene Debs – as well as other national political leaders such as William Jennings Bryan, Elihu Root, and Henry Cabot Lodge, had reflected at length on the controversy and had developed well-formed views on the desirability of the initiative, referendum, and recall. These leaders presented a range of perspectives on direct democracy, including competing conceptions of how, if adopted, it should be used.

The Populist Conception

Although the People's Party quickly disbanded, populist sentiments remained strong after the turn of the century and influenced the development of direct democracy. The populist conception of direct democracy was quite radical. According to this view, the common people were capable of governing themselves with little mediation by representatives and should be allowed to override their representatives whenever they wished. Bryan, the nation's best-known populist orator as well as the Democratic Party's presidential nominee in 1896, 1900, and 1908, traveled from state to state expounding this populist conception of direct democracy. In Bryan's view, the people should be trusted to make law directly. They were competent "to sit in judgment on every question which has arisen or which will arise, no matter how long our government will endure."[36] Bryan also maintained that the great political questions were in fact moral questions and that the intuitions of the people were as good as almost any degree of experience.[37]

At the 1912 Ohio constitutional convention, the Great Commoner delivered his famous "People's Law" speech, in which he described the initiative as "the most useful governmental invention which the people of the various states have had under consideration in recent years. It is the most effective means yet for giving the people absolute control over their government." Whereas Bryan understood that the initiative could not fully replace the representative system, he believed that it should be made as robust as possible so that the majority could have its way.[38]

---

[35] Piott, *Giving Voters a Voice*, 143–5, 167–8; John M. Allswang, *The Initiative and Referendum in California, 1898–1998* (Stanford: Stanford University Press, 2000), 13–17.

[36] Hofstadter, *Age of Reform*, 262.

[37] Ibid.

[38] William Jennings Bryan, "People's Law," published in 63rd Congress, 2nd Session. S. Doc. 523, 1914. Moreover, during this period, the Socialist Party, led by the labor organizer Eugene V. Debs, shared a populist conception of direct democracy and pushed it to its logical extreme. Debs and the Socialists won nearly six percent of the national presidential vote in 1912 running on a platform that starkly rejected Madisonian institutions and presented radical alternatives. While demanding the abolition of the Electoral College, the U.S. Senate, the presidential veto,

The Progressive Conception

Mainstream Progressives, especially in the East, distanced themselves from the populist view of direct democracy. Instead, they believed direct democracy should be used sparingly, and mainly for the purpose of restoring the health of the representative system. By 1912, Woodrow Wilson had become a leading proponent of this more modest conception of direct democracy. Wilson was a late convert to the direct democracy movement. During his career as a political scientist, he had refused to embrace initiative, referendum, and recall, but, as governor of New Jersey, he experienced a change of heart. In a 1911 interview, Wilson explained, "For twenty years I preached to the students of Princeton that the Referendum and Recall was bosh," he said. "I have since investigated, and I want to apologize to those students. It is the safeguard of politics. It takes power from the boss and places it in the hands of the people. I want to say with all my power that I favor it."[39] The new convert helped to define a nuanced progressive understanding of "power in the hands of the people" that was distinct from the populist conception.

Wilson began with the premise that representative democracy is the ideal form of government. The problem, however, was that representative institutions had become so tightly controlled and manipulated by powerful minority interests that they could no longer be called representative. "We have so complicated our machinery of government," Wilson argued, "we have made it so difficult, so full of ambushes and hiding-places, so indirect, that instead of having true representative government we have a great inextricable jungle of organization intervening between the people and the processes of their government; so that by stages, without intending it, without being aware of it, we have lost the purity and directness of representative government."[40] The reformers' challenge, Wilson said, was not to eliminate representative institutions, but to redeem them.[41] Rightly understood, the initiative, referendum, and recall provided the means to that end. Wilson went out of his way to rebut the charge that the new devices of direct democracy constituted "radical programmes" or were "meant to change the very character of our government." To the contrary, he argued that "the most ardent and successful advocates of the initiative and referendum regard them as a sobering means of obtaining genuine representative action on the part of legislative bodies."[42]

judicial review, and the Article V process for constitutional amendment, the platform also demanded initiative, referendum, and recall, both at the state and national levels. "Socialist Platform of 1912" in Johnson and Porter, eds., *National Party Platforms*, 188–91.

[39] Woodrow Wilson, quoted in Burton J. Hendrick, "The Initiative and Referendum and How Oregon Got Them," *McClure's Magazine*, July 1911, 235.

[40] Woodrow Wilson, "The Issues of Reform," in William Bennett Munro, ed. *The Initiative, Referendum, and Recall* (New York: D. Appleton and Co., 1912), 84 (reprinted in part from *North American Review*, May 1910 and in part from an address on "The Issues of Reform," delivered in Kansas City on May 5, 1911).

[41] Ibid., 84–5.

[42] Ibid., 87–8.

The leading Progressive Republican, Theodore Roosevelt, also joined the direct democracy movement in the lead-up to the 1912 election.[43] Like Wilson, Roosevelt was attracted to reforms that would make government more responsive to the majority. In a series of speeches in 1912, including his widely noted "Charter of Democracy" speech to the Ohio state constitutional convention, Roosevelt embraced the initiative and referendum as useful expedients that, he said, "should not be used to destroy representative government, but to correct it whenever it becomes misrepresentative. . . . [I]t has been found in very many States that legislative bodies have not been responsive to the popular will. Therefore I believe that the State should provide for the possibility of direct popular action in order to make good such legislative failure."[44]

A month later, at New York's Carnegie Hall, Roosevelt challenged those who said the new forms of direct democracy threatened majority tyranny. "I have scant patience with this talk of the tyranny of the majority," Roosevelt thundered. "Whenever there is tyranny of the majority, I shall protest against it with all my heart and soul. But we are to-day suffering from the tyranny of minorities. . . . No sane man who has been familiar with the government of this country for the last twenty years will complain that we have had too much of the rule of the majority."[45]

Although he supported initiative and referendum, Roosevelt harbored a certain skepticism about their ultimate benefits and cautioned that they should not be used "wantonly or in a spirit of levity." If they become too easy to invoke, he warned, "the result can be only mischievous."[46] Roosevelt recognized that some Progressives, especially in the East, had deep reservations about direct democracy. He assured them that although he would like to see the new forms of direct democracy widely adopted at the state level, "with proper safeguards," he did not intend "to part company from other Progressives who fail to sympathize with me in [this] view." He insisted that "each device is a device and nothing more, is a means and not an end. The end is good government, obtained through genuine popular rule."[47]

---

[43] Accounts of the timing of Roosevelt's conversion vary. Some place the date as early as 1910 when Roosevelt addressed the question before the Colorado state legislature, interpreting his remarks as an endorsement of initiative and referendum. But, others suggest that at that point his support remained equivocal. See Daniel A. Smith and Joseph Lubinski, "Direct Democracy During the Progressive Era: A Crack in the Populist Veneer?" *The Journal of Political History* 14, no. 4 (2002): 354, 376; Lloyd K. Musselman, "Governor John F. Shafroth and the Colorado Progressives: Their Fight for Direct Legislation, 1909–1910" (MA thesis, University of Denver, 1961), 86–9.

[44] Theodore Roosevelt, "'A Charter of Democracy': Address before the Ohio Constitutional Convention at Columbus, Ohio, February 21, 1912," reprinted in Theodore Roosevelt, *Progressive Principles: Selections form Addresses Made During the Presidential Campaign of 1912* (New York: Progressive National Service, 1913), 65.

[45] Theodore Roosevelt, "'The Right of the People to Rule': Address at Carnegie Hall, New York City, Under the Auspices of the Civic Forum, Wednesday Evening, March 20, 1912," reprinted in Roosevelt, *Progressive Principles*, 19–20.

[46] Theodore Roosevelt, "Nationalism and Popular Rule," *The Outlook* (January 21, 1911).

[47] Roosevelt, "A Charter of Democracy," 65. Roosevelt's most notable contribution to the debate over direct democracy was his proposal for popular referenda of state court decisions that

The Opponents

As support for initiative and referendum spread, national leaders who opposed the reforms engaged the debate. The opposition was led by conservatives such as President William Howard Taft and U.S. Senators Elihu Root of New York and Henry Cabot Lodge of Massachusetts. Many reformers ridiculed these men as reactionaries and allies of the special interests, but a fair reading of their arguments shows they were making a principled defense of Madisonian constitutionalism.

President Taft, in particular, paid a price for his stance. His strong opposition to direct democracy deepened his estrangement from Roosevelt and others in the Progressive wing of the Republican Party and contributed to his repudiation at the polls in November 1912. Taft was well aware of the cost: "Of course, I understand the penalty that one has to undergo in taking this position, of being charged with prejudice in favor of special interests, and against popular government, and with failing to recognize the great change which has come over the people.... I am not blind at all to the strength of the movement for the initiative, referendum, and recall. I am quite aware that I am swimming against the stream but this does not discourage me or make my conviction less strong."[48]

Taft swam against the stream with some vigor. He vetoed the Arizona statehood resolution on the grounds that the proposed state constitution provided for recall of judges; vociferously attacked Theodore Roosevelt's plan for popular referenda of state judicial decisions; and, in numerous speeches, voiced his opposition to the spread of initiative and referendum.[49]

After his electoral humiliation in November 1912, Taft assumed a faculty position at Yale Law School and delivered a series of lectures explaining in more detail his support for constitutional orthodoxy and his opposition to direct democracy. In lectures entitled "The Representative System," "The Initiative and the Referendum," and "The Initiative, the Referendum, the Recall," Taft established four main lines of attack against the new devices that remain relevant today.

First, Taft argued that citizens do not need direct democracy to control the government. If citizens are "sluggish" and offer their tacit assent, government

---

invalidated laws. In his February 1912 "Charter of Democracy" speech, Roosevelt unveiled a dramatic proposal to place a majoritarian check on courts by allowing voters to override state court decisions that declare laws unconstitutional. The plan became a central plank of the 1912 Progressive ("Bull Moose") Party platform. For details of Roosevelt's proposed popular check on the courts, see Chapter 7.

[48] William Howard Taft, "The Initiative, the Referendum, the Recall," in *Popular Government: Its Essence, Its Permanence, and Its Perils* (New Haven: Yale University Press, 1913), reprinted in David H. Burton, ed., *The Collected Works of William Howard Taft*, Vol. V (Athens: Ohio University Press, 2003), 63–4, 67–8.

[49] Ibid. See also William Howard Taft, "Veto Message [Returning without approval a joint resolution for the admission of the Territories of New Mexico and Arizona into the Union as States], August 22, 1911" in David H. Burton, ed., *The Collected Works of William Howard Taft*, Vol. IV (Athens: Ohio University Press, 2002), 149.

may be captured by special interests. But, if the people mobilize, they can force representatives to comply with the majority will. Indeed, the major reforms of the past decade had demonstrated that representative institutions will respond to an energized citizenry. "There is nothing to show that all legitimate governmental purposes sought by the so-called Progressives may not be promoted and brought about under the representative system," Taft argued. Although pursuing change through legislatures may be "somewhat more slow in its results" than adopting an initiative, this route will ensure wiser policies, especially in the details, because the legislative process will have included greater deliberation. "Great reforms should not be brought about overnight," Taft said. "They need time. They should be marked by careful consideration."[50]

Second, it was a delusion to believe that direct democracy would somehow "redeem" or otherwise improve representative institutions. Just the opposite was true. Direct democracy's real impact was to "minimize [the legislature's] power, to take away its courage and independence of action, to destroy its sense of responsibility, and to hold it up as unworthy of confidence. Nothing would more certainly destroy the character of a law-making body."[51]

Third, it was naïve to believe that initiative and referendum would magically protect government from interest group influence. The same powerful interests that had created boss rule could easily manipulate the initiative and referendum to achieve their ends. "[I]f we had another system, [special interests would] address themselves to its weaknesses and bring about a result quite as disheartening."[52]

Finally, Taft warned that direct democracy would threaten individual rights. He alleged that a "new school of political thinkers believed so strongly in popular rule that no right was beyond the peoples' absolute power to modify, impair, or abolish." Direct amendment of constitutions could thus lead to the casual destruction of fundamental rights. This was "a very different doctrine" than that of the Declaration of Independence, the Constitution, and the Bill of Rights.[53] Taft was especially concerned that direct democracy would threaten rights of property, in part because he believed that many reformers were driven by socialist impulses. But, he warned that it could also threaten other rights, as well.[54]

Meanwhile, in his 1913 Princeton lectures, Senator Elihu Root argued that the initiative process provides inadequate opportunities for deliberation and refinement of proposals, especially on complex issues. Root believed that the advocates of direct democracy had mistaken what he called the "true difficulty"

---

[50] William Howard Taft, "The Representative System," in Taft, *Popular Government*, reprinted in Burton, ed., *The Collected Works of William Howard Taft*, Vol. V, 37.

[51] Taft, "The Initiative and the Referendum," in Taft, *Popular Government*, reprinted in Burton, ed., *The Collected Works of William Howard Taft*, Vol. V, 51.

[52] Taft, "The Representative System," 37.

[53] Ibid., 52–3.

[54] Taft, "The Initiative, the Referendum, the Recall," 52–3.

of crafting wise laws, which was "not to determine what ought to be accomplished but to determine how to accomplish it." Proposed laws can have perfectly good intentions, but do harm if they are poorly written. Whereas the legislative process is designed to improve the quality of laws through "full discussion, comparison of views, modification and amendment . . . in the light of discussion and the contribution and conflict of many minds," the initiative process is incapable of achieving the same quality of deliberation.[55] "In ordinary cases the voters will not and cannot possibly bring to the consideration of proposed statutes the time, attention, and knowledge required to determine whether such statutes will accomplish what they are intended to accomplish," he argued. Moreover, "the vote usually will turn upon the avowed intention of such proposals rather than upon their adequacy to give effect to the intention."[56]

Senator Henry Cabot Lodge was also convinced that voters lacked the capacity to make proper legislation. "My objection [to the initiative and referendum] is the fundamental one," Lodge wrote. "[T]he mass of voters (and I include myself) are unable to legislate by a 'Yes' or 'No' vote at the polls. I do not believe that you can get good legislation in that way. It is a good deal easier to get a good representative than it is to pass a complicated law which very few people can understand unless they have given it particular attention."[57]

Applying Madisonian analysis, Taft, Root, and Lodge set forth the basic objections to direct democracy that persist to this day. To summarize:

- Direct lawmaking provides an inferior form of deliberation;
- Voters are incompetent to enact complex initiative legislation;
- Special interests can manipulate the initiative process;
- Direct lawmaking undermines representative institutions; and
- The initiative process threatens individual and minority rights.

The Federal Constitutional Challenge: Article IV, Section 4

In a last-ditch effort to derail direct democracy, opponents turned to the courts and argued that direct democracy violated the federal Constitution. Article IV, section 4 of the Constitution declares: "The United States shall guarantee to every State in this Union a Republican Form of Government." This provision indicates that states must maintain governments "republican" in form, and that the federal government has a duty to prevent threats to the

---

55 Root, "Experiments in Government," 94–5.
56 Ibid., 95–6.
57 Henry Cabot Lodge, "Letter to Theodore Roosevelt, December 18, 1911," in Theodore Roosevelt and Henry Cabot Lodge, *Selections from the Correspondence of Theodore Roosevelt and Henry Cabot Lodge, 1884–1918*, Vol. II (New York: Charles Scribner's Sons, 1925), 417–18. For additional critique, see Henry Cabot Lodge, "The Constitution and Its Makers" (speech delivered November 11, 1911) reprinted in *The Democracy of the Constitution and Other Addresses and Essays* (New York: Charles Scribner's Sons, 1915), 52–87.

republican character of the states. But, the clause's terse language permits various interpretations.[58] The debate over the constitutional validity of direct democracy focused on two questions: Did these new devices render state governments non-republican? And who had authority to interpret and enforce the guarantee clause?

Addressing the first question, advocates of direct democracy urged a flexible reading of the guarantee clause. They argued that "republican government" can be interpreted broadly to mean "popular government" – as opposed, specifically, to monarchy – and can include a range of direct and indirect democratic forms. They noted that the framers had accepted the state governments as "republican" even though several of the states embraced some forms of direct democracy such as town meetings and popular votes on ratification of state constitutions. Moreover, Progressives argued that initiative and referendum were not intended to abolish representative government, but to repair and strengthen it. In their view, this limited use of direct democracy was faithful to the republican principle, broadly defined.

Conservatives would have none of it. They cited the records of the Philadelphia Convention and the pages of the *Federalist* to demonstrate that Madison and other delegates intended a specific definition of republican government. They gave great weight to Madison's statement in *Federalist* 10 that "a republic" meant "a government in which a scheme of representation takes place," and his clear distinction between "republican government" and "pure democracy." Moreover, the new forms of direct democracy were a far greater threat to republican government than local town meetings or legislative referrals because these new devices had no limits. Over time, the initiative process would undermine representative institutions. Surely, they argued, this prospect of unfettered majoritarianism violated the principle of Article IV, section 4.[59]

Direct democracy's opponents believed they had a compelling argument that these devices violated the federal Constitution's guarantee clause, but they faced a second, procedural question: who would enforce this view? Would courts declare use of initiative, referendum, and recall unconstitutional and void?

State courts refused to do so. The first and most important case was *Kadderly v. City of Portland* (1903).[60] In that case, the Oregon Supreme Court

---

[58] Charles O. Lerche, Jr., "The Guarantee Clause in Constitutional Law," *Western Political Quarterly* 2, no. 3, (Sept. 1949): 358.

[59] The Progressive historian Charles Beard acknowledged that "from the tone of the Convention, one may reasonably infer that [the Founders] would have looked upon [initiative and referendum] with a feeling akin to horror . . . one of their chief purposes in framing the federal constitution was to devise a series of checks and balances which would effectively prevent direct majority rule in any form. . . . [N]o one has any warrant for assuming that the founders of our federal system would have shown the slightest countenance of a system of initiative and applied either to state or national affairs." Beard and Shultz, *Documents on the Statewide Initiative, Referendum, and Recall*, 28–9.

[60] *Kadderly v. City of Portland*, 44 Ore. 118 (1903).

affirmed the constitutionality of the state's initiative and referendum devices, concluding that they did not destroy the state's republican character. The Oregon court held:

> No particular style of government is designated in the constitution as republican, nor is its exact form in any way prescribed. Now, the initiative and referendum amendment does not abolish or destroy the republican form of government, or substitute another in its place. The representative character of the government still remains. The people have simply reserved to themselves a larger share of the legislative power, but they have not overthrown the republican form of the government, or substituted another in its place. The government is still divided into the legislative, executive, and judicial departments, the duties of which are discharged by representatives selected by the people.[61]

Courts in other states, including California, Washington, Oklahoma, and Kansas, cited *Kadderly* in upholding state or local initiative and referendum devices against constitutional attack.[62]

The controversy then shifted to the federal arena, and the question became: Did *federal* courts have authority to determine whether initiative and referendum violated the guarantee clause? A line of Supreme Court precedents suggested they did not. Beginning with *Luther v. Borden* (1848), the Court had consistently determined that the federal government's interpretation and enforcement of the guarantee clause was a "political question" that fell within the authority of Congress, not the courts.[63] Congress, however, was unwilling to address the question.[64] The opponents' last hope was to convince the

---

[61] Ibid., 144.

[62] The Washington Supreme Court also rejected an Art. IV guarantee clause challenge to initiative lawmaking in *Hartig v. City of Seattle* 53 Wash. 432, 102 P.2d 408 (1909); in addition, the California Supreme Court upheld the City of Los Angeles' local initiative and referendum process against constitutional challenge in *In re Pfahler*, 150 Cal. 71 (1906). See also *Ex Parte Wagner*, 95 P. 435 (Okla. 1908), upholding local referendum process; *State ex rel. Foote v. Board of City Commissioners*, 144 P. 241 (Kan. 1914), upholding local initiative procedure.

[63] *Luther v. Borden*, 48 U.S. (7 Howard) 1 (1849). The case arose from the Dorr Rebellion in Rhode Island, a fight between two groups – one, the existing charter government; the other, a rival "government" established by a voluntary convention – both claiming to be the legal and republican government of the state. When the controversy reached the Supreme Court, Chief Justice Roger Taney, writing for the Court, refused to resolve the dispute or establish any criteria for determining what constitutes a republican government. Instead, the Court declared that the dispute was a political question, and dismissed the case for lack of jurisdiction. In subsequent cases, the Court made small departures from *Luther's* bright-line rule, but the case's central holding remained an obstacle for those who argued that courts should abolish the initiative and referendum. See, e.g., *Texas v. White*, 74 U.S. (7 Wallace) 700 (1869), a Reconstruction-era case involving the status of provisional governments established by Congress and the President after the Civil War. In holding that the provisional government was valid and that the Congress is supreme in interpreting and enforcing the guarantee clause, the Court nevertheless held that congressional action under the clause was nevertheless subject to judicial scrutiny. For a discussion of this line of cases, see Lerche, "The Guarantee Clause in Constitutional Law," 358–74.

[64] It would have been difficult, to say the least, for Congress to have refused to recognize representatives from states such as South Dakota, Oregon, and Utah that had adopted initiative and

Supreme Court to overrule or distinguish *Luther* and issue a decision declaring that initiative and referendum violated Article IV, section 4.

Pacific States Telephone and Telegraph Co. v. Oregon (1912). The case that would settle the question, *Pacific States Telephone and Telegraph Company v. Oregon*, reached the U.S. Supreme Court in its October 1911 term.[65]

The facts of *Pacific States* conveniently framed the issue. In 1906, four years after Oregon adopted the initiative and referendum, voters approved an initiative imposing on telephone and telegraph companies a two percent tax on gross receipts from business done in the state. Pacific States refused to pay the tax, and Oregon sued for delinquency. The company's primary defense was that the tax was invalid because it had been enacted through an unconstitutional process – that is, by direct initiative rather than by the legislature. After the Oregon courts rejected this theory, the U.S. Supreme Court agreed to hear the case. In their brief, lawyers for Pacific States argued that (1) the Court had the authority to enforce the guarantee clause; and (2) the initiative process itself and the particular tax measure enacted through that process violated the federal constitutional guarantee of republican government.[66]

In a unanimous decision handed down in February 1912, the Court disagreed with the first contention and refused to reach the second. In the Court's view, the controlling question was whether it had the authority to determine whether a state government was republican in form. The Court said the issue had been long settled by *Luther*, "the leading and absolutely controlling case," which conclusively established that Congress, not the Court, had the power to determine the "purely political question" of the legal existence of a state government. The Court opined that if it were to decide otherwise, it would create "an inconceivable expansion of the judicial power and the ruinous destruction of the legislative authority in matters purely political."[67]

As a practical matter, *Pacific States* protected state and local initiative and referendum processes from legal challenge on federal constitutional grounds, an outcome widely interpreted to bestow constitutional legitimacy on the new devices.[68] Individual initiatives or referenda could face legal challenge, but the constitutional validity of the processes themselves was now secure.

referendum. And, if Congress was naturally unwilling to take measures to enforce the guarantee clause against existing states, how could it refuse admission to new states, such as Oklahoma and Arizona, which wanted to include initiative, referendum, and recall in their constitutions? President Taft's veto of the Arizona statehood resolution was the most serious federal attempt to resist direct democracy, but even Taft did not demand that Arizona strike the initiative and referendum provisions from its new state constitution, only that it exempt judges from recall.

[65] *Pacific States Telephone and Telegraph Company v. Oregon*, 223 U.S. 118 (1912).

[66] E.S. Pillsbury and Oscar Sutro, "Brief of Pacific States Telephone and Telegraph Company in *Pacific States Telephone and Telegraph Company v. State of Oregon*," summarized in ibid.

[67] *Pacific States*, 141.

[68] David B. Magleby, *Direct Legislation: Voting on Ballot Propositions in the United States* (Baltimore: The Johns Hopkins Press, 1984), 48.

What If? This outcome, although decisive, was not inevitable. Despite the Court's protestations in *Pacific States* that its hands were tied, it surely possessed the power to reverse or distinguish the *Luther* line of cases and declare that the initiative and referendum violated Article IV, section 4. It is worth considering what might have happened if the Court had declared direct democracy unconstitutional in 1912. Such a ruling surely would have provoked opposition in many quarters, especially in the Western states. But, it is unclear whether popular anger could have overturned the Court's ruling. The decision might have generated efforts to amend the federal Constitution to allow for initiative and referendum at the state and local levels, but there is no certainty that such an attempt would have cleared the high hurdles of the Article V amendment process, given the regional opposition to initiative and referendum in the East and South. In any event, as we examine other conflicts between direct democracy and the courts, it will be important to remember that the U.S. Supreme Court and state supreme courts protected direct democracy from the charge that it violates the Constitution of the United States.

OUTCOME OF THE PROGRESSIVE ERA DEBATE

The direct democracy movement approached its Progressive Era peak in 1912. That year, in addition to the crucial victory in *Pacific States*, activists won adoption of the statewide initiative process in five new states – Idaho, Nebraska, Nevada, Ohio, and Washington – and the recall in Arizona, Colorado, Nevada, and Washington. After these successes, however, the movement began to wane. Only three additional states – North Dakota (1914), Mississippi (1914), and Massachusetts (1918) – adopted the initiative process in the last years of the Progressive Era, and Mississippi's initiative process was invalidated in 1922. Since then, only five states have adopted the initiative process: Alaska (1959), Florida (1968), Wyoming (1968), Illinois (1970), and, again, Mississippi (1992).[69]

At present, twenty-four states have adopted some version of the statewide initiative process; twenty-four states allow citizens to demand popular referendum of laws enacted by the legislature; and eighteen states provide for recall of state-level elected officials.[70]

The Progressive Era contest over direct democracy thus ended in a split decision. The proponents achieved major victories, winning adoption of the

---

[69] In addition, New Mexico (1911), Kentucky (1915), and Maryland (1915) adopted the referendum, but not the initiative.

[70] Three states (Florida, Illinois, and Mississippi) have initiative, but no referendum; three (Kentucky, Maryland, and New Mexico) have referendum, but no initiative. The states that allow for recall of statewide elected officials are Alaska, Arizona, California, Colorado, Georgia, Idaho, Kansas, Louisiana, Michigan, Minnesota, Montana, Nevada, New Jersey, North Dakota, Oregon, Rhode Island, Washington, and Wisconsin. See Cronin, *Direct Democracy*, 51, 126–7; M. Dane Waters, ed., *Initiative and Referendum Almanac* (Durham: Carolina Academic Press, 2003), 12.

TABLE I.I. *State Adoptions of the Initiative Process*

State	Year
South Dakota	1898
Utah	1900
Oregon	1902
Montana	1906
Oklahoma	1907
Maine	1908
Michigan	1908
Missouri	1908
Arkansas	1910
Colorado	1910
Arizona	1911[a]
California	1911
Idaho	1912
Nebraska	1912
Nevada	1912
Ohio	1912
Washington	1912
North Dakota	1914
Mississippi	1914[b]
Massachusetts	1918
Alaska	1959
Florida	1968
Wyoming	1968
Illinois	1970
Mississippi	1992

[a] Whereas Arizona voters adopted the initiative in their state-hood constitution of 1911, the state was not admitted to the Union until 1912.

[b] Mississippi's 1914 initiative and referendum amendment was invalidated by the Mississippi Supreme Court in *Power v. Robertson*, 130 Miss. 188 (1922); the state readopted the initiative process in 1992.

The District of Columbia obtained initiative and referendum in 1977.

new devices in many states, and, crucially, securing direct democracy's constitutional legitimacy. But, their success was far from complete. Opponents effectively raised concerns about the new devices, blocked their adoption at the state level in most states outside the West, and prevented any realistic hope for their adoption at the national level.[71] Moreover, several states that adopted initiative and referendum imposed important restrictions on their use, including

[71] During the Progressive Era, proposals for a national initiative and referendum achieved little traction. The most serious proposal was the so-called War Referendum, which would have amended the federal constitution to require popular authorization for the United States to declare war, except when the country was attacked or invaded. During the period prior to

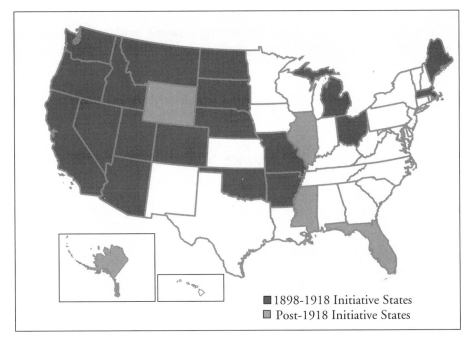

FIGURE I.I. Geographic Distribution of Initiative States.

super-majority vote requirements, subject matter restrictions, and other procedural hurdles that significantly limited direct democracy's potential in those states.

The Political Geography of Direct Democracy

A map of initiative states demonstrates that the outcome of the Progressive Era debate had a strong geographic dimension. Most notably, advocates of the new devices had much greater success in the West than in other regions of the country.

Several factors help explain this geographic divide. The new political institutions in the West were more fluid than in the South or East. Westerners were less attached to traditional forms and more open to political innovation. The West's egalitarian political culture was also receptive to populist ideology; indeed, a deep commitment to popular sovereignty and direct democracy became a defining feature of the more populist "Western" form of Progressivism. Moreover, few Western states were dominated by an entrenched political party or party machine, and legislatures were more likely to embrace direct democracy in

World War I, William Jennings Bryan and Wisconsin Senator Robert La Follette prominently advocated the proposal, and it was revived, again without success, during the 1930s. Cronin, *Direct Democracy*, 164–71; Ernest C. Bolt, Jr., *Ballots Before Bullets: The War Referendum Approach to Peace in America*, 1914–1941 (Charlottesville: University Press of Virginia, 1977).

states where there was party competition.[72] The West's fluid party system also allowed new interest groups to emerge, including many that saw direct democracy as a way to achieve their goals.[73] Together, these factors helped advocates of direct democracy secure adoption of the new devices in nearly every Western state.

The East proved more resistant. Only Maine and Massachusetts in New England, and Ohio and Michigan on the western edge of the region, adopted the statewide initiative and referendum. And in two of these states (Massachusetts and Ohio), proponents secured the new devices through state constitutional conventions rather than by convincing legislatures to devolve lawmaking power to the people.

Direct democracy failed to gain a stronger foothold in the Eastern states for a number of reasons. Party organizations were stronger in these states than in the West, populist sentiment weaker, and reformers were generally more inclined to attack boss rule by means other than initiative and referendum. The Eastern reform model emphasized the establishment of direct primaries, the creation of professional, nonpartisan agencies and commissions, and the strengthening of executives.[74] Eastern Progressives' ambivalence toward direct democracy, combined with strong party and other institutional resistance, limited the system's spread in the Eastern states.

The South also resisted direct democracy. Whereas the South had populist leaders such as Tom Watson and a deep populist streak, several factors conspired to limit direct democracy's success in the region. Southern states had few of the labor organizations and reform groups that successfully advocated direct democracy elsewhere; they also had a conservative political class, a one-party monopoly, and Jim Crow.[75] Most importantly, Southern politics was driven by the desire to preserve existing power relationships. Between 1890 and 1910, the same period when direct democracy was spreading in other states, the Old Confederacy was restricting the vote through poll taxes, literacy tests, hereditary or grandfather clauses, and other pernicious devices.[76] In short, the

[72] Daniel A. Smith and Dustin Fridkin, "Delegating Direct Democracy: Interparty Legislative Competition and the Adoption of Direct Democracy in the American States," *American Political Science Review* 102, no. 3 (Aug. 2008): 333–50.

[73] Thomas Goebel, *A Government by the People: Direct Democracy in America, 1890–1940* (Chapel Hill: University of North Carolina Press, 2002), 70; Piott, *Giving Voters a Voice*, 139.

[74] Nathaniel A. Persily, "The Peculiar Geography of Direct Democracy: Why the Initiative, Referendum, and Recall Developed in the American West," 2 MICH. L. & POL'Y. REV. 11 (1997), 24–7; David D. Schmidt, *Citizen Lawmakers: The Ballot Initiative Revolution* (Philadelphia: Temple University Press, 1989), 10–12.

[75] Goebel, *A Government by the People*, 92–9; see also Smith and Fridkin, "Delegating Direct Democracy" on the relationship between one-party dominance in state legislatures and resistance to direct democracy.

[76] Ibid., 91–92; Charles Sumner Lobingier, *The People's Law or Popular Participation in Lawmaking* (New York: The Macmillan Company, 1909), 301–19. In 1911, the Progressive journal *Equity* stated: "Many conscientious southerners oppose direct legislation because they fear this process of government would increase the power of the Negro, and therefore increase the danger of Negro domination." *Equity*, January 11, 1913, 19, cited in Schmidt, *Citizen Lawmakers*, 13.

South was moving in a direction quite contrary to direct democracy. Southern Democrats confirmed this sentiment by blocking the 1912 Democratic National Convention from adopting a direct democracy plank in the party platform.[77]

Despite these adverse conditions, the movement achieved some successes in the region. Most notably, Oklahoma entered the Union in 1907 with a new state constitution that included initiative and referendum and Arkansas adopted initiative and referendum in 1910.[78] In 1914, voters in Mississippi approved an amendment to the state constitution to allow initiative and referendum, but this achievement was short lived. In one of the most consequential early conflicts between direct democracy and the courts, the Mississippi Supreme Court struck down the state's initiative and referendum amendment. In *Power v. Robertson* (1922), the court held that the amendment was improperly submitted to voters because it contained multiple subjects. The legislature failed to respond with new amendments and it took seventy years, until 1992, for the state to adopt a new, highly restrictive, initiative process.[79]

As a result of these regional differences, Americans throughout most of the West were able to enact laws directly through the ballot, whereas most of their fellow citizens living in the East and South lacked this power. Initiative and referendum had become largely, although not exclusively, a Western phenomenon.

Other Important Differences Between States

The mixed outcome of the direct democracy debate can also be seen in the rules governing these devices. Subject matter restrictions, signature and vote requirements, provisions for post-election amendment, and other rules varied significantly between states – and these differences have consequences. In California, for example, Governor Hiram Johnson promoted rules for the initiative process that permitted both statutory and constitutional initiatives, protected initiative statutes from being amended or repealed by the legislature, and established straightforward procedures for qualifying and adopting measures. These generous provisions have helped make California's initiative process one of the strongest in the nation. In some other states, however, legislatures made the power difficult or impossible to use. Utah is perhaps the most dramatic example. After that state adopted the initiative process in 1900, the legislature refused to pass workable implementing legislation. Instead, the legislature enacted highly restrictive rules, including a requirement that all initiative petitions be signed "in the office and in the presence of an officer competent to

---

[77] Goebel, *A Government by the People*, 93.
[78] Ibid., 95.
[79] *Power v. Robertson*, 130 Miss. 188 (1922). Goebel, *A Government by the People*, 96–7; Piott *Giving the Voters a Voice*, 139–40. Meanwhile, in 1968, Florida became the only other Southern state to adopt the initiative process. Cronin, *Direct Democracy*, 51.

administer oaths."[80] These restrictions disabled Utah's initiative process. Similarly, other states imposed burdensome signature requirements, super-majority vote rules, or broad restrictions on the initiative subject matter.

Perhaps the most crucial issue was whether to allow initiative constitutional amendment (ICA), the most powerful form of direct democracy. Most states that allowed citizens to initiate statutes also allowed for ICA, but a few did not. Utah, Washington, Idaho, and Maine – as well as Alaska and Wyoming, which became initiative states after the Progressive Era – authorized initiative statutes, but not ICAs.[81]

These differences again demonstrate the mixed outcome of the controversy. Some states, like Oregon and California, adopted the strongest forms of direct democracy and enacted rules designed to implement their use. Other states, especially in the South and East, rejected direct democracy altogether. And, still others fell somewhere in the middle, with proponents winning adoption of some forms of direct democracy but not others, and opponents imposing various constraints on their use.

CONCLUSION

By winning adoption of direct democracy in many states, the Progressive Era reformers modified the Madisonian system, but they failed to resolve how these experiments in government would be used. Would direct democracy be invoked cautiously, as Progressives like Wilson and Roosevelt suggested, only to "correct" and "strengthen" representative institutions? Or would it be exercised in a more radical populist way to enable citizens to take the reins of power, bypass their elected representatives, and make law directly on a wide range of policy matters? Even more fundamentally, the debate failed to finally settle the most enduring question of American politics: What is the proper balance between popular sovereignty and limits on majority rule? The Progressive Era had renewed the founding era's intense debate on these questions and had apparently shifted the balance in favor of direct rule by popular majorities. But, it remained to be seen how this experiment would develop over time as citizens exercised the newly established powers.

[80] See Waters, *Initiative and Referendum Almanac*, 400. After World War II, the Utah legislature eased the restrictions, but still made it comparatively difficult to qualify initiatives.
[81] Ibid., 12. Montana and South Dakota adopted the initiative constitutional amendment process in 1972.

2

Direct Democracy Gathers Force

In 1970, an *American Political Science Review* article asked, "What ever happened to direct democracy?"[1] By the late 1960s, the initiative process seemed to be moribund in most states and many scholars had come to believe that direct citizen lawmaking, like the horse and buggy, was a relic of history. According to the prevailing view, "[t]he Madisons and Burkes who feared the excesses of democracy may rest in peace."[2] But, the requiems were, of course, premature. Even as the article circulated, the initiative power was poised to begin a dramatic and sustained resurgence.

This brief story demonstrates direct democracy's resilience. Once embedded in a state's constitutional structure, the process can fall dormant, but later revive. This chapter traces the varying strength of direct citizen lawmaking over time and across states, from its early flourishing in the Progressive Era, through its mid-century decline, to its more recent renewal.

CHANGES IN INITIATIVE USE OVER TIME

Figure 2.1 provides an overview of varying levels of initiative use over time by presenting the total number of statewide initiatives adopted in the twenty-four initiative states, by decade, over the past century.

1900s–1910s: "The Oregon System" and Progressive Era Enthusiasm

Citizens in Oregon adopted twenty-five statewide initiatives between 1904 and 1910 and remained the only voters to enact initiatives until Oklahomans adopted two in 1910. Across the country, initiative and referendum soon

---

[1] Howard D. Hamilton, "Direct Legislation: Some Implications of Open Housing Referenda," *American Political Science Review*, 64, no. 1 (Mar. 1970): 124.
[2] Ibid., 124–5.

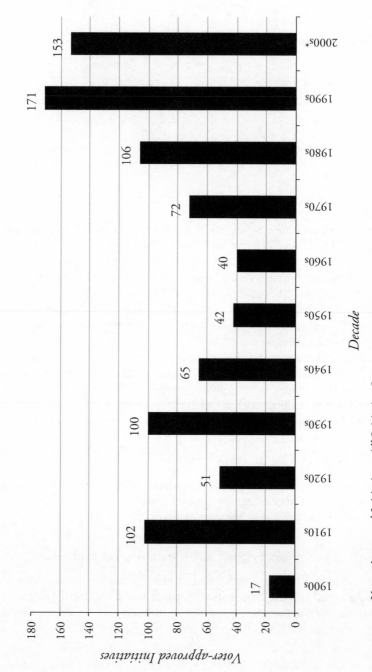

FIGURE 2.1. Voter-Approved Initiatives, All Initiative States, 1900s–2000s.
* 2000s data include initiatives adopted through 2008.

became known as "the Oregon system." In this one state laboratory, the aggressive, populist vision for direct citizen lawmaking first competed, in practice, with the more reserved conception of the initiative as "the medicine of the constitution, cautiously administered when the occasion might require."[3]

Oregon's great champion of direct democracy, William S. U'Ren, argued for frequent use of the new process. "We should do something with the power as soon as possible and should continue doing," U'Ren said. "When a farm machinery agent has a good machine, he always wants you to see it work in the field. We believe our new machine is a good one for making laws. Let us offer the field tests."[4]

U'Ren and his Direct Legislation League thus promoted numerous ballot measures and contributed to the state's early, ambitious experiments in initiative lawmaking. The initiatives adopted between 1904 and 1908 established direct primaries, granted home rule to local governments, extended the initiative and referendum to the local level, provided voters the power to recall public officials, enacted comprehensive new campaign finance rules, regulated railroads, and imposed taxes on a range of corporations, among other achievements. Oregon's active use of the process continued into the next decade, peaking in November 1912 when the statewide ballot contained a record twenty-eight citizen-initiated measures. Starting in 1912, some other states began to use the process in a similarly vigorous way. That year, Coloradans voted on twenty statewide initiatives; in 1914, Californians voted on seventeen and Arizonans fifteen. Counting all states, the number of initiatives on statewide ballots reached its Progressive Era peak of ninety in 1914.

Although many enthusiasts of direct democracy were delighted by this early flurry of activity, others thought it was excessive.[5] For example, by 1909, *The Oregonian*, the state's leading newspaper and an early supporter of initiative and referendum, concluded it had been "fallacious" to hope "there would be so much consideration and self-restraint on all sides that the new methods would not be pushed to the extreme, but would be used only on rare occasions and for remedial purposes."[6] Similarly, in *The Operation of the Initiative, Referendum, and Recall in Oregon* (1915), University of Oregon Professor James D. Barnett worried that the "multiplicity of measures" placed too heavy a burden on voters. Whether from the system's novelty, failures by the legislature, the "extreme ease of securing signatures," or the extraordinary role of activists like U'Ren, Barnett believed the system was being used in an unsustainable way. Barnett described some possible remedies for this excess, such as increasing signature requirements, prohibiting the resubmission of defeated proposals,

---

3 *The Oregonian* (February 18, 1908), 8, cited in James D. Barnett, *The Operation of the Initiative, Referendum, and Recall in Oregon* (New York: Macmillan, 1915), 78.

4 W. S. U'Ren, *Direct Legislation Record*, Vol. 7 (1901), 160, cited in Barnett, *The Operation*, 83.

5 Richard J. Ellis, *Democratic Delusions: The Initiative Process in America* (Lawrence: University Press of Kansas, 2002), 32–4.

6 *The Oregonian* (July 6, 1909), 8, cited in Barnett, *The Operation*, 78.

and limiting the number of measures on the ballot.[7] But, when initiative use dropped sharply in 1918, calls for restrictions subsided.

1920s–1960s: Stages of Decline

Direct democracy's decline occurred in stages. During the 1920s, voters approved fewer than half as many initiatives as in the prior decade.[8] Citizen lawmaking revived briefly in the early 1930s as public demand for Depression-era reforms, including repeal of prohibition, helped produce a spike in use, especially during in the 1932–1934 cycles. This increase did not last, however, and initiative use fell over the next three decades. By the 1960s, the process was nearly moribund. Except in a few states such as Washington, Arizona, North Dakota, and Arkansas, voters approved far fewer initiatives during the 1950s and 1960s than in prior years. How deep was direct democracy's nadir? During the entire decade of the 1960s, Oregonians – the former trailblazers of this process – adopted zero initiatives and Californians adopted only three.

There is no conclusive explanation for direct democracy's mid-century decline, although various observers have suggested a number of plausible reasons. The simplest account is that citizens simply lost interest in the process. As the 1970 *American Political Science Review* article noted, direct lawmaking came to be seen, at least in some quarters, as anachronistic in an era of increasingly professionalized government administration.[9] Others suggest that demand for direct democracy is inversely related to public trust in representative government.[10] If so, direct democracy's decline can be explained by the public's rising confidence in government during the post-World War II period. According to this theory, citizens who trusted their representatives were disinclined to use direct democracy to correct or constrain them.

California's experience offers support for this view. The state's use of the initiative process hit bottom in the 1950s and 1960s, during what journalist Peter Schrag calls a "golden moment" in California history – a time of relative prosperity, optimism, public investment, and confidence in state government.[11]

---

[7] Ibid., 82–5.

[8] North Dakota, California, and Montana were the only states to adopt more initiatives in the 1920s than in the 1910s.

[9] Hamilton, "Direct Legislation," 125.

[10] For a discussion of the inverse relationship between trust in government and initiative use, see David B. Magleby, *Direct Legislation: Voting on Ballot Propositions in the United States* (Baltimore: Johns Hopkins University Press, 1984), 14–15. Political scientist Caroline Tolbert further develops this thesis by linking increased initiative use to low voter trust in government during periods of rapid socioeconomic change. Caroline J. Tolbert, "Public Policymaking and Direct Democracy in the Twentieth Century: The More Things Change, the More They Stay the Same," in M. Dane Waters, ed., *The Battle Over Citizen Lawmaking: An In-Depth Review of the Growing Trend to Regulate the People's Tool of Self Government: The Initiative and Referendum Process* (Durham: Carolina Academic Press, 2001), 40–1.

[11] Peter Schrag, *Paradise Lost: California's Experience, America's Future* (New York: The New Press, 1998), 27–52.

During these years, the legislature worked with the governor to build the state's public university system to a position of national preeminence, construct hundreds of new elementary and secondary schools, acquire new parklands, and greatly expand its famed system of highways and aqueducts. Partly as a result of these achievements, confidence in representative institutions ran high. California's leading legislator of the period, Jesse Unruh, seized this moment to strengthen and institutionalize the state legislature. In the mid-1960s, Unruh organized a blue-ribbon constitutional revision commission to develop plans for a full-time professional legislature. Among other things, the proposed constitutional revisions and accompanying reforms provided for year-round, full-time sessions, statutory increases in legislators' pay, new funding for district offices, and increased legislative staff, including nonpartisan research staff. In 1966, the legislature asked voters to ratify this ambitious blueprint for professionalized representative government. The proponents' ballot statement, signed by both Democratic Governor Edmund G. "Pat" Brown and his Republican challenger, Ronald Reagan, argued "[i]f states are to survive and prosper in our system, they need the tools of effective government."[12] Californians approved the measure by a 75 percent vote.[13] This outcome made California's legislature the most highly-professionalized in the nation and signified the peak of Californians' support for representative government – again, at the very moment that their use of the initiative process hit its lowest point.[14]

Although this explanation best fits the California experience, a similar pattern could be seen elsewhere. Richard Ellis notes that Oregon's initiative process declined during the 1950s and 1960s, a time when "Oregonians took great pride in their government, turned out to vote in large numbers, and had high levels of trust in public officials."[15] But, the "trust in government" explanation cannot explain all fluctuations in initiative use. There is no evidence, for example, that voters in Washington, Arizona, or North Dakota lacked the high levels of trust in government that generally characterized the 1950s and early 1960s, yet they approved initiatives during this period at approximately the same rates as they did throughout the century.[16] Moreover, whereas initiative

---

[12] California Secretary of State, *Proposed Amendments to the Constitution, Propositions and Proposed Laws Together with Arguments, General Election November 8, 1966*, 1–2. *http://traynor.uchastings.edu/ballot_pdf/1966g.pdf*. See Bernard L. Hyink, "California Revises its Constitution," *Western Political Quarterly* 22, no. 3 (Sept. 1969): 637–54; Eugene C. Lee, "The Revision of California's Constitution," 3 *CPS Brief* (California Policy Seminar, April 1991), 3–6.

[13] The vote was 4,156,416 Yes to 1,499,675 No (75%–25%). California Secretary of State, *California Statement of Vote and Supplement, November 8, 1966 General Election*, 35.

[14] John Burns and the Citizens Conference on State Legislatures, *The Sometime Governments: A Critical Study of the 50 American Legislatures* (New York: Bantam, 1971), 48–54. This comprehensive study determined the California legislature to be the nation's best at the beginning of the 1970s. For an account of how the California legislature flourished in the decade after the 1960s reforms, see William K. Muir, Jr., *Legislature: California's School for Politics* (Chicago: University of Chicago Press, 1982).

[15] Ellis, *Democratic Delusions*, 34.

[16] Between 1914 and 2008 Washington voters approved 78 statewide initiatives, averaging approximately eight initiatives per decade. In the 1960s, Washington voters exceeded this

use increased in some states during the 1970s, just as trust in government plummeted, it did not do so in other initiative states.[17]

Others have looked to structural factors to help explain direct democracy's mid-century decline. For example, David Schmidt argues that during the 1950s and 1960s, signature requirements became so burdensome that they severely restricted access to the initiative process.[18] It is true that signature thresholds rose during this period because they are linked to the number of votes cast in prior elections, and those numbers increased in tandem with the post-war population boom. But, although these rising thresholds may have prevented certain low-budget groups from qualifying initiatives, they can hardly account for the dormancy of the initiative process at mid-century. Today, signature requirements in most initiative states are far greater than they were in the 1960s, yet these hurdles have not prevented a dramatic surge in initiative lawmaking.

1970s–2000s: Resurgence

By all accounts, in the 1970s, the initiative process staged a dramatic revival. A quick glance at the nationwide figures reveals steep decade-over-decade increases in voter-approved statewide initiatives starting in the 1970s. From a low point in the 1960s through the peak in the 1990s, the number of statewide initiatives adopted per decade increased from 40 to 72 to 106 to 171 – an overall four-fold increase during this period. Initiative use for the 2000s fell below the peak of the 1990s, but remained at a historically high level. Thus, for a period of more than three decades, citizens have used the initiative process more frequently and across a greater number of states than at any other time in the initiative era. This period of heavy, sustained initiative use is far different from the brief spikes of initiative use in the 1910s and early 1930s, both of which were quickly followed by sharp declines.

What caused the initiative process to revive after the 1960s and gain unprecedented strength thereafter? Many observers attribute the initiative's renewed vitality to a single measure, California's legendary Proposition 13 of 1978.[19] On

---

average by adopting nine statewide initiatives. By the same measure, between 1912 and 2008, Arizona voters approved approximately seven statewide initiatives per decade; they adopted seven measures in the 1960s. The figures for North Dakota are approximately nine initiatives per decade and eight in the 1960s.

[17] The University of Michigan's biennial election studies have tracked levels of trust in government since 1964. Favorable responses dropped substantially between 1964 and 1978. For a discussion, see David O. Sears and Jack Citrin, *Tax Revolt: Something for Nothing in California*, enlarged edition (Cambridge, MA: Harvard University Press, 1985), 24–5. Yet, the number of voter-approved statewide initiatives fell between the 1960s and 1970s in five states (Arkansas, Arizona, Nebraska, Nevada, and North Dakota).

[18] David D. Schmidt, *Citizen Lawmakers: The Ballot Initiative Revolution* (Philadelphia: Temple University Press, 1989), 21.

[19] See, e.g., David S. Broder, *Democracy Derailed: Initiative Campaigns and the Power of Money* (New York: Harcourt, 2000), 7: "Whether true or false populism, Prop. 13 revived interest in the initiative process. After Proposition 13, use of the initiative became much more frequent in the twenty-four states, plus the District of Columbia, where it is available."

close analysis, the famous citizen tax revolt measure does not fully explain the revival of the initiative power, but the myth of Proposition 13's impact is pervasive because it contains elements of truth.

Proposition 13 – also known as the "Jarvis-Gann initiative" in recognition of its primary sponsors, Howard Jarvis and Paul Gann – emerged during a period of double-digit price inflation, increasingly burdensome property taxes, and declining trust in government.[20] The measure was radical in several respects: it promised to roll back property assessments to former levels; limit future increases of the property's assessed value to 2 percent per year until the property is sold; restrict tax rates to 1 percent of a property's assessed value; and, crucially, require a two-thirds vote of the legislature to increase statewide taxes and a two-thirds vote of the people to increase taxes at the local level.[21] The state's legislative analyst predicted Proposition 13 would reduce property tax revenues in the first year by approximately $7 billion.[22] More importantly, in the long term, the measure would significantly restrict the future taxing powers of the state legislature and local governments.

California voters had rejected similar proposals in the late 1960s and early 1970s, but the measure's most prominent advocate, Howard Jarvis, was undeterred.[23] Jarvis, an entrepreneur and conservative political operative, resembled an Anti-Federalist or populist agitator as he artfully fused attacks on rising taxes with a more general assault on representative elites and the "big government" they controlled. In Jarvis' account, representatives had become arrogant, grasping, unresponsive, corrupt, and wasteful – in a word, tyrannical. He was "mad as hell" about this turn of events and urged the people to use the initiative power to regain control of government and reduce their burdensome taxes.[24] The ballot argument for Proposition 13 sounded these populist themes:

The Legislature will not act to reduce your property taxes...

More than 15% of all government spending is wasted! Wasted on huge pensions for politicians which sometimes approach $80,000 per year! Wasted on limousines for elected officials or taxpayer paid junkets. Now we have the opportunity to trade waste for property tax relief! If we want to permanently cut property taxes about 67% we must do it ourselves.[25]

---

[20] Periodic polling by the Field Institute showed a decline in Californians' confidence in government throughout the 1970s, bottoming out in 1978. See The Field Institute, "A Digest Describing the Public's Confidence in Institutions," *California Opinion Index*, vol. 6 (October 1981).

[21] California Secretary of State, *California Voters Pamphlet, Primary Election, June 6, 1978*, 56–7. http://traynor.uchastings.edu/ballot_pdf/1978p.pdf.

[22] Ibid.

[23] Sears and Citrin, *Tax Revolt*, 19–31; Schrag, *Paradise Lost*, 129–51.

[24] For Jarvis' account, see Howard Jarvis with Robert Pack, *I'm Mad as Hell* (New York: Times Books, 1979).

[25] John V. Briggs, "Arguments in Favor of Proposition 13," California Secretary of State, *California Voters Pamphlet, Primary Election, June 6, 1978*, 58.

Meanwhile, almost the entire California political establishment – its government, academic, business, and media leaders – opposed Proposition 13. The
bipartisan ballot argument opposing the measure soberly warned that Proposition 13 was "irresponsible" and "poorly drafted" and that it would "seriously
cripple" essential government services, deepen inequalities, and produce a host
of other negative consequences.[26] On Election Day, however, a large cross section of California voters disregarded these warnings and approved the measure
by a decisive 65 percent of the vote.

Proposition 13's success captured national attention and helped fuel
widespread demands for tax relief.[27] It also fully demonstrated the awesome
power of direct democracy.[28] In the face of strong opposition by most of
the state's leaders, ordinary citizens had used the initiative process to achieve
sweeping, fundamental, and lasting policy change.

This display of the initiative's potential immediately caused other groups
to consider bypassing the legislature to achieve their policy goals.[29] At the
same time, it energized California's network of attorneys, political consultants,
petition-gathering firms, and other professionals who grasped the initiative process's potential to generate profits for those who ran the campaigns.[30] Before
long, the initiative consultants took an increasingly proactive stance, generating
their own ideas for ballot measures and selling them to interest groups.[31] Moreover, many voters, flush with the excitement of having achieved a revolution
in tax policy through the ballot box, embraced the prospect of becoming more
active citizen lawmakers. It is thus no surprise that many close observers believe
Proposition 13 was instrumental in ushering in California's present era of frequent and consequential use of the initiative process.[32]

But, whereas Proposition 13 clearly contributed to the revival of the initiative
power, the historical record suggests that other factors were also at play. The
first stirrings of the initiative revival occurred before Proposition 13 reached the
ballot in 1978. As Richard Ellis has noted, Californians were already placing
more initiatives on the ballot in the early 1970s. Ten initiatives reached the
California ballot in 1972, the most in one year in any state since the early
1920s. Across the nation, the number of initiatives on statewide ballots reached

---

[26] Houston I. Flournoy, Tom Bradley, and Gary Sirbu, "Argument against Proposition 13,"
California Secretary of State, *California Voters Pamphlet, Primary Election, June 6, 1978* 59.
Former state controller Flournoy, the 1974 GOP nominee for governor, was one of many
leading Republicans, including future Governors George Deukmejian and Pete Wilson, who
opposed Proposition 13.

[27] Sears and Citrin, *Tax Revolt*, 40–2.

[28] Cronin, *Direct Democracy*, 3.

[29] Ibid.

[30] Magleby, *Direct Legislation*, 59–76; Schrag, *Paradise Lost*, 188–9.

[31] Jim Shultz, *The Initiative Cookbook: Recipes and Stories from California's Ballot Wars* (San
Francisco: Democracy Center, 1996), 81–2.

[32] Jack Citrin, "Who's The Boss? Direct Democracy and Popular Control of Government" in
Stephen C. Craig, ed., *Broken Contract?: Changing Relationships Between Americans and
Their Government* (Boulder, CO: Westview, 1996), 282.

fifty-two in the 1976–1977 cycle, the most since 1938–1939.[33] The initiative was already reviving in California and some other states when Proposition 13 added a substantial burst of energy.

Moreover, although it is widely believed that Proposition 13 quickly spurred citizen lawmaking across the country,[34] the history is again more complex. Several states were indeed inspired by Proposition 13's success to attempt similar measures. For example, in 1980, an antitax crusader in Massachusetts named Barbara Anderson drew inspiration from Proposition 13 in promoting Proposition 2½, a successful measure to reduce property taxes in the Commonwealth. "Our fight is not mainly about money," she said. "It's about control. *They* (the legislators) have to learn once and for all it's *our* government."[35] The same year, citizens in Missouri adopted an initiative called "the Hancock Amendment" which limited state taxes and required super-majority voter approval for most local tax hikes. And Montanans approved a tax indexing initiative in 1980 and an initiative freezing property taxes in 1986. However, states such as Nebraska, Colorado, Oregon, and Washington took more than a decade to adopt Proposition 13-type tax limitation initiatives, whereas many other states never did.[36]

More broadly, although Proposition 13 surely had a stimulating effect on overall initiative use in California, its contribution to the national surge in citizen lawmaking is less certain. Whereas initiatives adopted in California tripled between the 1970s and 1980s (from seven to twenty-one), eight initiative states – Alaska, Colorado, Michigan, Mississippi, Ohio, Utah, Washington, and Wyoming – saw no increase or even a decrease in voter-approved initiatives in the decade after Proposition 13. In several states, such as Alaska, Arizona, Colorado, Florida, and Nevada, a surge in initiative use did not occur until the 1990s, by which time new catalysts for initiative lawmaking had appeared.[37] And, in other states, the surge never came.

---

[33] Ellis, *Democratic Delusions*, 36.

[34] See, e.g., Broder, *Democracy Derailed*, 7.

[35] Quoted in Jack Citrin, "Introduction: The Legacy of Proposition 13," in Terry Schwadron, ed., *California and the American Tax Revolt: Proposition 13 Five Years Later* (Berkeley: University of California Press, 1984), 7 (emphasis in original). For a discussion of the Massachusetts Proposition 2½ campaign, see Daniel A. Smith, *Tax Crusaders and the Politics of Direct Democracy* (New York: Routledge, 1998), 85–127. Nearly a decade later, Barbara Anderson reflected on the importance of Proposition 13 to the Proposition 2½ effort: "We couldn't have [enacted Proposition 2½] if Proposition 13 had not passed in California. Massachusetts is not as adventurous as California. Certainly, the big argument we used was, 'California did it and they didn't fall into the ocean.'" Rebecca LaVally and Russell Snyder, "Proposition 13 Paved the Way for Tax Revolts Across U.S.," *Los Angeles Times*, February 14, 1988, A3, quoted in Smith, *Tax Crusaders*, 85.

[36] For an overview of tax limitation initiatives, see Pete Sepp, "A Brief History of I & R and the Tax Revolt" in M. Dane Waters, ed., *Initiative and Referendum Almanac* (Durham: Carolina Academic Press, 2003), 496–99.

[37] Averaging all initiative states, the per-decade increase in successful initiatives rose from 1.58 in the 1980s to 2.75 in the 1990s.

TABLE 2.1. *State Ranking, Voter-Approved Initiatives, 1904–2008*

State	1900s	10s	20s	30s	40s	50s	60s	70s	80s	90s	2000s*	Total
OR	17	24	4	7	6	7	–	7	14	22	16	124
CA	–	8	10	10	6	2	3	7	21	24	20	111
ND	–	7	11	22	10	5	8	4	5	5	5	82
WA	–	2	1	12	4	5	9	11	6	11	17	78
CO	–	15	4	8	2	3	3	6	6	14	11	72
AZ	–	16	–	3	10	3	7	2	4	13	12	70
AR	–	9	6	9	11	7	4	1	4	4	4	59
MT	–	6	5	1	–	1	–	6	8	7	8	42
MA	–	–	2	5	1	2	2	2	4	11	5	34
MO	–	–	5	4	1	–	–	3	4	8	6	31
MI	–	1	–	4	3	2	1	8	2	2	5	28
OK	–	5	3	5	5	–	–	1	3	4	1	27
FL	–	–	–	–	–	–	–	1	2	7	14	24
AK	–	–	–	–	–	–	–	4	4	9	5	22
ME	–	1	–	1	–	–	–	3	5	7	2	19
NV ‡	–	1	–	1	1	2	1	–	1	5	7	19
OH	–	4	–	4	3	–	–	1	–	4	3	19
NE	–	1	–	3	1	2	1	–	2	3	5	18
SD	–	2	–	–	–	–	–	1	6	5	4	18
ID	–	–	–	1	1	1	–	3	4	3	1	14
UT	–	–	–	–	–	–	1	1	–	–	2	4
WY	–	–	–	–	–	–	–	–	–	3	–	3
IL	–	–	–	–	–	–	–	–	1	–	–	1
MS	–	–	–	–	–	–	–	–	–	–	–	–
TOTAL	17	102	51	100	65	42	40	72	106	171	153	919

* 2000s data include initiatives adopted through 2008.

‡ After 1960, Nevada Initiative Constitutional Amendments required affirmative votes in two consecutive elections. See Nevada Constitution art: 19, Sec. 2 (4). This table counts only the second affirmative vote on these measures.

DIFFERENCES BETWEEN INITATIVE STATES

Overall Use

The uneven quality of the post-1970 initiative revival points to a more fundamental fact about the initiative power: For every initiative state that has used the process frequently and in consequential ways, another has used it infrequently if at all. In particular, Utah, Wyoming, Illinois, and Mississippi must be considered nominal initiative states because their highly restrictive rules have prevented citizens from actively exercising the initiative power.[38] But, other long-dormant initiative states, such as Maine, South Dakota, and Nevada, have

---

[38] For a discussion of state-by-state variation in the difficulty of qualifying ballot initiatives, see Shaun Bowler and Todd Donovan, "Measuring the Effect of Direct Democracy on State Policy:

begun to stir and Montana, Florida, and Alaska have developed active initiative systems. Conversely, North Dakota and Arkansas have experienced a decline in initiative use and have fallen from the top rank.

With these shifts, approximately fifteen states now reside in direct democracy's middle range, averaging between two and eight voter-approved initiatives per decade. In these mid-tier states, the initiative process arguably reflects the Progressive vision of direct democracy whereby citizens use the process in moderation to make occasional changes in institutions or policy. But, in the five strongest initiative states, citizens have used the initiative power with greater frequency and impact.

The Five Strongest Initiative States

California, Oregon, Washington, Colorado, and Arizona have emerged over time as the five strongest initiative states. They are distinguished in part by their high historical rates of initiative adoptions as well as by their heavy use of the process in the post-1970 period. Citizens in these states have adopted almost exactly half of all statewide initiatives over the past century. Moreover, they have led the recent national surge in citizen lawmaking by adopting more initiatives in the four decades between 1970 and 2008 than they did in the prior seven decades.

The strongest initiative states are distinguished by a number of characteristics. These states have constitutional provisions that allow the initiative process to operate freely.[39] They have a political environment of weak party organizations and vigorous interest groups. And, perhaps most importantly, they have repeat players and campaign professionals who, in the spirit of Oregon's U'Ren, "want to do something with the power . . . and continue doing."[40]

Repeat players include interest groups, politicians, and initiative entrepreneurs who understand how to navigate the complex and expensive process of qualifying a measure for the ballot and promoting it in a statewide election. California has developed the deepest pool of sophisticated initiative proponents. The state's initiative entrepreneurs have included tax crusaders Howard Jarvis and Paul Gann; Ward Connerly (a lead proponent of the state's anti-affirmative action initiative, a racial privacy initiative, and similar measures in several other states); conservative activist Ted Costa (the sponsor of numerous initiatives as well as the 2003 recall of Governor Gray Davis); Gerald Meral (an innovative sponsor of several environmental initiatives); and the actor Rob Reiner (sponsor of two tobacco tax measures). California also has many interest

Not all Initiatives are Created Equal," *State Politics and Policy Quarterly* 4, no. 3 (Fall 2004): 345–63.

[39] The one notable exception is that citizens in Washington may not initiate constitutional amendments.

[40] Charles M. Price, "The Initiative: A Comparative State Analysis and Reassessment of a Western Phenomenon," *Western Political Quarterly* 28, no. 2 (June 1975): 250–5; Barnett, *The Operation*, 83.

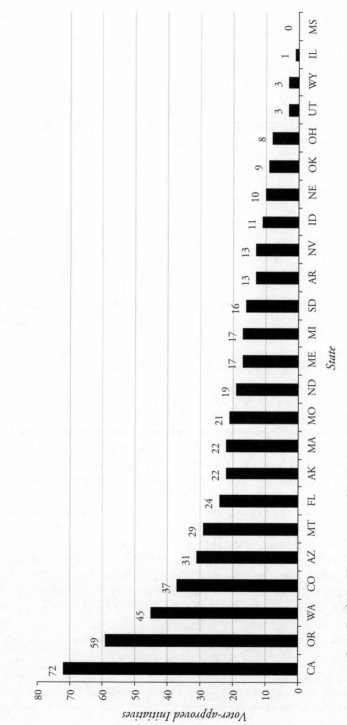

FIGURE 2.2. State Ranking, Voter-Approved Initiatives, 1970–2008.

groups, including public employee unions, Indian tribes, and professional associations, that understand the power of the state's initiative process and have invoked it on multiple occasions. Finally, the state's elected officials, including state legislators and governors, have frequently turned to the initiative process to pursue various electoral and policy objectives. Governor Pete Wilson was especially attached to direct democracy, either sponsoring or serving as a lead proponent of more than a half-dozen initiatives during the 1990s. More recently, Governor Arnold Schwarzenegger used a successful 2002 initiative to launch his career in state politics, won office through an extraordinary 2003 recall election, and, as governor, relied heavily on the initiative process to promote his policy agenda.[41]

California has also developed an "initiative industry," a sophisticated network of specialized professionals to assist initiative proponents.[42] California's initiative industry dates back to the 1930s and the founding of Whitaker & Baxter's Campaigns, Inc., a path-breaking political consulting firm that for more than two decades handled numerous initiative as well as candidate campaigns.[43] In the wake of Proposition 13, the industry matured and became more specialized. Today, one of its most important components is the "initiative bar" – attorneys who advise clients on initiative strategy, draft the text of proposed measures, negotiate or litigate pre-election questions such as the wording of a ballot title, help clients comply with campaign finance laws, and participate in defending the measure if it is challenged in court after the election. The lawyers are joined by experienced political consultants who provide a range of services to initiative proponents, including polling, voter targeting, direct mail, media relations, and the like. Finally, the initiative industry includes several companies that specialize in providing initiative proponents the necessary number of petition signatures to qualify an initiative, often at a rate of

---

[41] Richard Ellis noted that in California during the 1970s–1980s, more than one-third of all statewide initiatives were sponsored by elected officials or candidates for office; in 1988–90 their share rose to one-half. Ellis, *Democratic Delusions*, 80–1. For discussion of Pete Wilson's strategic use of the initiative process, see e.g. Lydia Chávez, *The Color Bind: California's Battle to End Affirmative Action* (Berkeley: University of California Press, 1998); Gerald C. Lubenow, ed., *California Votes: The 1994 Governor's Race: An Inside Look at the Candidates and Their Campaigns by the People Who Managed Them* (Berkeley: Institute of Governmental Studies Press, 1995). Arnold Schwarzenegger's embrace of direct democracy between 2002 and 2005 is recounted in Joe Mathews, *The People's Machine: Arnold Schwarzenegger and the Rise of Blockbuster Democracy* (New York: Public Affairs, 2006) and Peter Schrag, *California: America's High-Stakes Experiment* (Berkeley: University of California Press, 2006).

[42] For more detailed discussion and analysis of the state's initiative industry, see, e.g., David McCuan, Shaun Bowler, Todd Donovan, and Ken Fernandez, "California's Political Warriors: Campaign Professionals and the Initiative Process," in Shaun Bowler, Todd Donovan, and Caroline J. Tolbert, eds., *Citizens as Legislators: Direct Democracy in the United States* (Columbus: The Ohio State University Press, 1998), 55–79. See also Broder, *Democracy Derailed*, 43–89.

[43] See Carey McWilliams, "Government by Whitaker and Baxter," *The Nation* (April 14, April 21, May 5, 1951).

two dollars per signature or more, depending on market conditions.[44] California's network of repeat players and campaign professionals has sustained the state's heavy use of the initiative power over the past several decades and can be expected to continue to do so.

No other state has yet developed such an extensive support system for citizen lawmaking, but the other leading states do have sophisticated repeat players, some of whom are more prolific than any in California. For example, Oregon's Bill Sizemore made himself as a one-man initiative machine. A quintessential antigovernment populist and initiative entrepreneur, Sizemore not only sponsored numerous initiatives, but also formed a petition gathering firm, I & R Petition Services, to qualify his own measures as well as those of other initiative proponents. In the 2000 election cycle alone, Sizemore qualified six measures for the Oregon ballot and nearly matched that feat by qualifying five measures in 2008.[45] Other important repeat players in Oregon have included Lon Mabon (proponent of socially-conservative measures to restrict abortion and limit homosexual rights) and Lloyd Marbet (proponent of multiple initiatives to close the Trojan nuclear power plant), and conservative state legislator-turned-initiative practitioner Kevin Mannix.[46] In Colorado, the leading repeat player is initiative entrepreneur Doug Bruce, who has placed numerous measures on the state ballot, including the landmark Amendment 1 of 1992, a constitutional amendment that capped state taxing and spending and required voter approval for new tax increases.[47] In Washington, initiative entrepreneur Tim Eyman qualified a series of initiatives that limited taxes and spending and restricted government taxing authority.[48] And, in Arizona, leading entrepreneurs have included John Kromko, the state's "Mr. Initiative" in the 1970s and 1980s, and, more recently, Mark Osterloh, Nathan Sproul, and Jeff Singer.[49] Although many of the repeat players in high-use states have been conservative or libertarian antitax activists, initiative entrepreneurs can emerge from across the political spectrum. For every conservative initiative activist such as Howard Jarvis, there is a potential liberal counterpart such as Gerald Meral or Rob Reiner.

One additional factor contributing to the national surge in initiative use is the rise of organizations that pursue initiative campaigns in multiple states. A

---

[44] For analyses of the petition industry, see, e.g., Richard J. Ellis, "Signature Gathering in the Initiative Process: How Democratic Is It?" 64 MONT. L. REV 35 (2003); Frederick J. Boehmke, R. Michael Alvarez, "The Influence of Initiative Signature Gathering Campaigns on Political Participation. Caltech/MIT Voting Technology Project Working Paper # 27 (March 2005), http://www.vote.caltech.edu/media/documents/wps/vtp_wp27.pdf.

[45] Ellis, *Democratic Delusions*, 90–5; Edward Walsh, "Voters Say No but Sizemore Fights On," *The Sunday Oregonian*, Sept. 7, 2008, B-1.

[46] Broder, *Democracy Derailed*, 199–202, 214–5.

[47] Smith, *Tax Crusaders*, 128–56; Ellis, *Democratic Delusions*, 95–7.

[48] Ellis, *Democratic Delusions*, 98–102.

[49] Waters, *Initiative and Referendum Almanac*, 49–50. For a brief discussion of Osterloh's activities, see Dave Maass, "The Mark of a Clean Election," *Tucson Weekly* (May 30, 2002).

prominent example is U.S. Term Limits, Inc., an organization that coordinated efforts to qualify and defend term limits initiatives in most initiative states during the 1990s.[50] The Campaign for New Drug Policies, an organization funded by billionaire George Soros, has run initiative campaigns in several states to liberalize drug laws.[51] The Humane Society and the Fund for Animal Rights have pursued an effective multistate strategy to ban certain hunting practices and enact other legal protections for animals.[52] And a conservative umbrella organization called The Arlington Group coordinated a multistate effort to adopt defense of marriage initiatives.[53]

INITIATIVE SUBJECT MATTER

Citizens have used the initiative power to impose their will across the wide range of issues that fall within state authority. Later, we will see that courts have struck down many of these measures after their adoption. But, to understand the stakes in this conflict, we first need to survey the range of policies citizens have directly enacted.

Citizen initiatives have clustered in seven broad policy areas:

- Political and government reform
- Health, welfare, and morals
- Economic regulation
- Environment
- Tax
- Criminal procedure and punishment
- Education

Voter-approved initiatives have distributed among these seven categories as follows:

Political and Government Reform

Measures to reform politics and government have been the most common initiative type over the past century, accounting for more than 40 percent of all citizen lawmaking nationally and nearly one-third in the leading initiative states. This category of initiatives most clearly demonstrates the ongoing struggle between competing conceptions of direct democracy.

---

[50] Paul Jacob, "Term Limits and the I & R Process," in Waters, *Initiative and Referendum Almanac*, 505–8.

[51] Scott Ehlers, "Drug Policy Reform Initiatives and Referenda," in Waters, *Initiative and Referendum Almanac*, 484–7.

[52] Wayne Pacelle, "The Animal Protection Movement: A Modern-Day *Model* Use of the Initiative Process," in Waters, *The Battle Over Citizen Lawmaking*, 109–9.

[53] Sue O'Connell, "The Money Behind the 2004 Marriage Amendments," (Helena, MT: Institute on Money in State Politics, 2006). http://www.followthemoney.org/press/Reports/200601271.pdf.

TABLE 2.2. *Initiatives by Subject Category, 1904–2008*

State	PGR	HWM	Econ Reg.	Tax	Env.	Education	Crime	Total
OR	44	20	16	11	14	6	13	124
CA	30	19	18	8	12	10	14	111
WA	16	15	11	17	12	4	3	78
CO	34	16	9	5	5	3	–	72
AZ	23	13	14	7	5	4	4	70
ND	35	11	14	10	1	11	–	82
AR	29	5	10	6	1	7	1	59
MT	16	8	6	7	3	2	–	42
MA	12	5	6	5	5	1	–	34
MO	12	3	6	3	6	1	–	31
MI	9	6	5	5	1	1	1	28
OK	11	5	1	4	1	5	–	27
FL	6	6	4	2	3	3	–	24
AK	15	2	2	1	2	–	–	22
ME	9	1	3	2	3	1	–	19
NV	6	5	3	3	1	1	–	19
OH	7	5	2	5	–	–	–	19
NE	9	2	6	1	–	–	–	18
SD	7	–	5	2	3	1	–	18
ID	5	2	3	2	2	–	–	14
UT	2	1	1	–	–	–	–	4
WY	1	–	2	–	–	–	–	3
IL	1	–	–	–	–	–	–	1
MS	–	–	–	–	–	–	–	–
TOTAL	339	150	147	106	80	61	36	919

The strand of Progressivism that has sought to "redeem" and strengthen government has driven much citizen lawmaking from the earliest Oregon initiatives to the present day. Voters have used the initiative process to expand voting rights, mandate direct primaries, reorganize government agencies and the judicial system, establish or strengthen the civil service, create new regulatory commissions, require open meetings and disclosure of public records, regulate lobbyists, and limit campaign contributions.[54] Today, heirs of the Progressive tradition such as the League of Women Voters and Common Cause continue to promote these so-called good government initiatives with frequent success.

---

[54] A few examples from the leading states: Arizona's 1912 Proposition 300 provided women the right to vote; California's Proposition 12 of 1922 granted the governor new budget powers including the line item veto; Washington state's Initiative 207 of 1960 created a state civil service system and a state personnel board; Colorado's 1972 Amendment 9 required open meetings, financial disclosure by public officials, and lobbyist registration; and Oregon Measure 60 of 1998 created the state's innovative vote-by-mail system.

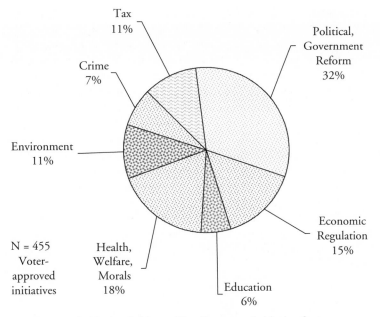

FIGURE 2.3. Initiative Subjects, Five Strongest Initiative States, 1904–2008.

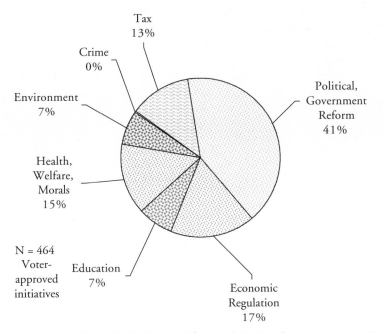

FIGURE 2.4. Initiative Subjects, Other 19 Initiative States, 1904–2008.

At the same time, however, citizens have used the initiative process to satisfy the competing, populist desire to restrict the power of representatives. Citizen lawmakers have a history of binding their representatives by limiting their discretionary authority to tax, spend, borrow, and budget. In addition, voters have adopted measures that more personally target legislators and the legislative body.[55] Most notably, during the 1990s, voters enthusiastically embraced the term limits movement. Between 1990 and 2000, citizens in twenty-one states adopted forty-three separate term limits initiatives.[56] These measures placed term limits on state legislators, state constitutional officers, or members of Congress, or threatened to put a "scarlet letter" on the ballot next to candidates who failed to support term limits. Not surprisingly, these restrictions were more popular with voters than with representatives. Almost all term limits laws were enacted through the initiative process; members of Congress and state legislators generally refused to adopt these reforms.[57] Access to the initiative made the difference: the process empowered voters to impose this reform over the objections of their representatives.

Health, Welfare, and Morals

A second large category of citizen-enacted laws has shaped public policy in the areas of public health, welfare, and morals. These initiatives have accounted for slightly more than one-sixth of all citizen lawmaking in the leading initiative states, a slightly higher percentage than in the other initiative states.

In the first third of the twentieth century, citizen lawmaking in this area was dominated by the peculiar issue of prohibition. Temperance activists believed that alcohol abuse and the culture of the saloon were serious threats to public health, welfare, and morals. Restricting alcohol, in their view, was integrally related to the era's larger program of social and humanitarian reform.[58] When

---

[55] For example, during the Great Depression, Arizona voters adopted an initiative that reduced the size of the legislature, slashed legislators' salaries, and limited the number and salaries of legislative staff. Similarly, in 1932, citizens in North Dakota adopted several initiatives reducing pay of government officials and, in 1934, Nebraskans adopted the initiative that replaced the state's bicameral legislature with a unicameral body.

[56] For further discussion of the term limits movement, see Chapter 6. See also National Conference of State Legislatures, "Legislative Term Limits: An Overview," http://www.ncsl.org/programs/legismgt/ABOUT/termlimit.htm; Thad Kousser, *Term Limits and the Dismantling of Legislative Professionalism* (New York: Cambridge University Press, 2005), 7–12.

[57] See Kousser, *Term Limits*, 9–10. Of all the 24 initiative states, only the two weakest, Illinois and Mississippi, did not adopt term limits. In Utah, legislators capitulated to citizen demands for term limits, but only under the threat of an initiative. Louisiana was the only state where legislators imposed term limits on themselves without the prod of the initiative process. The New Hampshire state legislature adopted term limits on the state's representatives in Congress, but not on themselves, in 1995. For further discussion of the adoption of term limits measures and the courts' response, see Chapter 6.

[58] Peter H. Odegard, *Pressure Politics: The Story of the Anti-Saloon League* (New York: Columbia University Press, 1928), 176; Richard Hofstadter, *The Age of Reform: From Bryan to F.D.R.*

legislatures defeated prohibition measures, activists turned to the initiative process, where they won narrow, state-by-state victories and built momentum toward national prohibition.

Between 1904 and 1942, citizens across the U.S. adopted 30 initiatives related to the regulation or prohibition of intoxicating liquors, including 19 measures in the five leading initiative states. These initiatives pursued various approaches, including "local option," statewide prohibition, and later, when public sentiment shifted, repeal. In 1930–1933, voters in seven states, including all the leading initiative states, used the initiative process to repeal state prohibition laws.[59]

During this early period, citizens in several states also used the initiative process to establish state-level social safety nets. Starting with a 1912 Colorado initiative providing state support for neglected and dependent children, voters in the leading initiative states adopted seventeen initiatives to establish and fund state programs to support indigent mothers and their children, war veterans and their widows, the blind, the insane, victims of tuberculosis, and the aged. Citizens in several other states, including Ohio, Oklahoma, North Dakota, Idaho, Nevada, and Massachusetts, adopted similar initiatives.

Ballot measures related to health, welfare, and morals have reemerged in recent years as voters have used the initiative power to enact new and controversial policies in this area. For example, in 1994, Oregon voters narrowly approved Measure 16, the nation's first law authorizing physician-assisted suicide for terminally ill adults. In 2008, Washington voters adopted a similar measure. In 1996, citizen lawmakers in Arizona and California authorized the medical use of marijuana, and, by 2008, voters in nine states had adopted medical marijuana laws.[60] In 2004, California voters approved Proposition 71, a measure that established a state constitutional right to conduct embryonic stem cell research and authorized $3 billion in state bonds to fund this research. And, in an echo of the prohibition movement, voters in several states have sought to ameliorate the evils of smoking by taxing tobacco, funding antismoking and related health programs, and restricting the places people may legally smoke.

Most recent measures in this category have advanced liberal goals, but voters have also adopted initiatives to reinforce traditional definitions of marriage

---

(New York: Vintage Books, 1955), 289–93. The movement was also driven in part by a nativist aversion to what Hofstadter called "the immigrant drinking masses." Hofstadter, *The Age of Reform*, 289–93.

59 Massachusetts voters adopted an initiative in 1930 to repeal the state's prohibition laws by a 64 percent vote. The percentage yes votes for the 1932 initiatives repealing prohibition were: California 69, Arizona 64, Washington 62, Oregon 60, North Dakota 58, and Colorado 56.

60 Voters approved medical marijuana initiatives in Arizona (1996), California (1996), Alaska (1998), Oregon (1998), Maine (1999), Nevada (1998/2000), Colorado (2000), Montana (2004), and Michigan (2008). For a discussion of the strategic use of initiatives by the medical marijuana movement, see Frederick J. Boehmke, *The Indirect Effect of Direct Legislation: How Institutions Shape Interest Group Systems* (Columbus: The Ohio State University Press, 2005), 3–7, 79, 145.

and family. Between 2000 and 2008, voters in eleven states used the initiative process to restrict marriage to a union between a man and a woman.[61] And, in 2008, voters in Arkansas adopted an initiative banning adoptions by individuals who are cohabiting outside of a valid marriage.[62]

Finally, citizen lawmakers have occasionally wrestled with abortion policy. Although the U.S. Supreme Court's decision in *Roe v. Wade* has significantly limited democratic policy making in this area, activists on both sides of the issue have qualified a number of measures designed either to expand or restrict abortion rights. Divided electorates have rejected most abortion-related initiatives, but there have been a few exceptions. In 1991, citizens in Washington adopted an initiative to codify abortion rights and require public funding for abortions for poor women. Conversely, in Colorado, voters adopted initiatives to restrict public funding for abortions (1984) and to require minors to notify their parents and wait 48 hours before the procedure (1998). Similarly, in 1988, Arkansas voters adopted an initiative to restrict public funding for abortions.[63]

Economic Regulation

A third type of initiative in some way regulates economic activity. Economic regulation measures have accounted for approximately 15 percent of voter-approved initiatives, both nationally and in the five leading initiative states.

During the first half of the twentieth century, the initiative process was an important arena for battles over employment regulation, with labor occasionally achieving victories at the polls. Progressive Era initiatives established maximum hour laws, an anti-blacklisting policy, and a landmark employer liability act. By mid-century, however, voters increasingly sided with management by adopting measures that limited workers compensation, mandated the open shop, restricted picketing and secondary boycotts, and prohibited the practice of "featherbedding" on railroad crews.[64]

After 1970, the total number of economic regulation initiatives tapered off. During this period, the most contentious initiatives in this category expanded and regulated the gambling industry, including lotteries, pari-mutuel betting,

---

[61] By 2008, voters in nineteen other states had adopted state "Defense of Marriage Amendments" or "DOMAs" through the legislative constitutional amendment (LCA) process. For further discussion and a listing of state DOMAs, see Chapter 7.

[62] The adoption restriction, Arkansas Initiative Act No. 1 of 2008, was approved by a 57–43 percent vote. Arkansas Secretary of State, "Elections," http://www.sos.arkansas.gov/elections_election_results.html.

[63] See Washington I-120 (1991); Colorado A-2 (1984) (funding restriction); Colorado A-12 (1998) (48-hour waiting period); Arkansas A-3 (1988) (funding restrictions.) As discussed in Chapter 5, the Colorado and Arkansas initiatives were all invalidated either in part or in their entirety.

[64] "Featherbedding" is a pejorative term usually describing efforts by unions to create more jobs than is necessary for a task. See, e.g., *Brotherhood of Locomotive Firemen and Enginemen v. Chicago, Rock Island & Pacific Railroad Co.*, 393 U.S. 129 (1968).

and casinos.[65] Less controversial were initiatives to increase the minimum wage. Between 1988 and 2006, citizens in ten states, including the five leading states, increased the state minimum wage through the initiative process.[66] Voters rarely approved more ambitious attempts to regulate business, but one important exception was California's Proposition 103 of 1988. That measure, backed by consumer advocate Ralph Nader, rolled back automobile insurance rates, restricted future rate increases, and created an elected office of state insurance commissioner to enforce the measure's new, complex regulations.

Environment

Although environmental measures have appeared on ballots throughout the initiative era, they increased dramatically after 1970 with the emergence of the modern environmental movement, especially in the leading initiative states. Overall, environmental initiatives have accounted for more than one-tenth of all citizen lawmaking in the leading initiative states, a larger percentage than in the other states.

Early environmental initiatives primarily sought to protect rivers in the Pacific Coast region. Examples included several Oregon measures preventing overfishing of the Columbia and Rogue rivers, California's 1924 initiative prohibiting construction of dams on the Klamath River, and Washington's 1960 initiative limiting the height of dams on several rivers and streams. These early measures, although not trivial, were overshadowed by the post-1970s measures, which enacted numerous landmark environmental initiatives. A leading example came in 1972 when California voters approved Proposition 1, the state's coastal zone protection act. This initiative placed heavy restrictions on development of the state's coastal areas and established a powerful commission to enforce its provisions. Voters subsequently approved measures that regulated toxic substances, required state agencies to act in more environmentally responsible ways, and mandated funding for a range of environmental priorities, including new water quality programs and the purchase and protection of wetlands and parklands. In addition, in recent decades, this category has expanded to include animal rights initiatives that outlawed cockfighting, dog racing, certain forms of hunting and fishing, and other practices.[67]

---

[65] Citizens in 12 states (Arizona, California, Colorado, Florida, Idaho, Maine, Michigan, Missouri, North Dakota, Oklahoma, Oregon, and South Dakota) adopted 24 gaming-related initiatives between 1980 and 2004.

[66] The minimum wage initiatives were adopted by Washington (1988, 1998), California (1996), Oregon (1996, 2002), Florida (2004), Nevada (2004/2006), Arizona (2006), Colorado (2006), Missouri (2006), Montana (2006), and Ohio (2006).

[67] For a discussion of the animal rights activists' strategic use of the initiative process during the 1990s, see Pacelle, "The Animal Protection Movement," 109–19.

Taxation

Tax policy has long had a prominent place on initiative ballots, accounting for 10 percent of initiatives adopted in the high-use states and slightly more in the other initiative states. These measures have usually, but not always, limited, reduced, or abolished taxes. As we have seen, the most prominent example is California's Proposition 13 of 1978, which both rolled back property taxes and limited the state's future taxing authority. Other measures have reduced or abolished state property, income, inheritance, sales, vehicle, and head or poll taxes. More importantly, initiatives have also placed limits on government's ability to impose future tax increases.[68]

Voters have sometimes adopted initiatives to raise taxes. Citizen-initiated tax increases were fairly common across the initiative states from the Progressive Era through the 1940s. In the 1920s, for example, North Dakota and Missouri adopted citizen-initiated gas taxes, Montana adopted a metal mining tax initiative, and Arkansas adopted citizen-initiated property tax to aid industries. Similarly, in 1932, voters in Washington State used the initiative process to adopt a graduated income tax. But, as a rule, voters have approved tax increases only when the levy is limited to a narrow group, good, or activity, and the revenues are earmarked for specific, popular purposes. The most successful of these targeted tax increases sought to "soak the smokers" by taxing tobacco products and earmarking the revenues for health or education programs. Between 1988 and 2006, voters in the leading initiative states, as well as Montana and Massachusetts, approved nine such measures.

Notably, however, voters have generally declined to use direct democracy to target the wealthiest segment of the community, far more often rejecting than approving proposed tax hikes on corporations or the rich. Even during the Progressive Era, when voters used the initiative to impose gross earnings taxes on railroads and other corporations, they repeatedly rejected initiatives proposing more radical redistributive tax policies such as Henry George's "single tax."[69] More recent attempts to tax the rich have achieved only mixed success. In 2004, California voters approved Proposition 63, which increased income tax rates for wealthy state residents and earmarked the revenues to pay for mental health programs, but such outcomes remain rare. Although citizen initiatives have occasionally imposed new tax burdens on the "few," they have

---

[68] See, e.g., Oregon Measure 5 of 1990 and Colorado Amendment 1 of 1992 (limiting property tax); Washington Initiative 402 of 1981 and California Proposition 6 of 1982 (abolishing state inheritance tax); California Proposition 7 of 1982 (indexing state income tax to inflation); California Proposition 62 of 1986 and Proposition 218 of 1996 (restricting local taxes); Washington Initiative 695 of 1999 and I-722 of 2000 (reducing vehicle license tax).

[69] The "single tax" idea, devised by Henry George (1839–97), would have placed a heavy tax on the value of land and eliminated all other forms of taxation. Relentless proponents qualified numerous single-tax initiatives in Oregon between 1908 and 1914, and no fewer than seven in California between 1912 and 1938. Voters rejected them all. Goebel, *A Government of the People*, 81–2, 163–71.

more generally limited the taxes of the "many" and constrained the government's future taxing power.

Criminal Procedure and Punishment

The most evident difference between initiative states is in the area of criminal law. Through 2008, citizens in California, Oregon, Washington, and Arizona adopted thirty-four crime-related initiatives, accounting for approximately 7 percent of all voter-approved initiatives in the high-use states. But, criminal justice initiatives were almost unknown elsewhere. The exceptions were a 1934 Arkansas criminal procedure initiative and a 1978 Michigan initiative requiring minimum sentences for violent offenders.

Early in the initiative era, Arizona and Oregon wrestled with one of the most controversial questions of criminal justice policy – the legality of capital punishment. In 1916, Arizona voters, by a bare majority, approved an initiative abolishing capital punishment; two years later, they reversed course and decisively approved a measure reinstating it. Similarly, Oregon voters narrowly approved a 1914 initiative to abolish the death penalty, but six years later approved a legislative referral reversing that decision. The few other criminal justice initiatives during the early period focused on questions of criminal procedure.[70]

After 1970, citizens used the initiative power to adopt a string of tough-on-crime measures. As Chapter 7 discusses in more detail, citizens reinstated the death penalty after courts had declared it unconstitutional. They also approved a number of other measures to enhance prosecutors' powers, restrict bail and parole, expand victims' rights to restitution, allow some juveniles to be tried and punished as adults, and dramatically increase sentences for a range of offenses.

The spike in tough-on-crime initiatives can be attributed to voter concerns over rising crime rates and the perception that the criminal justice system was soft on criminals.[71] In the mid-1990s, citizen legislators initiated an important shift in criminal justice policy when they enacted so-called three-strikes-and-you're-out sentencing laws for recidivist offenders. Washington voters adopted

---

[70] In 1934, California voters adopted Proposition 5, the most consequential criminal procedure initiative of the era. That measure, among other things, authorized prosecutors to comment on a criminal defendant's decision not to testify at trial, a policy that raised difficult constitutional questions.

[71] In the early 1990s, Americans were intently focused on chronically high crime rates and, more specifically, violent crimes committed by released felons. The Gallup Organization noted the growing salience of the crime issue: whereas in 1965, only 4 percent of respondents identified crime as "the most important problem facing the nation today," twenty-seven percent considered it the most important problem in 1995. Franklin E. Zimring, Gordon Hawkins, and Sam Kamin, *Punishment and Democracy: Three Strikes and You're Out in California* (New York: Oxford University Press, 2001), 178–9. In California, an August 1994 Field Poll reported that seventy-nine percent of respondents reported being "extremely concerned" with "crime and law enforcement." The Field Institute, *The Field Poll* (August 1994).

the nation's first three-strikes law, I-593, in 1993. Shortly thereafter, the three-strikes movement gained momentum when Richard Allen Davis was arrested in California for the kidnapping, rape, and murder of twelve-year-old Polly Klaas. Many were outraged by this infamous crime, especially when they learned the state had granted the killer an early release from prison despite his long history of violent offenses. California's three-strikes advocates, long rebuffed in the legislature, quickly gathered enough signatures to qualify an initiative for the 1994 ballot. This initiative, the most stringent of its kind in the nation, doubled prison sentences for "second strike" repeat offenses and required sentences of twenty-five-years-to-life for even a minor "third strike" offense following convictions for two "serious" or "violent" felonies. California voters adopted the measure by a 72-percent vote and rejected all later attempts to weaken it.[72] Moreover, these outcomes were part of a pattern of voter support for initiatives that enhanced criminal punishments or strengthened the prosecutor's hand. Through 2008, Californians qualified twelve tough-on-crime initiatives for the statewide ballot and approved eleven of them, usually by large margins. Similarly, voters in Arizona, Oregon, and Washington collectively approved fifteen tough-on-crime initiatives.[73] In the main exception to this tough-on-crime pattern, voters approved several initiatives that softened penalties for drug offenses. A prominent example was California's Proposition 36 (2000), which permitted drug offenders to receive treatment rather than punishment for their crimes.

Education

The fourth initiative type establishes funding levels and other policies for public education. Education initiatives have accounted for just above 5 percent of citizen lawmaking both nationally and in the leading initiative states. Many of these measures have mandated increased funding for public schools. In his book *For the Many or the Few*, economist John Matsusaka explained why advocates of increased school spending often turned to the initiative process during the first half of the twentieth century. In Matsusaka's account, urban voters generally wanted state governments to spend more money on public education than rural voters did. Although city dwellers had become the electoral majority in many states, their power in the legislature was diluted by malapportioned districts. As legislatures fell out of step with majority sentiment, urban voters

---

[72] For the lead proponents' account of the California Three Strikes campaign, see Mike Reynolds and Bill Jones with Dan Evans, *Three Strikes and You're Out! A Promise to Kimber: The Chronicle of America's Toughest Anti-Crime Law* (Fresno, CA: Quill Driver Books, 1996); for other analyses see, e.g., Zimring, Hawkins, and Kamin, *Punishment and Democracy*; Joe Domanick, *Cruel Justice: Three Strikes and the Politics of Crime in America's Golden State* (Berkeley: University of California Press, 2004).

[73] Colorado is the only one of the strongest initiative states that has not adopted any tough-on-crime initiative.

turned to the initiative process where they were able to secure more funding for public schools.[74]

More recently, many proponents of public education have again argued that schools are under-resourced and have returned to the initiative process to secure new education funding. A decade after Proposition 13, voters in California narrowly approved Proposition 98 (1988), an initiative that locked in a minimum 40 percent of the state's budget each year for the state's public schools and community colleges. In 2000, voters in Oregon, Colorado, and Washington adopted initiatives designed to commit additional resources to public schools, and Maine (2004) and Nevada (2004/2006) adopted similar measures. Thus, although voters have been reluctant to increase taxes, they have not hesitated to mandate spending on certain priorities – including, especially, public education.

Education policy has often been intertwined with other social issues, such as race relations, immigration, and religion. Citizen lawmakers have occasionally sought to dictate outcomes at the intersection of education and social policy. In 1922, Oregon voters approved an initiative requiring parents to send their children to public schools, a measure widely understood to target Roman Catholics who wanted to send their children to parochial schools. In 1928, citizens in Arkansas banned the teaching of evolution in the classroom. Two years later, they required the reading of the Bible in the public schools. In 1948, North Dakota voters prohibited public school teachers from wearing religious dress while at work. Citizens in Oklahoma (1946) and Arkansas (1956) adopted initiatives to reinforce segregation of the public schools. In the 1970s, voters in California, Colorado, and Washington adopted measures to end court-ordered busing for purposes of school desegregation. In the early 1990s, California voters adopted Proposition 187, a measure which, among other provisions, sought to deny public education to illegal immigrants. And, more recently, voters in California (1998) and Arizona (2000) adopted initiatives to require public schools to use English immersion rather than bilingual education as its primary means for teaching students with limited English proficiency.

THE INITIATIVE POWER'S IMPACT

During the Progressive Era, both supporters and critics of direct democracy made extreme predictions regarding its likely impact. By contrast, Theodore Roosevelt argued that the initiative and referendum's "success or failure is to be determined not on *a priori* reasoning but by actually testing how they work under varying conditions."[75] A century later, we know much more about how the initiative process operates, but scholars and practitioners continue to debate its effects.

[74] John G. Matsusaka, *For the Many or the Few: The Initiative, Public Policy, and American Democracy* (Chicago: University of Chicago Press, 2004), 94–100.
[75] Theodore Roosevelt, "Nationalism and Popular Rule," *The Outlook* (January 21, 1911).

Early Assessments

In the early decades of the twentieth century, most scholars agreed that direct democracy had not met expectations. In a 1932 article entitled "Thirty Years of the People's Rule in Oregon," political scientist Waldo Schumacher concluded that, even in that leading state, "the initiative and referendum have not produced the results that their friends and sponsors claimed for them.... [T]he people of Oregon have had too much faith in the wonder-working power of mere institutions – such as the initiative and referendum – in bringing about better government."[76] Similarly, in a detailed and influential 1939 study of the California initiative process, political scientists V. O. Key, Jr. and Winston Crouch argued that neither the proponents' hopes for direct democracy nor the opponents' fears of majority tyranny had materialized.[77] Proponents of direct democracy had been mistaken in believing that citizen lawmaking would somehow originate with "the people" and reliably work to the benefit of the public good. Instead, interest groups had quickly adapted to the new devices and become the main driving force behind citizen lawmaking. Moreover, Key and Crouch argued, direct democracy had neither significantly realigned power relationships nor "had a very profound effect on the great body of legislation." Contrary to Progressive Era expectations, "the conservatives have not been greatly injured by the use of the initiative and the referendum and the liberals have not been greatly aided."[78]

At the same time, Key and Crouch concluded that "[t]he tyranny of the majority has failed to materialize," mainly because voters in California had been reluctant to adopt measures that faced intense resistance. Well-resourced minorities, such as business and financial interests, had been especially adept at defeating initiatives they strongly opposed.[79] More generally, the evidence suggested that the electorate had been "no more precipitous in injuring [minorities] than the representative body."[80]

In 1950, political scientists Joseph G. LaPalombara and Charles B. Hagan were similarly sanguine, concluding that the fears of representative democracy's demise "were, to put the matter mildly, exaggerated."[81] Most mid-century scholars shared this benign view of the initiative power, if they considered it

---

[76] Waldo Schumacher, "Thirty Years of the People's Rule in Oregon: An Analysis," *Political Science Quarterly* 47, no. 2 (June 1932): 257–8.

[77] V. O. Key, Jr. and Winston W. Crouch, *The Initiative and the Referendum in California* (Berkeley: University of California Press, 1939), 572.

[78] Ibid., 565–75. Thomas Goebel underscores these points, noting that "the voting behavior of the public turned out to be much more conservative and reluctant to endorse radical changes than anticipated by direct legislation friends and foes alike." Goebel, *A Government by the People*, 153.

[79] Key and Crouch, *The Initiative and the Referendum in California*, 450.

[80] Ibid., 488.

[81] Joseph G. LaPalombara and Charles B. Hagan, "Direct Legislation: An Appraisal and a Suggestion," *American Political Science Review* 45, no. 2 (June 1951): 404.

at all. As the 1970 *APSR* article noted, the conventional view was that "the Madisons and Burkes who feared the excesses of democracy may rest in peace." This conclusion was reasonable considering direct democracy's relatively modest impact through much of the twentieth century.

Post-1970 Assessments

After 1970, however, scholars were forced to reconsider this view. In the aftermath of California's Proposition 13 of 1978, it became clear that, at least in the strongest initiative states, citizen lawmaking was significantly reshaping institutions and policy and generating a range of important indirect effects. A telling indicator was that more and more groups with varying political ideologies and agendas were turning to the initiative process rather than the legislature to achieve their goals. In this new environment, citizen lawmakers – not representatives – were increasingly setting the policy agenda, framing policy options, and making the key decisions across the policy terrain. With apparent relish, voters altered tax rates, spending priorities, campaign laws, environmental policies, criminal punishments, and the structure of government itself. These and other changes were not merely symbolic; careful analysis revealed that the initiative power was having a measurable impact.[82]

It is difficult to find consensus about the wisdom of individual policies enacted through the initiative process. Initiatives, like other forms of legislation, involve prudential judgments in situations where no solution is self-evidently correct. Reasonable people continue to disagree, for example, whether Proposition 13 has been a net benefit or burden to California, and one could surely say the same for most other citizen-enacted laws. But, the most troubling questions about the initiative process go beyond the details of individual ballot measures. The more profound concerns are whether direct democracy, over time and perhaps unintentionally, undermines institutions of representative government, and whether it poses a systematic threat to minority and individual rights.

Impact on Representative Government. In several states, the initiative power has significantly altered the powers of representative institutions, especially legislatures. These impacts have not occurred all at once, but in increments, as one

---

[82] Scholars have carefully compared initiative with non-initiative states and determined to measure these impacts. For example, John Matsusaka has found that initiative states have become more fiscally conservative as measured by reduced taxes and spending and increased reliance on user fees. Matsusaka, *For the Many or the Few*, 29–52. In addition, Elisabeth Gerber has shown that initiative states have adhered more closely than non-initiative states to majority voter preferences in a number of policy areas including abortion and the death penalty. Elisabeth R. Gerber, *The Populist Paradox: Interest Group Influence and the Promise of Direct Legislation* (Princeton: Princeton University Press, 1999), 121–36. And, Caroline Tolbert has analyzed how initiative states now operate under more restrictive governance policies than non-initiative states. Caroline J. Tolbert, "Changing Roles for State Legislatures: Direct Democracy and Governance Policies," in Bowler, Donovan, and Tolbert, *Citizens as Legislators*, 171–90.

initiative after another has restricted representatives' discretion and undercut their authority. These cumulative effects are perhaps most apparent in the context of the state budget process. Historically, a legislature's signal responsibility has been to enact the budget bill, a task that requires members to balance a multitude of competing interests and to anticipate emerging needs. Over the past generation, however, voters have increasingly limited that authority by engaging in "ballot-box budgeting." More specifically, they have restricted legislatures' budgetary discretion by adopting tax and expenditure limitation initiatives (TELs), and by earmarking large portions of state revenues for particular purposes.[83] By 1990, California's Legislative Analyst had reported that "[b]y our estimates, approximately 75 percent of the state's General Fund expenditure is not subject to legislative control through the budget process. More than half of this restriction is due to initiatives."[84] More recently, economist John Matsusaka has argued that these estimates are exaggerated, but no one can dispute that a large share of the state's budget is restricted by voter mandates.[85]

Ballot box budgeting is insidious because its negative effects occur gradually. Voters are often attracted to initiatives that limit taxes or mandate spending priorities, but fail to consider how these measures, in aggregate, distort the budget process. This problem has spread beyond California to other high-use initiative states where it has created one of the initiative power's most important and troubling impacts.

Similarly, term limits for elected officials, perhaps the most popular state-level institutional change in the past generation, have weakened legislatures in at least some states. Many of today's voters, like their Anti-Federalist predecessors, believe long-term incumbency corrupts representatives and makes them unresponsive to their constituents. But, it is also true that term limits can seriously impair a legislature. As Nelson W. Polsby argued, a "transformative

[83] See, e.g., Michael J. New, "Limiting Government Through Direct Democracy," *Policy Analysis*, No. 420 (Washington, D.C.: Cato Institute, Dec. 13, 2001), 1–17.
[84] Elizabeth G. Hill, *Ballot Box Budgeting* (Menlo Park: EdSource Publications, 1990), 3. See also Bruce E. Cain, Sara Ferejohn, Margarita Najar, and Mary Walther, "Constitutional Change: Is It Too Easy to Amend our State Constitution?" in Bruce E. Cain and Roger G. Noll, eds., *Constitutional Reform in California: Making State Government More Effective and Responsive* (Berkeley: Institute of Governmental Studies Press, 1995), 265, 289. Cain et al. noted that "some of the most critical fiscal decisions have been put into the Constitution by the [Initiative Constitutional Amendment] process, and this has limited the ability of elected officials to deal with fiscal crises." Some scholars argue that at least some legislatures have been able to circumvent voter-initiated tax and expenditure limitations. See, e.g., Thad Kousser, Mathew D. McCubbins, and Kaj Rozga, "When Does the Ballot Box Limit the Budget? Politics and Spending Limits in California, Colorado, Utah and Washington," in Elizabeth Garrett, Elizabeth Graddy, and Howell Jackson, eds., *Fiscal Challenges: An Inter-Disciplinary Approach to Budget Policy* (New York: Cambridge University Press, 2008). But, even if legislators are sometimes able to "work around" voter-imposed tax and expenditures limitations, these restrictions nevertheless constrain legislative discretion and responsibility.
[85] John G. Matsusaka, "Direct Democracy and Fiscal Gridlock: Have Voter Initiatives Paralyzed the California Budget? *State Politics and Policy Quarterly* 5, no. 3 (2005): 248–64, arguing that 32 percent of the California state budget is constrained by voter mandates.

legislature" – that is, a body that has "independent capacity, frequently exercised, to mold or transform proposals from whatever source into laws" and does not merely react to the executive – requires, among other things, member expertise that comes from years of experience in office.[86] Severe term limits undermine that capacity.

Wise term limits would balance the benefits of rotation with the need for institutional stability and expertise. But, the term limits citizens imposed in the 1990s err on the short side – they typically allow representatives to serve no more than six or eight years in the lower house of a legislature and eight years in the upper chamber. In several states, these restrictions have undermined legislative professionalism by creating an institutional culture of the revolving door; with short time horizons, few members develop policy expertise and almost all are distracted by the search for the next office.[87] Especially in combination with the erosion of legislative budget authority, the 1990s-era term limits initiatives present a long-term threat to representative institutions.

Impact on Rights. The second broad concern is whether the initiative power poses a systemic threat to individual and minority rights. Mid-century scholars such as V. O. Key, Jr. were impressed that the initiative process had not created a tyranny of the majority.[88] Key and others were principally focused on the absence of meaningful threats to property rights and to the rich. More recently, however, attention has turned to direct democracy's threat to the civil rights of other minority groups, such as racial minorities, aliens, and homosexuals.[89] Scholars have disagreed whether these latter groups face greater risk from the initiative process than from legislatures.[90] But, all can point to examples of antiminority initiatives that won popular approval. In the early

---

[86] Nelson W. Polsby, "Legislatures," in Fred L. Greenstein and Nelson W. Polsby, eds., *Handbook of Political Science*, Vol. 3 (Reading, MA: Addison-Wesley, 1975), 277. See also Nelson W. Polsby, "Some Arguments Against Congressional Term Limits," 16 HARV. J. L. & PUB. POL'Y 101 (1993).

[87] For a detailed analysis of the impact of term limits on state legislatures, see Thad Kousser, *Term Limits and the Dismantling of State Legislative Professionalism* (Cambridge, MA: Cambridge University Press, 2005). For more specific discussion of the impacts in California, see Bruce E. Cain and Thad Kousser, *Adapting to Term Limits: Recent Experiences and New Directions* (San Francisco: Public Policy Institute of California, 2004); Schrag, *California: America's High Stakes Experiment*, 150–4.

[88] Key and Crouch, *The Initiative and the Referendum in California*, 450.

[89] See, e.g., Derrick A. Bell, Jr. "The Referendum: Democracy's Barrier to Racial Equality," 54 WASH. L. REV. 1 (1978); Julian N. Eule, "Judicial Review of Direct Democracy," 99 YALE L.J. 1503 (1990); Hans A. Linde, "When Initiative Lawmaking Is Not 'Republican Government': The Campaign Against Homosexuality," 72 ORE. L. REV. 19 (1993).

[90] For empirical analyses of how minorities fare under initiated measures, see Barbara S. Gamble, "Putting Civil Rights to a Popular Vote," *American Journal of Political Science*. 41, no. 1 (1997): 245–69; Todd Donovan and Shaun Bowler, "Direct Democracy and Minority Rights: An Extension," *American Journal of Political Science* 42, no. 3 (1998); and Zoltan L. Hajnal, Elisabeth R. Gerber, and Hugh Louch, "Minorities and Direct Legislation: Evidence from California Ballot Proposition Elections," *Journal of Politics* 64, no. 1 (2002): 154–77.

years of the initiative era, voters enacted a number of initiatives that targeted vulnerable minorities, including African Americans, Japanese immigrants, and Roman Catholics. As the initiative process has gained strength, electoral majorities have continued to enact initiatives that appear to threaten minorities, often in highly-polarized campaigns. As we will see, the question of whether individual measures have actually violated rights is quite controversial, but the post-1970 initiative surge has clearly produced a series of contentious campaigns that have tested the boundaries of minority and individual rights – certainly a potentially troubling impact.

CONCLUSION

Both its supporters and critics understand that direct democracy has become far more than just a "safety valve" or a "cautiously administered medicine." In the states where it is strongest, the initiative process has become no less than a fourth branch of government, a status that surely exceeds the modest expectations of Eastern Progressives and more closely conforms to the more radical, populist vision that seeks to restrict representatives and introduce "the people's rule."[91] These developments have forced a new generation to confront fundamental questions regarding direct democracy's nature and impact that were first raised in a serious way in the Progressive Era debate. Legal scholars, political scientists, and economists have used an expanding array of methodological approaches to analyze whether initiatives increase voter education and engagement; whether ordinary citizens are competent to enact complex initiative legislation; whether special interests have co-opted the initiative process; and whether initiatives have a positive or adverse impact on specific policies, institutions, and groups. The question of whether the initiative power is a desirable tool of self-government or a flawed and dangerous distortion of democracy is far from resolved.

It goes without saying that the initiative process has many defenders. Stable majorities of voters in initiative states value the process and jealously guard it. For years, most survey respondents have agreed with the proposition that citizens are better than legislators at deciding important policy questions.[92] And,

---

[91] See Peter Schrag, "The Fourth Branch of Government? You Bet," 41 *Santa Clara L. Rev.* 937–49 (2001). For further discussion of the triumph of the populist conception of direct democracy, see Bruce E. Cain and Kenneth P. Miller: "The Populist Legacy: Initiatives and the Undermining of Representative Government," in Larry J. Sabato, Howard R. Ernst, and Bruce A. Larson, eds. *Dangerous Democracy?: The Battle Over Ballot Initiatives in America* (Lanham, MD: Rowman & Littlefield, 2001), 38–48.

[92] Matsusaka, *For the Many or the Few*, 1, 130–1. For a summary of a recent survey, see Public Policy Institute of California, *Just the Facts: Californians and the Initiative Process* (San Francisco: Public Policy Institute of California, 2006). The survey found that "Californians are highly supportive of the initiative process.... Six in 10 residents (59%) and likely voters (60%) believe that public policy decisions made by voters through the initiative process are probably better than policy decision made by the governor and state legislature. Only one in four thinks that voter decisions are probably worse. Majorities across party lines trust decisions made by the public more than those made by elected officials."

although voters may be willing to consider small reforms to the initiative process, they emphatically oppose weakening or abandoning it.[93] Moreover, political leaders and interest groups from across the ideological spectrum defend the initiative process, in part because they cherish the ability to override representative government when it frustrates their goals. And, numerous scholars have, in recent years, offered at least qualified support for a strong initiative system, arguing that it effectively promotes popular sovereignty by increasing citizens' knowledge of issues and participation in elections, and by making government more responsive to majority preferences.[94]

However, at the same time, the revival has produced fresh evidence of direct democracy's structural shortcomings and potential abuses.[95] Most importantly, the recent growth of the initiative power has renewed historic concerns that the process undermines representative government and places minority and individual rights at risk.

We now must ask: To what extent are these fears warranted? Is direct democracy, in fact, dangerous and out of control? Or has the Madisonian system managed to mitigate its potential harms?

---

[93] Ibid.

[94] See, e.g., Daniel A. Smith and Caroline J. Tolbert, *Educated by Initiative: The Effects of Direct Democracy on Citizens and Political Organizations in the United States* (Ann Arbor: The University of Michigan Press, 2004); Shaun Bowler and Todd Donovan, "Institutions and Attitudes about Citizen Influence on Government," *British Journal of Political Science* 32 (2002): 371–90; Elisabeth R. Gerber, "Legislative Response to the Threat of Popular Initiatives," *American Journal of Political Science* 40, no. 1 (1996): 99–128.

[95] For example, recent studies have highlighted ways the initiative process in practice violates many basic democratic norms, such as refinement of proposals, informed deliberation, consensus-building, compromise, and accountability. See, e.g., Cain and Miller, "The Populist Legacy," 43–8; Richard B. Collins and Dale Oesterle, "Governing By Initiative: Structuring the Ballot Initiative: Procedures that Do and Don't Work," 66 U. Colo. L. Rev. 47, 76–81 (1995); Magleby, *Direct Legislation*, 180–4. These recent studies build on earlier empirically based critiques of the initiative process' procedural deficiencies, including Key and Crouch, *Initiative and Referendum in California*, 568–69. Moreover, in recent decades, public choice theorists have shed new critical light on the initiative process by demonstrating that its structural limitations often prevent voters from expressing their true priorities and preferences among issues. For an overview of this argument, see John Haskell, *Direct Democracy or Representative Government?: Dispelling the Populist Myth* (Boulder, CO: Westview Press, 2001) or Sherman J. Clark, "A Populist Critique of Direct Democracy," 112 Harv. L. Rev. 434 (1998).

PART II

COUNTERING THE MAJORITY

3

The Counter-Majoritarian Power

Direct democracy was grafted into a larger constitutional system defined by checks and balances. Because that system matches power with counter-power, one could expect direct democracy to meet opposition from other branches of government. But, in many states, the reformers specifically designed the initiative process to bypass external checks. The question thus became: Could the Madisonian system effectively limit citizen lawmaking? This chapter examines the capacity of various institutions to counter the initiative power and discusses why courts are best positioned to exercise this check.

POTENTIAL INSTITUTIONAL COUNTER-POWERS

The Legislature

Legislatures see direct democracy as a rival power. This natural animosity makes it all the more surprising that reformers convinced *any* legislature to devolve lawmaking authority to the people.[1] Following the Progressive Era, legislatures strengthened their resistance to the people's rule. After 1918, only a handful of legislatures offered voters a chance to adopt the initiative process and, in those rare instances, imposed severe restrictions on its use. More often, legislatures sought to limit the initiative power where it already existed. Over time, legislatures have attempted to constrain the initiative power in three primary ways: by enacting laws that impede the people's ability to use the process; by repealing or amending voter-approved initiatives; or, short of repeal, by failing to implement initiatives as their proponents intended.

---

[1] For an analysis of factors that caused some legislatures to cede lawmaking power to citizens, see Daniel A. Smith and Dustin Fridkin, "Delegating Direct Democracy: Interparty Legislative Competition and the Adoption of Direct Democracy in the American States," *American Political Science Review* 102, no. 3 (Aug. 2008): 333–50.

Restrictions on the Initiative Process. First, a legislature can impose various restrictions on the process itself. Legislators often promote initiative regulations as necessary to prevent abuse of the process, but the restrictions can also be seen as thinly veiled efforts to weaken a rival.[2] In particular, legislatures have increased the signature requirements for qualifying an initiative, required greater geographic distribution of signatures, shortened the period for collecting signatures, restricted paid signature gatherers, increased the percentage vote required for enacting certain types of initiatives, and limited financial contributions to initiative campaigns.[3] As we shall see, however, many of these impediments were unenforceable because they conflicted with emerging judicial interpretations of First Amendment rights. Moreover, in some states, regulations on the initiative process require voter approval, and voters have generally rejected legislative proposals to limit their lawmaking power.

Repeal of Initiatives. Second, in most states, the legislature can repeal a voter-approved initiative or subject it to hostile amendment.[4] But, this power, too, is often limited. The constitutions of several states prevent the legislature from repealing or amending an initiative for a period of years or with less than a supermajority vote. For example, Nevada prevents the legislature from repealing or amending an initiative for three years after its adoption; Alaska and Wyoming impose a similar prohibition that lasts two years; Arkansas requires a two-thirds vote of both houses to repeal or amend an initiative; Michigan requires a three-fourths vote of both houses for repeal or amendment; Arizona prohibits repeal, but allows amendment by a three-fourths vote of both houses if the amendment "furthers the purpose of the initiative"; Washington requires a two-thirds vote for repeal or amendment for the first two years after enactment; and so on.[5] Most notably, California Constitution art. II, sec. 10(c) prevents the legislature from *ever* repealing or amending a voter-approved statutory initiative unless the initiative, by its terms, so allows.[6] Drafters of California initiatives sometimes allow the legislature to amend the measure after the election, but usually only if the amendment furthers the initiative's purposes and

---

[2] For an initiative activist's view, see Paul Jacob, "Silence Isn't Golden: The Legislative Assault on Citizen Initiatives," in M. Dane Waters, ed. *The Battle Over Citizen Lawmaking: An In-Depth Review of the Growing Trend to Regulate the People's Tool of Self Government: The Initiative and Referendum Process* (Durham: Carolina Academic Press, 2001), 97–107.

[3] Jennie Drage, "State Efforts to Regulate the Initiative Process," in Waters, ed., *The Battle Over Citizen Lawmaking,* 229–35.

[4] For decisions confirming the legislature's power to amend or repeal laws enacted through the initiative process, see, e.g., *Kadderly v. City of Portland,* 44 Ore. 118 (1903); *State v. Roach,* 230 Mo. 408 (1910); *In re Senate Resolution No. 4,* 54 Colo. 262 (1913); *Richards v. Whisman,* 36 S.D. 260 (1915); *State ex rel. Goodman v. Stewart,* 57 Mont. 144 (1920); *Luker v. Curtis,* 64 Idaho 703 (1943).

[5] For a state-by-state listing of rules for legislative repeal or amendment of voter-approved initiatives, see M. Dane Waters, ed., *Initiative and Referendum Almanac,* (Durham: Carolina Academic Press, 2003), 27. See also Chapter 1, n. 70.

[6] See CAL. CONST., art. II, sec. 10 (c).

the legislature approves the change by a supermajority vote. By design, California's rule protects statutory initiatives from legislative override. It is one of the reasons that California has become one of the strongest initiative states.[7]

California's three-strikes-and-you're-out sentencing law illustrates the importance of this rule. As we have seen, Californians expressed strong support for tough-on-crime sentencing laws. Following the notorious murder of Polly Klaas, Mike Reynolds (the father of another young murder victim) successfully completed a petition drive to qualify the three-strikes initiative for the state's November 1994 ballot. In the spring of 1994, the California legislature responded to this public demand by enacting a three-strikes law that was virtually identical to the pending initiative. But, despite this legislative action, Reynolds was unwilling to withdraw support for the ballot measure. He understood that rules matter: the legislature could always amend or repeal a three-strikes law of its own making, but it could not touch a comparable version directly enacted by the people. And, indeed, when voters approved Reynolds' initiative by a 72 percent vote, they effectively entrenched the law. The Democratic-controlled legislature has long believed that the state's three-strikes provisions are too severe and should be modified, but, it is powerless to do so. Instead, critics of the law must appeal to the people. In 2004, activists qualified Proposition 66, a measure that sought, among other things, to reduce the list of offenses that qualify as strikes as well as those that can count as a third strike. Voters, however, rejected the proposal and thus preserved three-strikes in its original form.[8]

Even when a legislature is formally able to amend or repeal a voter-approved initiative, many members are reluctant to counter the majority in such a direct way. On occasion, legislators have set aside these concerns and voted to repeal a popular initiative, especially when the measure struck directly at their self-interests. In 1956, for example, voters in Washington passed an initiative designed to redraw the state's legislative districts on an equal population basis, but the following year, the legislature reversed the voters' decision and preserved the status quo.[9] Similarly, in the 1990s, citizens in Idaho and Utah used the initiative power to impose term limits on their elected officials. But, in 2002, the Idaho legislature repealed the voter-imposed limits and, in 2003, the Utah legislature did the same.[10] In these cases, representatives were prepared

---

[7] V. O. Key, Jr. and Winston W. Crouch, *The Initiative and the Referendum in California* (Berkeley: University of California Press, 1939), 486.

[8] Voters rejected Proposition 66 by a margin of 47 to 53 percent. California Secretary of State, *Statement of Vote*, November 8, 1994 General Election, 107.

[9] The Washington legislature effectively overturned Initiative 199 of 1956. See *Washington Laws* of 1957, Chapter 5, p. 11, cited in Robert B. McKay, *Reapportionment: The Law of Politics and Equal Representation* (New York: Twentieth Century Fund, 1965), 444. See also Daniel A. Smith, "Homeward Bound? Micro-level Legislative Responsiveness to Ballot Initiatives," *State Politics and Policy Quarterly* 1, no. 1 (2001): 50–61.

[10] For a discussion, see Daniel A. Smith, "Overturning Term Limits: The Legislature's Own Private Idaho?" *PS: Political Science and Politics* 36, no. 2 (2003): 215, 215–16.

to risk voter anger rather than submit to career-threatening redistricting or term limitations. More often, individual legislators are reluctant to exercise this direct form of counter-majoritarian power, especially when the initiative has won majority support within the member's own district.[11]

Citizen lawmakers nevertheless clearly distrust legislatures and have often taken steps to prevent them from repealing or amending an initiative. The most effective strategy has been to qualify the initiative as a constitutional amendment (ICA) rather than as a statute in those states where this is an option. When citizens can embed an initiative into the state constitution, they protect it from legislative repeal. This incentive causes many ordinary laws to be elevated to constitutional status, removing them from the sphere of legislative discretion and normal politics.

Resistance at the Implementation Stage. Third, if a legislature dislikes an initiative, it can sometimes quietly resist the measure during the implementation stage. In their book *Stealing the Initiative*, political scientists Elisabeth Gerber, Arthur Lupia, Mathew D. McCubbins, and D. Roderick Kiewiet studied the ability of legislators and other government actors to subvert or "steal" voter-approved initiatives. Analyzing the aftermath of several initiatives approved by California voters between 1979 and 1998, these scholars searched for evidence that the legislature or some other branch of government failed to implement an initiative as its supporters likely intended. Arguing that "government actors must choose to comply with an initiative if it is to affect policy," the authors found that these actors "regularly reinterpret, and sometimes reverse, electoral outcomes."[12] But, they also acknowledged that a legislature's ability to resist the electoral mandate is greatest when the initiative's terms are vague. When an initiative is clear and essentially self-executing, it is far harder for the legislature to subvert it in this way.

To summarize, legislatures can occasionally, and by various means, apply a check on the initiative power, but their ability to do so is constrained both by practical political considerations and by the design of the initiative process itself.

The Executive

Governors are less likely than legislatures to be hostile to the initiative process, partly because governors answer to the same statewide electorate that adopts ballot measures, whereas legislators are chosen from districts that can be far

---

[11] A legislator is more likely to support a bill that thwarts the will of the statewide majority if the member's own constituency opposed the initiative. See Daniel A. Smith, "Homeward Bound?"; Todd Donovan, "Direct Democracy as 'Super-Precedent'? Political Constraints of Citizen-Initiated Laws," 43 WILLAMETTE L. REV. 191, 227–30 (2007), discussing the circumstances under which legislators are more apt to override voter-approved initiatives.

[12] Elisabeth R. Gerber, Arthur Lupia, Mathew D. McCubbins, and D. Roderick Kiewiet, *Stealing the Initiative: How State Government Responds to Direct Democracy.* (Upper Saddle River, NJ: Prentice Hall, 2001), vii.

removed from statewide majority preferences. A number of factors – including, historically, malapportionment, or, more recently, gerrymandered districts or districts with disproportionately low voting rates – can cause the legislature as a whole to fall out of step with the sentiments of the broader state electorate.[13] Governors, however, are chosen in statewide elections and are less likely to find themselves in a counter-majoritarian relationship with a state's voters. It is thus understandable that some governors, such as California's Pete Wilson and Arnold Schwarzenegger, have embraced the initiative process and used it strategically in conflicts with the legislature.

Of course, some governors have had a very difficult relationship with the initiative system, especially when high-powered populist initiative entrepreneurs such as California's Howard Jarvis, Colorado's Doug Bruce, or Oregon's Bill Sizemore have used the process to seize the governor's power to set the policy agenda. During the 1990s, Sizemore used the initiative process so persistently that Oregon's governor John Kitzhaber was largely reduced to resisting a steady stream of initiatives.[14] But, as a rule, governors are unwilling to oppose the initiative electorate when it speaks. One thinks of California's governor Jerry Brown who, in 1978, strongly opposed Proposition 13 until it received 65 percent voter approval. Overnight, Brown converted into a "born-again tax cutter."[15]

Moreover, even if governors want to resist an initiative, they have limited ability to do so. The initiative power prohibits the executive veto – a design feature that again demonstrates how the initiative process seeks to evade checks and balances. Lacking a veto power, the governor has no direct institutional role in the process of citizen lawmaking. In some circumstances, the governor can join other government actors to subvert the implementation of an initiative, but meaningful resistance is not always possible, and, where possible, can pose risk of political reprisal. In combination, these factors seriously limit the executive's capacity to check the initiative power.

The Courts

Courts are best-positioned to place a check on initiatives because they possess the power to review the constitutional validity of all laws, including laws enacted directly by the people, and have greatly expanded the scope of this supervisory power.[16] The broad reach of the judicial check on the initiative

---

[13] For discussion of this "two constituencies" dynamic in California, see Bruce E. Cain, "Epilogue: Seeking Consensus among Conflicting Electorates," in Gerald C. Lubenow and Bruce E. Cain, eds., *Governing California: Politics, Government, and Public Policy in the Golden State* (Berkeley, CA: Institute of Governmental Studies Press, 1997), 331–43.

[14] Richard J. Ellis, *Democratic Delusions*: The Initiative Process in America (Lawrence: University Press of Kansas, 2002), 93–4.

[15] Peter Schrag, *Paradise Lost: California's Experience, America's Future* (New York: The New Press, 1998), 153.

[16] Some early advocates of direct democracy feared that courts would use judicial review to thwart the initiative power and sought to prevent them from doing so. For example, direct democracy

power can best be understood by seeing how judicial review developed as a counter-majoritarian force within the broader Madisonian system.

THE POWER OF JUDICIAL REVIEW

Founding Era Debate

The Founders struggled to define the judicial power. The logic of checks and balances seemed to call for an independent judiciary with the capacity to exert a counter-power against other branches of the national government as well as against the states, but it took time to settle the question. At the Philadelphia Convention, the delegates rejected Madison's proposal for a Council of Revision, comprised of the executive and members of the judiciary, which would exercise at least a limited veto over acts of Congress. Instead, they established an executive veto and debated granting courts a separate power to strike down laws inconsistent with the Constitution. In the end, they omitted from the Constitution any direct reference to judicial review. Although scholars today continue to disagree about the Founders' intentions, the weight of the evidence indicates that, as Alexander Bickel put it, "the Framers of the Constitution specifically, if tacitly, expected that the federal courts would assume a power – of whatever exact dimensions – to pass on the constitutionality of actions of the Congress and the President, as well as of the several states."[17] As Professor Edwin S. Corwin concluded, the proponents of the Constitution did not conceal their intentions and "judicial review was universally regarded as a feature of the new system while its adoption was pending."[18]

During the ratification period and shortly thereafter, Hamilton and Madison described the judicial power with the metaphors "bulwark" and "guardian." In *Federalist* 78, Hamilton described judges as "the bulwarks of a limited constitution against legislative encroachments."[19] Similarly, when shepherding

---

advocates in Nevada secured a state constitutional provision exempting citizen initiatives from judicial review, just as they had exempted initiatives from the executive veto. This effort was ultimately ineffective, however, and in every initiative state, courts retain the power to invalidate laws enacted by the people. See Julian N. Eule, *Judicial Review of Direct Democracy*, 99 Yale L. J. 1503, 1546 (1990), citing *Caine v. Robbins*, 61 Nev. 416 (1942).

[17] Alexander M. Bickel, *The Least Dangerous Branch: The Supreme Court at the Bar of Politics* (Indianapolis: Bobbs-Merrill, 1962), 15. See also Charles A. Beard, *The Supreme Court and the Constitution* (New York: Macmillan, 1912), 51; Edwin S. Corwin, *The Doctrine of Judicial Review: Its Historical and Legal Basis and Other Essays* (Princeton: Princeton University Press, 1914), 10; David P. Currie, "The Constitution in the Supreme Court: The Powers of the Federal Courts, 1801–1835," 49 U. Chi. L. Rev. 646 (Summer 1982), 655–56. See also Hamilton, *Federalist* 78 (supporting judicial review); Brutus, XI (13 January 1788), XII (February 7 and 14, 1788), and XV (20 March 1788), in Herbert J. Storing, ed., *The Anti-Federalist: Writings by the Opponents of the Constitution* (Chicago: University of Chicago Press), 162–73, 182–87 (warning of the dangers of judicial review).

[18] Corwin, *The Doctrine of Judicial Review*, 17, 65–6.

[19] Hamilton, *Federalist* 78, 464.

the Bill of Rights through the First Congress, Madison suggested that the courts would "consider themselves in a peculiar manner the guardians of those rights; they will be an impenetrable bulwark against every assumption of power in the legislative and the executive; they will be naturally led to resist every encroachment upon rights expressly stipulated for in the constitution by the declaration of rights."[20]

But, when the Anti-Federalists envisioned this plan, they saw the potential for judicial tyranny. Anti-Federalists believed it was dangerous to allow an unelected and largely unaccountable body to overturn the decisions of an elected and accountable legislature. Brutus, one of the most perceptive Anti-Federalists, hammered on this point. "[T]he supreme court under this constitution would be exalted over all other power in the government, and subject to no controul," Brutus argued. "I question whether the world ever saw, in any period of it, a court of justice invested with such immense powers, and yet placed in a situation so little responsible."[21] He contended that the Court would "have a right, independent of the legislature, to give a construction to the constitution and every part of it, and there is no power provided in this system to correct their construction or do it away. If, therefore, the legislature pass any laws, inconsistent with the sense the judges put on the constitution, they will declare it void; and therefore in this respect their power is superior to that of the legislature."[22]

Hamilton was compelled to deny that judicial review would destroy the popular nature of the Constitution by subordinating the legislature to the judicial power. In *Federalist* 78, he artfully distanced the people from their representatives and located the will of the people not in the legislature, but in the Constitution itself. In Hamilton's account, the Constitution embodies the full expression of the people's will, and any legislative action in conflict with the Constitution violates that will. Courts thus serve as the people's guardians against the legislature – they are "an intermediate body between the people and the legislature in order, among other things, to keep the latter within the limits assigned to their authority."[23] According to Hamilton, this system does not "by any means suppose a superiority of the judicial to the legislative power. It only supposes that the power of the people is superior to both, and that where

---

[20] James Madison, Speech in the House of Representatives, June 8, 1789, in James Madison, *Papers of Madison*, Vol. 12, Robert Allen Rutland, ed. (Charlottesville: University Press of Virginia, 1979), 206–7. Madison's views on the judicial enforcement of a declaration of rights seem to have been influenced by Jefferson. On March 15, 1789, Jefferson had written to Madison, "In the arguments in favor of a declaration of rights you omit one which has great weight with me, the legal check which it puts in the hands of the judiciary." Ibid., 13. For a discussion, see Jack N. Rakove, "Parchment Barriers and the Politics of Rights," in Michael J. Lacey and Knud Haakonssen, eds., *A Culture of Rights: The Bill of Rights in Philosophy, Politics, and Law – 1791 and 1991* (New York: Cambridge University Press, 1991), 140–42.

[21] Brutus, XV, 20 March 1788, in Storing, *The Anti-Federalist*, 182–3.

[22] Brutus, XV, 182–3, 185.

[23] Hamilton, *Federalist* 78, 466.

the will of the legislature, declared in its statutes, stands in opposition to that of the people, declared in the Constitution, the judges ought to be governed by the latter rather than the former."[24] Fifteen years later, Chief Justice Marshall adopted Hamilton's logic when asserting the Court's power of judicial review in *Marbury v. Madison* (1803).[25]

Alexander Bickel later argued, however, that it was specious for Hamilton and Marshall to downplay the counter-majoritarian nature of judicial review. When they invoked "the people" in the "mystic sense" to refer to those who in the past drafted and ratified the Constitution, Bickel argued, they "obscure[d] the reality that when the Supreme Court declares unconstitutional a legislative act or the action of an elected executive, it thwarts the will of representatives of the actual people of the here and now; it exercises control, not on behalf of the prevailing majority, but against it. That, without mystic overtones, is what happens."[26]

But, at times, Hamilton *did* candidly acknowledge the courts' counter-majoritarian function. Whereas the "*Marbury* theory" of judicial review is the better-known theme of *Federalist 78*, Hamilton also argued in that essay that courts were a necessary check on the people themselves. More specifically, Hamilton wrote that an independent judicial power was needed "to guard the Constitution and the rights of individuals from the effects of those ill humors which the arts of designing men, or the influence of particular conjunctures, sometimes disseminate among the people themselves, and which, although they speedily give place to better information, and more deliberate reflection, have a tendency, in the meantime, to occasion dangerous innovations in the government, and serious oppressions of the minor party in the community."[27]

Hamilton thus suggested that judicial power had a dual function. It not only prevented errant legislators from violating the "mystic" or permanent will of the people as expressed in the Constitution, but also checked the contemporaneous will of "the people themselves" when, seized by "ill humors," they desire acts contrary to the higher law. In the latter, explicitly counter-majoritarian rationale for judicial review, Hamilton again revealed the Founders' fear that temporary majorities could threaten rights and other constitutional norms. Independent judges were needed to serve as "faithful guardians of the Constitution" where "legislative invasions of it have been instigated by the major voice of the community."[28]

Although most participants in the constitutional debates assumed that courts would place a check on the legislative power, they were less certain how strong that check would be. Convention delegate James Wilson, for one, thought the

---

[24] Ibid.
[25] *Marbury v. Madison*, 5 U.S. (1 Cranch) 137, 177 (1803). Marshall wrote: "Certainly all those who have framed written constitutions contemplate them as forming the fundamental and paramount law of the nation, and consequently the theory of every such government must be, that an act of the legislature, repugnant to the constitution, is void."
[26] Bickel, *The Least Dangerous Branch*, 16–17.
[27] Hamilton, *Federalist 78*, 468.
[28] Ibid., 468–9.

power of judicial review would be too weak because the legislature could enact ill-considered, destructive and dangerous laws, but not so "unconstitutional as to justify the judges in refusing to give them effect."[29] Conversely, the Anti-Federalist Brutus feared unaccountable judges would become oppressive. If judges failed to restrain themselves, Brutus argued, they could extend the power of judicial review beyond reasonable limits and be "exalted above all other power in the government."[30]

The evidence suggests that Madison and Hamilton believed judicial review would likely be a limited power, held mainly in reserve. It is clear they tried to design the *entire* republican structure to prevent tyranny, secure rights, and preserve other constitutional norms; they had no expectation that the courts would assume an exclusive, or even principal, guardianship of these responsibilities.[31] Although Madison argued on the House floor that courts would act as guardians of the Bill of Rights, he did not expect courts to enlarge the definitions of rights or actively enforce these norms against the rest of the government.[32] Hamilton and Madison did not expect, as the Anti-Federalists alleged, that courts would usurp the legislative power or, as Hamilton put it, "on the pretense of a repugnancy...substitute their own pleasure to the constitutional intentions of the legislature."[33] Instead, Hamilton believed courts would avoid this form of "arbitrary discretion," because they were "bound down by strict rules and precedents which serve to define and point out their duty in every case that comes before them."[34] Indeed, it was the limited nature of the judicial function that made the courts "beyond comparison the weakest of the three departments" and "the least dangerous."[35]

THE RISE OF THE JUDICIAL POWER

The development of judicial review comprises a rich and complex history too extensive to examine in full detail here. Instead, the following discussion briefly highlights how its power has expanded over time.

Early Period: The Principle of Restraint

The Supreme Court's decisions in *Marbury v. Madison* (1803) and *Fletcher v. Peck* (1810) settled any remaining questions about its power to nullify,

---

[29] James Wilson (July 21, 1787), quoted in Jonathan Elliot, ed., *Debates on the Federal Constitution in the Convention Held at Philadelphia in 1787*, Vol. V (New York: Burt Franklin, 1888), 344. See also Thayer, "The Origin and Scope of the American Doctrine of Constitutional Law," 7 HARV. L. REV. 129, 140–1 (1893).
[30] Brutus, XV, 20 March 1788, in Storing, *The Anti-Federalist*, 182.
[31] Hamilton, *Federalist* 84, 514.
[32] Rakove, "Parchment Barriers," 141.
[33] Hamilton, *Federalist* 78, 467.
[34] Ibid., 470.
[35] Ibid., 464–70.

respectively, federal and state laws.[36] By 1803, courts in eight states had claimed the power of judicial review and courts in other states eventually followed.[37] After establishing the power, courts had to determine standards for its use. Specifically, under what circumstances should a court declare a law void?

In the 1890s, Harvard law professor James Bradley Thayer concluded that judges' dominant "rule of administration" of judicial review in the century after the founding was *restraint*. According to this norm, courts yielded to the legislature's judgment regarding a statute's constitutionality except "when those who have the right to make laws have not merely made a mistake, but have made a very clear one, so that it is not open to rational question."[38] Thayer assembled evidence from several states to show that this norm of judicial restraint began "very early" – as early as the 1790s, and was well established by the 1810s.[39] Professor Thayer noted numerous instances where courts embraced the principle of judicial restraint. He argued that this sentiment was "early, constant, and emphatic," "definite," and "adopted with too general an agreement and insisted on quite too emphatically, to allow us to think it a mere courteous and smoothly transmitted platitude." Indeed, he observed, judges had to defend the principle of judicial restraint against "denial and dispute" by numerous litigants.[40]

Partly as a result of this norm of judicial restraint, many of the nation's early and profound constitutional debates were resolved outside the courts.[41] Although it seems strange from today's perspective, during the nineteenth century, courts rarely enforced the Bill of Rights. Instead, most disputes

---

[36] *Marbury* (1803) (voiding section of Judiciary Act of 1789); *Fletcher v. Peck*, 10 U.S. (6 Cranch) 87 (1810) (invalidating Georgia law that sought to void land purchase contracts). Prior to 1803, the Supreme Court passed on the constitutionality of a number of laws (see, e.g., *Hylton v. United States*, 3 U.S. (3 Dall.) 171 (1796), affirming the constitutional validity of a federal tax on carriages), but *Marbury* was the first case in which the Court nullified an act of Congress and provided an extended defense of this power.

[37] Corwin, *Doctrine of Judicial Review*, 75–6. Corwin dated the state-level establishment of judicial review as follows: North Carolina (1787), Virginia (1788), New Hampshire (1791), South Carolina (1792), Pennsylvania (1793), New Jersey (1796), Kentucky (1801), Maryland (1802). He noted possible alternative dates for Virginia (1793) and Pennsylvania (1799).

[38] Thayer, "The Origin and Scope of the American Doctrine of Constitutional Law," 144.

[39] Thayer cited a South Carolina case, *Adm'rs of Byrne v. Adm'rs of Stewart*, 3 Des. 466 (1812), in which the judge struck a balance between asserting the power of judicial review and conceding that it should be used with reserve. The legislative power is due "high deference," the judge wrote. "It is supreme in all cases where it is not restrained by the constitution, and it is the duty of legislators as well as judges to consult this and conform their acts to it, so it should be presumed that all their acts do conform to it unless the contrary is manifest." Ibid., 141–2.

[40] Ibid., 144–5.

[41] A primary example is the controversy over the Alien and Sedition Acts. The constitutional validity of these acts was not tested in the Supreme Court; instead, their validity was debated and resolved largely through the political branches, culminating in the elections of 1800. John Chester Miller, *Crisis in Freedom: The Alien and Sedition Acts* (Boston: Little Brown, 1951), 136–9. The Alien Act expired in 1800 and the Sedition Act in 1801. The Alien Enemies Act was finally reviewed and upheld by the Supreme Court in 1948 and remains part of federal law.

regarding alleged government violations of rights were resolved through representative institutions. Legislatures, not courts, were the primary venue for interpreting and securing rights, both at the national and state levels.[42]

Meanwhile, state courts exercised judicial review in widely varying ways. The courts of New York and Massachusetts exercised the power most aggressively, whereas courts in other states invoked it hardly at all.[43] New York, in particular, was prominent in its use of the power and in its contribution to nineteenth century constitutional law, whereas courts in Virginia invalidated only two state laws between 1793 and 1860.[44] In most states, the judicial function was largely limited to the resolution of questions related to common law or statutory interpretation, and courts largely deferred to the legislature and executive on questions of constitutional interpretation.[45] Thus, throughout most of the nineteenth century, in most corners of the country, courts exercised judicial review with considerable restraint, reducing the great counter-majoritarian power to the point of dormancy.

1890s–Present: Judicial Enforcement of Rights

In the 1890s, however, the judiciary began to emerge as a strong counter-majoritarian, rights-enforcing power. A number of factors contributed to this change. First, the Reconstruction-Era amendments had expanded the range of potentially justiciable federal constitutional constraints on state governments, including requirements that states grant persons within their jurisdictions "due process of law" and "equal protection of the laws." The U.S. Supreme Court initially interpreted these provisions narrowly, but the clauses later provided the necessary means for aggressive federal judicial intervention against state legislative power.

Second, at the end of the nineteenth century, the nation's rapid industrialization changed the legal environment by calling into question long-established principles of property rights and limited government. Populist and socialist movements were mobilizing during this period to advocate fundamental economic reforms. These movements were often frustrated by what they saw as the government's lack of responsiveness to their demands, but in fact, legislatures were beginning to enact laws imposing broad regulations on economic activity. The judiciary as a whole was so philosophically opposed to these trends that it discarded is historic rule of deference and developed constitutional doctrines designed to constrain the legislative power.

---

[42] See John J. Dinan, *Keeping the People's Liberties: Legislators, Citizens, and Judges as Guardians of Rights* (Lawrence: University Press of Kansas, 1998), 31.

[43] See, for example, *Wynehamer v. People*, 13 N.Y. (3 Kern) 378 (1856). In this case, the New York court invalided a prohibition law for violating the tavern owner's due process rights to practice a livelihood, a decision that preceded the U.S. Supreme Court's development of economic substantive due process.

[44] Corwin, *Doctrine of Judicial Review*, 77–8.

[45] Dinan, *Keeping the People's Liberties*, 19.

An important landmark came in *Allgeyer v. Louisiana* (1897) when a unanimous Supreme Court first interpreted the word "liberty" in the Fourteenth Amendment's due process clause to include a "right to contract" – a doctrine that courts used repeatedly to strike down state statutes regulating labor-management relations and other economic relationships.[46] In addition, in the mid. 1890s, the Court for the first time applied the takings clause of the Fifth Amendment against the states to strike down economic regulation on property rights grounds. In a series of other cases, the Court enforced similar restrictions against congressional actions.[47]

These assertive Supreme Court rulings were part of a larger erosion of judicial deference to the majority will. Starting in the 1890s, state courts also invoked provisions of state constitutions and the U.S. Constitution to strike down laws providing for minimum wages, maximum hours, employer compensation for injured workers, and other protections for labor. Legal scholar Edwin S. Corwin found that, by contrast to earlier decades, the period after 1890 was marked by "a tremendous expansion of judicial review in all jurisdictions" driven by "modern definitions of 'liberty,' 'property,' and 'due process of law.'"[48]

As we shall see in Chapter 7, this expansion of counter-majoritarian judicial power forced a crisis during the Progressive Era as reformers sharply attacked courts and sought to place popular checks on them. The conflict was not resolved until the 1930s, when the courts finally yielded to the legislative power on questions of economic regulation. Yet, the courts did not abandon the power of judicial review. Instead, in the transitional case of *U.S. v. Carolene Products* (1938), the Supreme Court signaled that even as it was ceding power in the economic realm, it would reposition itself as guardian of civil rights and liberties.[49]

The idea that courts would actively enforce civil rights and liberties had begun to emerge in the 1920s. During World War I and its aftermath, the U.S. Supreme Court began re-envisioning the Bill of Rights as a judicially enforceable check on the federal government, and, later, the states.[50] The Court

---

[46] *Allgeyer v. Louisiana*, 165 U.S. 578 (1897). The era of judicial activism in the defense of economic rights was defined by the Court's decision in *Lochner v. New York*, 198 U.S. 145 (1905), striking down a state law limiting maximum hours for bakery workers.

[47] See *Missouri Pacific Railway Company V. Nebraska*, 164 U.S. 403 (1896) and *Chicago, Burlington & Quincy Railroad Company v. Chicago*, 166 U.S. 226 (1897), applying the takings clause of the Fifth Amendment against states. For an example of judicial invalidation of an act of Congress on "liberty of contract" grounds, see *Adair v. United States*, 208 U.S. 161 (1908).

[48] Corwin, *The Doctrine of Judicial Review*, 77.

[49] The Court famously signaled this intention through a footnote in *United States v. Carolene Products Co.*, 304 U.S. 144 (1938). For a leading analysis of footnote 4 and its significance, see John Hart Ely, *Democracy and Distrust: A Theory of Judicial Review* (Cambridge, MA: Harvard University Press, 1980), 73–104.

[50] Dinan, *Keeping the People's Liberties*, 117–22.

first enforced the free speech provisions of the First Amendment against the states in the late 1920s, and over the next several decades incorporated into the Fourteenth Amendment most other provisions of the Bill of Rights.[51] By the 1940s, the U.S. Supreme Court had so fully embraced this vision of a judicialized Bill of Rights that Justice Robert Jackson could declare in *Barnette* that the "purpose of a Bill of Rights was to place [certain subjects] beyond the reach of majorities and officials, and to establish them as legal principles to be applied by the courts."[52]

The Court also breathed new life into the equal protection clause of the Fourteenth Amendment. For years, the Court had largely ignored the clause; in 1920, Justice Holmes described it with contempt as "the last resort of constitutional arguments."[53] But at mid-century, courts began using equal protection principles to override state-level policies related not only to racial segregation, but also legislative apportionment, districting, and voting, as well as a range of policies that made distinctions on the basis of gender, and other characteristics.[54]

Finally, although abandoning the controversial doctrine of substantive due process in the economic realm, the Court continued to use the due process clause to define and protect other substantive rights, eventually including a constitutional right of privacy. This latter innovation provided judges a constitutional basis for overturning legislative enactments regarding, among other things, contraception, abortion, and marriage.

The growth of judicial power thus occurred in two primary movements. The first judicial expansion of rights, which extended from the 1890s to the 1930s, was designed to protect economic liberty, but eventually succumbed to popular opposition during the Great Depression. The second was marked by nationalization and judicial enforcement of the Bill of Rights, expanded judicial enforcement of equal protection, and, finally, revival of substantive due process in the service of personal privacy. Through this second movement, courts have firmly established themselves as the nation's dominant interpreters of the Constitution and the primary guardians of constitutional rights. As a consequence, litigation has become the crucial medium of rights-based politics and judges have become a formidable counter-power to both legislatures and the initiative system.[55]

---

[51] For cases addressing incorporation of the First Amendment, see *Fiske v. Kansas*, 274 U.S. 380 (1927); *Gilbert v. Minnesota*, 254 U.S. 325 (1920) (dictum only); *Gitlow v. New York*, 268 U.S. 652 (1925) (dictum only). For a discussion of the Court's transition into a rights-enforcing institution, see Dinan, *Keeping the People's Liberties*, 117–22; Paul L. Murphy, *World War I and the Origin of Civil Liberties in the United States* (New York: W. W. Norton & Co., 1979), 71–132.

[52] *West Virginia Board of Education v. Barnette*, 319 U.S. 624, 638 (1943).

[53] *Buck v. Bell*, 274 U.S. 200, 208 (1927).

[54] *Brown v. Board of Education*, 347 U.S. 497 (1954).

[55] See Dinan, *Keeping the People's Liberties*, 116–66; Rainer Knopff, "Populism and the Politics of Rights: The Dual Attack on Representative Democracy," *Canadian Journal of Political Science* 31, no. 4 (Dec. 1998): 683–705.

JUDICIAL REVIEW OF DIRECT DEMOCRACY

The judicial check on direct democracy has a distinctive quality. Although most theories of judicial review discuss its use in representative context, judicial review of direct legislation involves a different dynamic. When a court strikes down a voter-approved initiative, it is not checking a coordinate department of representative government, but the people themselves. Hamilton argued in *Federalist* 78 that courts may overturn acts of the coordinate body – the legislature – without violating the will of the people because there can be a lack of identity between the people and their representatives. But, this formulation collapses when the people bypass the legislature and enact law directly. In the latter context, the court is no longer an intermediary between the sovereign people and their representatives; instead, it rises above the people to enforce its interpretation of the Constitution against the express will of the majority. Judicial review of direct democracy is thus a naked case of the courts vs. the people – Bickel's counter-majoritarian difficulty in the extreme.

Although the standard *"Marbury"* reading of *Federalist* 78 provides an inadequate theoretical justification for judicial review of direct democracy, the alternative reading more readily supports this highly counter-majoritarian act. Again, in the "non-*Marbury*" passages, Hamilton argued that courts needed power to "guard the Constitution and the rights of individuals" from "the people themselves" when they agitate for unconstitutional acts. Hamilton suggested that "infractions in this shape" are a different problem from those proceeding "wholly from the cabals of the representative body" – but the judge's duty is to safeguard the Constitution in either case.[56] Although Hamilton did not expressly discuss the problem of judicial review of direct democracy, the counter-majoritarian sections of *Federalist* 78 suggest he would have considered judicial vigilance in reviewing direct legislation not only legitimate, but essential.

As direct democracy has gathered force in recent decades, a number of judges and legal scholars have devoted increased attention to the problem of judicial review of initiatives. As Thayer would put it, the debate has turned on what "rule of administration" judges should apply when reviewing citizen-enacted laws. More specifically, should courts treat initiatives the same as they would a law enacted by a legislature or should they use different standards when reviewing citizen-enacted law? Although the prevailing rule is that courts should review an initiative no differently than they would any other law, a range of voices have proposed alternative standards of review.[57] Some have

---

[56] Hamilton, *Federalist* 78, 468–69.

[57] For recitation of the current standard of review, see, e.g., *U.S. Term Limits v. Thornton*, 514 U.S. 779, 809 (1995): "We are aware of no case that would even suggest that the validity of a state law under the Federal Constitution would depend at all on whether the state law was passed by the state legislature or by the people directly through amendment of the state constitution." See also, *Citizens Against Rent Control/Coalition for Fair Housing v. City of Berkeley*, 454 U.S. 290, 295 (1981): "[For purposes of judicial review] it is irrelevant that the voters rather than the legislative body enacted [the challenged law]."

asserted that courts should exercise *more* deference when reviewing initiatives than they do when reviewing ordinary legislation, whereas others have argued that courts should give *less* deference to direct legislation.

The Relationship Between Ideology and Standard of Review

It is perhaps no surprise that one's views about the proper relationship between courts and direct democracy are often tied to one's broader ideological commitments. In recent decades, as many of the most consequential initiatives have advanced conservative goals, political conservatives have advocated special judicial deference to the initiative power. Conversely, most contemporary scholars and judges who want courts to exercise heightened scrutiny of initiatives are liberals who oppose the substance of these measures.

It is important to remember, however, that the present alignment is not fixed. The initiative power is not necessarily a conservative force, nor is the judicial power necessarily liberal – indeed, a century ago the alignment was just the opposite. During the Progressive Era, initiative and referendum were largely supported by liberal elements in the society – economic populists, Socialists, and Progressives – and opposed by conservatives like William Howard Taft who feared that direct democracy would threaten rights of property and contract. Courts were the conservative stronghold of the government, and the term "judicial review of direct democracy" called forth images of a conservative court striking down a liberal ballot measure. Over the past century, however, the institutions have realigned in such a way that "judicial review of direct democracy" now more readily suggests a liberal court invalidating a conservative initiative.

Because the current alignments are not set in stone, one could someday see liberal academics calling for greater judicial deference to citizen-enacted laws and conservatives demanding heightened judicial scrutiny. But, the present alignment helps explain why it is liberals who now support a strong judicial check on direct democracy and conservatives who counsel greater judicial deference to the initiative power.

The Argument for Greater Deference

The theory that courts should exercise increased deference when reviewing initiatives is based almost exclusively on the principle of popular sovereignty. The theory asserts that citizens have not only "the right to make laws" but a *sovereign* and *reserved* right to do so, superior to any power they delegate to the legislature. In this view, the people as principals have a superior claim to deference than does their mere agent, the legislature. Indeed, the people are superior to both court and legislature, and courts should exercise maximum restraint when passing on the validity of the laws the people directly enact.

This view finds little support in the contemporary legal academy. A few scholars have suggested initiatives might warrant greater deference than acts of legislatures in a limited category of cases, namely in situations where an initiative seeks to address a problem of legislative self-entrenchment.[58] But, as a rule, scholars reject diminished judicial scrutiny of laws enacted directly by the people.

Some judges, however, have embraced the view that courts should use extra restraint when reviewing citizen-enacted laws. One notable example was U.S. Supreme Court Justice Hugo Black. Justice Black confronted the issue in *Reitman v. Mulkey* (1967), a case testing the constitutional validity of California's Proposition 14 of 1964, the controversial initiative that sought to repeal the state's fair housing law and ban future such enactments. In oral argument, Solicitor General Thurgood Marshall contended that the challenge had greater force because the law had been adopted by the people directly, rather than by the legislature. Justice Black flatly disagreed and suggested, to the contrary, that the challenge should have less force "because here, it's moving in the direction of letting the people of the State – the voters of the State – establish their policy, which is as near to a democracy as you can get."[59] Black dissented from the Court's decision invalidating the initiative. In two other landmark challenges to voter-approved initiatives, *Hunter v. Erickson* (1969) and *James v. Valtierra* (1971), he reiterated his view that courts should show special deference to direct democracy.[60]

A number of state judges have shared this perspective. For example, in a series of cases during the 1970s and 1980s, California Supreme Court Justice Frank Richardson argued that the court had a "solemn duty to jealously guard the initiative process," was "required to resolve any reasonable doubts in favor of this precious right," and owed initiatives "very special and very favored treatment."[61] Similarly, Washington Supreme Court Justice Richard Sanders argued that his court should treat citizen-enacted laws with the greatest

---

[58] A number of policies, including legislative redistricting, term limitations, and campaign finance regulation, either directly or indirectly affect citizens' ability to displace incumbent legislators. In this view, self-interested legislators can craft laws in these areas that improperly entrench their power, whereas the problem of self-dealing is eliminated when voters are the ones making the law. This structural difference arguably supports a claim for differential review in favor of citizen lawmakers. See, Michael J. Klarman, "Majoritarian Judicial Review: The Entrenchment Problem." 85 GEO. L. J. 491 (1997). But, as a rule, scholars reject loosening judicial scrutiny of initiatives either in this limited category or more broadly. Instead, the argument for extra deference is much more frequently advanced by initiative advocates who are infuriated when courts invalidate laws adopted by the people.

[59] *Reitman v. Mulkey*, 387 U.S. 369 (1967). This exchange between Marshall and Black is recorded in Philip B. Kurland and Gerhard Casper, eds., *Landmark Briefs and Arguments of the Supreme Court of the United States*, Vol. 64, (Arlington, VA: University Publications of America, 1975), 668.

[60] *Hunter v. Erickson*, 393 U.S. 385, 397 (1969), Black, J., dissenting; *James v. Valtierra*, 402 U.S. 137, 141 (1971).

[61] *Amador Valley Joint Union High School District v. State Board of Equalization*, 22 Cal. 3d 208, 248 (1978) (upholding the Jarvis-Gann initiative, Proposition 13 of 1978); *Brosnahan v. Brown*, 32 Cal. 3d 236, 241 (1982) (rejecting a pre-election challenge to a crime victims' initiative, Proposition 8 of 1982); *Legislature v. Deukmejian*, 34 Cal. 3d 658, 683 (1983) (invalidating a redistricting initiative before the election), Richardson, J., dissenting.

respect.[62] In one case, Saunders chided the court majority for overturning the state's voter-approved term limits law, complaining that "[t]oday, six votes on this court are the undoing of 1,119,985 votes that Washingtonians cast at the polls."[63] And in *Marriage Cases*, California Supreme Court Justice Marvin Baxter attacked the court's lack of deference to citizen lawmakers by arguing that it had "substituted, by judicial fiat, its own social policy views for those expressed by the People themselves."[64]

The Argument for Less Deference

The theory that courts should give *less* deference to citizen-enacted law is based on very different premises. Those who hold this view celebrate the courts as strong guardians of rights and, crucially, they disparage the initiative process, at least as it is currently practiced in the high-use states. The specifics of their critique have taken various and sometimes contradictory forms. At times, they have argued that direct democracy is, in fact, *un*democratic. Initiative lawmaking, from this perspective, fails to enact the will of the people, either because the process is dominated by special interests, or because it inadequately aggregates voter preferences, or for various other reasons.[65] Alternatively, these judges and scholars have suggested that direct democracy is *too* democratic, meaning that the initiative process too easily translates dangerous majority sentiments into law and thus facilitates majority tyranny.

In an influential 1978 article, law professor Derrick A. Bell, Jr. emphasized the latter concern. "Direct democracy," he wrote, "carried out in the privacy of the voting booth . . . enables the voters' racial beliefs and fears to be recorded and tabulated in their pure form [and] has been a more effective facilitator of that bias, discrimination, and prejudice which has marred American democracy from its earliest day. . . . The record of recent ballot legislation reflects all too accurately the conservative, even intolerant, attitudes citizens display when given the chance to vote their fears and prejudices, especially when exposed to expensive media campaigns. The security of minority rights and the value of racial equality which those rights affirm are endangered by the possibility of popular repeal."[66] Bell was among the first to argue that direct democracy's threat to minorities required a strong judicial response. "The evidence, both historical and contemporary, justifies a heightened scrutiny of ballot legislation similar to that recognized as appropriate when the normal legislative process carries potential harm to the rights of minority individuals," Bell wrote. "This

---

[62] See *Gerberding v. Munro*, 134 Wn.2d 188, 211 (1998); *Amalgamated Transit Union Local 587 v. State of Washington*, 142 Wn.2d 183 (2000).

[63] Ibid., 229–30.

[64] *In re Marriage Cases*, 43 Cal.4th 757, 863, Baxter, J. dissenting.

[65] For a public choice perspective on the democratic deficiencies of direct democracy, see Sherman J. Clark, "A Populist Critique of Direct Democracy," 112 Harv. L. Rev. 434 (1998).

[66] Derrick A. Bell, Jr., "The Referendum: Democracy's Barrier to Racial Equality," 54 Wash. L. Rev. 1, 14–15, 20–1 (1978).

protection should be provided as a logical development of existing Supreme Court doctrine."[67]

Similarly, in a much-cited 1990 *Yale Law Journal* article, Julian N. Eule argued that when laws are enacted directly by the people through a process without internal checks or filters, "courts must play a larger role . . . because the judiciary stands *alone* in guarding against the evils incident to transient, impassioned majorities that the Constitution seeks to dissipate."[68] By this "larger role," Eule meant that courts should subject certain initiatives to heightened review. The level of this review could not be reduced to a precise formulation like "strict scrutiny," Eule argued, but should be understood as a "hard look" – essentially caution, or suspicion, or less deferential review.

Notably, Eule believed the courts should use this heightened review only for some initiatives, not others. Because direct democracy's primary threat is to "individual rights and equal application of laws," he suggested, "it is principally in these areas that courts should treat [initiatives] with particular suspicion." But, the courts should also apply heightened review to other seemingly neutral initiatives like redistricting reform or middle-class tax cuts that, in his view, disenfranchised minorities or imposed economic burdens on the "underrepresented poor" and racial minorities.[69] By contrast, Eule argued, certain other initiatives, including those that "enforce ethics in government, regulate lobbyists, or reform campaign finance practices" do not warrant heightened scrutiny because they "pose no distinctive threat of majoritarian tyranny."[70] Eule's argument generated much interest, although critics objected that the standards he proposed were not easily administrable and would provide judges arbitrary license to privilege certain citizen-enacted policies over others.[71]

Other critics of the initiative power searched for a specific constitutional basis for heightened judicial review. In particular, former Oregon Supreme Court Justice Hans A. Linde wrote a series of law review articles advancing the theory that state courts should invoke the federal Constitution's Art. IV guarantee clause to strike down initiatives that conflict with republican principles, especially those that appeal to popular passion to restrict the rights of unpopular minorities.[72] Linde argued that despite the U.S. Supreme Court's

---

[67] Ibid., 23.

[68] Eule, "Judicial Review of Direct Democracy," 1525.

[69] Ibid., 1558–60.

[70] Ibid.

[71] For critical discussions of Eule's approach, see, e.g., Mark Tushnet, "Fear of Voting: Differential Standards of Judicial Review of Direct Legislation." 1 N.Y.U. J. Legis & Pub. Pol'y 1, 4–5 (1997); Robin Charlow, "Judicial Review, Equal Protection, and the Problem with Plebiscites," 79 Cornell L. Rev. 527, 550–5 (1994).

[72] See, e.g., Hans A. Linde, "Who Is Responsible for Republican Government?" 65 U. Colo. L. Rev. 709 (1994); Hans A. Linde, "When Initiative Lawmaking Is Not 'Republican Government': The Campaign against Homosexuality," 72 Ore. L. Rev. 19 (1993); Hans A. Linde, "When is Initiative Lawmaking Not 'Republican Government'?" 17 Hastings Const. L. Q. 159 (1989); David B. Frohnmayer and Hans A. Linde, "Initiating 'Laws' in the Form of 'Constitutional Amendments': An Amicus Brief" 34 Willamette L. Rev. 749 (1998). For a critique of this

holding in *Pacific States* that the constitutional validity of the initiative process is non-justiciable, state courts have an independent responsibility to enforce the clause against initiatives that threaten principles of republican government.[73]

Evidence of Heightened Scrutiny of Initiatives

Have courts, in practice, subjected initiatives to heightened scrutiny? This is somewhat difficult to determine because a judge may apply different standards of review without saying so.[74] We know that no court has embraced Linde's argument that state courts should strike down certain types of initiatives on guarantee clause grounds, and none has explicitly adopted the Bell-Eule view that a law should receive heightened scrutiny or a "hard look" simply because it was enacted by the people directly. Nevertheless, there is evidence that some judges are hostile to direct legislation.

Judicial Commentary. A number of judicial opinions are illustrative. For example, dissenting in *Brosnahan v. Brown* (1982), a case upholding a citizen-approved "Victims' Rights" initiative, California Chief Justice Rose Bird attacked the manner in which the law was enacted.[75] "[I]nitiatives are drafted only by their proponents, so there is usually no independent review by anyone else," she wrote. "There are no public hearings. The draftsmen so monopolize the process that they completely control who is given the opportunity to comment on or criticize the proposal before it appears on the ballot." Moreover, she wrote, "[t]he voters have no opportunity to propose amendment or revisions . . . [the] only expression left to all other interested parties who are not proponents is the 'yes' or 'no' vote they cast. Since the only people who have input into the drafting of the measure are its proponents, there is no opportunity for compromise or negotiation." The consequence of this "inflexibility," Bird concluded, is that "more often than not a proposed initiative represents the most extreme form of law which is considered politically expedient."[76]

---

approach, see, e.g., Jesse H. Choper, "Observations on the Guarantee Clause – As Thoughtfully Addressed by Justice Linde and Professor Eule," 65 U. COLO. L. REV. 741 (1994).

[73] See, e.g., *Lowe v. Kiesling*, 882 P.2d 991 (Ore. App. 1994) (declining to invoke the guarantee clause to remove from the ballot Oregon Measure 9 of 1992, a measure which would have restricted the rights of homosexuals.) Jeffrey T. Even, a Washington Assistant Attorney General, surmised: "At this juncture, it would be astonishing if the courts were suddenly to announce that the Guarantee Clause prohibited or severely restricted the ability of the people to exercise a legislative function they have utilized for nearly a century." Jeffrey T. Even, "Direct Democracy in Washington: A Discourse on the Peoples' Powers of Initiative and Referendum," 32 GONZ. L. REV. 247, 256 (1996–97). For another practitioner's view, *see* Hardy Myers, "The Guarantee Clause and Direct Democracy," 34 WILLAMETTE L. REV. 659 (1998) (observing that "the relationship between the Guarantee Clause and the initiative process . . . may be the greatest undefined relationship between the U.S. Constitution and state lawmaking.") Ibid., 662.

[74] Julian N. Eule, "Representative Government: The People's Choice," 67 CHI.-KENT L. REV. 777, 780–82 (1991).

[75] *Brosnahan v. Brown*, 32 Cal.3d 236 (1982), Bird, C.J. dissenting.

[76] Ibid., 266, internal citations omitted.

In the same case, California Supreme Court Justices Stanley Mosk and Allen Broussard complained that "initiative promoters may obtain signatures for any proposal, however radical in concept and effect, and if they can persuade 51 percent of those who vote at an ensuing election to say 'aye,' the measure becomes law regardless of how patently it may offend constitutional limitations. The new rule is that the fleeting whims of public opinion and prejudice are controlling over specific constitutional provisions."[77]

Justice Mosk was more blunt. In a dissent from the California Supreme Court's 1991 decision upholding Proposition 140, the state's voter-approved term limits initiative, Justice Mosk wrote: "The initiative process is out of control in California."[78]

Opponents of Proposition 140 later challenged the measure in federal court. When the case reached a three-judge panel of the Ninth Circuit Court of Appeals, Judges Stephen Reinhardt and Betty B. Fletcher renewed the judicial attack on the state's initiative process. In *Jones v. Bates* (1997), Judges Reinhardt and Fletcher remarkably ruled that the vote on Proposition 140 violated the due process clause of the Fourteenth Amendment because voters had been inadequately informed of the consequences of their vote – namely, that Proposition 140 imposed a lifetime limit on the terms of elected officials.

To support this ruling, Judge Reinhardt wrote that "direct ballot measures lack the kinds of critical, deliberative filters that the Framers contemplated and that, to some extent, the Constitution created as prerequisites to the passing of legislation. The public ... generally lacks legal or legislative expertise – or even a duty (as legislators have under Article VI) to support the Constitution. It lacks the ability to collect and to study information that is utilized routinely by legislative bodies. Thus, at least in instances like this, in which the measure raises serious constitutional questions, our usual assumption that laws passed represent careful drafting and consideration does not obtain."[79]

An *en banc* panel of the Ninth Circuit quickly intervened, vacated the Reinhardt-Fletcher decision, and reinstated California's term limits initiative.[80] Concurring in this latter judgment, Judge Diarmuid F. O'Scannlain repudiated his colleagues' distrust of the initiative power: "Searching the Constitution ... I am unable to locate an 'ignorant voter clause' that vests federal courts with the power to review voter-enacted legislation to ensure that enough people were capable of understanding what they voted for at the ballot."[81]

The Reinhardt-Fletcher "ignorant voter" theory was an unsuccessful judicial attempt to limit the initiative power. But, the courts have developed other, more effective, constraints on direct legislation, including the "political structure"

---

[77] Ibid., 297–98, Mosk and Broussard, J., dissenting. Former California Supreme Court Justice Joseph Grodin expressed similar views. See Joseph R. Grodin, *In Pursuit of Justice: Reflections of a State Supreme Court Justice* (Berkeley: University of California Press, 1989), 102, 107.

[78] *Legislature v. Eu*, 54 Cal.3d 492 (1991), Mosk, J., dissenting.

[79] *Jones v. Bates*, 127 F.3d 839, 859-860 (9th Cir. 1997).

[80] *Bates v. Jones*, 131 F.3d 843 (9th Cir. *en banc* 1997).

[81] Ibid., 853, O'Scannlain, J., concurring.

theory of equal protection and strict enforcement of state constitutional rules for initiative lawmaking.

"Political Structure" Equal Protection Doctrine. The U.S. Supreme Court first invoked the political structure equal protection doctrine in *Hunter v. Erickson* (1969), a case invalidating a local citizen initiative in Akron, Ohio, that prevented the city council from enacting, without voter approval, ordinances against racial discrimination in housing. In *Hunter*, the Court held that the Akron initiative reallocated decision-making authority in a way that specifically disadvantaged racial minorities who benefited from anti-discrimination laws.[82] The Court further developed this doctrine in *Washington v. Seattle School District, No 1* (1982) when it struck down Washington Initiative 350, a citizen-enacted law designed to override Seattle's desegregation plan and end mandatory busing in the state's public schools.[83] Writing for the Court in *Seattle*, Justice Harry Blackmun argued that in adopting I-350, the statewide electorate had discriminated against minorities "by lodging decision making authority over the question [of racial assignments] to a new and remote level of government" defeat the district's desegregation plan.[84]

The political structure theory, also known as the *Hunter-Seattle* doctrine, rests on the premise that racial minorities are entitled to pursue beneficial legislation (such as, fair housing laws, desegregative busing, and affirmative action) and that laws that make it structurally more difficult for them to do so should be subject to heightened judicial scrutiny. Put another way, whereas "conventional" equal protection analysis looks to the substance of the law that is being challenged, "political structure" equal protection analysis asks whether a majority has created political obstacles that prevents minorities from seeking legal protections.

Justice Lewis Powell criticized the theory for unduly restricting the power of a statewide majority to exercise legitimate sovereignty over local policy.[85] And, clearly, the political structure doctrine evinces distrust of direct democracy. As Julian Eule argued, the Court in *Seattle* invoked structural equal protection analysis to invalidate I-350 not merely because it repealed a school integration program, but because of "the manner by which it was achieved."[86] In Eule's view, the Court was disturbed by Washington voters' use of the initiative power and exercised a "hard judicial look," deciding that "we know what's going on here and we won't allow any of it."[87] In theory, courts could use the *Hunter-Seattle* doctrine to invalidate legislative enactments, but in practice, they have

---

[82] *Hunter v. Erickson*, 387.
[83] *Washington v. Seattle School District No. 1*, 458 U.S. 457 (1982).
[84] Ibid., 483.
[85] Ibid., 494–95.
[86] Eule, "Judicial Review of Direct Democracy," 1565.
[87] Ibid., 1573.

invoked it against citizen-enacted laws. Perhaps for that reason, the political structure cases have occasioned some of the most pointed debates regarding judicial review of the initiative power.

James v. Valtierra (1971), for example, was a political structure challenge to California Proposition 10 (1950), an initiative that required local governments to obtain voter approval before building low-income housing projects. Justice Black, writing for the court's majority, defended the people's right to vote on these matters. "Provisions for referendums demonstrate devotion to democracy," Justice Black wrote, "not to bias, discrimination, or prejudice."[88] Professor Bell sharply attacked the decision, arguing that "Justice Black's declaration . . . is in fact almost opposite of the truth when the issue submitted to the voters suggests, even subtly, that majority interests can be furthered by the sacrifice of minority rights."[89] In Bell's view, "The *Valtierra* decision was not only wrong; it was, in the context of other equal protection decisions affecting poor and minority groups, also capricious because it eschewed even the most casual equal protection scrutiny. The decision can be explained only by a deep-seated faith in the sanctity of referenda results, even when the action taken seriously disadvantages minorities and the poor."[90]

Similarly, when California voters adopted Proposition 209 (1996), an initiative constitutional amendment banning affirmative action programs in state employment, contracting, and university admissions, its opponents immediately challenged it in federal court on structural equal protection grounds. Federal district Judge Thelton Henderson issued a preliminary injunction, declaring that the initiative violated the equal protection clause under the *Hunter-Seattle* doctrine. In his decision, Judge Henderson rejected the view that citizen-enacted laws are entitled to special deference. "The issue is not whether one judge can thwart the will of the people" he wrote, "rather, the issue is whether the challenged enactment complies with our Constitution and Bill of Rights. Without a doubt, federal courts have no duty more important than to protect the rights and liberties of all Americans by considering and ruling on such issues, no matter how contentious or controversial they may be. This duty is certainly undiminished where the law under consideration comes directly from the ballot box and without benefit of the legislative process."[91]

When the state appealed, a Ninth Circuit panel vacated Henderson's ruling and reinstated the initiative. Judge O'Scannlain, writing for the appellate court, criticized Henderson's use of political structure theory to overturn the will of the people. "No doubt the district court is correct," O'Scannlain wrote. "Judges apply the law; they do not *sua sponte* thwart wills. If Proposition 209 affronts the federal Constitution – the Constitution which the people of the United States themselves ordained and established – the court merely reminds the

---

[88] *James v. Valtierra*, 141.
[89] Bell, *The Referendum*, 28.
[90] Ibid., 5.
[91] *Coalition for Economic Equity, v. Wilson*, 946 F. Supp. 1480, 1489 (N.D. Cal. 1996) (reversed by 122 F.3d 692).

people that they must govern themselves in accordance with the principles of their own choosing. If, however, the court relies on an erroneous legal premise, the decision operates to thwart the will of the people in the most literal sense: What the people of California willed to do is frustrated on the basis of principles that the people of the United States neither ordained nor established. A system which permits one judge to block with the stroke of a pen what 4,736,180 state residents voted to enact as law tests the integrity of our constitutional democracy."[92]

As the federal courts have become less receptive to race-conscious remedies, the *Hunter-Seattle* doctrine has lost favor in racial contexts. However, as we will see in Chapter 5, the theory has reemerged elsewhere, most notably in the litigation challenging Colorado's Amendment 2 of 1992, a voter-approved initiative banning laws protecting persons from discrimination on the basis of sexual orientation. Amendment 2 more specifically sought to impose a statewide rule that "homosexual, lesbian, or bisexual orientation, conduct, practices or relationships shall [not]...entitle any person or class of persons to have or claim any minority status, quota preferences, protected status, or claim of discrimination."[93] Several local governments in Colorado – including Denver, Boulder, and Aspen – had enacted ordinances prohibiting discrimination on the basis of sexual orientation in employment, housing, and public accommodations. Amendment 2 was designed to repeal these laws and prohibit future enactment of similar statutes or regulations.

Soon after voters approved the initiative, opponents challenged it on a number of theories, including structural equal protection grounds. In *Evans v. Romer*, the Colorado Supreme Court applied the *Hunter-Seattle* doctrine to strike down the measure.[94] When the case reached the U.S. Supreme Court in *Romer v. Evans* (1996), a divided Court presented competing views of this exercise of the initiative power.[95] Justices Antonin Scalia, William Rehnquist, and Clarence Thomas argued that Amendment 2 was "not the manifestation of a 'bare...desire to harm' homosexuals, but...rather a modest attempt by seemingly tolerant Coloradans to preserve traditional sexual mores against the efforts of a politically powerful minority to revise those mores through the use of the laws...[Amendment 2] put directly, to all the citizens of the State, the question: Should homosexuality be given special protection? They answered no. The Court today asserts that this most democratic of procedures is unconstitutional."[96]

But, Justice Anthony Kennedy, writing the majority opinion declaring Amendment 2 unconstitutional, displayed distrust of direct democracy. Although Kennedy did not claim to apply the *Hunter-Seattle* doctrine to reach

---

92 *Coalition for Economic Equity. v. Wilson*, 122 F.3d 692, 699 (9th Cir. 1997). The "Yes" vote for Proposition 209 in fact was 5,268,462.
93 Colorado Amendment 2 (1992).
94 *Evans v. Romer*, 854 P.2d 1270 (Colo. 1993).
95 *Romer v. Evans*, 517 U.S. 620 (1996).
96 Ibid., 647.

the judgment, his opinion embraced its logic. In Justice Kennedy's view, "laws of the kind now before us raise the inevitable inference that the disadvantage imposed is born of animosity toward the class of persons affected." More specifically, Amendment 2 "identifie[d] persons by a single trait and then denie[d] them the possibility of protection across the board.... A law declaring that in general it shall be more difficult for one group of citizens than for all others to seek aid from the government is itself a denial of equal protection of the laws in the most literal sense."[97]

As these examples suggest, the political structure cases have revealed competing judicial attitudes toward the initiative process. Judges who believe direct democracy poses a distinct threat to minorities have used the doctrine to place a heightened check on certain citizen-enacted laws. By contrast, more conservative judges have rejected the political structure doctrine, believing it unduly restricts voter sovereignty.

Strict Enforcement of Initiative Rules. In addition, judicial attitudes toward the initiative power are sometimes revealed in cases interpreting and enforcing a state's rules for initiative lawmaking. Examples include the rule that an initiative may contain only one subject, or that the people may not use the initiative process to revise the state's constitution. As we shall discuss in more detail in Chapter 6, initiative opponents regularly challenge ballot measures on the basis that they violate these types of rules. Judges can interpret such rules in widely divergent ways and, as we shall see, a court's attitude toward the initiative power can sometimes be discerned by how strictly it enforces them. If a court mistrusts the initiative power and wants to constrain it, the court can strike down an initiative on technical grounds. Conversely, a court that is more sympathetic to the initiative power will be more likely to uphold an initiative against this form of attack.

Pre-Election Review

A final, related question is whether courts should pass on the validity of an initiative prior to the election. As James D. Gordon and David B. Magleby have noted, "[a] lawsuit to strike an initiative or referendum from a ballot is one of the deadliest weapons in the arsenal of the measure's political opponents."[98] Aggressive pre-election judicial review can significantly constrain the initiative power. Recognizing this fact, initiative opponents have often pursued pre-election litigation to attempt to kill measures before they reach the ballot.

Pre-election challenges to initiatives fall into three categories. The first type attacks the measure for failure to comply with procedural rules of the initiative

---

[97] Ibid., 633, 634.
[98] James D. Gordon III and David B. Magleby, "Pre-Election Judicial Review of Initiatives and Referendums," 64 NOTRE DAME L. REV. 298 (1989).

process, such as the form of the petition, the sufficiency of signatures, and the language of the title and summary. Most states allow pre-election review of procedural compliance, and, in many states, this review is mandatory.[99] The second type of pre-election challenge asserts that the initiative contains improper subject matter, such as multiple subjects, a revision rather than an amendment to the state constitution, or substantive policies that the state constitution excludes from the initiative process. Courts in most states will review these types of challenges before the election. Finally, some pre-election challenges attack the initiative on substantive constitutional grounds. Courts in most initiative states are reluctant to resolve these questions before the election.

This principle of restraint is based on the doctrine of ripeness, the general rule against advisory opinions, and other related considerations of separation of powers and judicial economy.[100] Although courts developed this approach in the context of bills pending in a legislature, they have generally applied it to initiatives, as well.

However, courts in several states have rejected this view. In Arkansas, Oklahoma, Missouri, Montana, Nebraska, and Utah, courts will consider facial constitutional challenges to initiatives before the election, and, in Florida, the state constitution mandates this form of pre-election review.[101]

A number of judges and legal scholars, viewing the issue through the framework of the judicial guardianship of rights, believe courts should be willing to intervene before the election to remove an unconstitutional initiative from the ballot. Former Oregon Supreme Court Justice Hans Linde has been a leading advocate of this view. Linde argued, for example, that the Oregon high court should have intervened to strike from the ballot a measure restricting the rights of homosexuals.[102] Proposals to prevent citizens from voting on controversial measures affecting minority rights again reflect the view that direct democracy is dangerous and that courts should exercise heightened vigilance to constrain it.

Although some courts have invalidated initiatives before the election on various grounds, they have more often exercised the judicial check after the people have voted.[103]

---

[99] Courts often review pre-election challenges to initiatives to determine whether the proponents have met procedural requirements. See Douglas Michael, "Judicial Review of Initiative Constitutional Amendments, 14 U.C. DAVIS L. REV. 461, 468–74 (1980).

[100] Gordon and Magleby, "Pre-Election Judicial Review," 304–20. Colorado is one of the few states that allows for advisory opinions, but they must be requested by the legislature.

[101] For a concise overview of pre-election review of initiatives in various states, see Philip L. DuBois and Floyd Feeney, *Lawmaking by Initiative: Issues, Options, and Comparisons* (New York: Agathon Press, 1998), 43–5.

[102] See Linde, "When Initiative Lawmaking Is Not 'Republican Government,'" 19.

[103] Gordon and Magleby, "Pre-Election Judicial Review," 303. See, e.g., *Lowe v. Keisling*, 130 Ore. App. 1, 17–18 (1994), rejecting plaintiffs' argument that allowing a vote on an initiative to restrict homosexual rights would in itself violate the guarantee clause, which, following Linde's theory, forbids states from holding an election on "any proposed laws aimed at restricting the substantive rights of unpopular minority groups."

CONCLUSION

The doctrine of judicial review and an expanding conception of judicial power have placed courts in a strong position to counter initiatives. In determining how to exercise this responsibility, courts have a range of choice. The prevailing rule is that judges should review initiatives using the same standards they use when reviewing acts of legislatures. But, as we have seen, strong theoretical undercurrents pull the courts in different directions. According to one view, courts should give greater deference to initiatives because they reflect the will of the sovereign people; the contrary view asserts that citizen lawmaking is dangerous and should be given less deference than ordinary legislation.

These competing views provide a theoretical framework for understanding the court's check on direct democracy. We now need to turn from theoretical debates to the historical record and ask: How *have* courts treated the initiative power and the broad range of citizen-enacted laws?

4

The Courts at Work

Have courts, in fact, countered direct democracy? The short answer is "yes," but the full story is more complex. An accurate assessment requires us to consider the various ways courts have interacted with the initiative power. Courts have both defended the initiative process against various threats and taken a heavy toll on individual initiatives. This chapter begins by discussing how courts have often protected the initiative process, then turns to the litigation record to show how judicial review of individual initiatives has placed a strong check on the initiative power.

JUDICIAL PROTECTION OF THE INITIATIVE PROCESS

At crucial moments, courts have defended direct democracy from attack. Most importantly, courts protected the initiative process when the reformers first grafted it onto the representative system. By refusing to rule that direct citizen lawmaking violates the guarantee clause, the U.S. Supreme Court in *Pacific States* (1912) and several state courts defeated the constitutional challenge to direct democracy.[1]

More recently, courts have struck down numerous attempts by state legislatures to "reform" – and thereby weaken – direct democracy. As we have seen, legislatures have sought to limit contributions to ballot measure campaigns, ban payments to signature gatherers, require petitioners to be registered to vote in the state, and limit the locations where petitioners can operate.[2]

---

[1] *Pacific States Telephone and Telegraph Company v. Oregon*, 223 U.S. 118 (1912); see also *Kadderly v. City of Portland*, 44 Ore. 118 (1903); *In re Pfahler*, 150 Cal. 71 (1906); *Ex Parte Wagner*, 95 P. 435 (Okla. 1908); *Hartig v. City of Seattle*, 53 Wash. 432 (1909).

[2] See M. Dane Waters, ed. *The Battle Over Citizen Lawmaking: An In-Depth Review of the Growing Trend to Regulate the People's Tool of Self-Government: The Initiative and Referendum* (Durham: Carolina Academic Press, 2001), 282–85.

If allowed to stand, these types of restrictions could seriously inhibit the exercise of direct democracy. But, the courts have frequently declared them void.

For example, in the 1970s, the Massachusetts legislature enacted a statute prohibiting corporations from spending corporate funds to influence the vote on ballot measures, unless the measure "materially affect[ed] any of the property, business, or assets of the corporation."[3] But, in *First National Bank of Boston v. Bellotti* (1978), the U.S. Supreme Court invoked the First Amendment to strike down this restriction.[4] Similarly, in *Citizens Against Rent Control/ Coalition for Fair Housing v. City of Berkeley* (1981), the Court invalidated a Berkeley, California city ordinance limiting contributions to committees formed to support or oppose local ballot measures.[5] And, in *Meyer v. Grant* (1988), the Court declared that initiative sponsors have a First Amendment right to pay persons to collect signatures on initiative petitions, thus striking down a law enacted by the Colorado legislature to ban that practice.[6] Courts have also invalidated laws requiring petitioners to reside or to be registered to vote in the state or county where they are circulating initiative petitions, or to disclose by wearing a badge or by other means that they are being paid to collect signatures.[7] Through these and related decisions, courts have protected the exercise of direct democracy.

Courts also supervise pre-election procedures for qualifying individual measures for the ballot. Here, judicial protection of direct democracy has been less consistent. On purely procedural matters, such as challenges to the sufficiency of petition signatures, courts have generally interpreted the requirements liberally to prevent a measure's opponent from seizing on technicalities to block an election.[8] But, when a challenge to an initiative combines procedural and

---

[3] *Mass. Gen. Laws Ann.* Ch. 55 § 8 (West Supp. 1977).
[4] *First National Bank of Boston v. Bellotti*, 435 U.S. 765 (1978).
[5] *Citizens Against Rent Control/Coalition for Fair Housing v. City of Berkeley*, 454 U.S. 290 (1981).
[6] *Meyer v. Grant*, 486 U.S. 414 (1988), striking down *Colorado Rev. Stat.* § 1-40-110 (1980).
[7] See, e.g., *State ex rel. Stenberg v. Beermann*, 240 Neb. 754 (1992); *Bernbeck v. Moore*, 126 F.3d 1114 (8th Cir. 1997); *Buckley v. American Constitutional Law Foundation, Inc.*, 525 U.S. 182 (1999). For listing and analysis of cases relating to regulations of the initiative process, see Joseph F. Zimmerman, *The Initiative: Citizen Law-making* (Westport, CT: Prager, 1999), 57–88; M. Dane Waters, ed. *Initiative and Referendum Almanac* (Durham: Carolina Academic Press, 2003), 461–67.
[8] The courts' deferential review of purely procedural aspects of the initiative process is similar to their review of popular referendum and recall. The flurry of litigation surrounding the recall of California Governor Gray Davis in 2003 illustrated the limits of judicial review of the procedural aspects of direct democracy. In the summer of 2003, opponents filed more than ten cases in state and federal court challenging various aspects of the recall and seeking to prevent or delay the election. Because the basis for the recall was non-reviewable, opponents could only challenge the validity of the procedures governing its use. While the Davis recall litigation was intense and produced some moments of uncertainty, the courts eventually construed the procedural rules liberally to allow the election to proceed without interference. For further discussion of

substantive elements, the courts have sometimes offered greater resistance. Pre-election review of ballot titles and summaries is a notable example.

In most initiative states, a Title Board, the Attorney General, or the Secretary of State has initial responsibility for drafting an initiative's title and summary, but if interested parties object to the wording, they can challenge it in court.[9] The stakes are high because the specific language of the title and summary sends important cues to voters and can sometimes determine a measure's success or failure. In recent decades, activists have often filed pre-election lawsuits to challenge phrasing – to fight, for example, for the ballot title to say "affirmative action" instead of "racial preferences."

The level of judicial involvement of these matters varies from state to state. In some states, courts have become enmeshed in lengthy disputes over the text of ballot titles. Richard Ellis has documented how the Oregon high court's docket became clogged with ballot title disputes in the 1990s. During the 1999–2000 election cycle, various parties appealed ninety-two of the titles certified by the attorney general's office, and the court ended up rewriting half of these titles. During March and April 2000, the court devoted almost all of its time to reviewing ballot titles, and from 1998 to 2000, fully one-fifth of its decisions involved these disputes.[10]

Other courts have shown greater deference toward the drafting agency's decisions, but during the 1990s, the titling process in several states, including Colorado, Washington, and Arizona, became increasingly litigious. The Colorado Supreme Court, in particular, began second-guessing the Colorado Title Board's judgments with increasing frequency.[11] The trend toward judicial revision of initiative titles and summaries raised concerns regarding separation of powers because, in some cases courts, the were interpreting voter-approved initiatives based in part on the summary they had written before the election.[12]

The greatest controversies surrounding judicial oversight of title and summary arose in states such as Florida where proponents are responsible for writing their own ballot titles and courts have blocked initiatives from the ballot on the grounds that the title was inadequate.[13] In addition, as we shall see, some courts also used pre-election review of the initiative's compliance with

the judicial role in the Davis recall and the distinctions between judicial review of initiatives and other forms of direct democracy, see Kenneth P. Miller, "The Davis Recall and the Courts," *American Politics Research* 33, no. 2 (March 2005): 135–162.

9 For a state-by-state listing of title and summary procedures, see Waters, ed., *Initiative and Referendum Almanac*, 18–19.

10 Richard J. Ellis, *Democratic Delusions: The Initiative Process in America* (Lawrence: University Press of Kansas, 2002), 148–151.

11 Ibid., 152–157.

12 Ibid., 150–151.

13 Ibid., 157–166.

the single-subject rule to block measures from the ballot. The evidence indicates that some courts are now offering greater resistance to direct democracy through the pre-election enforcement of rules for the initiative process.

JUDICIAL REVIEW OF VOTER-APPROVED INITIATIVES

The courts' most comprehensive check on the initiative power is judicial review of voter-approved initiatives. In Chapter 2, we traced the growth of citizen lawmaking in the five strongest initiative states – California, Oregon, Washington, Colorado, and Arizona – over the past century. We can now examine how frequently, and on what basis, courts countered these initiatives through post-election judicial review. The record of post-election initiative challenges reveals that courts have exercised a strong check on the initiative power across states and over time.[14]

Challenges and Invalidations

Legal challenges to voter-approved initiatives started right away. In 1904, Oregon voters adopted the nation's first two statewide initiatives – one establishing the state's direct primary system, the other authorizing local option on the prohibition question. Shortly after the election, opponents challenged the prohibition initiative, arguing that the measure violated a number of state and federal constitutional provisions.[15] The challenges failed, but the pattern had been set: Initiative opponents would not hesitate to ask courts to counter the will of the people.

In the century that followed, over 40 percent of all voter-approved initiatives in the strongest initiative states faced post-election challenges. Initiative litigation rates in these states hovered around 30 percent through the 1930s then declined at mid-century. After 1970, however, the rates sharply increased, with more than half (56 percent) of all initiatives adopted between 1970 and the end of the 1990s facing post-election judicial review. Initiative litigation reached all-time highs in the 1990s in both absolute and percentage terms.

---

[14] The chapter analyzes post-election challenges to the validity of voter-approved initiatives. The analysis excludes cases that were filed prior to the election, or that sought judicial interpretation or enforcement of initiatives rather than their invalidation, or that were withdrawn, dismissed, or otherwise resolved without producing a reported decision. The outcomes are sorted into four categories: "upheld," "invalidated in part," "invalidated in entirety," and "pending." The record of initiative litigation is not fixed, especially for the most recent period, because there is an inevitable delay between voter approval of initiatives and resolution of post-election challenges.

[15] See *Sandys v. Williams*, 46 Ore. 327 (1905); *Fouts v. Hood River*, 46 Ore. 492 (1905); *State ex rel. Gibson v. Richardson*, 48 Ore. 309 (1906); *State v. Kline*, 50 Ore. 426 (1907); *State v. Langworthy*, 55 Ore. 303 (1909).

Opponents challenged over 60 percent of all initiatives adopted that decade in the strongest initiative states – a remarkable level of litigation.

Invalidations are an even better measure of the courts' check on the initiative power.[16] In the leading states, courts struck down, in whole or in part, 44 percent of the initiatives that faced post-election challenges. This meant that, overall, nearly one-fifth (18 percent) of all initiatives adopted by voters in these states were invalidated either in part or in their entirety. Moreover, the invalidation rates increased sharply between the 1960s and the 1990s as conflict between citizen lawmakers and courts escalated. Courts invalidated, in whole or in part, nearly one third (31 percent) of the 84 initiatives adopted in these states during the 1990s.

Table 4.1 and Figure 4.1 display the overall trends in the number of initiatives approved, challenged, and invalidated in the strongest initiative states throughout the first century of the initiative era. Initiative use reached historic highs in the 1990s, both nationally and in the strongest initiative states. The numbers declined in the 2000s, but the drop-off was far less than in other periods, such as the 1920s or 1950s–1960s. Aside from the 1990s, initiative use was higher in the 2000s than in any other decade during the past century.

Table 4.1 and Figure 4.1 also show that the judicial check on citizen-enacted laws more than kept pace with the dramatic expansion of the initiative power through the 1990s, with the rate of initiative challenges and invalidations rising to historic highs in that decade.

---

[16] Another way to measure the judicial check on initiatives is to compare it with the courts' check on acts of the legislature. All evidence suggests that a citizen initiative is much more likely than a legislative act to be challenged and invalidated. One study by political scientist Craig Emmert reported that, in the early 1980s (1981–1985), state supreme courts invalidated, on average, 2.4 laws per year, which was a 22.7 percent mean invalidation rate for laws challenged in state high courts during that period. As legislatures have a far greater output than the initiative process, the overall invalidation rate for legislative acts is far lower than the invalidation rate for citizen initiatives. Craig F. Emmert, "Judicial Review in State Supreme Courts: Opportunity and Activism," (Paper presented at the 1988 Annual Meeting of the Midwest Political Science Association, Chicago, IL). Emmert also found large variations in invalidation rates both by state and by policy area. See also Laura Langer, *Judicial Review in State Supreme Courts: A Comparative Study* (Albany: State University of New York Press, 2002). For discussion of the distinction between judicial invalidation of initiatives and legislative acts, see Mathew Manweller, *The People Versus The Courts: Initiative Elites, Judicial Review, and Direct Democracy in the American Legal System* (Bethesda, MD: Academica Press, LLC, 2005), 8. It would also be useful to compare litigation rates for initiatives with those for measures placed on the ballot by legislatures. Although there are no large-scale empirical studies of these differences, it is likely that legislative referenda, like other legislative acts, are challenged and invalidated at lower rates than citizen-initiated law. As Julian Eule noted, legislative referenda are, on average, more carefully vetted and less controversial than citizen-initiatives. Julian N. Eule, "Judicial Review of Direct Democracy," 99 YALE L. J. 1503, 1573 (1990). These factors suggest that legislative referenda are less likely than initiatives to face post-election legal attack.

TABLE 4.1. *Post-election Initiative Challenges and Invalidations by Decade, Five Strongest Initiative States, 1904–2008*

Decade Adopted	Total Voter-Approved Initiatives	Number Challenged	Litigation Outcome				Challenge Rate	Invalidation Rate (of Challenged)[b]	Invalidation Rate (of Total)
			U	IE	IP	Pn			
1900s	17	7	6	–	1	–	.41	.14	.06
1910s	65	21	9	7	5	–	.32	.57	.18
1920s	19	6	3	2	1	–	.32	.50	.16
1930s	40	14	11	2	1	–	.35	.21	.08
1940s	28	7	5	2	–	–	.25	.29	.07
1950s	20	4	3	1	–	–	.20	.25	.05
1960s	22	6	2	3	1	–	.27	.67	.18
1970s	33	17	9	3	5	–	.52	.47	.24
1980s	51	26	13	6	7	–	.51	.50	.25
1990s	84	51	24	14	12	1	.61	.52	.31
2000s[a]	76	26	15	4	3	4	.34	.32	.09
TOTALS	455	185	100	44	36	5	.41	.44	.18

[a] Data for 2000s include voter-approved initiatives from 2000–2008 and initiative litigation through 2008.
[b] Resolved challenges; pending litigation excluded.
U = Upheld; IE = Invalidated in entirety; IP = Invalidated in part; Pn = Pending.

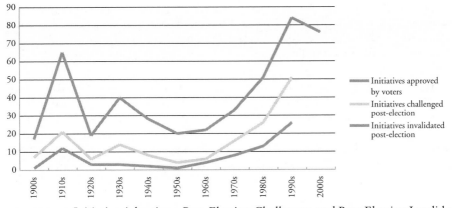

FIGURE 4.1. Initiative Adoptions, Post-Election Challenges, and Post-Election Invalidations, Five Strongest Initiative States, 1900s–2000s.

Initiative Litigation Data: 1900s–1990s

The frequency and outcomes of challenges to initiatives adopted in the 2000s remain uncertain. The record takes time to develop because there is a delay between voter approval of initiatives and resolution of post-election litigation. These lag times can vary significantly. In *Coalition for Economic Equity v. Wilson* (1997), for example, Ninth Circuit Judge Diarmuid O'Scannlain remarked that "[t]he ink on Proposition 209 was barely dry when plaintiffs filed this lawsuit."[17] Similarly, opponents of California's Proposition 8 filed three separate lawsuits challenging the initiative on November 5, 2008, the day after the election.[18] But, at other times, opponents bring challenges years after the people have voted, once new developments generate fresh legal theories. For example, in *James v. Valtierra* (1971), opponents challenged California's Proposition 10 of 1950 two decades after the measure was adopted, only after equal protection theories had expanded to the point where it became plausible to argue that poverty is a "suspect classification."[19] Accordingly, we can make only tentative observations regarding the judicial check on recently enacted initiatives.

It is likely that the rate of post-election challenges to initiatives adopted in the 2000s will drop from the 1990s peak, but it will take time to see how sharp the decline will be. Much depends on developments in the law. Notably, if the U.S. Supreme Court were to declare that same-sex couples have a *federal*

---

[17] *Coalition for Economic Equity v. Wilson*, 122 F.3d 692, 700 (9th Cir. 1997).

[18] *Strauss v. Horton*, California Supreme Court Case No. S168047; *Tyler v. State of California*, California Supreme Court Case No. S168066; *City and County of San Francisco v. Horton*, California Supreme Court Case No. S168078. These three challenges to Proposition 8 were filed on November 5, 2008, the day after the vote on Proposition 8 and before the election's results were certified.

[19] *James v. Valtierra*, 402 U.S. 137 (1971).

constitutional right to marry, it would immediately invalidate eleven initiatives adopted in the 2000s in Arkansas, California, Colorado, Florida, Michigan, Montana, Nebraska, Nevada, North Dakota, Ohio, and Oregon. And the development of new legal theories could generate fresh challenges to other initiatives, as well.

More than anything, the litigation record demonstrates the incredibly high level of conflict between the initiative power and the courts during the 1990s. The spike can be attributed to specific developments during that decade, most notably the term limits movement. Between 1990 and 2000, term limits activists generated forty-three separate initiatives in twenty-one states. Opponents challenged almost all of these initiatives on a range of legal theories and courts invalidated most of them. In just one case, *U.S. Term Limits, Inc. v. Thornton* (1995), the U.S. Supreme Court struck down congressional term limits initiatives adopted in twenty states (Alaska, Arizona, Arkansas, California, Colorado, Florida, Idaho, Maine, Massachusetts, Michigan, Missouri, Montana, Nebraska, North Dakota, Ohio, Oklahoma, Oregon, South Dakota, Washington, and Wyoming), as well as an additional initiative in Nevada that had received the first of two required affirmative votes.[20] Similarly, the Court's decision in *Cook v. Gralike* (2001) invalidated scarlet letter initiatives adopted in the 1990s in Alaska, Missouri, and Nevada.[21] And, in a flurry of litigation, state courts invalidated several other term limits initiatives.[22] This mass conflict between citizen lawmakers and the courts was unprecedented and greatly contributed to the high rates of initiative challenges and invalidations in the 1990s.

But, term limits initiatives were not the only source of conflict during that decade. Citizen lawmakers and courts sparred over many other hot-button issues, including criminal sentencing, affirmative action, public benefits for illegal immigrants, the rights of homosexuals, and the regulation of campaign finance. Many of these issues remain contested, and will almost certainly

---

[20] *U.S. Term Limits Inc. v. Thornton*, 514 U.S. 779 (1995).

[21] *Cook v. Gralike*, 531 U.S. 510 (2001).

[22] Cases invalidating state term limit initiatives included *League of Women Voters vs. Secretary of the Commonwealth*, 425 Mass. 424 (1997); *Duggan v. Beermann*, 249 Neb. 411 (1996); *Lehman v. Bradbury*, 333 Ore. 231 (2002); *Cathcart v. Meyer*, 88 P.3d 1050 (Wy. 2004). Cases invalidating "scarlet letter" initiatives included *Bramberg v. Jones*, 20 Cal.4th 1045 (1999); *Morrissey v. State*, 951 P.2d 911 (S. Ct. Colo. 1998); *Donovan v. Priest*, 326 Ark. 353 (1996); *Barker v. Hazeltine*, 3 F.Supp.2d 1088 (Dist. S.D. 1998); *Miller v. Moore*, 169 F.3d 1119 (8th Cir. 1999); *Simpson v. Cenarrusa*, 130 Idaho 609 (1997). A "self-limit" initiative was invalidated in *Van Valkenburgh v. Citizens for Term Limits*, 135 Idaho 121 (2000). In addition, courts in some states used pre-election review to strike down term limits initiatives. These cases included *Alaskans for Legislative Reform v. State*, 887 P.2d 960 (Alaska 1994); *The Chicago Bar Association v. Illinois State Board of Elections*, 161 Ill.2d 502, 509 (1994) (term limits on state elected officials); and *In re Initiative Petition No. 364*, 1996 Ok. 129 (1996) ("scarlet letter").

continue to generate new initiatives and initiative challenges. Whereas over-all initiative adoptions, challenges, and invalidations have declined since their historic highs of the 1990s, there is little evidence that either direct democracy or the judicial power is in retreat.

Differences Between States

The judicial check on initiatives has varied from state to state, with different initiative states experiencing noticeably different rates of initiative challenges and invalidations.

California initiatives have been challenged and invalidated at the highest rates. By the 1990s, it seemed that post-election litigation had become an institutionalized feature of the state's initiative system. Opponents challenged 69 percent of all California initiatives adopted from the 1970s through the 1990s, and courts invalidated, in part or in whole, 38 percent of all initiatives adopted in the state during these years. A number of factors help explain these remarkably high initiative litigation rates. Most importantly, California initiatives have raised difficult constitutional issues in areas including criminal procedure and punishment, campaign finance reform, busing, affirmative action, immigrant rights, and the definition of marriage.[23] And, at the same time, state and federal judges in California have actively expanded and enforced rights. This combination of factors has made post-election litigation a regular strategy for initiative opponents, and a strong check on the California initiative process.

Although the other leading initiative states had lower litigation rates than California, conflicts between citizen lawmakers and courts increased in those states, as well. Oregon, for example, saw a large spike in initiative litigation in the 1990s. In earlier decades, courts had exercised a relatively light check on the state's initiative process, invalidating less than 10 percent of all initiatives adopted between 1904 and the end of the 1980s. But, in the 1990s, all of that changed. Courts invalidated, in whole or in part, over one-fourth of all Oregon initiatives adopted in the 1990s, with the Oregon Supreme Court, in particular, more aggressively countering the state's initiative process. Meanwhile, the rates of initiative challenges and invalidations also rose during the 1990s in Washington, Arizona, and Colorado.

Outcomes in State vs. Federal Courts

The difference between state and federal court checks on direct democracy is an area of both theoretical and practical importance. The most basic distinction is jurisdictional. Although state courts have general subject matter jurisdiction,

---

[23] See, e.g., Craig B. Holman and Robert Stern, "Judicial Review of Ballot Initiatives: The Changing Role of State and Federal Courts," 31 LOY. L.A. L. REV. 1239, 1256–1257 (1998).

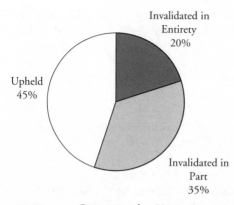

Upheld
45%

Invalidated in
Entirety
20%

Invalidated in
Part
35%

FIGURE 4.2. Outcomes for Voter-Approved Initiatives Challenged in Federal Court, Five Strongest Initiative States, 1912–2008 N = 55 challenged initiatives.

federal courts have limited jurisdiction and will review an initiative challenge only if the challenge raises a federal question. Initiative opponents may always choose to bring suit in state court, but must present a federal question to challenge the measure in federal court. When opponents have a choice between state and federal court, they must decide which is more likely to invalidate the measure.

One prominent theory suggests that federal courts are more willing than state courts to strike down citizen-enacted laws.[24] This view has a plausible theoretical basis because federal judges are less politically accountable than state court judges. Article III of the Constitution provides federal judges institutional independence to render unpopular decisions without fear of political reprisal.[25] By contrast, states have chosen to make their judges accountable to the people through various forms of election and, in some states, judicial recall. In light of these differences, one might conclude that state court judges are less likely than federal judges to invalidate voter-approved measures, and that opponents should bring initiative challenges in the federal courts whenever possible. The record, however, offers a more complex picture.

[24] See Holman and Stern, "Judicial Review of Ballot Initiatives," 1258; Gerald F. Uelmen, "Crocodiles in the Bathtub: Maintaining the Independence of State Supreme Courts in an Era of Judicial Politicization," 72 (NOTRE DAME L. REV.) 1133 (1997); Julian Eule, "Crocodiles in the Bathtub: State Courts, Voter Initiatives, and the Threat of Electoral Reprisal," 65 U. COLO. L. REV. 733, 735–740 (1994); Michael Vitiello and Andrew J. Glendon, "Article III Judges and the Initiative Process: Are Article III Judges Hopelessly Elitist?" 31 LOY. L.A. L. REV. 1275 (1998).

[25] Hamilton argued in *Federalist* 78 that "If...the courts of justice are to be considered as the bulwarks of a limited Constitution against legislative encroachments, this consideration will afford a strong argument for the permanent tenure of judicial offices, since nothing will contribute so much as this to that independent spirit in the judges which must be essential to the faithful performance of so arduous a duty." *Federalist* 78, 468.

In the leading states, opponents challenged initiatives three times more often in state court than in federal court.[26] The preference for state court litigation was more pronounced in the early period. Opponents long opted to pursue initiative challenges in the state courts even when the challenges raised federal constitutional claims. Beginning in the 1980s, however, opponents turned more frequently to the federal courts, a trend that accelerated in the 1990s. The most striking shift to the federal courts occurred in California. Before 1990, opponents of California initiatives almost always brought challenges to state court (approximately 90 percent of the time from the 1910s through the 1980s). In the 1990s, however, one-half of all challenges to California initiatives were brought to federal court.[27] In the other leading states, litigation increasingly shifted to federal court, as well. The trend was clear: When initiatives raised federal constitutional questions, opponents increasingly sought to bring their claims before federal judges.

Was it a smart strategy? At first glance, the record suggests that it was. In the leading states, initiatives challenged in federal courts were invalidated, in whole or in part, 55 percent of the time. By contrast, initiatives challenged in state court were invalidated, in whole or in part, 39 percent of the time. These outcomes offer support for the view that federal courts have been somewhat more willing to strike down voter-approved initiatives. But if we analyze the outcomes more closely, we see that when federal courts invalidated an initiative, they were more likely to strike it down only in part. State courts, by contrast, were more likely to invalidate an initiative in its entirety, often on technical state constitutional grounds. These outcomes demonstrate that state

[26] The figures were 127 voter-approved initiative challenges in state court; 37 challenged in federal court; and 17 challenged in both state and federal courts. The distinction between "state" and federal" challenge is complicated when cases are filed in state courts but ultimately resolved in the federal courts. This happened most frequently when state challenges were reviewed by the U.S. Supreme Court. For purposes of this analysis, the category "state challenge" includes most cases filed in state courts but ultimately resolved by the U.S. Supreme Court. However, a few cases that originated outside of the five strongest initiative states and then reached the U.S. Supreme Court are characterized as "federal." The main example is *U.S. Term Limits v. Thornton*, 514 U.S. 779 (1995). That case originated in the Arkansas state courts, but produced a decision in the U.S. Supreme Court that struck down congressional term limits initiatives in all five of the states in this study. Finally, initiative challenges arising from criminal cases originally filed in state courts but later transferred to federal courts through petition for writ of *habeas corpus* are treated as federal challenges.

[27] Craig Holman and Robert Stern lamented the shift in initiative litigation to federal courts, arguing that federal judges had shown insufficient deference to California initiatives. Holman and Stern, "Judicial Review of Ballot Initiatives," 1255–56. In response, election law expert Richard Hasen suggested that the pool of cases was too small to draw meaningful conclusions, and that the outcomes could be distorted by selection bias. In other words, initiative opponents might have been bringing the more meritorious claims in federal court. See Richard A. Hasen, "Judging the Judges of Initiatives: A Comment on Holman and Stern," 31 Loy. L.A. L. Rev. 1267, 1268–1270 (1998). By expanding the number of cases, we are able to make a broader comparison between state and federal court treatment of initiatives across states and over time.

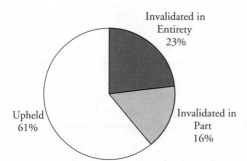

FIGURE 4.3. Outcomes for Voter-Approved Initiatives Challenged in State Court, Five Strongest Initiative States, 1904–2008 N = 144 challenged initiatives. *Percentages reflect resolved challenges; pending litigation excluded.*

judges applied a strong check on voter-approved initiatives, even in the face of possible voter retribution.

Outcomes by Initiative Subject Matter

Courts have scrutinized laws in certain policy areas more closely than in others, and the focus of their concerns has changed over time. As we have seen, between the 1890s and the mid-1930s, courts placed significant constitutional limits on economic regulation, but after the New Deal crisis, they largely deferred to lawmakers in this area. Conversely, beginning in the 1960s, courts increased their scrutiny of policy in areas such as political regulation and criminal procedure. These broad developments in constitutional law suggest that we should notice variations in initiative challenges and invalidations depending on the subject matter of the initiative.

Chapter 2 grouped voter-approved initiatives into the following seven broad policy categories:

- Political and government reform
- Health, welfare, and morals
- Economic regulation
- Environment
- Tax
- Criminal procedure and punishment
- Education

Analyzing initiative litigation outcomes in these categories reveals notable differences.

Crime. Initiatives that enacted criminal justice policy faced the highest rate of post-election challenges. Nearly three-fourths of the thirty-four crime initiatives adopted in the leading states through 2008 were challenged after the election, usually by a criminal defendant who argued that an initiative violated his state or federal constitutional rights. Courts upheld many of these initiatives against constitutional attack, including some very tough measures like California's three-strikes sentencing law. But, they also invalidated nine crime measures (26 percent of the total adopted), in whole or in part, on a range of state and federal constitutional grounds.

Political and Government Reform. Initiatives in the largest subject category, political and government reform, faced the greatest number of challenges, and the second-highest litigation rate. Two types of initiatives in this category – campaign finance reform and term limits – were the most frequently challenged.

Campaign Finance Reform. Voters in the five leading initiative states adopted eighteen measures to limit political contributions or expenditures, require their disclosure, or otherwise regulate money in the political process. Opponents challenged all seventeen of the measures adopted through 2006 and courts invalidated, at least in part, fourteen of the seventeen (82 percent), usually on the grounds that one or more provisions of the measure violated state or federal protections on political speech. These outcomes placed a heavy constraint on citizen efforts to regulate money in politics.

Term Limits. As we have noted, the term limits movement won victories in almost all of the initiative states, including the five leading states. Voters in California, Oregon, Colorado, Washington, and Arizona collectively adopted ten initiatives to impose term limits on representatives or to pressure representatives to support term limits. Opponents challenged eight of these measures, and courts invalidated, at least in part, all eight. The U.S. Supreme Court invalidated all state-imposed term limits on members of Congress; the supreme courts of Oregon and Washington struck down initiatives imposing term limits on state officials, and various courts invalidated "scarlet letter" initiatives adopted in these states.[28]

Economic Regulation. Economic regulation initiatives were also challenged and invalidated at high rates – 35 percent and 24 percent, respectively. These outcomes are perhaps surprising until we see that most of the litigation occurred prior to the New Deal. Early in the twentieth century, courts struck down a number of economic regulation initiatives on rights-based theories, but after the 1930s, the number of initiatives in this category declined overall, as did litigation seeking to invalidate them.

---

[28] The only unchallenged term limits initiatives in these states were Colorado Amendment 5 of 1990, which was superseded by a more severe term limits initiative, and Colorado Amendment 18 of 1998, which authorized candidates for Congress to place a voluntary declaration on the ballot that they would serve no more than three terms in the House or two terms in the Senate. State term limits survived in Arizona, California, and Colorado. For a more detailed discussion, see Chapter 6.

TABLE 4.2. *Initiative Litigation Outcomes by Initiative Subject Matter, Five Strongest Initiative States, 1904–2008*

Subject Category	Total Voter-Approved Initiatives	Number Challenged	Litigation Outcome				Challenge Rate	Invalidation Rate (of Challenged)[a]	Invalidation Rate (of Total)
			U	IE	IP	Pn			
Crime	34	25	15	3	6	1	.74	.38	.26
Political/Gov't Reform	147	67	31	18	17	1	.46	.53	.24
Economic Regulation	68	24	8	12	4	–	.35	.67	.24
Education	27	7	3	2	2	–	.26	.57	.15
Tax	48	19	12	5	1	1	.40	.33	.13
Environment	48	16	12	1	3	–	.33	.25	.08
Health/Welfare/Morals	83	27	19	4	2	2	.33	.24	.07

[a] Resolved challenges; pending litigation has been excluded.

U = Upheld; IE = Invalidated in entirety; IP = Invalidated in part; Pn = Pending.

Other Subjects. Initiatives in the remaining categories – education, tax, environment, and health/welfare/morals – were also frequently challenged at high rates, but less frequently invalidated. Some of these measures produced intense litigation, including the education initiatives that sought to end desegregative busing and bilingual education, and the two Colorado initiatives to restrict abortion, which fell into the category of health/welfare/morals. But, for the most part, initiatives in these categories did not raise serious constitutional difficulties, and courts exercised a comparatively light check on them.

Legal Bases of Initiative Challenges and Invalidations

Finally, judicial decisions help us assess direct democracy's potential threats to constitutionally protected rights and powers because they provide accounts of each challenged initiative's alleged constitutional violations as well as analyses of these claims.

The bases for initiative challenges and invalidations can be divided into the two broad areas of constitutional law: rights and powers. Rights-based challenges have alleged that the initiative violated state or federal constitutional protections of property, contract, speech, petition, association, due process, equal protection, or the cluster of rights governing criminal procedure and punishment. Conversely, powers-based challenges have claimed that the measure violated federal constitutional provisions such as the Article IV guarantee of republican government, the Article V rules for constitutional amendments, the Article VI supremacy clause, state constitutional provisions related to the powers of government institutions or the scope of the initiative process.

In the leading states, opponents attacked initiatives slightly more often on powers-based than rights-based theories, with seventy-one challenges alleging that the initiative violated provisions for the distribution of power, sixty-one alleging that the initiative violated constitutionally-protected rights, and fifty-three alleging some combination of the two theories. However, courts were slightly more receptive to rights-based challenges. Courts invalidated forty initiatives, in whole or in part, for violation of rights, thirty-three for violation of powers, and seven for a combination of the two.

Table 4.3 breaks down these broad categories to indicate the specific state and federal constitutional provisions that courts held the initiatives violated.

When invalidating initiatives for rights violations, the courts invoked federal constitutional rights four times more often than state constitutional rights. Of course, federal courts always enforced federal rather than state constitutional rights, but state courts usually did as well. Occasionally, the supreme courts of Oregon and California invoked state constitutional rights to strike down citizen-enacted laws, but even those courts more frequently relied on the rights provisions of the federal Constitution. The right most frequently invoked was the First Amendment, followed by the Fourteenth Amendment guarantees of

TABLE 4.3. *Specific Legal Bases for Invalidation of Voter-Approved Initiatives, Five Strongest Initiative States, 1904–2008*

Rights

Federal		State	
1st Amendment	15	Free speech and related rights	3
14th Amendment equal protection clause	13	Equal protection	1
14th Amendment due process clause^a	9	Due process	3
8th Amendment	3	Other criminal justice rights	2
5th Amendment (self-incrimination)	1		
Contracts clause	3	Contracts clause	1
Other	–	Other	3

Powers

Federal		State	
Article VI supremacy clause	7	Separation of powers/legislature's powers/judicial powers	7
Qualifications clauses	5	Single-subject rule/separate vote requirement	7
Article V amendment rules	2	Title/summary/form of ballot measure	7
Commerce clause	2	2-in-conflict rule	3
Other	–	No-revision rule	1
		Other limits on the initiative power	3
		Other	8

^a The federal due process category does not include incorporation cases enforcing provisions of the federal Bill of Rights through the Fourteenth Amendment; these cases are separately listed in other categories.

equal protection and due process, the rights of criminal defendants, and the contracts clause.

Meanwhile, in cases involving conflicts over powers, courts held that a number of initiatives violated the supremacy clause of Article VI, and that others impermissibly sought to place restrictions on federal representatives in violation of the qualifications clauses or the Article V rules for federal constitutional amendments. More frequently, courts struck down initiatives for violating state constitutional provisions concerning separation of powers, the powers of representative institutions, or limitations on the initiative power, such as the single-subject rule, the no-revision rule, or the separate-vote requirement for state constitutional amendments.

INITIATIVE LITIGATION IN OTHER STATES

Although this analysis focuses on conflicts between direct democracy and courts in the five strongest initiative states, it is useful to compare patterns of litigation in other, lower-use initiative states. Although a complete record of initiative litigation has not been compiled for all twenty-four initiative states, it is possible to describe some features of the judicial check on initiatives in both the weakest and the mid-range initiative states.

Weakest Initiative States

Courts have exercised a check on direct democracy in all initiative states, including states where the initiative process is weakest. The four lowest-use initiative states – Illinois, Mississippi, Utah, and Wyoming – have an important history of initiative litigation. In 1994, for example, the Illinois Supreme Court invalidated a term limits initiative before it could reach the ballot. The rules for the Illinois initiative process are highly restrictive: Citizens may only adopt initiatives that related to "structural and procedural subjects" contained in Article IV or the Illinois Constitution, the article that defines the legislature's powers. Voters had successfully used the process only once, in 1980, to reduce the size of the state legislature.[29] Term limits activists believed that the term limits initiative also fit within the narrow scope of the Illinois initiative system. But, the Illinois Supreme Court held that "the eligibility or qualifications of an individual legislator does not involve the structure of the legislature *as an institution*."[30] Through this ruling, the court further limited the state's highly constrained initiative process. In a similar manner, the Mississippi Supreme

---

[29] The 1980 initiative constitutional amendment reduced the size of the Illinois House of Representatives from 177 to 118 members. See ILL. CONST. of 1970, art. IV, sec. 2 (1980).

[30] *The Chicago Bar Association v. Illinois State Board of Elections*, 161 Ill.2d 502, 509 (1994) (emphasis in original).

Court has used pre-election review of initiatives to reinforce the state's restrictive rules for initiative lawmaking.[31] And, in the other weakest initiative states, Utah and Wyoming, several citizen-initiated laws have faced legal challenges.[32]

Mid-Range States

In the mid-range initiative states, the dynamics between the initiative system and the courts has varied significantly. Four of these states, Arkansas, Alaska, North Dakota, and Florida, demonstrate some of these differences.

Arkansas. In Arkansas, direct democracy and the judicial power have engaged in long-term conflict and courts have exercised a check on the Arkansas initiatives comparable to those seen in the strongest initiative states. In the first years of the initiative era, nearly every Arkansas initiative was embroiled in litigation as initiative proponents fought with the state supreme court over the scope of the initiative process and restrictions on its use.[33] In 1928, Arkansas citizens adopted an initiative banning the teaching of evolution in the public schools and in 1930, adopted another initiative requiring the "reverent daily reading of the English Bible" in the public schools. The U.S. Supreme Court eventually invalidated both of these measures.[34] In the 1950s, Arkansas voters adopted measures to reinforce racial segregation in the public schools and preserve unequal population districts in the upper house of the state legislature, and courts invalidated these measures, as well.[35] More recently, courts have

---

[31] See, e.g., *In re Proposed Initiative Measure No. 20*, 774 So.2d 397 (Miss. 2000), striking down a proposed anti-gambling initiative because the proponent did not adequately disclose the measure's potential negative impacts on state revenues.

[32] See *Anderson v. Utah*, Slip. Op. No. 000909680 (D. Utah 2001), upholding Utah's 2000 "official English" initiative; *Cathcart v. Meyer*, 88 P.3d 1050 (Wy. 2004), invalidating Wyoming's citizen-initiated term limits on state legislators. See also *U.S. Term Limits, Inc. v. Thornton*, 514 U.S. 779 (1995), striking down citizen-initiated term limits on Wyoming's representatives in Congress.

[33] See, e.g., *State ex rel. Little Rock v. Donaghey*, 106 Ark. 56 (1912), determining that only three constitutional amendments may be adopted per election and invalidating on that basis two citizen-initiated amendments; *Hildreth v. Taylor*, 117 Ark. 465 (1915), striking down an initiative by holding that initiated constitutional amendments must receive a majority of all votes cast in the election, not just of the votes cast on the measure. These rulings placed heavy restrictions on the state's initiative process, but were later reversed by a specially appointed supreme court panel in *Brickhouse v. Hill*, 167 Ark. 513 (1925). For analysis of this early history, see David Y. Thomas, "Direct Legislation in Arkansas," *Political Science Quarterly* 29 (March 1914): 84–110; David Y. Thomas, "Initiative and Referendum in Arkansas Come of Age," *American Political Science Review* 27, no. 1 (Feb. 1933): 66–75.

[34] *Epperson v. State of Arkansas*, 393 U.S. 97 (1968), invalidated the 1928 Arkansas initiative restricting the teaching of evolution in the public schools; the 1930 Arkansas initiative requiring the daily reading of the Bible in public schools was invalidated by *Abington Township School District v. Schempp*, 374 U.S. 203 (1963). See also *McLean v. Arkansas Board of Education*, 529 F. Supp. 1255 (E.D. Ark. 1982).

[35] In 1956, citizens in Arkansas adopted an "interposition" initiative, instructing the legislature to oppose "the Un-Constitutional desegregation decisions of May 17, 1954 and May 31, 1955 of

invalidated, in whole or in part, Arkansas initiatives to restrict public funding for abortions, impose term limits on members of Congress, instruct candidates to support federal term limits, and establish campaign finance regulations.[36]

Alaska. Similarly, in Alaska, citizen-enacted initiatives have faced heavy post-election litigation. Opponents brought challenges against Alaska initiatives that established financial disclosure rules for candidates and elected officials, imposed term limits on the state's representatives in Congress, opened state lands for homesteading, instructed candidates to support a federal term limits amendment, established English as the state's official language, and restricted the possession of marijuana.[37] Notably, the conflict between citizens and the courts over marijuana regulation resembled fights in California and Oregon to define the scope of state constitutional rights. In *Ravin v. State* (1975), the Alaska Supreme Court declared that the Alaska Constitution's privacy clause (art. I, sec.22) protected a citizen's right to possess and use a limited amount of marijuana in his or her own home.[38] In 1990, Alaska citizens adopted an initiative to reverse the court and recriminalize this activity. But in *Noy v. State* (2003), the court invalidated the initiative, holding that because Alaska initiative process is limited to statutory initiatives, citizens could not amend the state constitution to reverse the court's decision and narrow the scope of

---

the United States Supreme Court." A federal court eventually declared this state constitutional amendment void on the basis that it violated the supremacy clause of the U.S. Constitution. *Dietz v. State of Arkansas*, 709 F. Supp. 902 (E.D. Ark. 1989). Also in 1956, Arkansas citizens adopted a school assignment initiative that had the effect of enforcing segregation. That statutory initiative was challenged in federal court, but was superseded by an act of the legislature before the litigation was completed. See *Dove v. Parham*, 181 F. Supp. 504 (E.D. Ark. 1960), appealed at 282 F.2d 256 (8th Cir. 1960). See also *Cooper v. Aaron*, 358 U.S. 1 (1958). After the U.S. Supreme Court's decision in *Baker v. Carr*, 369 U.S. 186 (1962), the federal courts invalidated in part the 1956 Arkansas redistricting initiative in *Yancey v. Faubus*, 238 F. Supp. 290 (E.D. Ark. 1965).

[36] *Dalton v. Little Rock Family Planning Services*, 516 U.S. 474 (1996), invalidating in part a 1988 initiative restricting abortion funding; *U.S. Term Limits, Inc. v. Hill*, 316 Ark. 251 (1994), striking down congressional term limits, affirmed by *U.S. Term Limits, Inc. v. Thornton*, 514 U.S. 779 (1995); *Russell v. Burris*, 146 F.3d 563 (8th Cir. 1998), invalidating in part a 1996 campaign finance reform initiative; *Donovan v. Priest*, 326 Ark. 353 (1996), invalidating a "scarlet letter" initiative.

[37] See *Falcon v. Alaska Public Offices Commission*, 570 P.2d 469 (Alaska 1977) and *Grimm v. Wagoner*, 77 P.3d 423 (Alaska 2003), challenging a 1974 initiative requiring the disclosure of personal finances of state officials and candidates for office; *Thomas v. Bailey*, 595 P.2d 1 (Alaska 1979), invalidating the 1978 homesteading initiative; *U.S. Term Limits, Inc. v. Thornton*, 514 U.S. 779 (1995), striking down Alaska's 1994 initiative imposing term limits on members of Congress; *Cook v. Gralike*, 531 U.S. 510 (2001), invalidating Alaska's "scarlet letter" initiative; *Alaskans for a Common Language, Inc. v. Kritz*, 170 P.3d 183 (Alaska 2007), invalidating in part a 1998 initiative declaring English the state's official language; and *Noy v. State of Alaska*, 83 P.3d 538 (Alaska 2003), invalidating an initiative to criminalize private possession and use of marijuana.

[38] *Ravin v. State of Alaska*, 537 P.2d 494 (Alaska 1975).

the privacy right.[39] Overall, courts invalidated, in part or in their entirety, approximately one-third of initiatives adopted by voters in Alaska – a rate comparable to those found in the strongest initiative states.

North Dakota. Although North Dakota's enthusiasm for direct democracy in the 1920s and 1930s placed it among the highest-use initiative states, the state now operates in the middle range, averaging five initiatives per decade. The state's initiative system has generated comparatively little conflict with courts. In large part, this is because citizens in North Dakota have generally avoided adopting initiatives that raise significant federal constitutional questions. The U.S. Supreme Court held that the state's 1920 "red flag" initiative violated the First Amendment, and that its 1992 congressional term limits initiative violated the federal Constitution's qualifications clauses.[40] And, someday, the Court may hold that its 2004 marriage initiative violates the federal constitutional rights of same-sex couples. But, few other North Dakota initiatives have raised serious constitutional concerns.[41] The state's citizens have not used the initiative process to restrict campaign finance, establish new criminal procedures or punishments, restrict abortion, end affirmative action, or declare English as the state's official language.[42] By avoiding these and other hotly contested constitutional issues, citizen lawmakers in North Dakota have generated relatively few conflicts with the courts. In addition, the North Dakota Supreme Court has not strictly enforced the state's single-subject rule or other rules governing the initiative process, thus further limiting conflict between the initiative system and the judicial power in the state.[43]

---

[39] *Noy v. State of Alaska*, 83 P.3d 538 (Alaska 2003).

[40] The "red flag" initiative prohibited the display of red and black flags or signs bearing anti-government inscriptions and prohibited the displaying of any flag other than the national flag or the flag of a friendly nation. Like other "red flag" laws, the North Dakota initiative was invalidated by the U.S. Supreme Court in *Stromberg v. California*, 283 U.S. 359 (1931). See also *U.S. Term Limits. Inc. v. Thornton*, 514 U.S. 779 (1995), invalidating the North Dakota term limits initiative.

[41] An exception was a 1996 North Dakota initiative restricting waste facilities. In *Municipal Services Corp. v. State*, 1996 U.S. Dist. LEXIS 22891 (D. N.D. 1996), a federal court invalidated the initiative on the grounds that it violated the federal commerce clause.

[42] In 1954, North Dakota voters adopted a conflict of interest initiative limiting the amount of business that legislators could do with the state. The initiative was challenged on the grounds that it violated due process, equal protection, and privileges and immunities protected by the U.S. and North Dakota Constitutions, but the North Dakota Supreme Court rejected the challenge. *Lindberg v. Benson*, 70 N.W. 2d 42 (N.D. 1955).

[43] See e.g., *Larkin v. Gronna*, 69 N.D. 234 (1939), upholding a voter-approved initiative against single subject and ballot title challenge; *State ex rel. Syvertson v. Jones*, 74 N.D. 465 (1946), upholding a statutory initiative against the claim that it exceeded constitutional powers; *City of Fargo v. Sathre*, 76 N.D. 341 (1949), upholding initiative against claim that it violated title rules as well as other constitutional provisions; *SunBehm Gas, Inc. v. Conrad*, 310 N.W. 2d 766 (N.D. 1981), upholding an initiative against the claim that it violated the single-subject rule and powers of the legislature.

Florida. The Florida Supreme Court has significantly weakened direct democracy in the state by strictly enforcing the rules governing the initiative process. The Florida Constitution requires the state supreme court to review each initiative before it reaches the ballot to determine whether it complies with the state's single-subject rule and other technical requirements.[44] Ever since its decision in *Fine v. Firestone* (1984), the court has strictly enforced the single-subject rule and thus prevented many initiatives from reaching the ballot.[45] In *Fine*, the court struck down a tax limitation measure for violating the single-subject rule. The proposed measure sought to restrict general taxes, user fees, and bond debt. Although courts in almost every other state would have held that these three topics form a common "subject," the Florida court held that they were three distinct subjects, and could not be included in the same initiative.[46] The rule of the case was that initiatives could not affect "multiple functions of government" – a barrier that Justice Leander Shaw called "practically insurmountable."[47]

The court candidly characterized the rule as a constraint on the initiative power, stating that "[the] single-subject provision is a rule of restraint designed to insulate Florida's organic law from precipitous and cataclysmic change."[48] The Florida court held that initiatives require "strict compliance" with the single-subject rule because "our constitution is the basic document that controls our governmental functions," and thus should not be easily amended.[49]

The practical consequence is that the Florida court has excluded from the ballot many initiatives that would have been submitted to voters in other states. Most notably, the court invoked the single-subject rule to prevent a vote on an initiative to ban state-sponsored affirmative action. In 1996, citizens in California adopted Proposition 209, an initiative that amended the state constitution to declare that "the state shall not discriminate against, or grant preferential treatment to, any individual or group on the basis of race, sex, color, ethnicity, or national origin in the operation of public employment, public education, or public contracting."[50] After the election, the measure's main proponent, Ward Connerly, mobilized an effort to place a similar initiative on the Florida ballot. To satisfy the Florida Supreme Court's strict reading of the state's single-subject rule, Connerly divided his proposal into four separate initiatives: one directed at public education; a second at pubic employment; a third at public contracting; and a fourth at affirmative action based on gender as well as race.[51] Despite

---

[44] See FLA. CONST. art. V, sec. 3. The single-subject rule for initiated amendments is FLA. CONST. art. XI, sec. 3.

[45] *Fine v. Firestone*, 448 So. 2d 984 (Fla. 1984).

[46] Ibid., 990–992.

[47] Ibid., 990; *Evans v. Firestone*, 457 So. 2d 1351, 1360 (Fla. 1984), Shaw, J., concurring.

[48] *In re Advisory Opinion to the Attorney General*, 636 So.2d 1336, 1339 (Fla. 1994).

[49] *Fine v. Firestone*, 989.

[50] California Proposition 209 (1996).

[51] William Yardley, "Drive to Alter Race Rules Advances," *St. Petersburg Times* (October 27, 1999), 1B.

this partition, the court held that each of the measures violated its "function of government" test for enforcing the single-subject rule and excluded all of them from the ballot.[52]

Citizens in Florida continue to qualify a substantial number of initiatives for the ballot, but the court's strict pre-election enforcement of technical rules has clearly limited the Florida initiative process and prevented it from becoming one of the strongest in the nation.

CONCLUSION

Although courts have protected citizen access to direct democracy, they have also always exercised a strong check on individual initiatives. The evidence from the strongest initiative states demonstrates that as the initiative power expanded in recent decades, the judicial check on initiatives more than kept pace. During the recent peak of initiative lawmaking in the 1990s, over 60 percent of all initiatives adopted in the five strongest initiative states were challenged after the election and over 30 percent of them were invalidated in part or in their entirety.

Litigation rates varied by state and policy area. California was the state with the highest rates of initiative litigation. Term limits, campaign finance reform, and criminal justice initiatives were challenged and invalidated at the highest rates.

Meanwhile, the bases for invalidations were nearly evenly divided between rights and powers. Rights-based challenges most frequently involved conflicts over federal First Amendment, equal protection, and due process rights, whereas some state courts also invoked state constitutional rights to strike down voter-approved initiatives. Powers-based challenges focused on federalism concerns such as conflicts between initiatives and federal law and the boundaries of state power to regulate federal elected officials, as well as state constitutional concerns such as separation of powers, the powers of representative institutions, and the limits of the initiative power.

Finally, courts have exercised a check on citizen lawmaking in the lower-use initiative states. The nature of the interaction between courts and the initiative process has varied from state to state, depending on several factors. These factors included the subject matter of voter-approved initiatives, the state's rules for the initiative process, the strictness of judicial enforcement of these rules, and the use of pre-election judicial review.

---

[52] *Advisory Opinion to the Attorney General Re: Amendment to Bar Government From Treating People Differently Based on Race in Public Education; Advisory Opinion to the Attorney General Re: Amendment to Bar Government From Treating People Differently Based on Race in Public Employment; Advisory Opinion to the Attorney General Re: Amendment to Bar Government From Treating People Differently Based on Race in Public Contracting; Advisory Opinion to the Attorney General Re: End Governmental Discrimination and Preferences Amendment,* 2000 Fla. LEXIS 1460 (2000).

Overall, the historical record indicates that courts have exercised a strong counter-majoritarian check on the people's rule. But, to assess whether these decisions have successfully mitigated direct democracy's threats to constitutional rights and powers, we must closely examine cases in these respective areas.

5

Conflicts Over Rights

Perhaps the most troubling allegation against direct democracy is that it places rights at risk. The fear that unfettered majorities will threaten individual and minority rights has persisted across generations, from the Founders to Progressive Era opponents like President Taft to more recent critics like Professors Bell, Eule, and Linde. Determining whether this fear is well-founded requires close analysis. Specifically, we want to know in what ways citizen lawmaking has, in practice, threatened rights and also to what extent courts have mitigated the danger.

We must begin, however, by noting that any such analyses are complicated by a lack of consensus on essential terms. Julian Eule clearly identified the problem: "Assessing the extent to which [initiatives] disregard the rights of minorities necessarily depends on judgments about whom we recognize as 'minorities,' what we view as their 'rights,' and how we measure voter 'disregard.'"[1] The definition of "right" is particularly contentious. As Mary Ann Glendon has argued, "In truth, there is very little agreement regarding *which* needs, goods, interests, or values should be characterized as 'rights.'"[2] This has long been so. Michael J. Lacey and Knud Haakonssen have observed that "the vocabulary of rights" is deeply embedded in American political culture and "has been worked especially hard in political debate" ever since the eighteenth century: "Slaves cited violations of their natural rights in hopeless petitions to Congress. Abolitionists and their states' rights adversaries both spoke in rights terms. Later on, when leaders of the union movement invoked labor's right to organize as the key to securing social justice for the new industrial working class, their opponents in the corporations invoked the individual's right to

---

[1] Julian N. Eule, "Judicial Review of Direct Democracy," 99 YALE L. J. 1503, 1552 (1990).

[2] Mary Ann Glendon, *Rights Talk: The Impoverishment of Political Discourse* (New York: The Free Press, 1991), 16.

work free of union obligations."[3] Moreover, as Glendon notes, "Occasions for conflict among rights multiply as catalogs of rights grow longer."[4] Opposing sides in debates over desegregative busing, affirmative action, criminal justice policy, abortion, and numerous other issues have made competing rights-based claims. The stakes are high because in a rights-honoring system, defining an interest as a right confers power on and protects the right-bearer.

Acknowledging this difficulty, we again examine rights-based court challenges to voter-approved initiatives. This approach inevitably narrows our focus to those rights that are at least arguably enforceable by courts and assumes that when an initiative conflicts with something viewed as a constitutional right, its opponents will likely file suit. But, despite this difficulty, the approach captures the broad range of direct democracy's potential threats to rights, identifies the most difficult and important conflicts, and provides historical context by highlighting changes in the definition of rights over the past century.

To begin, let us turn back the clock nearly a century to examine an early initiative that showed how direct democracy can indeed threaten minority rights, and how an expanding scope of judicially enforceable rights helped the courts mitigate that threat.

OREGON'S COMPULSORY PUBLIC SCHOOL INITIATIVE OF 1922

Oregon, the great laboratory of direct democracy, produced an early warning of direct democracy's potential threat to rights. In 1922, Oregon voters approved a ballot initiative that required children between the ages of 8 and 16 years to attend state-run schools. The law permitted only limited exceptions and imposed criminal penalties for violators.[5] Although this measure's language appeared relatively innocuous, it was in fact designed to shut down Oregon's private schools and clearly targeted the Roman Catholic institutions that enrolled a majority of the state's 12,000 private school students.[6]

---

[3] Michael J. Lacey and Knud Haakonssen, "History, Historicism, and the Culture of Rights," in Michael J. Lacey and Knud Haakonssen, eds., *A Culture of Rights: The Bill of Rights in Philosophy, Politics, and Law – 1791 and 1991* (New York: Cambridge University Press, 1991), 1.

[4] Glendon, *Rights Talk*, 16.

[5] The measure was listed on the November 7, 1922, Oregon ballot as no. 314. State of Oregon, *Proposed Constitutional Amendments and Measures (with Arguments) to be Submitted to the Voters of Oregon at the General Election, Tuesday, November 7, 1922*: 23. The initiative was codified as *Or. Laws* sec. 5259.

[6] M. Paul Holsinger, "The Oregon School Bill Controversy, 1922–1925," *The Pacific Historical Review* 37, no. 3 (Aug., 1968): 330. Holsinger notes that "of the estimated 12,031 students enrolled in Oregon private schools in 1922, 7,303 grade school age children were in Roman Catholic schools. Only 750 were in Adventist-controlled institutions and only 450 in Lutheran schools." Ibid.

Historian John Higham described the initiative as "certainly one of the most severe of the Americanization laws" during a period of much anti-immigrant sentiment.[7]

At first glance, Oregon in the 1920s seems an unlikely setting for an anti-minority initiative of this sort. The state's population was one of the most homogenous in the nation – overwhelmingly native born, white, Protestant, English speaking, and literate. As of 1920, only about 15 percent of the state's population was foreign born and less than 10 percent was Roman Catholic.[8] However, in the wake of World War I, strong nativist sentiments stirred throughout the United States, including in the Pacific Northwest. In Oregon, these passions were fueled by a resurgent Ku Klux Klan, which by 1922 claimed 14,000 members in the state. The Klan is best known for terrorizing blacks in the South, but, in the early 1920s, it spread across the country. In Oregon, its principal target was "foreign elements," including immigrants and Catholics.[9]

The Initiative Campaign

At the time, Klan members and sympathizers exerted influence in other institutions, including the Scottish Rite Masonic Order, the group that formally sponsored the Oregon initiative for compulsory public education. In their literature supporting the measure, the Masons fused nativist and populist themes. "We must now halt those coming to our country from forming groups, establishing schools, and thereby bringing up their children in an environment often antagonistic to the principles of our government," one of the Masons' tracts declared.[10] The initiative was thus designed to impose assimilation by requiring all children – including, especially, immigrants and religious minorities – to attend state-run schools where only the majority's values were taught. In the official voter's pamphlet, proponents argued that the voters should "[m]ix the children of the foreign born with the native born and the rich with the poor, mix those with prejudices in the public school melting pot for a few years while their minds are plastic and finally bring out the finished product – a true American."[11]

During the campaign, the Klan, the Masons, and other proponents effectively tapped into the sentiment that Oregon was more "purely and fundamentally

---

[7] John Higham, *Strangers in the Land: Patterns of American Nativism, 1860–1925* (New Brunswick: Rutgers University Press, 1955), 260.

[8] Holsinger, "The Oregon School Bill Controversy," 328; David B. Tyack, "The Perils of Pluralism: The Background of the Pierce Case," *The American Historical Review* 74, no. 1 (Oct. 1968): 75–6.

[9] William G. Ross, *Forging New Freedoms: Nativism, Education, and the Constitution, 1917–1927* (Lincoln: University of Nebraska Press, 1994), 148–50; Higham, *Strangers in the Land*, 296.

[10] Holsinger, "The Oregon School Bill Controversy," 331–2.

[11] State of Oregon, *Proposed Constitutional Amendments and Measures* (1922), 23.

American" than any other state and that voters should take steps to keep it that way.[12] Speaking on behalf of the measure, many proponents directly attacked Catholic schools and the immigrant Catholic population as threats to American values and social cohesion.[13] Debate over the measure dominated the Oregon governor's election of 1922. In the Republican primary, incumbent Governor Ben W. Olcott denounced the Klan and steadfastly opposed the school initiative, whereas his challenger, Charles Hall, endorsed the measure. Although Olcott won the primary, Hall made an unexpectedly strong showing. This outcome emboldened the initiative's supporters, who pressed the Democratic nominee, Walter M. Pierce, to support the measure's adoption. Two months before the general election, Pierce, facing long odds in a strongly Republican state, aligned with the anti-Catholic movement and announced his endorsement. "I am a Protestant, the ninth generation in America," Pierce said. "My wife and relatives are Protestants. Every one of our six children was educated in the public schools from the primary to the college and the university. I am in favor of and shall vote for the compulsory school bill."[14] Pierce's support for the initiative helped him win a decisive victory in the governor's race.[15]

Meanwhile, in the weeks before the election, the initiative's opponents attempted to mobilize public opinion against the measure. The local archbishop formed the Catholic Civil Rights Association of Oregon to fight the initiative through pamphlets, newspaper advertisements, lectures, and direct voter contact.[16] But, Catholics also knew they risked backlash if their opposition was seen as an assertion of Catholic power. Accordingly, they built a coalition to oppose the measure. During the campaign, a broad group of religious leaders, educators, publishers, businessmen, and public officials voiced their opposition, arguing that the initiative threatened, among other things, religious freedom and parental autonomy.[17] These warnings were unheeded, however, as Oregonians approved the measure by a 53 percent vote.[18]

After their loss on Election Day, the initiative's opponents had limited options. They could have promoted a new initiative to reverse the 1922 outcome or lobbied the Oregon legislature to repeal the voter-approved initiative before it went into effect, but neither option was particularly promising. It seemed improbable that voters would change their minds, and even less likely that the legislature would counter the voters' will, especially because in the

---

[12] Holsinger, "Oregon School Bill Controversy," 330.

[13] Ibid., 332; Ross, *Forging New Freedoms*, 149–50.

[14] Quoted in *The Oregonian*, Sept. 13, 1922: 11 and cited in Holsinger, "Oregon School Bill Controversy," 334–5.

[15] Pierce's margin of victory over incumbent Republican Governor Olcott was 133,392 to 99,164. Holsinger, "Oregon School Bill Controversy," 335; Oregon State Library, "Walter Marcus Pierce," http://www.osl.state.or.us/home/lib/governors/wmp.htm.

[16] Ross, *Forging New Freedoms*, 157.

[17] Tyack, "The Perils of Pluralism," 86–7.

[18] The vote on the measure was 115,506 to 103,685. Oregon Blue Book, "Initiative, Referendum, and Recall: 1922–1928," http://bluebook.state.or.us/state/elections/elections14.htm.

1922 election, Klan-backed candidates had won control of both houses of the legislature as well as the governor's office.[19]

With both direct and representative legislative channels apparently blocked, the measure's opponents instead pursued a litigation strategy. They would seek to define their threatened interests as judicially-enforceable rights and invoke the counter-majoritarian power of the courts to overturn the will of the people.

Pierce v. Society of Sisters. Two weeks after the election, Oregon's Catholic bishops began raising funds to support the litigation effort. In addition, they selected the Society of the Sisters of the Holy Names of Jesus and Mary, a Catholic teaching order that administered several parochial schools and academies in Oregon, to serve as plaintiff in an action to enjoin enforcement of the initiative. The Knights of Columbus, a Catholic lay organization, offered support in part by helping pay legal expenses of the Hill Military Academy, a nonsectarian, private school for boys that was also pursuing court action to block the law.[20] The plaintiffs then made another important decision. Believing that state judges might be comparatively unsympathetic to their claims, the plaintiffs decided to file their actions in federal district court.

As evidenced by the case briefs, the parties were uncertain how to frame the constitutional questions. Over the past generation, American courts had vigorously enforced economic rights, but had taken only a few tentative steps to protect civil rights and liberties. Importantly, in the early 1920s, the U.S. Supreme Court still maintained the view that the rights contained in the Bill of Rights (with the exception of the takings clause of the Fifth Amendment) were not judicially enforceable against the states.[21] Thus, although the initiative impaired free exercise of religion by preventing parents from sending their children to religious schools, the plaintiffs could not expect courts to invalidate it on that basis.[22] Indeed, attorneys for the state were able to argue that "[i]t is now definitely settled that the Fourteenth Amendment did not radically alter the relations between the federal and state governments, or make the provisions of the Bill of Rights in the United States Constitution binding upon the state governments."[23]

---

[19] Holsinger, "Oregon School Bill Controversy," 335–6.

[20] Ross, *Forging New Freedoms*, 161.

[21] See *Chicago, Burlington & Quincy Railroad Company v. Chicago*, 166 U.S. 226 (1897), enforcing the Fifth Amendment takings clause against state action. For a discussion of the incorporation controversy, see Henry J. Abraham and Barbara A. Perry, *Freedom and the Court: Civil Rights and Liberties in the United States*, Eighth Edition (Lawrence: University Press of Kansas, 2003), 33–105.

[22] For a discussion of the relationship between the *Pierce* case and enforcement of the free exercise clause, see Jay S. Bybee, "Substantive Due Process and Free Exercise of Religion: *Meyer, Pierce* and the Origins of *Wisconsin v. Yoder*," 25 CAP. U. L. REV. 887 (1996).

[23] "Brief of Appellant, the Governor of the State of Oregon, *Pierce v. Society of Sisters*," 18–19, reprinted in Philip B. Kurland and Gerhard Casper, eds., *Landmark Briefs and Arguments of the Supreme Court of the United States*, Vol. 23 (Arlington, VA: University Publications of America, 1975), 25–6.

The U.S. Supreme Court's precedents, however, offered alternative rights-based theories for challenging the initiative. First, plaintiffs were able to invoke the Court's prevailing doctrines of economic liberty to argue that the restriction on private schooling impaired their property rights in violation of the Fourteenth Amendment's due process clause. In addition, in an important move, the plaintiffs argued that the due process clause also protected noneconomic rights, and that the initiative violated those rights as well.

Crucially, just weeks before the plaintiffs challenged the Oregon school initiative, the U.S. Supreme Court had, for the first time, endorsed the theory that the substantive rights protected by the Fourteenth Amendment's due process clause protected not only economic rights of property and contract but also certain other fundamental rights. In *Meyer v. Nebraska* (1923), the Court had struck down a Nebraska law prohibiting foreign language instruction before the eighth grade in either public or private schools, holding that the restriction violated fundamental liberties protected by the due process clause.[24] The Oregon plaintiffs seized on this precedent and argued that the courts should use *Meyer's* new, expansive reading of the Fourteenth Amendment's due process clause to invalidate the compulsory public school initiative.[25]

Both the federal district court and the U.S. Supreme Court agreed. In *Pierce v. Society of Sisters of the Holy Names of Jesus and Mary* (1925), the Supreme Court unanimously held that the Oregon initiative violated not only property rights, but also noneconomic civil liberties – which, in this case, included "the liberty of parents and guardians to direct the upbringing and education of children within their control."[26] In the Court's view, "The fundamental theory of liberty upon which all governments in this Union repose excludes any general power of the State to standardize its children by forcing them to accept instruction from public teachers only."[27]

Pierce's Legacy. For two reasons, *Pierce* was a landmark case. With *Meyer*, it signaled the Court's assumption of responsibility for guarding noneconomic civil liberties – a highly consequential expansion of the judicial power that has continued to this day. In addition, the case offered an important demonstration of how courts can resist the initiative power when it threatens minority rights.[28] The record of initiative litigation over the past century reveals that *Pierce* indeed became a model: By enforcing an expanding sphere of rights, courts have placed a major constraint on the initiative power. To see this constraint operate in a number of areas, the balance of this chapter analyzes, in turn, conflicts between citizen initiatives and rights of property and contract,

[24] *Meyer v. Nebraska*, 262 U.S. 390 (1923).
[25] "Brief on Behalf of Appellee, *Pierce v. Society of Sisters*," 10–14, reprinted in Kurland and Casper, eds., *Landmark Briefs*, Vol. 23, 272–6.
[26] *Pierce v. Society of Sisters of the Holy Names of Jesus and Mary*, 268 U.S. 510, 534 (1925).
[27] Ibid., 534–5.
[28] See, e.g., Hans A. Linde, "When Initiative Lawmaking Is Not 'Republican Government': The Campaign Against Homosexuality," 72 ORE. L. REV. 19, 35–8 (1993).

speech and association, criminal procedure and punishment, equal protection, and due process.

RIGHTS OF PROPERTY AND CONTRACT

Given the legal environment of the early twentieth century, it is no surprise that initiative opponents challenged many voter-approved measures on the basis that they violated rights of property and contract.[29] If adopted today, many of these initiatives would go unchallenged, but during this earlier period, citizen attempts to regulate economic activity naturally gave rise to rights-based litigation.

Thus, when Oregon voters in 1912 adopted an initiative regulating railroad freight rates and setting maximum carload rates, the Southern Pacific Railroad immediately challenged the initiative in federal district court, arguing that the rate regulations constituted a taking of property without due process. The court sided with Southern Pacific and invalidated the initiative.[30] Similarly, the California Supreme Court partially invalidated a 1918 anti-usury initiative on the basis that it violated lenders' property and equal protection rights, and the Washington Supreme Court struck down on property rights grounds a 1932 initiative imposing a graduated state income tax.[31]

In addition, during this early period, courts invalidated some initiatives like the 1922 Oregon school initiative on the grounds that they violated both economic and noneconomic rights. But, after the Supreme Court's historic New Deal-era retreat from its defense of economic liberties, courts less frequently invoked property or contract rights to counter citizen initiatives. As a result, many recent initiatives – including, for example, minimum wage measures – that might once have faced rights-based litigation now go unchallenged. Although opponents still sometimes challenged voter-approved initiatives on the theory that they violate economic rights, these challenges now rarely succeed.[32]

FIRST AMENDMENT RIGHTS

The Supreme Court's decision to enforce First Amendment rights eventually placed a powerful check on citizen lawmaking, but the earliest First Amendment cases challenged laws enacted by legislatures, not by the people directly. As we have noted, for more than a century after the founding, courts declined to enforce the First Amendment; instead, they allowed the political process to

---

[29] The challenged initiatives, among other things, regulated railroad rates, limited maximum hours of employment, restricted interest and fees that lenders may charge borrowers, and banned the operation of employment agencies.

[30] *Southern Pacific Company v. Railroad Commission of Oregon*, 208 F. 926 (1913), invalidating Oregon Measure 29 [358] of 1912.

[31] *Culliton v. Chase*, 174 Wash. 363 (1933).

[32] A notable exception is California Proposition 103 (1988), an insurance initiative invalidated in part by *Calfarm Insurance Co. v. Deukmejran*, 48 Cal.3d 805 (1989).

define the balance between free expression and government restrictions. But, during World War I and its aftermath, governments sharply increased limits on dissent and courts reassessed their deferential posture. As the war became divisive, Congress enacted and President Wilson signed the Espionage Act (1917) and the Sedition Act (1918), which, among other things, criminalized speech critical of the government and the war effort. The latter act established penalties for "disloyal, profane, scurrilous, or abusive language about the form of government of the United States, or the Constitution of the United States, or the military or naval forces of the United States, or the flag of the United States, or the uniform of the Army or Navy of the United States."[33] Similarly, during this period many state legislatures repressed dissent through enactment of new antisedition laws. The Socialist labor organizer and presidential candidate Eugene V. Debs was one of many prosecuted for expressing prohibited forms of dissent. Debs delivered an antiwar speech before a crowd in Ohio in June 1918 and was convicted under the federal Espionage Act of obstructing recruiting and attempting to cause insubordination in the army. The Supreme Court affirmed his conviction in *Debs v. United States* (1919).[34]

But, critics of these policies, including the newly formed American Civil Liberties Union, argued that government suppression of dissent violated basic rights of free speech, and that courts should enforce the First Amendment to strike down convictions under these laws.[35] Justices Oliver Wendell Holmes Jr. and Louis Brandeis were among the first members of the Court to entertain this view. In 1920, Brandeis argued that courts must enforce the First Amendment because "an intolerant majority, swayed by passion or by fear, may...stamp as disloyal opinions with which it disagrees."[36] Later in the decade, Brandeis wrote that the purpose of the First Amendment is to guard against "the occasional tyrannies of governing majorities," by which he meant majorities operating through the medium of representative government.[37]

In *Gitlow v. New York* (1925), the Court stated for the first time in dictum that "freedom of speech and of the press – which are protected by the First Amendment from abridgement by Congress – are among the fundamental rights and 'liberties' protected by the due process clause of the Fourteenth Amendment from impairment by the States."[38] *Gitlow* thus set the Court on a course to enforce the First Amendment – and, eventually, most other provisions of the Bill of Rights – against states as well as the federal government.[39]

[33] *40 Stat. 553* (1918).

[34] *Debs v. United States*, 249 U.S. 211 (1919).

[35] John J. Dinan, *Keeping the People's Liberties, Legislators, Citizens, and Judges as Guardians of Rights*. (Lawrence: University Press of Kansas, 1998): 118.

[36] *Schaefer v. United States*, 251 U.S. 466, 495 (1920), Brandeis, J., dissenting.

[37] *Whitney v. California*, 274 U.S. 357, 376 (1927), Brandeis, J., dissenting.

[38] *Gitlow v. New York*, 268 U.S. 652, 666 (1925). In this case, the Court affirmed the conviction of a socialist agitator for distributing manifestos in violation of New York's criminal anarchy act, but announced in dictum the incorporation of First Amendment rights of free speech and free press.

[39] See Paul L. Murphy, *World War I and the Origin of Civil Liberties in the United States* (New York: W. W. Norton, 1979), 269.

For the most part, citizen lawmakers were not party to the earliest conflicts over judicial enforcement of the First Amendment because, during the 1910s and 1920s, voters enacted very few initiatives that specifically sought to silence dissent. The one notable exception occurred in 1920 when voters in North Dakota adopted an initiative to ban the display of red or black flags or signs bearing antigovernment inscriptions, and to prohibit carrying in a parade any flag other than the American flag or the flag of a friendly nation.[40] This initiative clearly suppressed free expression. But, thirty-two states passed "red flag" laws during the red scare of 1919 and 1920 and only one was enacted through the initiative process. Almost all of these restrictions on dissent were enacted by representatives rather than by the people themselves. In the landmark 1931 case *Stromberg v. California*, the U.S. Supreme Court declared that the red flag laws violated the First Amendment.[41]

Restrictions on Picketing

In the 1930s and 1940s, citizen-enacted laws more frequently conflicted with the courts' expanding interpretation of the First Amendment. During this period, judicial enforcement of First Amendment rights was closely tied to the emerging labor movement, as unions claimed that legal prohibitions on picketing violated their rights of free speech. Until 1940, the Supreme Court had held that the First Amendment did not protect picketing, which it characterized as a violent activity that governments could prohibit.[42] But, in 1940, after years of union effort, the Court reversed course and held that picketing was protected by the First Amendment.[43]

Although legislatures enacted most anti picketing laws, citizens also adopted several of them through the initiative process. In 1938, for example, Oregon voters approved an initiative to restrict picketing and boycotts by labor unions. But, the American Federation of Labor (AFL) challenged the initiative in the Oregon state courts, and in *American Federation of Labor v. Bain* (1940), the Oregon Supreme Court invoked the First Amendment to overturn the citizen-enacted law.[44] *Bain* marked the first time a court invalidated an initiative from the high-use states on First Amendment grounds. It would not be the last. Indeed, as courts expanded the First Amendment's

---

[40] See Thomas W. Howard, ed., *The North Dakota Political Tradition* (Ames, Iowa: Iowa State University Press, 1981).

[41] *Stromberg v. California*, 283 U.S. 359 (1931).

[42] *American Steel Foundries v. Tri-City Central Trades Council*, 257 U.S. 184 (1921), upholding an antipicketing statute.

[43] *Thornhill v. Alabama*, 310 U.S. 88 (1940).

[44] *American Federation of Labor v. Bain*, 165 Ore. 183 (1940), striking down Oregon Measure 9 [316] of 1938. Similarly, in 1952, Arizona voters adopted an antipicketing initiative (Proposition 312); the Arizona Supreme Court invalidated the measure on First and Fourteenth Amendment grounds in *Baldwin v. Arizona Flame Restaurant, Inc.*, 82 Ariz. 385 (1957).

reach, it became one of the most frequently invoked and powerful constraints on voter-approved initiatives.

Campaign Finance Regulations

Since the 1970s, courts have invoked the First Amendment to strike down numerous campaign finance reform initiatives. Controlling the influence of money in politics has long been a priority for Progressive Era reformers and their "good government" successors. Prior to the 1970s, several states and Congress imposed regulations on political contributions and expenditures without judicial interference. For example, in 1908, Oregon voters used the initiative power to adopt the state's "Corrupt Practices Act," which, among other provisions, strictly limited the amounts candidates could spend on campaigns.[45] Similarly, Congress adopted the federal Corrupt Practices Act of 1925, as amended by the Taft-Hartley Act of 1947, which prohibited corporations and labor unions from making contributions or expenditures in connection with federal elections. For decades, the Oregon initiative went unchallenged and the Supreme Court avoided passing on the constitutional validity of the federal regulations.[46] But, in the 1970s, litigants gained ground arguing that such laws violated constitutional rights of free speech. In *Deras v. Meyers* (1975), the Oregon Supreme Court held that the Corrupt Practices Act's updated expenditure limits violated the free speech provisions of the Oregon and U.S. Constitutions.[47] The following year, the U.S. Supreme Court issued its landmark decision in *Buckley v. Valeo* (1976), invalidating in part the Watergate-era Federal Election Campaign Act Amendments of 1974. The federal law had imposed new disclosure rules and limits on contributions and expenditures in federal elections.[48] In *Buckley*, the Court, for the first time, asserted a strong First Amendment check on such regulation, holding that political expenditures and contributions are political speech entitled to First Amendment protection.[49]

Judicial invalidation of campaign finance regulation on First Amendment grounds has generated much controversy. Many defend the Court's approach, arguing that campaign expenditures and contributions are individual liberties that require protection against undue government regulation.[50] But,

---

[45] Oregon 1908 Measure 16 [330]. Citizens in Montana adopted a similar initiative in 1912.

[46] See *United States v. Congress of Industrial Organizations*, 335 U.S. 106 (1948); *United States v. UAW-CIO*, 352 U.S. 567 (1957). But compare *State v. Pierce*, 163 Wis. 615 (1916), striking down Wisconsin's Corrupt Practices Act on state and federal constitutional grounds.

[47] *Deras v. Myers*, 272 Ore. 47 (1975).

[48] *Buckley v. Valeo*, 424 U.S. 1, 14–16 (1976).

[49] Ibid.

[50] See, e.g., Daniel D. Polsby, "*Buckley v. Valeo*: The Special Nature of Political Speech," *Supreme Court Review* 1976 (1976): 1–43; Kathleen M. Sullivan, "Political Money and Freedom of Speech," 30 U.C. Davis L. Rev. 663 (1997).

many reformers devoutly disagree, contending that regulation of campaign finance actually serves First Amendment values by restructuring the political process in a way that promotes the ability of more citizens to participate meaningfully in political debate.[51] *Buckley* has withstood this controversy for over a generation and reformers have been forced to struggle against its strictures in their efforts to regulate political money. Despite repeated setbacks, reformers have remained committed to this effort, often turning to the initiative process to pursue new restrictions. By 2008, citizens in eleven states had adopted twenty-seven campaign finance reform measures. Opponents challenged nearly all of these initiatives, including all fifteen adopted in the five leading initiative states. Remarkably, courts invalidated fourteen of the fifteen measures, in part or in their entirety, usually on the basis that they violated the First Amendment or its state constitutional counterparts.

Regulation of Party Primaries

Courts also invoked the First Amendment to strike down other political reform initiatives, including efforts to promote greater nonpartisanship in primary elections. In 1996, California voters adopted a measure to replace the state's closed primary with a so-called blanket primary system, an arrangement that allows voters to participate in any party's primary contests. The blanket primary had been used for many years in Washington and three other states without judicial interference, but when California voters adopted the system, the state's political parties filed suit in federal court alleging that it violated their First Amendment associational rights.[52] In *Democratic Party v. Jones* (2000), the Supreme Court agreed, invalidating not only the California initiative, but also Washington's venerable blanket primary system and similar arrangements in other states.[53]

In 2004, Washington voters responded by replacing the blanket primary with Initiative 872, a measure that established a so-called top-two system for primary elections. Under this system, the general election is a runoff between the two candidates who receive the highest vote totals in the primary, regardless of

---

[51] For a discussion of competing views, see Daniel Hays Lowenstein and Richard L. Hasen, eds., *Election Law: Cases and Materials*, Third Edition (Durham: Carolina Academic Press, 2004), 780–96.

[52] The California initiative, Proposition 198, was promoted by "good government" groups and approved by a 60 percent vote. For a series of essays on this initiative, see Bruce E. Cain and Elisabeth R. Gerber, eds., *Voting at the Political Fault Line: California's Experiment with the Blanket Primary* (Berkeley: University of California Press, 2002). The Washington blanket primary (1935 *Wash. Laws* 26) had been upheld in *Heavey v. Chapman*, 93 Wash.2d 700 (1980), but could not survive the U.S. Supreme Court's later scrutiny. For a discussion, see Bruce M. Botelho and Christine O. Gregoire, "Brief of the States of Washington and Alaska as Amici Curiae in Support of Respondents, *California Democratic Party v. Jones*, No. 99–401," 2000 U.S. S. Ct. Briefs Lexis 240 (March 30, 2000).

[53] *California Democratic Party v. Jones*, 530 U.S. 567 (2000).

their stated party affiliation.[54] The Ninth Circuit invoked the First Amendment to invalidate that initiative, but, in *Washington State Grange v. Washington State Republican Party* (2008), the U.S. Supreme Court reversed and upheld the measure.[55]

Persistent First Amendment challenges to campaign finance, party primary, and other political regulation initiatives have contributed to what election law scholar Richard Pildes calls the "constitutionalization of democratic politics," and have limited citizen capacity to enact political reform.[56]

Other First Amendment Conflicts

The remaining conflicts between initiatives and First Amendment challenges have covered a wide range, from California's Proposition 15 (1964), banning pay-for-view television, to Washington's Initiative 335 (1977), restricting pornography. Courts invalidated these and several other measures, asserting their strong and expanding guardianship of First Amendment rights.[57] But, the most persistent conflict between citizen lawmaking and the First Amendment has been in the area of political regulation, especially campaign finance reform, as courts doggedly enforced the doctrine of *Buckley*.

---

[54] Washington Initiative 872 of 2004.

[55] *Washington State Grange v. Washington State Republican Party*, 128 S. Ct. 1184 (2008), reversing *Washington State Republican Party v. State of Washington*, 460 F.3d 1108 (9th Cir. 2006).

[56] Richard H. Pildes, "Foreword: The Constitutionalization of Democratic Politics," 118 HARV. L. REV. 28, 31 (2004).

[57] Courts have invoked the First Amendment or state constitutional equivalents to invalidate (in part or in entirety) a 1964 California initiative banning pay-for-view television; a 1977 Washington initiative restricting pornographic theaters and publications; a 1984 Oregon initiative requiring utilities to disseminate information in billing envelopes; a 1988 Oregon initiative revoking an executive branch ban on discrimination based on sexual orientation; and a 1988 Arizona initiative requiring the state and its political subdivisions to "act" only in English. Initiative opponents have unsuccessfully challenged a number of other initiatives on First Amendment grounds, often in combination with other legal theories. It is worth noting that few cases have alleged that citizen initiatives violate religious liberties – and in the high use states, courts have invalidated no initiatives on that basis. High-use states have rarely enacted initiatives that even arguably infringe on religious liberties. Oregon voters produced two initiatives that gave rise to religious liberty challenges – the physician-assisted suicide initiative of 1994 and a 1998 measure requiring that adopted children be granted access to their birth certificates – but these challenges did not easily fit within the paradigm of religious liberties and were rejected in court. See *Lee v. Oregon*, 107 F.3d 1382 (9th Cir. 1997) upholding Oregon Measure 16 of 1994 and *Doe 1 v. State of Oregon*, 164 Ore. App. 543 (1999), upholding Measure 58 of 1998. But two Arkansas initiatives – one banning the teaching of evolution in the public schools and the other requiring the reading of the Bible in the public schools – were invalidated on First Amendment Establishment Clause grounds. *Epperson v. State of Arkansas*, 393 U.S. 97 (1968), invalidating the anti-evolution initiative; *Abington Township School District v. Schempp*, 374 U.S. 203 (1963), invalidating the Bible reading initiative, confirmed by *McLean v. Arkansas Board of Education*, 529 F. Supp. 1255 (E.D. Ark. 1982).

CRIMINAL JUSTICE RIGHTS

Conflict between citizen lawmakers and the courts over criminal justice policy did not emerge until the 1960s when the Supreme Court began enforcing the criminal justice provisions of the Bill of Rights against the states and, more intensely, in the 1970s when citizens in several states began enacting numerous tough-on-crime initiatives.

The federal Bill of Rights is largely devoted to protecting individuals from abuses of the criminal justice system. The specific rights prohibit, among other things, most warrantless searches or seizures; forced confessions; long imprisonment without trial; trials without juries; multiple prosecutions for the same offense; prosecutions without assistance of counsel; and, upon conviction, infliction of cruel and unusual punishment. The U.S. Supreme Court long hesitated to enforce these protections against the states. Instead, it preferred to allow the states to define the rights of criminal defendants and to determine the permissible scope of state criminal procedures and punishments. But, over the course of the twentieth century, and especially during the 1960s, the Court applied the criminal justice provisions of the Fourth, Fifth, Sixth, and Eighth Amendments, one by one, against the states. This redefinition of rights had direct consequences for citizen lawmaking.

Comment on Defendant's Refusal to Testify

The changing fate of one early California ballot measure helps illustrate the impact of the expanding judicial power. In 1934, California voters approved Proposition 5, an initiative constitutional amendment that authorized prosecutors and trial judges to comment at trial regarding a defendant's refusal to testify.[58] Several years later, the state brought murder charges against a man named Admiral Dewey Adamson. At trial, Adamson declined to take the witness stand and both the prosecutor and the judge made critical comments regarding his silence. The jury convicted Adamson and sentenced him to death. On appeal, Adamson's lawyers argued that the negative commentary concerning their client's refusal to testify violated his Fifth Amendment rights. But, in the landmark case of *Adamson v. California* (1947), a divided U.S. Supreme Court affirmed the conviction and allowed the rule to stand. The majority held that the Fifth Amendment right against self-incrimination was not enforceable against the states.[59]

Less than two decades later, however, the Court revisited the *Adamson* precedent and reached the opposite result. In *Malloy v. Hogan* (1964), the

---

[58] The initiative, which became art. I, sec. 13 of the California Constitution, read in relevant part: "[I]n any criminal case, whether the defendant testifies or not, his failure to explain or to deny by his testimony any evidence or facts in the case against him may be commented upon by the court and by counsel, and may be considered by the court or the jury."

[59] *Adamson v. California*, 332 U.S. 46 (1947). Adamson was later executed at San Quentin. For a more detailed discussion of the *Adamson* case, see Abraham and Perry, eds., *Freedom and the Court*, 41–4.

Court held that the Fifth Amendment right against self-incrimination is binding against the states through the Fourteenth Amendment and, shortly thereafter, in *Griffin v. California* (1965), it held that the Fifth Amendment right prevents comment on the defendant's refusal to testify. The latter decision thus invalidated the 1934 initiative.[60] These contrasting results again illustrated the impact of the judicial expansion of rights: What was permissible in 1947 became unconstitutional in 1965, even though neither the text of the citizen-enacted amendment, nor the relevant provisions of the federal Constitution, had changed during this period.

Capital Punishment

An early Arizona death penalty initiative provided a similar example. During the 1910s, the citizens of Arizona debated whether the new state should permit executions. In 1916, voters narrowly adopted an initiative to abolish capital punishment in the state. Then, two years later, they decisively approved another initiative to reinstate it. Among other implementing provisions, the 1918 initiative gave juries unlimited discretion in pronouncing death sentences for persons convicted of specified crimes.[61] This rule remained undisturbed for many years, largely because courts did not enforce the Eighth Amendment against the states until the 1960s.[62] In 1972, however, the Court issued its landmark decision in *Furman v. Georgia*, declaring that many existing procedures for imposing the death penalty (including unlimited jury discretion) violated the Eighth Amendment.[63] A year later, the Arizona Supreme Court held that *Furman* effectively invalidated the state's voter-mandated death penalty provisions.[64] In Chapter 7, we will more closely examine the intense conflict between citizen lawmakers and courts over the constitutional validity of capital punishment, but for now it is sufficient to note that the expanding judicial enforcement of the Eighth Amendment placed a new rights-based limit on citizen-enacted death penalty laws.

Shortly after *Furman*, citizens in California, Oregon, Washington, and Arizona contributed to this conflict by enacting a flurry of tough-on-crime measures.[65] As we have seen, the voters' enthusiasm for these measures can be explained in part by their fear of rising crime rates and their growing belief that legislatures, parole boards, and courts were more focused on protecting the rights of criminal defendants than on controlling crime. From the 1970s through the 2000s, voters supported a range of measures designed to reinstate

---

[60] *Malloy v. Hogan*, 378 U.S. 1 (1964); *Griffin v. California*, 380 U.S. 609 (1965).

[61] Arizona Proposition 306 (1918).

[62] See *Robinson v. California*, 370 U.S. 660 (1962) incorporating the Eighth Amendment.

[63] *Furman v. Georgia*, 408 U.S. 238 (1972).

[64] *State v. Endreson*, 109 Ariz. 117 (1973).

[65] In 1978, Michigan voters adopted a tough-on-crime measure designed to prevent early release of violent offenders. It was the only crime-related initiative adopted outside of the leading states during this period.

the death penalty, expand the range of offenses subject to capital punishment, increase the severity of noncapital sentences, and restrict certain rights of criminal defendants.[66]

Critics charged that citizen lawmakers' seizure of criminal justice policy produced unfair procedures and excessive punishments.[67] And, perhaps not surprisingly, every voter-approved, tough-on-crime initiative faced rights-based challenges on state or federal constitutional grounds, typically by a defendant who had been convicted or sentenced under the provisions of the initiative. Conflicts between voters and a rights-enforcing judiciary thus became an important arena for defining the balance between the state's power to control crime and the rights of criminal defendants. The litigation record shows that courts invalidated several death penalty initiatives, determining that they failed to meet the increasingly strict U.S. Supreme Court standards for capital punishment. Generally, however, courts upheld voter-initiated changes to rules of criminal procedure, as well as initiatives that mandated more severe, noncapital punishments for certain offenses.

Three-Strikes-And-You're-Out

Perhaps the most controversial of these tough-on-crime initiatives was California's three-strikes-and-you're-out sentencing law. After California voters approved this measure, it faced a series of challenges in state and federal courts.[68] The battle over the law's constitutional validity culminated in the case of Leandro Andrade.

Many considered Andrade an ideal party to challenge California's three-strikes law because under its provisions, a trial court sentenced him to prison for an extremely long term for minor triggering offenses (stealing videos from two Kmart stores in Southern California). Although the three-strikes law imposed a twenty-five-years-to-life sentence in state prison for a "third strike" conviction, Andrade faced *fifty*-years-to-life (two consecutive terms of twenty-five-years-to-life) because he had been convicted not only of a third strike, but also a fourth, for two separate petty thefts in November 1995. The length of his

---

[66] Most notably, during this period (1970–2008), Californians voted on ten initiatives that can be characterized as "tough-on-crime" and approved nine of them, usually by large margins.

[67] See, e.g., Franklin E. Zimring, Gordon Hawkins, and Sam Kamin, *Punishment and Democracy: Three Strikes and You're Out in California* (New York: Oxford University Press, 2001), 181–204.

[68] In one important case, the California Supreme Court used its interpretive powers to modify the three-strikes scheme. In *People vs. Superior Court (Romero)*, 13 Cal.4th 497 (1996), the court held that judges in three-strikes cases must have the authority to dismiss evidence of prior convictions on their motion, even when prosecutors object. California's three-strikes law contained no such provision, but instead provided only that "[t]he prosecuting attorney may move to dismiss or strike a prior felony conviction allegation in the furtherance of justice . . . or if there is insufficient evidence to prove the prior conviction." *Cal. Penal Code Sec. 667(f)(2).* But, the court insisted that trial judges must also have independent power to dismiss evidence of prior convictions. With this modification, the court upheld the law.

sentences meant Andrade would not be eligible for release until at least 2046 when he would be 87 years old.[69] Moreover, it was hard to believe that Andrade was among the most dangerous felons in California's prison system. Although he was a heroin addict and a habitual offender, his prior "strikes" were for residential burglary, a felony the California law classified as "serious," but not "violent," and his triggering offenses were comparatively trivial. For many critics, the lack of proportionality between Andrade's crimes and punishment demonstrated the excesses of California's three-strikes law.

After exhausting his appeals in the California state courts, Andrade challenged his fifty-years-to-life sentence in the federal courts through a petition for writ of *habeas corpus*. After the federal district court denied his petition, the Ninth Circuit reversed, holding that, as applied to Andrade, three-strikes violated the Eighth Amendment because his punishment was "grossly disproportionate" to his crimes.[70] However, in *Lockyer v. Andrade* (2003) and the companion case of *Ewing v. California* (2003), a narrowly divided U.S. Supreme Court upheld the three-strikes sentences against Eighth Amendment attack.[71] The Court's decisions made it clear that it was unwilling to invoke the Eighth Amendment to invalidate noncapital sentences, and signaled that citizen lawmakers may use the initiative power to impose noncapital sentencing policies without rights-based judicial constraints.[72]

Other Conflicts over Defendants' Rights

Starting in the 1980s, voters approved several initiatives restricting criminal defendants' procedural rights. Although Warren-Era Supreme Court rulings required all states to provide defendants the procedural rights enumerated in the Bill of Rights, some state courts granted defendants rights that exceeded federal constitutional minimums. As the tough-on-crime movement gained strength, however, citizen lawmakers sought to limit these state-level guarantees.

Some of the most important conflicts emerged in California. After the California Supreme Court issued a line of decisions expanding the state

[69] Andrade had prior convictions for misdemeanor theft, residential burglary (three counts), transportation of marijuana, and escape from prison. The residential burglaries counted as "serious felonies" and thus "strikes" under California's three-strikes law. See *Lockyer v. Andrade*, 538 U.S. 63 (2003).

[70] *Andrade v. Attorney General*, 270 F.3d 743 (9th Cir. 2001). The Ninth Circuit did not declare the three-strikes law facially unconstitutional, but more narrowly held that it violated the Eighth Amendment as applied to the circumstances of Andrade's case. 270 F.3d at 767.

[71] *Lockyer v. Andrade*, 538 U.S. 63 (2003).

[72] In a dissent joined by Justices John Paul Stevens, Ruth Bader Ginsburg, and Stephen Breyer, Justice David Souter argued that the Court's unwillingness to declare Andrade's sentence in violation of the Eighth Amendment meant there was no meaningful Eighth Amendment constraint on noncapital sentencing policies. "This is the rare sentence of demonstrable gross disproportionality," Souter wrote. "If Andrade's sentence is not grossly disproportionate, the principle has no meaning." *Lockyer*, 538 U.S. at 83, Souter, J., dissenting. See also the companion case, *Ewing v. California*, 538 U.S. 11 (2003).

constitutional rights of criminal defendants, California citizens adopted initiatives to restrict these rights. In 1982, California voters adopted Proposition 8, the Victims' Bill of Rights initiative. This measure placed restrictions on the court's expansive interpretations of the exclusionary rule, defendants' testimonial privileges, bail, and other provisions. The initiative was challenged, but the court upheld most of its provisions.[73] However, the court continued to expand defendants' rights in other areas and, in 1990, voters responded with Proposition 115, the Crime Victims' Justice Reform Act. This measure declared that the state constitution "shall not be construed by the courts to afford greater rights to criminal defendants than those afforded by the Constitution of the United States."[74] The state's high court quickly invalidated this limitation. In *Raven v. Deukmejian* (1990), the court held that a blanket restriction on its power to define and enforce state constitutional rights "unduly restrict[ed] the judicial power" and "severely limit[ed] the independent force of the California Constitution," thus effecting a revision of the state constitution beyond the permissible scope of the initiative power.[75] However, more modest citizen-initiated limits on the rights of criminal defendants have survived judicial scrutiny.

The history of conflict between citizen lawmakers and courts over criminal justice policy shows that the 1960s–1970s era marked a critical transition. Prior to that period, the initiative and judicial powers had little interaction in this area. But, when courts began expanding the rights of criminal defendants in the 1960s and voters responded by approving a flurry of tough-on-crime initiatives, the competing movements produced intense conflict. Courts applied a check on death penalty initiatives and on some initiatives that restricted rights of criminal defendants, but citizens countered with provisions that constrained the powers of courts and imposed harsh punishments on convicted criminals.

EQUAL PROTECTION RIGHTS

Throughout the first century of the initiative era, perhaps the most divisive voter-approved measures were those that generated equal protection challenges, as opponents alleged that the initiative discriminated against minorities or unequally allocated fundamental rights. Many of these measures presented

---

[73] *Brosnahan v. Brown*, 32 Cal.3d 236 (1982) upheld most of Proposition 8 of 1982, but invalidated Proposition 8's bail provisions because they were in conflict with a competing measure. For a discussion of Proposition 8 of 1982, see Barry Latzer, "California's Constitutional Counterrevolution," in G. Alan Tarr, ed., *Constitutional Politics in the States: Contemporary Controversies and Historical Patterns* (Westport, CT: Greenwood Press, 1996), 165–7. In 2008, California voters adopted Proposition 9, another victims' rights initiative. The measure, like its predecessors, was vulnerable to post-election challenge.

[74] California Proposition 115 (1990).

[75] *Raven v. Deukmejian*, 52 Cal. 3d 336 (1990), invalidating in part California Proposition 115 (1990). See John Dinan, "Court-constraining Amendments and the State Constitutional Tradition," 38 RUTGERS L. J. 983, 1009-16 (2007).

difficult equal protection questions that divided courts and established important precedents.

Judicial enforcement of equal protection followed the pattern of other rights in that the equal protection clause experienced a period of dormancy followed by dramatic revival. Whereas the Reconstruction-Era Congress had drafted the equal protection clause in expansive terms – "no state shall... deny to any person within its jurisdiction the equal protection of the laws" – courts long interpreted the clause through the framework of economic rights and enforced it narrowly on that basis. As the 1896 *Plessy* case signified, courts were unwilling to invoke equal protection to strike down state-sanctioned racial segregation, and otherwise allowed the clause to fall largely dormant.[76]

Beginning in the mid-twentieth century, however, courts revived the clause, using it to protect minorities and root out numerous forms of discrimination. Through several stages, courts developed the doctrine that race, in particular, is a constitutionally "suspect" classification, and that laws that make distinctions based on race are subject to strict judicial scrutiny. Other classifications, including alienage and gender, were either suspect or quasi-suspect and called for heightened levels of judicial review. Courts developed these doctrines in the belief that majoritarian political processes systematically disadvantaged certain minorities and that judicial protection helped compensate for this imbalance.

Meanwhile, in a separate line of cases, the Supreme Court developed the doctrine that the equal protection clause prohibits unequal allocation of "fundamental rights," especially in the area of voting. Most notably, in a series of decisions in the 1960s beginning with *Baker v. Carr* (1962), the Court read the clause to require that legislative districts be drawn on an equal population basis, a decision that launched the "reapportionment revolution."[77]

The judicial expansion of equal protection guarantees led in turn to an explosion of rights-based litigation that raised a wide range of vexing constitutional questions. For example, after holding that states may not discriminate against racial minorities, courts had to decide whether states may use race-based classifications for "benign" purposes, such as remedying the effects of past discrimination, promoting racial diversity in public institutions, or increasing minority political representation. Similarly, after courts determined that some groups – for example, racial minorities, legal aliens, and women – were entitled to heightened judicial protection against discrimination, they had to decide whether to grant similar protection to other groups such as illegal immigrants and homosexuals.

Citizen lawmakers contributed to these controversies by enacting numerous initiatives that tested equal protection limits. The resulting litigation raised

[76] See, e.g., *Plessy v. Ferguson*, 163 U.S. 537 (1896).
[77] See, Gordon E. Baker, *The Reapportionment Revolution: Representation, Political Power, and the Supreme Court* (New York: Random House, 1966), 111–41; Robert B. McKay, *Reapportionment: The Law of Politics and Equal Representation* (New York: Twentieth Century Fund, 1965), 71–98.

the following issues: 1) Did voters discriminate against a protected minority group? 2) Could voters repeal or ban government efforts to assist certain minority groups? 3) Did voters impermissibly discriminate against a nonprotected group? And 4) Could voters allocate fundamental rights in an unequal way? A closer look at the litigation history in these areas will help us determine the extent to which the initiative power has threatened minority rights and whether courts have effectively mitigated that threat.

Discrimination Against Protected Minorities

Over the past century, citizens have enacted only a few measures that expressly discriminated against legally protected minorities or created what courts have come to define as "suspect classifications." Two early examples were initiatives that targeted legal aliens: the 1914 Arizona initiative restricting employment of aliens and California's 1920 alien land law.

The 1914 Arizona initiative was a union-backed measure that limited the number of noncitizens an employer could hire.[78] As a consequence of this restriction, many immigrants legally residing in the state faced the loss of their jobs. One of them was Mike Raich, a legal immigrant from Austria who was employed as a cook. Raich challenged the initiative in federal district court in Arizona. The district court held that the initiative was unconstitutional and, in *Truax v. Raich* (1915), the U.S. Supreme Court affirmed.[79] Writing for the Court, Chief Justice Charles Evans Hughes noted that the Fourteenth Amendment requires a state to provide equal protection of the laws not only to "citizens" but to "persons" within its jurisdiction – including legal aliens.[80] Moreover, Hughes wrote, "the right to work for a living in the common occupations of the community is of the very essence of the personal freedom and opportunity that it was the purpose of the [Fourteenth] Amendment to secure. . . . If this could be refused solely on the ground of race or nationality, the prohibition of the denial to any person of the equal protection of the laws would be a barren form of words."[81]

However, courts were slow to strike down California's citizen-enacted alien land law of 1920. The California legislature had enacted the state's first alien land law in 1913 by wide margins in both houses.[82] The 1913 law prohibited

---

[78] Arizona Proposition 318 (1914).
[79] *Truax v. Raich*, 239 U.S. 33 (1915). See also Higham, *Strangers in the Land*, 183.
[80] Ibid., 39, citing *Yick Wo v. Hopkins*, 118 U.S. 356, 369 (1886).
[81] Ibid., 41 (internal citations omitted).
[82] The California legislature adopted the 1913 *Alien Land Law*, codified as Chapter 113 California statutes of 1913, by a vote of 35 to 2 in the Senate and 72 to 3 in the Assembly. Legislatures in twelve other states – Washington, Arizona, Oregon, Idaho, Nebraska, Texas, Kansas, Louisiana, Montana, New Mexico, Minnesota, and Missouri – also adopted similar restrictions. Ronald Takaki, *Strangers from a Different Shore: A History of Asian Americans* (New York: Little Brown, 1989), 203–7; see also Thomas E. Cronin, *Direct Democracy: The Politics of Initiative, Referendum, and Recall* (Cambridge, MA: Harvard University Press, 1989), 93.

land ownership by "aliens ineligible to citizenship" – which in practice meant Asians, because federal law had restricted naturalized citizenship to whites and persons of African nativity or descent. The act also prevented legal aliens from leasing agricultural land for a term of more than three years.

In time, however, it became apparent that California's 1913 restrictions contained loopholes that allowed Japanese farmers to possess land by placing title in the names of their U.S.-born children or by other means. By 1920, rising anti-Asian sentiment in California spurred an initiative campaign to tighten the law's restrictions. Under the provisions of Proposition 1, Asian immigrants could no longer purchase agricultural land under the names of American-born minors, nor acquire stock in any corporation owning real property, nor even lease agricultural land. Californians approved the initiative by a landslide 75 percent vote.[83]

After the election, Japanese immigrants challenged the initiative through a series of cases in federal court. The suits argued that the restrictions violated not only U.S. treaty agreements with Japan, but also the Japanese immigrants' property and equal protection rights under the Fourteenth Amendment. Several of these claims reached the U.S. Supreme Court in the 1920s, and the Court rejected each one.[84] However, in 1948, in the case of *Oyama v. California*, the Court finally struck down one of the law's key provisions – the restriction on land ownership by citizens who are children of aliens.[85] Shortly thereafter, the California Supreme Court invalidated the balance of the law, ruling that it violated both the equal protection and due process clauses.[86] Years later, in 1971, the U.S. Supreme Court cited its precedents in *Truax* and *Oyama* for the proposition that "classifications based on alienage, like those based on nationality or race, are inherently suspect and subject to close judicial scrutiny. Aliens as a class are a prime example of a 'discrete and insular' minority . . . for whom such heightened judicial solicitude is appropriate."[87]

Clearly, the 1920 California alien land law supports the charge that voters can use the initiative power to discriminate against unpopular and relatively powerless minorities and that courts can be slow to defend these groups. But, the incident needs to be placed in historical perspective. During the 1910s and 1920s, citizen lawmakers enacted few laws that discriminated against immigrants whereas Congress and state legislatures enacted many such laws.[88] And,

---

[83] Takaki, *Strangers from a Different Shore*, 203–5.
[84] See *Porterfield v. Webb*, 263 U.S. 225 (1923); *Frick v. Webb*, 263 U.S. 326 (1923); *Webb v. O'Brien*, 263 U.S. 313 (1923).
[85] *Oyama v. California*, 332 U.S. 633 (1948).
[86] *Sei Fujii v. State*, 38 Cal. 2d 718 (1952).
[87] *Graham v. Richardson*, 403 U.S. 365, 371–2 (1971), prohibiting states from denying welfare assistance to aliens legally residing in the United States.
[88] Examples include the federal *Cable Act of 1922*, which declared that an American woman who marries an alien ineligible to citizenship ceases to be a citizen of the United States; the *National Origins Act of 1924*, which prohibited Japanese immigration in the same way that the *Chinese Exclusion Act of 1882* restricted immigration from China; and numerous

albeit belatedly, courts did invalidate the voter-approved alien land law. Nevertheless, this exception provides the important warning that courts cannot always be counted upon to check the initiative power's threat to minority rights.

Reversal of Policies to Assist Minorities

Although citizen lawmakers adopted few initiatives that overtly discriminated against minorities, they more frequently enacted measures blocking government efforts to assist minorities. Beginning in the 1960s, as the civil rights movement gathered strength, many state and local governments began to enact policies designed to assist racial minorities and other groups that had faced discrimination. These policies included laws to prohibit private discrimination in housing; desegregate public schools through racial assignments of students (and sometimes through mandatory busing); pursue race- or gender-based affirmative action in state employment, contracting, and university admissions; and provide non-English speakers education and other services in their native languages. Because these programs were highly controversial, it is not surprising that electoral majorities sometimes adopted initiatives to repeal or ban them.

Fair Housing. A leading example came when the California legislature adopted the Rumford Fair Housing Act of 1963.[89] The statute prohibited racial discrimination by realtors and owners of apartments or publicly financed homes. Shortly after its enactment, opponents qualified Proposition 14, an initiative constitutional amendment that sought to repeal the act and prevent the state from enacting similar legislation. As the 1964 election approached, the fight over the initiative became highly polarized, with both sides appealing to voters in emotional and rights-laden language. In the ballot pamphlet, proponents tapped into populist sentiments: "The Rumford Act establishes a new principle in our law – that State appointed bureaucrats may force you, over your objections, to deal concerning your own property with the person they choose. This amounts to seizure of private property.... Your 'Yes' vote will prevent such tyranny." The opponents countered: "*Proposition 14 is immoral.* It would legalize and incite bigotry. At a time when our nation is moving ahead on civil

state alien land laws that discriminated against Asian immigrants. The *Cable Act*, 42 Stat. 1021, was amended in 1930 to allow U.S. women who married aliens to retain their citizenship. For a discussion of these restrictive laws, see Takaki, *Strangers from a Different Shore*, 14–15.

[89] For a more detailed discussion of the Rumford Act and the Proposition 14 campaign, see Thomas W. Casstevens, *Politics, Housing, and Race Relations: California's Rumford Act and Proposition 14* (Berkeley: Institute of Governmental Studies, 1967); Raymond E. Wolfinger and Fred I. Greenstein, "The Repeal of Fair Housing in California: An Analysis of Referendum Voting," *American Political Science Review* 62, no. 3 (Sept. 1968): 753–9.

rights, it proposes to convert California into another Mississippi or Alabama and to create an atmosphere for violence and hate."[90]

Californians approved the measure by a 65 percent vote. After the election, Proposition 14's opponents challenged the measure, and in *Reitman v. Mulkey* (1967), the U.S. Supreme Court invoked the equal protection clause to declare the measure void. The Court reasoned that if the state enforced the initiative, it would effectively authorize private discrimination against racial minorities in housing.[91]

Busing. Meanwhile, during this same period, numerous public school districts throughout the United States began implementing school desegregation plans. Districts began assigning students to schools on the basis of their race and often required them to attend schools far from their homes as a way to reverse established patterns of segregation. Many parents objected to these arrangements and formed grassroots antibusing movements. In three of the leading initiative states – California (1972), Colorado (1974), and Washington (1978) – voters adopted statewide initiatives to reverse these programs and ban racial assignments in public schools.[92]

However, when opponents challenged these initiatives on equal protection grounds, courts blocked their implementation.[93] Most notably, in *Washington v. Seattle School District No. 1* (1982), the U.S. Supreme Court applied "political structure" equal protection analysis to invalidate the Washington antibusing initiative.[94] As we have seen, the Court ruled that the statewide electorate had discriminated against minorities "by lodging decisionmaking authority over the question [of racial assignments to] a new and remote level of government" to defeat the district's desegregation plan.[95]

Affirmative Action. By the 1990s, the Court's equal protection jurisprudence with respect to race gradually shifted away from the 1960s-era, minority-rights paradigm toward a so-called color blind view of equal protection that generally disfavored race-conscious policies. The Court increasingly embraced the view

---

[90] California Secretary of State, *Proposed Amendments to the Constitutions, Propositions and Proposed Laws Together with Arguments to be Submitted to the Electors of the State of California at the General Election, Tuesday, Nov. 3, 1964*, 18–20. http://traynor.uchastings.edu/ballot_pdf/1964g.pdf.

[91] *Reitman v. Mulkey*, 387 U.S. 369, 380–1 (1967), affirming *Mulkey v. Reitman*, 64 Cal.2d 529 (1966).

[92] California Proposition 21 (1972); Colorado Amendment 8 (1974); Washington Initiative 350 (1978).

[93] *Santa Barbara School District v. Superior Court*, 13 Cal.3d 315 (1975); *Keyes v. School Dist. No. 1*, 119 F.3d 1437 (10th Cir. 1997); *Washington v. Seattle School District No. 1*, 458 U.S. 457 (1982). Courts invalidated the California and Washington initiatives; the Colorado initiative was not invalidated, but was limited by federal court enforcement of desegregation in the Denver schools.

[94] *Washington v. Seattle School District No. 1*, 458 U.S. 457 (1982).

[95] Ibid., 483.

that, absent compelling justification, the equal protection clause prohibits all forms of racial discrimination, including so-called benign discrimination.[96] This transition was well underway when California voters, in 1996, adopted Proposition 209, the state's landmark anti-affirmative action initiative. The day after the election, Proposition 209's opponents challenged the law in federal district court on "political structure" equal protection grounds.

As we noted in Chapter 3, Judge Thelton Henderson issued a temporary restraining order and preliminary injunction against enforcement of the initiative. Judge Henderson concluded that the initiative's ban on affirmative action violated the structural equal protection doctrine of *Hunter* and *Seattle* because it created race and gender classifications by placing special burdens on those seeking race and gender preferences. "After the passage of Proposition 209," Judge Henderson wrote, "women and minorities who wish to petition their government for race- or gender-conscious remedial programs face a considerably more daunting burden. Before such persons can approach their school district, city council, county government, or any other subdivision of government with such a proposal, they must first obtain an amendment to the California Constitution that would either (a) repeal Proposition 209, or (b) permit the specific government entity at issue to adopt a particular race- or gender-conscious affirmative action program."[97]

On appeal, however, a three-judge panel of the Ninth Circuit reversed on the grounds that Proposition 209 violated neither "conventional" nor "political structure" equal protection standards. Citing recent Supreme Court decisions in *City of Richmond v. J. A. Croson Co.* (1989) and *Adarand Constructors, Inc. v. Peña* (1995), Judge Diarmuid O'Scannlain wrote that the equal protection clause's guarantee against race- and gender-based discrimination "does not depend on the race or gender of those burdened or benefited by a particular classification."[98] Indeed, he wrote, "a law that prohibits the State from classifying individuals by race or gender *a fortiori* does not classify individuals by race or gender. Proposition 209's ban on race and gender preferences, as a

---

[96] See, e.g., *City of Richmond v. J. A. Croson Co.*, 488 U.S. 469, 494 (1989), *Adarand Constructors, Inc. v. Peña*, 515 U.S. 200, 226 (1995), *Gratz v. Bollinger*, 539 U.S. 244 (2003), *Parents Involved in Community Schools v. Seattle School District No. 1*, 551 U.S. 701 (2007), striking down affirmative action programs and other "benign" racial classifications. But compare, *Grutter v. Bollinger*, 539 U.S. 306 (2003) upholding the University of Michigan's undergraduate affirmative action admissions program.

[97] *Coalition for Economic Equity v. Wilson*, 946 F. Supp. 1480, 1498 (N.D. Cal. 1996).

[98] *Coalition for Economic Equity v. Wilson*, 122 F.3d 692, 702 (9th Cir. 1997), citing *City of Richmond*, 488 U.S. at 494 (plurality opinion) and *Adarand*, 515 U.S. at 229–30 (1995). In *Adarand*, the Court determined that all racial classifications, even for "benign" purposes, are subject to strict scrutiny. The decision overturned *Metro Broadcasting, Inc. v. Federal Communications Commission*, 497 U.S. 547 (1990). *Metro Broadcasting* had established a two-tiered system for reviewing racial classifications, requiring only intermediate scrutiny for "benign" classifications. In *Adarand*, the Court wrote: "Consistency does recognize that any individual suffers an injury when he or she is disadvantaged by the government because of his or her race." *Adarand*, 515 U.S. at 230.

matter of law and logic, does not violate the Equal Protection Clause in any conventional sense."[99]

Moreover, the Ninth Circuit rejected the equal protection challenge to Proposition 209 based on political structure analysis. "The alleged 'equal protection' burden that Proposition 209 imposes on those who would seek race and gender preferences," Judge O'Scannlain wrote, "is a burden that the Constitution itself imposes. The Equal Protection Clause, parked at our most 'distant and remote' level of government, singles out racial preferences for severe political burdens – it prohibits them in all but the most compelling circumstances."[100]

After losing in the Ninth Circuit, opponents of Proposition 209 sought review by the U.S. Supreme Court, but the Court denied their petition for certiorari. Proposition 209's survival against constitutional attack underscored the judicial power's emerging "neutral" or "color blind" conception of equal protection rights, marked the decline of the political structure theory in the area of race, and cleared the way for citizens in other states, including Washington (1998), Michigan (2006), and Nebraska (2008) to enact initiatives banning state-sponsored affirmative action.[101] The Michigan initiative, Proposition 2 of 2006, was also challenged on equal protection grounds, but the Tenth Circuit rejected the challenge. In *Coalition to Defend Affirmative Action v. Granholm* (2006), the court held that "[t]he First and Fourteenth Amendments to the United States Constitution . . . *permit* States to use racial and gender preferences under narrowly defined circumstances. But they do not *mandate* them, and accordingly they do not prohibit the State from eliminating them."[102]

Bilingual Education. Citizen lawmakers generated more equal protection litigation by overturning 1970s-era government policies designed to assist language minorities in the public schools. California voters adopted the first of these measures, Proposition 227, in 1998. At the time, 1.4 million children in California public schools were deemed to be "limited English proficient (LEP)," meaning that they did not understand English well enough to keep up in school. Under existing policies, many LEP students were taught in their "home" language. This measure was designed to abolish bilingual education in most instances and replace it with intensive sheltered English immersion.[103] After a contentious campaign, Proposition 227 won by a 61 percent vote. Opponents challenged the measure in federal courts on several theories, including structural equal protection grounds. But, the courts upheld the measure against

---

[99] Ibid., 702.

[100] Ibid., 708.

[101] Washington Initiative 200 of 1998; Michigan Proposal 2 of 2006; Nebraska Initiative 424 of 2008.

[102] *Coalition to Defend Affirmative Action v. Granholm*, 473 F.3d 237, 240 (10th Cir. 2006).

[103] See California Secretary of State, *California Voter Information Guide, Primary Election, June 2, 1998*, 32–35. http://traynor.uchastings.edu/ballot_pdf/1998p.pdf.

these challenges.[104] In 2002, citizens in Arizona and Massachusetts adopted similar initiatives.

Discrimination Against Non-Protected Minorities

Citizen lawmakers also approved a number of initiatives that arguably discriminated against groups such as the poor, illegal aliens, and homosexuals. Although these groups lacked protected status under the Fourteenth Amendment's equal protection clause, they nevertheless sought relief from courts on equal protection grounds. The resulting litigation produced mixed results.

The Poor. In *James v. Valtierra* (1971), the landmark case challenging California's Proposition 10 of 1950, the litigants were unable to convince the Court that the measure impermissibly discriminated against the poor. As we have seen, the initiative required local governments to obtain voter approval through a mandatory referendum before they constructed any new low-income public housing projects. Two justices, Thurgood Marshall and William Brennan, believed that this initiative established "an explicit classification on the basis of poverty – a suspect classification which demands exacting judicial scrutiny."[105] But, the Court's majority rejected the view that poverty is a suspect classification for purposes of equal protection review.[106]

Illegal Aliens. On occasion, minorities that lacked protected status won equal protection challenges to voter-approved initiatives. For example, federal courts relied in part on the equal protection clause to invalidate California's Proposition 187 of 1994, the controversial measure designed to deny public services to illegal aliens. The Supreme Court had established the legal context for this conflict in the early 1980s when, in *Plyler v. Doe* (1982), it struck down a Texas statute preventing illegal immigrant children from attending the public schools. Although the Court declined to grant protected status to aliens unlawfully living in the United States, it held that a policy barring their children from school could not survive rational basis equal protection review as it applies to nonsuspect classifications.[107]

---

[104] See *California Teachers Association v. State Board of Education*, 271 F.3d 1141 (9th Cir. 2001), upholding Proposition 227 against Fourteenth Amendment equal protection and First Amendment challenges; *Valeria v. Davis*, 307 F.3d 1036 (9th Cir. 2002), upholding the measure against a structural equal protection challenge. For a discussion of the political structure theory in the *Valeria* case, see Elizabeth T. Bangs, "Who Should Decide What is Best for California's LEP Students? Proposition 227, Structural Equal Protection, and Local Decision-Making Power," 11 La Raza Journal 113 (2000).
[105] *James v. Valtierra*, 402 U.S. 137, 144–5 (1971).
[106] Ibid., 141.
[107] *Plyler v. Doe*, 457 U.S. 202 (1982).

Voters in California tested these limits when they adopted Proposition 187. The initiative qualified for the ballot in the early 1990s, a period that, in some ways, resembled the early 1920s, with growing economic distress, historically high immigration rates, and rising passions regarding the impact of immigrants (now further fueled by nativist voices on the radio airwaves). Anti-immigrant sentiments were particularly strong in California and Arizona where large numbers of undocumented aliens from Mexico and Central America resided in violation of U.S. law. Proposition 187's proponents argued that the federal government had failed to guard the border and that California taxpayers thus bore the burden of providing social services to immigrants who were unlawfully living in the state. The initiative proposed a severe remedy: It denied illegal immigrants access to public services, including social services, health care, and education. The measure also required public employees to report suspected illegal aliens to state and federal enforcement agencies.

Following an emotionally charged campaign, the California electorate adopted Proposition 187 by a 59 percent vote. Immediately thereafter, a coalition of immigrant rights groups challenged the measure in federal district court in Los Angeles. In *League of United Latin American Citizens v. Wilson*, the federal court enjoined enforcement of Proposition 187 partly on the basis that most of its provisions were preempted by federal law – a topic we turn to in the following chapter – as well as on the separate ground that its denial of public education to undocumented immigrant children violated equal protection requirements as set forth in *Plyler*.[108] Proposition 187 was tied up in the federal courts for five years until newly elected governor Gray Davis (a Proposition 187 opponent) agreed to a mediated settlement that voided almost all of its provisions.[109]

Language Minorities. Over half of the states have joined in a movement to establish English as their official language. Citizens in California (1986), Colorado (1988), Florida (1988), Alaska (1998), and Utah (2000) adopted official English laws through the initiative process.[110] Opponents argue that these measures discriminate against language minorities and have challenged several of the initiatives on equal protection and First Amendment grounds. The Arizona Supreme Court invalidated the most restrictive of these measures, the Arizona Official English initiative, on a combination of equal protection and First Amendment grounds.[111] More recently, the Alaska

---

[108] *League of United Latin American Citizens v. Wilson*, 1998 U.S. Dist. LEXIS 3368 (C.D. Cal. 1998).

[109] The only provision that survived the challenge was an enhanced penalty for using false identification.

[110] For a discussion of this movement, see Jack Citrin, Beth Reingold, Evelyn Walters, and Donald P. Green, "The 'Official English' Movement and the Symbolic Politics of Language in the States, *Western Political Quarterly* 43, no. 3 (Sept. 1990): 535–59.

[111] *Ruiz v. Hull*, 191 Ariz. 441 (1998). See also *Arizonans for Official English v. Arizona*, 520 U.S. 43 (1996), dismissed for lack of standing.

Supreme Court struck down that state's Official English initiative on the basis that it violated the First Amendment.[112]

Gays and lesbians. In the early 1990s, Colorado's Amendment 2 tested the equal protection rights of gays and lesbians, another minority group that has historically lacked protected status. As we have seen, after Denver, Boulder, and Aspen enacted local ordinances prohibiting discrimination on the basis of sexual orientation, the statewide electorate sought to prohibit such laws by imposing a statewide rule that "homosexual, lesbian, or bisexual orientation, conduct, practices or relationships shall [not] ... entitle any persons or class of persons to have or claim any minority status, quota preferences, protected status or claim of discrimination."[113]

As evidenced by the majority opinion in *Romer v. Evans* (1996), Amendment 2 created difficulties for the Court. Those in the majority, led by Justice Kennedy, were clearly troubled by the initiative and believed it should be invalidated. However, they faced the problem that, for purposes of equal protection review, the Court had never recognized sexual orientation as a suspect classification nor homosexuals as a protected class.[114] Consequently, they had to rely on an alternative equal protection theory to invalidate the citizen-enacted law.

Commentators have struggled to explain Justice Kennedy's reasoning in the case. In announcing the judgment, he asserted that the Court merely subjected the initiative to low-level, rational basis equal protection review and found it invalid under that standard. But Justice Kennedy's opinion suggests he relied on the structural equal protection theory to invalidate Amendment 2 by essentially holding that the statewide electorate had impermissibly reallocated decision-making authority in a way that disadvantaged a vulnerable minority group – in this case, not racial minorities, but gay and lesbian persons.[115] In this view, the Court tacitly recognized sexual orientation as at least a quasi-suspect classification and homosexuals a protected class.[116]

In the early 2000s, the Court further recognized the rights claims of gays and lesbians when, in *Lawrence v. Texas* (2003), it invalidated a Texas statute that criminalized homosexual sodomy.[117] In dissent, Justice Scalia complained that

---

[112] *Alaskans for a Common Language, Inc. v. Kritz*, 170 P.3d 183 (Alaska 2007).

[113] Colorado Amendment 2 (1992).

[114] Indeed, at the time, *Bowers v. Hardwick*, 478 U.S. 186 (1986) (the case recognizing a state's authority to criminalize sodomy) remained good law. See *Romer v. Evans*, 517 U.S. 620, 636 (1996), Scalia, J., dissenting.

[115] *Romer*, 634.

[116] For competing interpretations of the holding and implications of *Romer v. Evans*, see, e.g., Louis Michael Seidman, "*Romer's* Radicalism: The Unexpected Revival of Warren Court Activism," 1996 Sup. Ct. Rev. 203 (1996); Andrew Koppelman, "*Romer v. Evans* and Invidious Intent," 6 Wm & Mary Bill of Rts J 89 (1997); Robert H. Bork, *Slouching Towards Gomorrah: Modern Liberalism and American Decline* (New York: ReganBooks 1996), 112–114.

[117] *Lawrence v. Texas*, 539 U.S. 558 (2003). The majority held that the law violated substantive due process, whereas in a concurring opinion Justice Sandra Day O'Connor argued it violated equal protection.

the Court was exercising the judicial power to expand the rights of gays and lesbians beyond what the Constitution required and contended that the logic of *Romer* and *Lawrence* was inexorably leading to creation of a constitutional right to same sex marriage.[118]

The California Supreme Court's 2008 decision in *In re Marriage Cases* was a milestone in this area of law. In addition to holding that same sex couples were entitled to marriage rights under the California Constitution, the court more broadly declared that sexual orientation was a suspect classification under the state constitution's equal protection clause. Henceforth, any state or local policies in California that made distinctions on the basis of sexual orientation would be subject to strict judicial scrutiny.[119] Although Proposition 8 reversed the specific outcome of *In re Marriage Cases* by inserting a "Defense of Marriage Amendment" into the California Constitution, the initiative did not affect the court's broader ruling that, under the state's constitution, sexual orientation was now a suspect classification. It remained to be seen whether other state courts, or the federal courts, would follow this lead.[120]

Allocation of "Fundamental Rights" – Voting

During the 1960s, yet another conflict arose between the initiative power and the courts, this time in the area of legislative redistricting. Prior to the 1960s, the Supreme Court had deferred to states in determining legislative district boundaries, considering the matter a non-justiciable political question.[121] States were thus able to maintain legislative districts with varying numbers of constituents, most commonly in the upper house of the state legislature. These so-called malapportioned districts generally favored rural constituencies and diluted the votes of urban residents, but were justified on the basis that less populated, rural regions had distinctive interests that would be disregarded in a legislature where both houses were apportioned on a purely equal population basis.

In several initiative states, citizen lawmakers participated in legislative redistricting. For example, in Arizona (1918, 1932), California (1926), Colorado (1932, 1962), Oregon (1952), and Washington (1956), citizens used the initiative power either to determine district lines or to establish new criteria for the legislature to follow when drawing districts. As a rule, these initiatives allowed for unequal population districts in the upper house, but required the lower house to be apportioned on an equal population basis. Sometimes, but not always, they established more equally apportioned districts than what

---

[118] Ibid., 604–5, Scalia, J., dissenting.

[119] *In re Marriage Cases*, 43 Cal.4th 757, 840, 854 (2008).

[120] *See Strauss v. Horton*, California Supreme Court Case No. S168047 (2009). In *Kerrigan v. Commissioner of Public Health*, 289 Conn. 135 (2008), the Connecticut Supreme Court held that under the Connecticut Constitution, sexual orientation, like gender, is a quasi-suspect classification, and that Connecticut laws that discriminate on the basis of sexual orientation would now be subject to heightened or "intermediate" scrutiny.

[121] See *Colegrove v. Green*, 328 U.S. 549 (1946).

legislators had created for themselves.[122] Notably, after California voters adopted the "Senate plan" formula for legislative apportionment in 1926, they rejected three subsequent initiatives (1948, 1960, 1962) seeking to change it.[123]

But, in the 1960s, the rights revolution entered this arena as well when the Supreme Court issued its landmark decisions in *Baker v. Carr* (1962) and *Reynolds v. Sims* (1964). In these cases, the Court held that because voting is an implied fundamental right, legislative districting is justiciable and subject to heightened judicial scrutiny. Henceforth, the Court would apply equal protection standards to districting plans to ensure that states do not dilute votes by creating unequal population districts. All districts would now have to adhere to the "one-person-one-vote" principle.[124] As soon as the Court issued its decision in *Baker v. Carr*, almost every legislative district map in the nation, including those created by citizen legislators, became constitutionally suspect.

Indeed, in *Lucas v. Forty-Fourth General Assembly of Colorado* (1964), the Court insisted that even when the state's majority wished to establish a system of representation resembling the U.S. Congress, with the upper house apportioned on factors other than strict population equality, the equal protection clause prohibited that choice. In *Lucas*, the Court struck down a 1962 Colorado initiative establishing a "federal model" plan for the state legislature that would create districts in the lower house based on population equality but senate districts based on geographic regions and other factors.[125] Colorado voters had been presented a choice in the 1962 election: approve either the federal model initiative or an alternative plan that would apportion seats in both houses on an equal population basis. They decisively preferred Amendment 7, the federal model option. The measure carried not only statewide (by 63 percent) but also in regions where votes would be "diluted" under the plan. The Court nevertheless disallowed the voter-approved initiative on the grounds that the plan violated the new one-person-one-vote equal protection standard, concluding that "[a]n individual's constitutionally protected right to cast an equally weighted vote cannot be denied even by a vote of a majority of the state's electorate, if the apportionment scheme adopted by the voters fails to measure up to the requirements of the Equal Protection Clause."[126]

MODERN SUBSTANTIVE DUE PROCESS RIGHTS – PRIVACY AND AUTONOMY

Finally, we return to conflicts between the initiative power and substantive due process rights. As we have seen, in *Meyer* and *Pierce*, the Supreme Court

---

[122] Citizen lawmakers in two other states, Arkansas (1936) and Michigan (1952), also accomplished redistricting through the initiative process. Baker, *The Reapportionment Revolution*, 112–113.

[123] Ibid., 113.

[124] *Baker v. Carr*, 369 U.S. 186 (1962); *Reynolds v. Sims*, 377 U.S. 533 (1964).

[125] *Lucas v. Forty-Fourth General Assembly of Colorado*, 377 U.S. 713 (1964).

[126] Ibid., 736.

developed the doctrine that the due process clause of the Fourteenth Amendment protects certain noneconomic fundamental rights – in particular, parents' substantive liberty to control their children's upbringing and education.[127] During the 1930s, the Court repudiated the doctrine of substantive due process in the economic realm, but *Meyer* and *Pierce* have retained their vitality. Beginning in the 1960s, the Court revived the *Meyer-Pierce* doctrine to enforce a constitutional "right of privacy" or, as the Court later put it, "[to place] limits on a state's right to interfere with a person's most basic decisions about family and parenthood."[128] The Court thus invoked the due process clause to strike down laws that outlawed contraceptives (1965), prohibited interracial marriage (1967), and restricted abortion (1973).[129]

Moreover, the California Supreme Court's decision in *Marriage Cases* shows how state supreme courts can independently expand state constitutional rights of privacy to dictate outcomes in controversial policy areas. The court invoked the California Constitution's due process and privacy clauses, rather than the due process provisions of the U.S. Constitution, to strike down the state's marriage laws.[130]

But, it was the U.S. Supreme Court's abortion decisions that marked the most dramatic expansion of the constitutional right of privacy and thus of the judicial power in the realm of social policy. Those decisions generated a massive popular backlash that has lasted for decades. It is remarkable, however, that the resulting controversy and grass-roots mobilization has produced very few successful citizen initiatives. In more than three decades after *Roe v. Wade*, voters adopted only four abortion-related initiatives – one in Washington to reinforce abortion rights, and two in Colorado and one in Arkansas to limit these rights. More specifically, Washington voters in 1991 narrowly adopted Initiative 120, a measure creating a state statutory right to birth control and abortion and requiring public funding for abortions for poor women, whereas voters in Colorado adopted Amendment 3 in 1984, which restricted public funding for abortions and Amendment 12 in 1998, which mandated parental notification and a 48-hour waiting period for unemancipated minors seeking abortion. Pro-choice activists challenged both of the Colorado initiatives in federal court. The Tenth Circuit partially invalidated the anti-funding initiative on federal preemption grounds and struck down the parental notification initiative on the basis that it violated the implied right of privacy protected

---

[127] *Pierce*, 534.
[128] See *Planned Parenthood of Southeastern Pennsylvania v. Casey*, 505 U.S. 833, 849 (1992).
[129] *Griswold v. Connecticut*, 381 U.S. 479 (1965); *Loving v. Virginia*, 388 U.S. 1 (1967); *Roe v. Wade*, 410 U.S. 113 (1973). In *Loving*, the Court held that antimiscegenation laws violated both the equal protection and due process clauses of the Fourteenth Amendment.
[130] *In re Marriage Cases*, 43 Cal.4th 757, 809–20 (2008). As noted above, in *Marriage Cases*, the California Supreme Court also invoked the state constitution's equal protection clause as a separate, independent basis for invalidating the state's restriction on same-sex marriage.

by the due process clause.[131] Arkansas was the only other state to adopt an abortion-related initiative, Amendment 3 of 1988. This initiative prohibited the use of public money to pay for any abortion, except to save the mother's life. The U.S. Supreme Court invalidated the measure's funding restrictions to the extent they conflicted with federal law.[132]

Despite several attempts by activists on both sides of the issue, voters in the other initiative states declined to adopt abortion-related initiatives. The restrictions on citizen lawmaking in this area again demonstrate that when courts declare a federal constitutional right, they almost always have the last word. If the Supreme Court were to reverse *Roe*, initiative contests could become intense battlegrounds for determining abortion policy, and, in some states, anti-abortion initiatives would likely generate protracted conflicts with state courts. But, under the present judicial constraints, direct democracy can have little policy impact in this controversial area.

CONCLUSION

When Elihu Root spoke in 1913 about the dangers and shortcomings of direct democracy, he added a word of consolation. The initiative power, he noted, operated within the protective constraints of the Fourteenth Amendment. "Since the adoption of the Fourteenth Amendment to the Constitution," Root observed, "the states are prohibited from violating in their own affairs the most important principles of the National Constitution."[133] When Root offered this assurance, the Fourteenth Amendment was comparatively weak, with its enforcement mainly limited to the protection of economic rights. Nearly a century later, judicial interpretation and enforcement of the Fourteenth Amendment have greatly expanded, through incorporation of the Bill of Rights, major expansion of the equal protection clause, and revival of substantive due process to protect rights of personal privacy and individual autonomy. Moreover, in recent decades, state supreme courts have moved beyond the boundaries of the federal Constitution to expand their enforcement of state constitutional rights.

Despite these developments, many remain convinced that direct democracy has undermined minority rights. A fair reading of the record suggests that direct democracy's most consequential impact on rights has been to limit the *expansion* of rights in a number of areas, including affirmative action, bilingual

---

[131] *Hern v. Beye*, 57 F.3d 906 (10th Cir. 1995), invalidating in part Colorado Amendment 3 (1984), prohibiting public funding for abortions; *Planned Parenthood of the Rocky Mountains Services Corporation v. Owens*, 287 F.3d 910 (10th Cir. 2002), invalidating Colorado Amendment 12 (1998), requiring parental notification and waiting period for unemancipated minors seeking abortion.

[132] *Dalton v. Little Rock Family Planning Services*, 516 U.S. 474 (1996).

[133] Elihu Root, "Experiments in Government and the Essentials of the Constitution," in Robert Bacon and James Brown Scott, eds., *Addresses on Government and Citizenship* (Cambridge, MA: Harvard University Press, 1916), 90.

education, marriage, and certain areas of criminal law. Because these controversies have involved competing rights claims, however, one's view of how seriously the initiative power has threatened rights may ultimately depend, as Professor Glendon put it, on one's view of "*which* needs, goods, interests, or values should be characterized as 'rights.'"[134]

More broadly, one can see that the growth of the initiative power – and its potential threat of majority tyranny – have been met by the rise of a rights-enforcing judicial power. And although the record of their conflict is complex, the frequency with which courts have invalidated initiatives on a range of rights-based theories suggests that, on balance, where direct democracy has threatened rights, the judicial power has effectively countered the threat.

[134] Glendon, *Rights Talk*, 16.

6

Conflicts Over Powers

Critics have also long argued that direct democracy undermines representative government. The initiative process, it is said, too easily allows fleeting majorities to alter powers of state government – or even, potentially, federal powers. This chapter examines how citizen initiatives have threatened to erode representative institutions and how, in turn, courts have responded to these threats.

CHANGING CONSTITUTIONAL DESIGN

Direct democracy's potential danger to representative government is greatest in states with initiative constitutional amendment (ICA), the process that permits citizens to propose state constitutional amendments and adopt them by simple majority vote. In the same way the ICA can limit state constitutional rights, it can erode the constitutional powers of state government.

Again, these dynamics are a sharp departure from the federal model of "higher law" constitutionalism. Any movement to modify *federal* institutions – for example, to abolish the Electoral College or impose term limits on members of Congress – must work its way through Article V's exacting, two-stage, super-majority amendment process. Amendments may be proposed only by a two-thirds vote of both houses of Congress or by a federal constitutional convention demanded by two-thirds of the state legislatures, while ratification requires approval of three-fourths of the states, either through their legislatures or state ratifying conventions.[1]

Madison argued that the Article V amendment procedure was "stamped with every mark of propriety. It guards equally against that extreme facility, which

---

[1] Although the Article V procedure for calling a constitutional convention has never been invoked, some efforts have come close. See *Uhler v. AFL-CIO*, 468 U.S. 1310, (1984). State legislatures have ratified twenty-six of twenty-seven amendments; the Twenty-First Amendment was the only one ratified through the state convention procedure. See Thomas F. Schaller, "Democracy at Rest: Strategic Ratification of the Twenty-First Amendment," *Publius* 28, no. 2 (Spring 1998): 81–97.

would render the Constitution too mutable; and that extreme difficulty, which might perpetuate its discovered faults."[2] In truth, Article V tips the balance toward "extreme difficulty" and has thwarted almost all popular movements for formal constitutional change. Since 1789, over 11,000 amendments have been introduced, but only 27 have been approved by Congress and ratified by the requisite number of states.[3]

The high barrier to federal constitutional amendment has always had detractors. Thomas Jefferson, for example, contended that constitutions should not be treated "like the ark of the covenant, too sacred to be touched."[4] Similarly, groups including Anti-Federalists, the People's Party, Socialists, and Progressives have complained that Article V unduly restricts the people's ability to change their government as they see fit. In 1912, the Progressive Party platform declared that "a free people should have the power from time to time to amend their fundamental law so as to adapt it progressively to the changing needs of people," and promised to provide "a more easy and expeditious method of amending the Federal Constitution."[5] These Progressive Era efforts failed. Congress rejected amendments offered by Senator Robert M. La Follette to liberalize the Article V procedure, and the U.S. Supreme Court struck down citizen efforts to vote on state ratification of federal constitutional amendments.[6]

---

[2] Madison, *Federalist* 43, 275. Similarly, Alexander Hamilton wrote that although "the right of the people to alter or abolish the established constitution whenever they find it inconsistent with their happiness" is a "fundamental principle of republican government," the Constitution should not be subject to change as a result of a "momentary inclination." Hamilton, *Federalist* 78, 468.

[3] According to U.S. Senate Historian Don Ritchie, 11,219 proposed Constitutional amendments were introduced in the Congress between 1789 and 2004. See "Odds Stacked Against Passage of Amendments," *The Seattle Post Intelligencer* (February 25, 2004).

[4] Thomas Jefferson, Letter to Samuel Kercheval (1816) in Andrew A. Lipscomb and Albert E. Bergh, eds., *The Writings of Thomas Jefferson*, Vol. 15 (Washington, D.C.: Thomas Jefferson Memorial Association, 1904), 40.

[5] Kirk H. Porter and Donald Bruce Johnson, eds., *National Party Platforms, 1840–1964* (Urbana: University of Illinois Press, 1966), 176. The Socialist Platform of 1912 was more specific, demanding "[a]bolition of the present restrictions upon the amendment of the constitution, so that instrument may be amendable by a majority of the voters in a majority of the states." Ibid., 190. Other critiques of Article V include "Letter of the Federal Farmer: IV," October 12, 1787, in Herbert J. Storing, ed., *The Anti-Federalist: Writings by the Opponents of the Constitution* (Chicago: University of Chicago Press, 1985), 59–60 and Herbert Croly, *Progressive Democracy* (New York: Macmillan, 1914), 230–44. For discussion, see William G. Ross, *A Muted Fury: Populists, Progressives, and Labor Unions Confront the Courts, 1890–1937* (Princeton: Princeton University Press, 1994), 149, 156–59.

[6] Senator La Follette's 1913 proposal to change Article V would have allowed amendments to be proposed by majority vote in both houses of Congress or through the application of ten states, with ratification by a majority of voters in a majority of states. See S.J. Res. 24, 63rd Congress, 1st sess. 1913. See also *Hawke v. Smith*, 253 U.S. 221 (1920), invalidating Ohio Issue No. 1 of 1918. The Court reaffirmed that states may not alter the Article V amendment process in *National Prohibition Cases*, 253 U.S. 350, 386 (1920) and *Leser v. Garnett*, 258 U.S. 130, 137 (1922). See also *Prior v. Noland*, 68 Colo. 263, 270 (Colo. 1920).

By contrast, state constitutions have long been more mutable. Although the federal Constitution has been amended on just 27 occasions, most state constitutions have been amended at least 100 times, including the California Constitution of 1879, which has been amended over 500 times.[7] Indeed, the "lower" or "popular" constitutional tradition in the states has always been more receptive to institutional change than the "higher law" federal constitutional tradition. However, it is important to distinguish between different forms of state constitutional amendment. Most amendments to state constitutions are proposed by legislatures, and only then submitted to the people for ratification.[8] Whereas this process is less exacting than the federal Article V procedure, it requires legislative deliberation and broad consensus between the legislature and the people. By contrast, the ICA method, available in its most direct form in 16 states, allows citizens to amend the state constitution, usually by simple majority vote, over the objections of representatives and with minimal deliberation.[9] By permitting the electorate to attack government institutions in a moment of haste, anger, or even inattention, this method places the powers of the legislature, the courts, and other government institutions at risk.

Two other dynamics are important to note. First, ICAs pose a greater challenge to representative government than statutory initiatives do. Statutory initiatives can sometimes undermine the powers of representatives, but they are vulnerable to repeal by the legislature or invalidation by the courts. These differences demonstrate, again, that not all initiative states are alike. Citizens can more easily remake representative government if they are in a state with ICA than if they are in a state that only allows statutory initiatives.

Second, although the U.S. Constitution provides strong protection of federal powers, it provides only limited protection for the institutional powers of *state* governments. Whereas the U.S. Constitution provides an umbrella of rights that protects individuals at the state level (largely through the Fourteenth Amendment), it does not provide comparable protection for the powers of state government institutions.

---

[7] As of 2007, the California Constitution had been amended 514 times. The Council of State Governments, *The Book of the States* Vol. 39 (Lexington, KY: The Council of State Governments, 2007), 9. For a discussion of amendment patterns, see Donald S. Lutz, "Patterns in Amending of American State Constitutions," in G. Alan Tarr, ed., *Constitutional Politics in the States: Contemporary Controversies and Historical Patterns* (Westport, CT: Greenwood Press, 1996), 24–46; Bruce E. Cain, Sara Ferejohn, Margarita Najar, and Mary Walther, "Constitutional Change: Is It Too Easy to Amend our State Constitution?" in Bruce E. Cain and Roger G. Noll, eds., *Constitutional Reform in California: Making State Government More Effective and Responsive* (Berkeley: Institute of Governmental Studies Press, 1995), 265–90.

[8] Council of State Governments, *Book of the States* Vol. 39, 11–16.

[9] The sixteen states with a direct form of Initiative Constitutional Amendment are Arkansas, Arizona, California, Colorado, Florida, Illinois, Missouri, Michigan, Montana, Nebraska, Nevada, North Dakota, Ohio, Oklahoma, Oregon, and South Dakota. Two additional states, Massachusetts and Mississippi, have an indirect form of ICA. M. Dane Waters, ed. *Initiative and Referendum Almanac.* (Durham, N.C.: Carolina Academic Press, 2003), 12.

With these factors in mind, we can now ask: How effectively have courts defended state and federal representative institutions against the initiative power? To explore this question, we begin by revisiting one of the most dramatic citizen-initiated attempts to alter the powers of both state and federal institutions: the term limits movement of the 1990s. Because this controversy encompassed many of the dynamics this chapter seeks to address, we will examine it in some detail.

THE TERM LIMITS MOVEMENT

In the early 1990s, an antigovernment, populist mood spread through much of the nation. A series of scandals in Congress and state legislatures fueled popular suspicion that far too many representatives had become corrupt. At the same time, however, most incumbent legislators enjoyed enormous financial and other advantages against prospective challengers. Many citizens concluded that, under these conditions, periodic elections no longer provided a sufficient popular check on representatives. Term limits, they believed, were needed to control the vices of long-term incumbency. A movement thus quickly emerged to impose mandatory term limits on both state legislators and members of Congress.

Defenders of the existing constitutional design objected that term limits would devastate legislatures. Political scientist Nelson Polsby argued that "the main effect of [congressional term limits was] overwhelmingly likely to be the weakening of Congress in the overall scheme of national policymaking" as power migrated to "unelected bureaucrats and congressional staff, the admittedly elected but far more distant president and his largely unaccountable entourage of appointed officials, and, most unacceptably, lobbyists and interest group specialists in public policy."[10] Term limits, Polsby argued, would deny members of Congress the capacity to maintain "an arm's length independence" from these other powers.[11]

Similarly, opponents of state-level term limits feared they would undermine the hard-won professionalization of state legislatures. Just a generation earlier, reformers had convinced voters to support state constitutional changes designed to reduce excessive turnover and amateurism in state capitals. Mandatory term limits, many argued, would almost surely reverse these gains.

In response, term limits advocates pointed to the rule's ancient provenance, which dated back to the classical republics of Greece and Rome.[12] Term limits

---

[10] Nelson W. Polsby, "Term Limits" in Alan Brinkley, Nelson W. Polsby, and Kathleen M. Sullivan, *New Federalist Papers: Essays in Defense of the Constitution* (New York: W.W. Norton & Co., 1997), 70.

[11] Ibid.

[12] Mark P. Petracca, "Rotation in Office: The History of an Idea," in Gerald Benjamin and Michael J. Malbin, eds., *Limiting Legislative Terms* (Washington, D.C.: CQ Press, 1992), 19–21.

were also well known during the founding era, when the concept was called "rotation in office." The Articles of Confederation embraced the principle by requiring that "no person shall be capable of being a delegate for more than three years in any term of six years."[13] However, in drafting the Constitution, the Framers rejected the term limits rule, concluding that that the short length of House terms and other features of the constitutional design made mandatory term limits unnecessary.[14]

In the ratification debates, the Anti-Federalists attacked the Constitution's failure to impose a rotation requirement, especially for U.S. senators.[15] At the New York ratifying convention, Gilbert Livingston moved the adoption of an amendment providing that "[n]o person shall be eligible as a senator for more than six years in any term of twelve years."[16] Similarly, at the North Carolina and Virginia ratifying conventions, advocates of term limits proposed that the Constitution be amended to provide that members of Congress "at fixed periods, be reduced to a private station."[17] These efforts ultimately failed and the Constitution was ratified with no restrictions on re-eligibility for election to federal office.[18]

During much of the nineteenth century, an informal norm of rotation in Congress prevailed, with many members serving only one term before returning to private life in their home states. Between 40 and 50 percent of Congress left office each election cycle and the attrition rate sometimes reached 70 percent.[19] However, around the turn of the twentieth century, as the power of the federal government expanded and service in Congress became more

---

[13] Articles of Confederation, Section V (1777). In addition, rotation was an important principle at the state level. The Pennsylvania Constitution of 1776, for example, required rotation in office for all state-elected officials to guard against "the danger of an inconvenient aristocracy." See Petracca, "Rotation in Office," 27.

[14] Petracca, "Rotation in Office," 31. See text of Section 4 of the Virginia Plan presented by Edmund Randolph to the Federal Convention, May 29, 1787, in Gaillard Hunt and James B. Scott, eds., *Debates in the Federal Convention of 1787 Reported by James Madison* (Buffalo, New York: Prometheus Books, 1920), 23–6.

[15] See, Herbert J. Storing, ed., *The Complete Anti-Federalist* (Chicago: University of Chicago Press, 1981), section 2.8.147 (The Federal Farmer supporting term limits); section 2.9.201 (Brutus supporting term limits). See also Gordon S. Wood, *The Creation of the American Republic, 1776–1787* (Chapel Hill: University of North Carolina Press, 1969), 520–22.

[16] Gilbert Livingston, in Jonathan Elliot, ed., *The Debates of the Several State Conventions on the Adoption of the Constitution* Vol. II (New York: Burt Franklin, 1888), 289.

[17] Ibid., Vol. III, 657–658 (Virginia); Ibid., Vol. IV, 243 (North Carolina).

[18] See, e.g., Brutus, XVI, 10 April 1788, in Storing, ed., *The Anti-Federalist:* 189–90. See also Charles Kesler, "Bad Housekeeping: The Case Against Congressional Term Limits," The Heritage Foundation *Policy Review*, (Summer 1990), reprinted in Benjamin and Malbin, eds., *Limiting Legislative Terms*, 242–43. In addition, the First Congress debated but rejected a constitutional amendment that would have limited representatives to three terms during any eight-year period. 1 *Annals of Congress* 790 (1789).

[19] For a discussion of this history by an opponent of term limits, see Kesler, "The Case Against Congressional Term Limits," 244.

attractive, legislative careers lengthened and turnover declined.[20] These changes professionalized Congress, but also entrenched members and insulated them from shifts in public opinion. The only way to break the power of incumbency, activists argued, was to establish mandatory limits on representatives' terms. Although the movement's primary objective was to establish congressional term limits, it also sought to limit the service of state-level elected officials and thus replace long-term careerist incumbents with "citizen legislators" at both the state and federal level.

The term limits movement quickly exposed a divide between citizens and their representatives. In 1990, a national poll showed that citizens supported term limits for members of Congress by a 61-to-21 percent margin, a view that was remarkably consistent across demographic groups.[21] By contrast, in a separate 1990 survey of U.S. House members, 66 percent admitted they opposed limitations on the number of terms members could serve.[22] Most state legislators also predictably opposed limits on their terms. This opposition created an enormous obstacle. Although proponents introduced term limits amendments in statehouses around the country, legislators consistently killed the proposals. It was thus not surprising that the movement decided to bypass legislatures and instead impose term limits on state and federal representatives directly, through the initiative process, in every state where that was an option.

Term Limits Initiatives

Proponents qualified the first term limits initiatives in 1990 in Oklahoma, Colorado, and California. Oklahomans were first in line, adopting a term limits initiative in September 1990 by a 67 percent vote.[23] Six weeks later, voters in Colorado approved Amendment 5, an initiative imposing term limits on both state-level elected officials and Colorado's representatives in Congress, by a 70 percent vote. California voters also adopted a term limits initiative, Proposition 140, by a narrower 52-to-48 percent margin. Proposition 140 imposed lifetime term limits on the state's elected officials, cut the legislature's budget by 40 percent, and abolished legislators' pensions.[24]

[20] Nelson W. Polsby, "The Institutionalization of the U.S. House of Representatives," *American Political Science Review* 62, no. 1 (March 1968): 144–68.

[21] John H. Fund, "Term Limitation: An Idea Whose Time Has Come," in Benjamin and Malbin, eds., *Limiting Legislative Terms*, 227, citing *New York Times*/CBS survey of 1,515 adults, conducted March 30–April 2, 1990.

[22] Fund, "Term Limitation," 225, citing Gallup Organization, "Poll for the National Federation of Independent Business," (Princeton, N.J.: Gallup, January 1990), 6.

[23] Oklahoma State Question 632 imposed a twelve-year limit on state legislative service – either in the state house, the state senate, or the two combined. See Gary W. Copeland, "Term Limitations and Political Careers in Oklahoma: In, Out, Up, or Down," in Benjamin and Malbin, eds., *Limiting Legislative Terms*, 141.

[24] The California Supreme Court later invalidated Proposition 140's elimination of legislative pensions as applied to incumbent legislators. *Legislature v. Eu*, 54 Cal.3d 492, 530 (1991). For

The next major test came when activists qualified a term limits initiative for the 1991 Washington state ballot. Initiative 553 sought to impose term limits on both state officials and Washington's representatives in Congress. The measure was designed to apply retroactively and, by its terms, would have barred U.S. House Speaker Tom Foley (D-WA), then serving his fourteenth term, from seeking reelection after 1992. I-553 faced intense opposition from Common Cause, the League of Women Voters, labor organizations, business interests, and, not least, Speaker Foley. The measure failed, 46 to 54 percent.[25]

In 1992, however, the movement regrouped and imposed term limits on members of Congress, state officials, or both, in thirteen states, all through the initiative process. These outcomes included a decisive victory in Washington, reversing the defeat of 1991, and in California, where voters extended term limits to the state's representatives in Congress. Citizen lawmakers also approved term limits measures in Arizona, Arkansas, Florida, Michigan, Missouri, Montana, Nebraska, North Dakota, Ohio, Oregon, South Dakota, and even Wyoming, a state that had never adopted an initiative until that year.[26]

Over the next two years, support for term limits continued to build. In 1993, voters in Maine adopted limits for state legislators and, in 1994, voters in eight states – Alaska, Colorado, Idaho, Maine, Massachusetts, Nebraska, Nevada, and Oklahoma – adopted new or more stringent term limits initiatives. By 1995, twenty-one states had adopted term limits on state elected officials and twenty-three states had imposed limits on their representatives in Congress, in almost every case through ballot initiatives. This wave of term limits initiatives greatly contributed to the high rates of initiative use in the 1990s and constituted one of the most successful political mobilizations in U.S. history.[27]

Outside the initiative states, however, the term limits movement made virtually no gains.[28] Despite the strong popular demand for these reforms, most legislatures refused to adopt them, causing term limits activist Paul Jacob to conclude that "[w]ithout the citizen initiative process, there would be no term limits movement."[29] To be sure, congressional Republicans, seeking to break

a discussion of the Proposition 140 campaign, see Schrag, *Paradise Lost,* 241–43; Charles M. Price, "The Guillotine Comes to California: Term-Limits Politics in the Golden State," in Benjamin and Malbin, eds., *Limiting Legislative Terms,* 117–24.

[25] David J. Olson, "Term Limits Fail in Washington: The 1991 Battleground" in Benjamin and Malbin, eds., *Limiting Legislative Terms,* 82. See also Stuart Rothenberg, "Transplanting Term Limits: Political Mobilization and Grass-Roots Politics," in ibid., 97–113.

[26] M. Dane Waters, *Initiative and Referendum Almanac* (Durham: Carolina Academic Press, 2003), 445–46; 505–08.

[27] Ibid., 505–08.

[28] Only a few legislatures adopted term limits. The Utah legislature adopted a weak form of term limits in 1994, but repealed them in 2003. Louisiana lawmakers adopted a weak version of term limits in 1995. And the same year, the New Hampshire legislature imposed term limits on the state's representatives in Congress, but not on themselves.

[29] Paul Jacob, "Term Limits and the I & R Process," in Waters, ed., *Initiative and Referendum Almanac,* 505.

TABLE 6.1. *Term Limit States*

State	Initiative State	Congressional Limits (Year adopted)	Congressional Limits (House/Senate)	State Legislative Limits (Year adopted)	State Limits (lower/upper house)	State Limits Repealed by Legislature or Invalidated by Court
Alaska	x	1994	6/12	–	8/8	¥
Arizona	x	1992	6/12	1992	8/8	
Arkansas	x	1992	6/12	1992	6/8 (L)	
California	x	1992	6/12	1990	6/8 (L)	
Colorado	x	1990/94	6/12	1990	8/8	
Florida	x	1992	8/12	1992	8/8	
Idaho	x	1994	6/12	1994	8/8	*Repealed 2002*
Louisiana		–	–	1995^a	12/12	*Invalidated 1997*
Maine	x	1994	6/12	1993	8/8	
Massachusetts	x	1994	6/12	1994	8/8	
Michigan	x	1992	6/12	1992	6/8 (L)	
Missouri	x	1992	8/12	1992	8/8 (L)	
Montana	x	1992	6/12	1992	8/8	
Nebraska	x	1994/96	6/12	1994/96^c/00	8	
New Hampshire		1995^a	6/12	–	–	
Nevada	x	1994^d	6/12	1994/96	12/12 (L)	
North Dakota	x	1992	12/12	–	–	
Ohio	x	1992	8/12	1992	8/8	
Oklahoma	x	1994	6/12	1990	12 (total) (L)	*Invalidated 2002*
Oregon	x	1992	6/12	1992	6/8 (L)	
South Dakota	x	1992	12/12	1992	8/8	
Utah	x	1994^a	12/12	1994	12/12	*Repealed 2003*
Washington	x	1992	6/12	1992	6/8	*Invalidated 1998*
Wyoming	x	1992	6/12	1992	12/12^b	*Invalidated 2004*

All congressional term limits invalidated by the U.S. Supreme Court in *U.S. Term Limits v. Thornton* (1995).

¥ Alaska's state term limits initiative invalidated before the election, in *Alaskans for Legislative Reform v. State*, 887 P.2d 960 (Alaska 1994).

L = lifetime limit on state legislators.

a = adopted by legislature, not through initiative process.

b = Wyoming legislature amended citizen-enacted term limits extending limit in lower house from six to twelve years.

c = Nebraska's state term limits were twice invalidated by the Nebraska Supreme Court, but readopted in 2000. *Duggan v. Beermann*, 245 Neb. 907 (1994); *Duggan v. Beermann*, 249 Neb. 411 (1996).

d = Congressional term limits declared unconstitutional by U.S. Supreme Court before second vote required for adoption of Nevada initiatives.

Sources: Waters, ed., *Initiative and Referendum Almanac*, 507–508; Kousser, *Term Limits*, 12; National Conference of State Legislatures, "Legislative Term Limits: An Overview."

the Democrats' control of the House of Representatives, seized on term limits as the centerpiece of their "Contract with America." Led by House Minority Leader Newt Gingrich, Republican House candidates pledged to bring a term limits amendment to the floor for a vote within the first 100 days of the 104th Congress.[30] Resulting from, in part, their identification with this pledge, Republicans gained fifty-four House seats in the 1994 elections and won control of the House for the first time in four decades. But, after their sweeping victory, many Republican members lost their enthusiasm for the term limits principle.

The Republican leadership brought term limits amendments to the House floor in March 1995, but several influential members of the new majority, including Representative Henry Hyde (R-IL), steadfastly resisted them. Hyde reminded his colleagues of the importance of experience in office and urged them not to succumb to "the angry, pessimistic, populism that drives this movement."[31] The House rejected four separate term limits amendments: only one gained a bare majority and all fell far short of the two-thirds vote required for referral to the states for ratification.[32] The day after the vote, Republican strategist Bill Kristol said, "One reason there wasn't so much pressure yesterday is that the people of 22 states have already imposed term limits on their elected officials. The key issue is what the Supreme Court decides later this year."[33] And, indeed, many members of Congress looked to the Court to invalidate the voter-imposed limitations on their terms.

U.S. Term Limits v. Thornton. The case that would determine the validity of the congressional term limits measures, *U.S. Term Limits v. Thornton* (1995), originated in Arkansas.[34] In November 1992, voters in that state joined the term limits movement by adopting Amendment 73. Like term limits measures in several other states, the Arkansas initiative placed limits on elected members of the state executive branch, on members of the state legislature, and on the state's representatives in Congress.[35] Amendment 73 stated in its preamble: "[E]lected officials who remain in office too long become preoccupied with reelection and ignore their duties as representatives of the people. Entrenched incumbency

---

[30] "Republican Contract with America," http://www.house.gov/house/Contract/CONTRACT. html.

[31] Janet Hook, "House Votes Down Term Limits, Deals Setback to GOP Congress," *The Los Angeles Times* (March 30, 1995), A-1.

[32] Katharine Q. Seelye, "House Turns Back Measures to Limit Terms in Congress," *The New York Times* (March 30, 1995), A-1.

[33] "Term Limits: Full Scope of Defeat May Wait Until '96," *The Hotline* (March 30, 1995).

[34] *U.S. Term Limits, Inc. v. Thornton*, 514 U.S. 779 (1995).

[35] Amendment 73 imposed the following term limits: statewide office (8 years); state legislature (6/8 years); Congress (6/12 years). Arkansas Secretary of State, "Amendment 73. Arkansas Term Limitation Amendment," http://www.sos.arkansas.gov/ar-constitution/arcamend73/ arcamend73.htm. The amendment characterized the limits as ballot access restrictions, but it was clear that the provisions would effectively force incumbents from office.

has reduced voter participation and has led to an electoral system that is less free, less competitive, and less representative than the system established by the Founding Fathers. Therefore, the people of Arkansas, exercising their reserved powers, herein limit the terms of elected officials."[36] Voters approved the initiative by a 67 percent vote.

Shortly after the election, term limits opponents challenged the measure and two years later, the case, titled *U.S. Term Limits, Inc. v. Thornton*, reached the U.S. Supreme Court.[37] In May 1995, by a narrow 5-to-4 vote, the Court declared that state-imposed congressional term limits were unconstitutional.

Writing for the majority, Justice John Paul Stevens determined that congressional term limit laws sought to impose new qualifications for members of Congress. Article I of the Constitution provides short lists of qualifications for representatives and senators related to age, citizenship, and residency. The case's central question was whether these qualifications are exclusive or whether states may add additional qualifications. The Constitution does not expressly address the question, but the Court determined that a restrictive reading of the qualifications clauses can be inferred from the text and structure of the Constitution, the history surrounding its drafting and ratification, and the nature of the federal system.[38]

Consequently, the Court held that the only permissible way to establish congressional term limits was through a federal constitutional amendment. "[A]llowing the several States to adopt term limits for congressional service would effect a fundamental change in the constitutional framework," Justice Stevens wrote. "Any such change must come not by legislation adopted either by Congress or by an individual State, but rather – as have other important changes in the electoral process – through the amendment procedures set forth in Article V."[39]

The Court's decision provoked a vigorous and lengthy (eighty-eight page) dissent. Justice Clarence Thomas, joined by Chief Justice William Rehnquist and Justices Sandra Day O'Connor and Antonin Scalia, attacked the majority's interpretation of the constitutional text and history, as well as its view of the federal system. Asserting the priority of state citizenship over national citizenship, the dissenters contended that the people, acting through the states, have a reserved power, guaranteed by the Tenth Amendment, to impose term

---

[36] Ibid.

[37] *U.S. Term Limits, Inc. v. Thornton*, 779.

[38] U.S. Const. art. I, sec. 2 requires that representatives be at least 25 years old, a U.S. citizen for at least seven years, and an inhabitant of the state of election. Art. I, sec. 3 requires that senators be at least 30 years old, a U.S. citizen for at least nine years, and an inhabitant of the state of election.

[39] *U.S. Term Limits, Inc. v. Thornton*, 837. The Court further reasoned that allowing individual states to adopt term limits for congressional service would create a "patchwork" of qualifications that would undermine "the uniformity and national character that the Framers envisioned and sought to ensure." Ibid., 822.

limits on their respective members of Congress. The dissenters emphasized that the Constitution nowhere prevents states from establishing additional eligibility requirements for members of Congress. "The Constitution is simply silent on this question," the dissenters argued. "And where the Constitution is silent, it raises no bar to action by the States or the people."[40]

Justice Thomas further observed that "[i]t is ironic that the Court bases today's decision on the right of the people to 'choose whom they please to govern them' . . . by invalidating [a ballot initiative] that won nearly 60% of the votes cast in a direct election and that carried every congressional district in the State."[41]

By the narrowest of margins, however, the Court rejected these criticisms and declared that an institutional change of this order required a federal constitutional amendment. In defending the Congress against state-imposed term limits, the Court overturned laws adopted by 23 states – which in turn represented the votes of nearly 25 million citizens and a sizeable majority in nearly every state where voters were allowed to determine the question. *U.S. Term Limits v. Thornton* was thus demonstrably one of the most counter-majoritarian decisions in the Court's history.

Indeed, *U.S. Term Limits* merits recognition as one of the most consequential judicial decisions in U.S. history. If just one justice in the majority had voted the other way, term limits would have quickly taken effect on representatives from nearly half of the states, with countless unforeseeable consequences. And, even if these changes damaged the Congress, they would have been difficult to repeal on a state-by-state basis, especially at a time when antigovernment sentiments continued to run high. It was only through the Court's intervention – and only by a single vote – that Congress and the federal constitutional design were spared fundamental alteration through a process far removed from the Founders' expectations.

"Scarlet Letter" Initiatives

Although the Court's ruling in *U.S. Term Limits* was a mortal wound, activists sought to keep the congressional term limits movement alive – again, through the initiative process. In 1996 and 1998, activists qualified a wave of new initiatives instructing legislators to support a federal term limits amendment and threatening punishment if they failed to do so. In Colorado, for example, Amendment 12 (1996) directed the state's legislators and representatives in Congress to support a federal amendment limiting U.S. Senators to twelve years in office and House members to six. The measure instructed members of the state legislature to call for a federal constitutional convention to adopt this amendment and required Colorado's representatives in

---

40 Ibid.
41 Ibid.

Congress to perform a number of specific actions to secure the amendment's adoption.

The measure was called the "scarlet letter initiative," because of its punishment for those who failed to comply. Election officials were required to place the phrase "DISREGARDED VOTERS' INSTRUCTIONS ON TERM LIMITS" on future ballots next to the names of state legislators and members of Congress who failed to meet the initiative's demands.[42]

Scarlet letter initiatives won voter approval in ten states – Alaska, Arkansas, California, Colorado, Idaho, Maine, Missouri, Nebraska, Nevada, and South Dakota.[43] But in a flurry of litigation, state and federal courts invalidated them all. Most courts held that issuing instructions to representatives and threatening them with the "scarlet letter" violated the principles of the Article V amendment process.[44] The Colorado Supreme Court, for example, held that by instructing lawmakers "to proceed on a precise and inflexible course of action" the initiative violated "the strict language of Article V, which precludes state citizens from direct participation in the amendment process."[45]

After courts in several other states issued similar rulings, the U.S. Supreme Court struck down the last remaining scarlet letter initiatives. *In Cook v. Gralike* (2001), the Court ruled that the scarlet letter initiatives violated the states' authority under the U.S. Constitution's elections clause (Art. I, sec. 4, cl. 1) to regulate the time, manner, and place of federal elections. The court further held that the instructions impermissibly favored candidates who supported a particular term limits proposal. Writing for the majority, Justice Stevens observed that imposing binding instructions on federal representatives was inconsistent with the Constitution's theories of federalism, representation, and legislative deliberation.[46]

---

[42] In addition, the initiative instructed nonincumbent candidates for office to support this specific term limits amendment. If they failed to do so, the secretary of state would place the phrase "DECLINED TO SUPPORT TERM LIMITS" next to their names on the ballot. See Colorado Amendment 12 (1996).

[43] Waters, ed. *Initiative and Referendum Almanac*, 506–08.

[44] See, e.g., *Donovan v. Priest*, 326 Ark. 353 (1996) (invalidating Arkansas initiative on Article V grounds); *League of Women Voters of Maine v. Gwadosky*, 966 F.Supp. 52 (D. Me. 1997) (invalidating Maine initiative on Article V grounds); *Simpson v. Cenarrusa*, 130 Idaho 609 (1997) (invalidating Idaho initiative on speech or debate clause and state constitutional grounds); *Barker v. Hazeltine*, 3 F.Supp.2d 1088 (D. S.D. 1998) (invalidating South Dakota initiative on speech or debate clause, Article V, First Amendment and due process grounds); *Morrissey v. State*, 951 P.2d 911 (Colo. 1998) (invalidating Colorado initiative on guarantee clause and Article V grounds); and *Miller v. Moore*, 169 F.3d 1119 (8th Cir. 1999) (invalidating Nebraska initiative on right-to-vote and Article V grounds). In addition, the Oklahoma Supreme Court invalidated that state's scarlet letter initiative prior to the election on Article V and state constitutional grounds. *In re Initiative Petition No. 364*, 930 P.2d 186 (Okla. 1996).

[45] *Morrissey v. State*, 915. Although the court rested its decision on Article V, and declined to reach the question of whether Article IV, section 4 is justiciable, it observed that "[t]his coercion of legislators is itself inconsistent with Article IV, section 4." Ibid., 917.

[46] *Cook v. Gralike*, 531 U.S. 510 (2001).

Meanwhile, both the House of Representatives and the Senate held several more votes on term limits amendments, but none came close to the two-thirds needed to refer an amendment to the states. Although polls continued to show public support for term limits, by 1997 a Republican strategist conceded that "the intensity [for term limits] is gone. The anger is gone."[47]

Challenges to Term Limits on State Officials

Although the U.S. Supreme Court protected Congress from mandatory term limits, it did not similarly protect state legislatures. Defenders of these institutions were thus forced to bring separate state-by-state challenges. These cases raised several distinctive state constitutional questions, but the central issue was whether citizens could legitimately invoke the initiative power to make fundamental change to a state legislature. Cases in three of the top five initiative states – California, Washington, and Oregon – illustrated the range of state constitutional challenges to these measures.

California. The California legislature and allied petitioners brought the first challenge to a voter-approved term limits initiative in *Legislature v. Eu*, (1991).[48] This case presented several state constitutional claims, most importantly that Proposition 140 constituted an impermissible revision of the state constitution.[49] The definition of "revision" was crucial because in California, as we have noted, citizens may *amend* the constitution through the initiative process, but they may not *revise* it by direct vote. Revisions are considered to be more fundamental or comprehensive than amendments and may be adopted only with the legislature's participation.[50] According to the California Supreme Court, the distinction between amendment and revision is based on the premise that comprehensive changes to the constitution "require more formality, discussion, and deliberation than is available through the initiative process."[51]

Proposition 140's challengers alleged that the measure made such a drastic change to California's basic governmental plan that it violated the no-revision rule. Under "harsh term limits," they argued, "the Legislature will be unable

---

[47] Jill Lawrence, "Favorable Conditions Make Amendments Moot: Public Approves of GOP Goals, but 'Intensity is Gone,'" *USA Today* (Feb. 25, 1997), 6A.

[48] *Legislature v. Eu*, 492.

[49] The petitioners also argued that Proposition 140 violated the single-subject rule, impaired the obligation of contracts, and constituted an unlawful bill of attainder. The court rejected all of these theories except the contracts clause claim, and on that basis invalidated the measure's denial of pensions to incumbent legislators. Ibid., 532.

[50] CAL. CONST. art. II, sec. 8(a) provides that "[t]he initiative is the power of the electors to propose statutes and amendments to the Constitution and to adopt or reject them." By contrast, revisions to the California Constitution may be proposed in two ways, by a two thirds vote of both houses of the legislature, or by a constitutional convention called by the Legislature with the approval of the people. Any proposed revision must be ratified by a vote of the people. See CAL. CONST. art. XVIII.

[51] *Legislature v. Eu*, 506, citing *Raven v. Deukmejian*, 52 Cal.3d 336, 349–50 (1990).

to discharge its traditional duties as policymaker, keeper of the purse, and counterweight to the executive branch in the way the Constitution intends. The result is a change so profound in the structure of our government that it constitutes a revision."[52]

But, the California Supreme Court rejected this view. "Proposition 140 on its face does not affect either the structure or foundational powers of the Legislature, which remains free to enact whatever laws it deems appropriate," the court wrote. "The relationships between the three governmental branches, and their respective powers, remain untouched."[53]

Justice Stanley Mosk issued a pointed dissent, arguing that Proposition 140 was an impermissible revision because "the change that would be effected by Proposition 140 would be substantial. In the state's history, only two such changes have clearly been of this sort: the movement from a full-time Legislature with broad powers to a part-time body subject to narrow limitations, which was effected when the present constitution superseded the original instrument in 1879; and a movement in the opposite direction, which was accomplished under the successful proposal of the California Constitutional Revision Commission in 1966. The change here would be of similar magnitude."[54]

Washington. Opponents had more success in Washington. In *Gerberding v. Munro* (1998), the Washington Supreme Court invalidated citizen-imposed term limits on state officials.[55] The central issue in *Gerberding* was whether term limits may be adopted only by state constitutional amendment. The resolution of this issue was critical because Washington is one of six initiative states – including Alaska, Idaho, Maine, Utah, and Wyoming – that do not allow constitutional amendment through the initiative process. Declaring that legislative terms have constitutional status and may be changed only by constitutional amendment, the court invalidated the state's term limits initiative.[56]

Justice Richard Sanders objected that Washington voters should be allowed to impose term limits through the initiative process. "To strike down term limits because they interfere with our constitutional system is indeed anomalous as term limits are overtly a restraint on career politicians and serve as an indirect check on the legislative branch," Sanders wrote. "[Term limits] are specifically consistent with our citizens' historically populist mistrust of the legislature."[57] Sanders lamented that "[t]oday, 6 votes on this court are the undoing of the 1,119,985 votes that Washingtonians cast at the polls in favor of term limits."[58]

---

[52] Ibid., 507.
[53] Ibid., 509. Moreover, the court rejected the petitioners' claim that the initiative violated the state constitutional requirement that an initiative embrace only one subject, thus underscoring the California courts' liberal interpretation of the state's single-subject rule.
[54] Ibid., 543 (Mosk, J., dissenting).
[55] *Gerberding v. Munro*, 134 Wn.2d 188 (1998).
[56] Ibid., 211.
[57] Ibid., 228–29 (Sanders, J., dissenting).
[58] Ibid., 231.

As it turned out, the Washington court's logic prevailed in nearly every state where the issue arose. In Massachusetts, the Supreme Judicial Court held that term limits could only be imposed through a constitutional amendment.[59] Similarly, the Alaska Supreme Court ruled that voters could not enact term limits through an initiative statute.[60] And the Wyoming Supreme Court struck down that state's term limits initiative on similar grounds.[61] Only the supreme court of Maine took the opposite view, upholding a statutory initiative that imposed term limits on that state's elected officials.[62]

Oregon. The Oregon Supreme Court invalidated that state's term limits initiative on the grounds that it combined multiple amendments to the state constitution in a single initiative. Measure 3 of 1992, adopted by a 70 percent vote, had imposed term limits on Oregon's representatives in Congress as well as on the state's elected officials. After *U.S. Term Limits* invalidated Measure 3's limits on congressional terms, opponents challenged the surviving limits on state officials. In *Lehman v. Bradbury* (2002), the Oregon Supreme Court struck down these remaining provisions.[63] The *Lehman* case turned on whether Measure 3 complied with the Oregon court's new, strict interpretation of the state constitution's separate-vote requirement.[64] We will later examine more closely the court's controversial interpretation of this rule. Briefly stated, the issue in this case was whether state term limits and federal term limits were "separate amendments" and thus needed to be submitted to the voters as separate initiatives. Rejecting the contention that Measure 3 was "a cohesive combination of provisions" on a "discrete subject," the court held that it impermissibly contained multiple amendments and thus was void in its entirety.[65]

Term limits proponents were outraged by the *Lehman* decision. In their view, a hostile court had improperly enforced a technical rule to overturn the will of the people. Initiative activist Bill Sizemore said, "The overall decision is absurd and the basis for it is a complete fabrication on the part of the court.... They are simply making this law up."[66] But, the frustrated activists could not overcome this setback. By the time the Oregon Supreme Court issued its decision, support for term limits had dissipated and new initiatives to impose them failed.[67]

---

[59] *League of Women Voters v. Secretary of the Commonwealth*, 425 Mass. 424 (1997).
[60] *Alaskans for Legislative Reform v. State*, 887 P.2d 960 (Alaska 1994).
[61] *Cathcart v. Meyer*, 88 P.3d 1050 (Wy. 2004).
[62] *League of Women Voters v. Secretary of State*, 683 A.2d 769 (Me. 1996).
[63] *Lehman v. Bradbury*, 333 Ore. 231 (2002).
[64] ORE. CONST. art. XVII, sec. 1.
[65] *Lehman v. Bradbury*, 244, 248–49, 251.
[66] Ashbel S. Green and Lisa Grace Lednicer, "State High Court Strikes Term Limits," *The Oregonian* (January 17, 2002), A-1.
[67] In 2002, term limits activists mounted a petition drive to place a new term limits initiative on the Oregon ballot, but failed to gain the necessary signatures. In 2006, a new term limits initiative, Measure 45, qualified for the ballot, but was defeated 788,895 to 555,016.

The Judicial Check on Term Limits Initiatives

For over a decade, citizen lawmakers and courts engaged in conflict over the constitutional validity of term limits initiatives. Most importantly, courts invalidated all voter-approved initiatives that imposed term limits on members of Congress or that sought to coerce public officials to support adoption of a federal term limits amendment. The judicial defense of the federal constitutional design proved too strong for the term limits movement to overcome. However, judicial review of term limits on state officials produced more mixed results, with the outcome of challenges usually turning on whether citizens had adopted the measure through an ICA.

OTHER CONFLICTS OVER FEDERAL POWERS

Although the term limits movement provides the most dramatic example of direct democracy's threat to constitutional powers, other citizen-enacted laws have raised similar concerns. The balance of the chapter analyzes how courts have addressed these threats. We begin by examining a range of cases involving federal powers – specifically, the federal powers of state legislatures and the supremacy of federal over state law.

Federal Powers of State Legislatures

Article V. Under the U.S. Constitution's Article V application clause, state legislatures can collectively force Congress to call a federal constitutional convention. This clause, which has never been successfully invoked, provides that "Congress . . . on the Application of the Legislatures of two thirds of the several States, shall call a Convention for proposing Amendments."[68]

Citizens have occasionally attempted to insert themselves directly into the Article V application process, but courts have prevented them from doing so. A notable example occurred in the early 1980s, when citizens engaged a movement to promote a federal balanced budget amendment. Unable to win sufficient support in Congress, the movement turned to the Article V application procedure. Thirty-two legislatures supported the call for a constitutional convention, just two short of the required number. The remaining legislatures balked, however, and proponents invoked the initiative process to force action by two holdout states. Activists qualified initiatives in California and Montana instructing legislatures in these states to make the necessary applications. The measures threatened lawmakers with loss of pay and other sanctions if they failed to act and, if necessary, instructed the respective secretaries of state to submit applications to Congress directly on behalf of the people.[69]

---

[68] U.S. Const. art. V.
[69] See California Proposition 35 of 1984; Montana Constitutional Initiative No. 23 of 1984.

However, courts in these states struck the measures from the ballot. The California Supreme Court declared that the proposed initiative violated the Article V application clause procedure. "Article V provides for applications by the 'Legislatures of two-thirds the several States,' not by the people through the initiative," the court held. "[I]t envisions legislators free to vote their best judgment, responsible to their constituents through the electoral process, not puppet legislators coerced or compelled by loss of salary or otherwise to vote in favor of a proposal they may believe unwise."[70] The Montana court reached a similar conclusion.[71] As a consequence, the balanced budget movement stalled and never reached the necessary thirty-four-state threshold.

In this episode, as well as in the later "scarlet letter," congressional term limits cases, courts prevented citizens from forcing Congress to call a federal constitutional convention. These outcomes complemented earlier decisions that prevented direct citizen action at the Article V ratification stage.[72] Courts have thus steadfastly preserved legislatures' powers at both ends of the federal constitutional amendment process.

Electoral College. A related question is whether courts will allow citizen lawmakers to modify a state's rules for allocating presidential electors. Article II, section 1 of the Constitution provides that "[e]ach State shall appoint, in such Manner as the Legislature thereof may direct, a Number of Electors, equal to the whole Number of Senators and Representatives to which the State may be entitled in the Congress."[73]

Although the Electoral College has many detractors, the rigors of the Article V amendment process have protected it from abolition. In recent years, activists have promoted various ideas for modifying the presidential election system without having to resort to Article V. Under one scheme, states would enter a compact to award the presidency to the candidate who wins the national popular vote. The agreement would require electors to cast their votes for the national popular vote winner, even if that candidate lost the popular vote in

---

[70] *AFL-CIO v. Eu*, 36 Cal.3d 687, 694 (1984). Proponents of the California measure appealed to the U.S. Supreme Court to stay the California Supreme Court's ruling, but Justice Rehnquist denied the application. Although Rehnquist wrote that interpretation of the term "Legislatures" in the Article V application clause remained unsettled, the initiative was also invalidated on independent state grounds, and thus was not appropriate for Supreme Court review. *Uhler v. AFL-CIO*, 468 U.S. 1310, 1311 (1984).

[71] *State of Montana, ex rel., Harper v. Waltermire*, 213 Mont. 425 (1984).

[72] See, e.g., *Hawke v. Smith*, 221.

[73] Two amendments have modified the Electoral College: Amendment XII (distinct votes for president and vice president) and Amendment XXIII (electoral votes for the District of Columbia). Over 1,000 other proposed constitutional amendments to change the presidential selection process have failed. See Donald S. Lutz, "The Electoral College in Historical and Philosophical Perspective" in Paul D. Schumaker and Burdett A Loomis, eds., *Choosing a President: The Electoral College and Beyond* (New York: Chatham House Publishers/Seven Bridges Press, 2002), 45–46.

their state.[74] Proponents of this plan have considered pursuing it through the initiative process in some states.[75]

Other activists have used the initiative process to seek to change rules for allocation of electoral votes in individual states. In 2004, for example, Democrats in Colorado qualified Amendment 36, an initiative that would have divided the state's nine electoral votes based on the candidate's share of the statewide popular vote. Voters defeated the measure, but other such proposals will likely arise.[76] Any changes enacted through the initiative process will certainly face court challenges on the ground that only legislatures, not citizens, may determine a state's rules for selecting presidential electors.[77]

Federal Supremacy Over State Laws

Meanwhile, several voter-approved initiatives have been challenged and invalidated on the basis that they were preempted by federal law. The supremacy clause of Article VI declares that "[t]his Constitution, and the Laws of the United States which shall be made in Pursuance thereof; and all Treaties made, or which shall be made, under the Authority of the United States, shall be the supreme Law of the Land; and the Judges in every State shall be bound

---

[74] The proposal for an interstate compact was first developed by Northwestern University law professor Robert W. Bennett and then advanced by the Amar brothers. See Robert W. Bennett, "Popular Election of the President without a Constitutional Amendment," 4 GREEN BAG 2d 241 (2001); Akhil Reed Amar and Vikram David Amar, "How to Achieve Direct National Election of the President without Amending the Constitution," Findlaw, Dec. 28, 2001, http://writ.news.findlaw.com/amar/20011228.html. For a discussion, see Stanley Chang, "Updating the Electoral College: The National Popular Vote Legislation," 44 HARV. J ON LEGIS. 205, 210–29 (2007).

[75] In California, for example, the legislature adopted the interstate compact plan in 2006, but Governor Arnold Schwarzenegger vetoed the bill. See California Assembly Bill 2948 (2006). Activists later turned to the initiative process. See "Letter from Tom Steyer to Patricia Galvan, Initiative Coordinator, Office of the Attorney General of the State of California, August 20, 2007" available at http://ag.ca.gov/cms_attachments/initiatives/pdfs/2007-08-21_07-0048_Initiative.pdf. For the activists' view of the national popular vote movement, see John R. Koza, Barry Fadem, Mark Grueskin, Michael S. Mandell, Robert Richie, and Joseph Zimmerman, *Every Vote Equal: A State-Based Plan for Electing the President by National Popular Vote* (Los Altos, CA: National Popular Vote Press, 2006).

[76] See Kirk Johnson, "Coloradans to Consider Splitting Electoral College Votes," *The New York Times* (September 19, 2004), A-22. All but two states allocate their electoral votes to presidential candidates on a winner-take-all basis. Nebraska and Maine award one electoral vote for the presidential vote winner in each congressional district, with the remaining two votes going to the winner of the statewide presidential vote. In the 2008 election cycle, Republican activists in California floated a proposed initiative requiring the state to switch to the Nebraska-Maine system, but the measure failed to reach the ballot.

[77] For similar reasons, Alaska Proposition 4 of 2004 could be vulnerable to constitutional challenge. Through this initiative, citizens of Alaska changed the rules for filling a U.S. Senate seat in the event of a vacancy. The initiative arguably usurps the legislature's powers under the Seventeenth Amendment.

thereby, any Thing in the Constitution or the Laws in any State notwithstanding."[78]

Numerous voter-approved initiatives have conflicted with this clause.[79] Measures seeking to reshape immigration and drug policies are perhaps the most notable examples.[80]

Immigration. When they adopted Proposition 187 in 1994, California voters asserted themselves in immigration policy, an area of federal responsibility. Voters believed that both federal and state officials had failed to meet their obligation to enforce federal immigration laws. The ballot argument in favor of Proposition 187 hammered on this point:

"If the citizens and the taxpayers of our state wait for the politicians in Washington and Sacramento to stop the incredible flow of ILLEGAL ALIENS, California will be in economic and social bankruptcy. We have to ACT NOW! On our ballot, Proposition 187 will be the first giant stride in actually ending the ILLEGAL ALIEN invasion. The federal government and the state government have been derelict in their duty to control our borders.... Vote YES ON PROPOSITION 187. ENOUGH IS ENOUGH!"[81]

By its terms, Proposition 187 sought to restrict illegal immigration into California by requiring public employees to verify the immigration status of persons with whom they come in contact, to report suspected illegal immigrants to state and federal officials, and to deny those persons state-funded social services, health care, and education.[82]

Opponents argued, however, that these citizen-enacted regulations not only violated rights, but also were preempted by federal immigration law. And, indeed, federal Judge Mariana R. Pfaelzer enjoined enforcement of the measure

---

[78] U.S. Const. art. VI, sec. 2.
[79] A number of initiatives have petitioned the federal government to change federal policy. During the 1980s, for example, voters adopted several statewide initiatives demanding a bilateral nuclear freeze between the United States and the Soviet Union. The Reagan Administration denounced this and other nuclear freeze initiatives, but because the measures were nonbinding, they never faced legal challenge. See also *National Audubon Society v. Davis*, 307 F.3d 835 (9th Cir. 2002); (declaring California Proposition 4 of 1998; which banned certain animal traps, preempted in part by federal law); and *U.S. v. Hunt*, 19 F.2d 634 (D. Ariz. 1927) (declaring Arizona Proposition 306 of 1916, which imposed restrictions on hunting and fishing, invalid as applied to federal lands), modified by *Hunt v. United States*, 278 U.S. 96 (1928).
[80] An example from another policy area is Washington Initiative 383 of 1980, a measure that banned the importation and storage of radioactive wastes generated outside the state. The measure directly conflicted with federal laws, including the federal *Atomic Energy Act*, the *Low-Level Radioactive Waste Policy Act*, and the *Hazardous Waste Materials Transportation Act*. I-383 was quickly challenged and invalidated on the grounds that it violated the federal supremacy and commerce clauses. *Washington State Building and Construction Trades Council, AFL-CIO v. Spellman*, 684 F.2d 627 (9th Cir. 1982).
[81] Dick Mountjoy, Ronald Prince, and Barbara Kiley, "Argument in Favor of Proposition 187," California Secretary of State, *California Ballot Pamphlet, General Election, November 8, 1994*, 54.
[82] California Proposition 187 (1994).

largely on federal preemption grounds. In *League of United Latin American Citizens v. Wilson* (1995), Judge Pfaelzer held that Proposition 187's verification, notification, and reporting requirements "[were] aimed solely at regulating immigration" and were preempted by the federal government's delegated power to regulate immigration and naturalization.[83] In addition, the judge held that federal law preempted most of the measure's provisions denying public benefits to illegal immigrants.[84]

In her ruling, Judge Pfaelzer observed that "California voters' overwhelming approval of Proposition 187 reflects their justifiable frustration with the federal government's inability to enforce the immigration laws effectively." However, she noted that "the authority to regulate immigration belongs exclusively to the federal government and state agencies are not permitted to assume that authority. The State is powerless to enact its own scheme to regulate immigration or to devise immigration regulations which run parallel to or purport to supplement the federal immigration laws."[85]

In 1996, although the Proposition 187 litigation was still pending, Congress enacted landmark federal welfare and immigration reform legislation.[86] Among other provisions, these acts made legal immigration status a condition for the receipt of public benefits, with limited exceptions such as for emergency medical care.[87] After Congress enacted these laws, Judge Pfaelzer held that the federal government had now fully preempted the issue of alien eligibility for public benefits and she entered a final order enjoining enforcement of almost all provisions of Proposition 187.[88] Thus, whereas Proposition 187 put illegal immigration on the national agenda and spurred congressional action, the court prevented voters from directly enacting policy in an area of federal responsibility.

Marijuana. Another high-profile conflict between initiative power and federal authority emerged over the regulation of marijuana. In 1970, President Richard Nixon launched the federal "War on Drugs" by signing the Comprehensive Drug Abuse Prevention and Control Act, which is now called the "Controlled Substances Act." Among other restrictions, the 1970 statute for the first time

---

[83] *League of United Latin American Citizens v. Wilson*, 908 F.Supp. 755, 771 (C.D. Cal. 1995).

[84] Ibid., 771–86. The court held that the state could not deny illegal aliens benefits from programs supported by federal funds.

[85] Ibid., 786.

[86] *Personal Responsibility and Work Opportunity Act of 1996*, 110 Stat. 2105 (Sections 400–51); *Illegal Immigration Reform and Responsibility Act of 1996*, 110 Stat. 3009 (Sections 501–05).

[87] Ibid.

[88] *League of United Latin American Citizens v. Wilson*, 997 F.Supp. 1244 (C.D. Cal. 1997); *League of United Latin American Citizens v. Wilson*, 1998 WL 141325 (C.D. Cal. 1998). As noted in Chapter 5, Governor Gray Davis brought an end to five years of litigation over the validity of Proposition 187 by agreeing to a mediated settlement that essentially adopted the district court's ruling. See "Federal Judge Issues Final Ruling on Immigrant Initiative," Associated Press State and Local Wire (September 13, 1999).

made possession of marijuana a federal crime.[89] The Act listed marijuana as a "Schedule I" controlled substance, a designation reserved for drugs that have "high potential for abuse," have no "currently accepted medical use in treatment in the United States," and lack "accepted safety for use . . . under medical supervision."[90] Despite sustained efforts, activists have failed to persuade Congress to change this designation.[91]

Frustrated in the federal arena, activists turned to the initiative process to liberalize state-level restrictions on marijuana. California voters adopted the first of these initiatives, Proposition 215, in 1996. This measure provided that California's drug control laws "shall not apply to a patient, or to a patient's primary caregiver, who possesses or cultivates marijuana for the personal medical purposes of the patient upon the written or oral recommendation or approval of a physician."[92] By 2008, voters in nine other states had adopted similar initiatives.[93]

Medical marijuana initiatives clearly conflicted with the federal war on drugs and, more specifically, the Controlled Substances Act. Litigation predictably ensued. Two of the cases, *United States v. Oakland Cannabis Buyers' Cooperative (2001)* and *Gonzales v. Raich* (2005), eventually reached the U.S. Supreme Court.[94]

The first case arose when federal agents sought court orders enjoining cannabis clubs in California from manufacturing and distributing marijuana. The federal government did not ask the courts to invalidate Proposition 215, but only to enforce the federal restrictions. After a federal judge in Northern California granted a preliminary injunction against the marijuana distributors, the U.S. Supreme Court affirmed.[95]

The tension between state and federal policy persisted, however, as California law enforcement officials continued to observe the medical exemptions of Proposition 215, whereas federal agencies insisted that any possession or distribution of marijuana violated federal law. The next major skirmish arose in *Raich* when local officials in California determined that Angel Raich and Diane Monson were authorized by Proposition 215 to cultivate cannabis plants, but federal officials seized and destroyed the plants. This case again did not focus

---

[89] 28 U.S.C. 841(a)(1) of the Act made it a federal crime to "manufacture, distribute, or dispense, or possess with intent to manufacture, distribute, or dispense, a controlled substance."

[90] 28 U.S.C. 812(b)(1).

[91] See K.K. DuVivier, "State Ballot Initiatives in the Federal Preemption Equation: A Medical Marijuana Case Study," 40 WAKE FOREST L. REV. 221, 281–83 (2005).

[92] California Proposition 215 of 1996.

[93] Between 1996 and 2008, voters in Alaska, Arizona, California, Colorado, Maine, Michigan, Montana, Nevada, Oregon, and Washington adopted medical marijuana initiatives. Legislatures in a few other states (Hawaii, New Mexico, Rhode Island, and Vermont) adopted similar measures. See *Gonzales v. Raich*, 545 U.S. 1, 5 (2005). In 2008, voters in Massachusetts adopted an initiative decriminalizing possession of one ounce or less of marijuana.

[94] *United States v. Oakland Cannabis Buyers' Cooperative*, 532 U.S. 483 (2001).

[95] Ibid., 499. See also *United States v. Cannabis Cultivators Club*, 5 F.Supp.2d 1086, 1105 (N.D. Cal. 1998).

on the validity of Proposition 215, but rather on the enforceability of the federal drug laws. The U.S. Supreme Court held that the Article I commerce clause gave Congress the necessary authority to prohibit the cultivation and personal use of marijuana.[96] Although the Court did not invalidate medical marijuana initiatives, it preserved the power of federal agencies to override these policies and enforce federal drug laws.[97]

The outcomes of federal preemption cases are more complex than the cases striking down congressional term limits, but, in both contexts, courts have prevented citizen initiatives from encroaching on federal powers.

OTHER CONFLICTS OVER STATE POWERS

Courts have less reliably countered direct democracy's threat to the institutional powers of state government. A number of factors explain the comparative weakness of this protection.

Limits of Federal Constitutional Protection

Aside from its protection of the *federal* powers of state legislatures, the U.S. Constitution provides virtually no protection to state legislatures or other state institutions when they are threatened by direct democracy. Courts could conceivably use the federal Article IV guarantee clause to guard the powers of state-level republican institutions, but, as we have seen, they have consistently determined that the clause is non-justiciable. No other federal constitutional provision offers comparable protection.

Limits of State Constitutional Protection

Moreover, state constitutions offer state institutions only limited defenses against ICAs. This is because, once properly adopted, ICAs become part of the state constitution and are thus protected against state constitutional challenge. Two California initiatives – Proposition 24 of 1984 and Proposition 140 of 1990 – further illustrate the practical difference between constitutional and statutory initiatives.

Proposition 24 was a statutory initiative that established internal rules for the state legislature. Among other provisions, it imposed new procedures for selecting legislative leaders and for determining the membership and powers of legislative committees. The measure also cut the legislature's budget by 30 percent. However, after voters approved the measure, state Superior Court Judge James Ford declared it void on the basis that it conflicted with the

---

[96] *Gonzales v. Raich*, 545 U.S. 1, 33.

[97] By comparison, the Supreme Court has held that the federal government may not invoke the Controlled Substances Act to override Oregon's voter-adopted, physician-assisted suicide law, Measure 16 of 1994. See *Gonzales v. Oregon*, 546 U.S. 243 (2006).

provision of the California Constitution that "[e]ach House shall determine the rules of its own proceedings."[98]

After handing down his decision, Judge Ford suggested that the case was straightforward because statutes are subordinate to constitutions. "[I]t really comes down to the Constitution of this state," he said. "We are governed by that document."[99] Clearly, however, this rationale would have collapsed if California voters had adopted Proposition 24's restrictions through an ICA rather than through a statutory initiative.

Activists learned the lesson. Six years later, they qualified Proposition 140, the initiative that imposed term limits and other restrictions on the legislature, as an ICA. Unlike Proposition 24, Proposition 140 largely survived post-election challenges. These different outcomes demonstrate again why citizen lawmakers often prefer to present their proposals as ICAs rather than as statutory initiatives.

Limits of Judicial Review

Most fundamentally, the courts' ability to defend the powers of representative government against citizen initiatives is limited by the nature of judicial review. Judges do not sit on a Council of Revision with plenary power to veto legislation. Instead, their power is designed to be more modest. Courts may legitimately judge a law's constitutionality, but not its wisdom. As the founder James Wilson anticipated, courts are sometimes obliged to uphold laws they consider dangerous and destructive, but "[not so] unconstitutional as to justify the judges in refusing to give them effect."[100]

New Judicial Attempts to Constrain the Initiative Power

After 1970, a number of judges despaired at the growing impact of the initiative power. California Supreme Court Justice Stanley Mosk declared that "the initiative process is out of control," and some judges in other states shared his

---

[98] *People's Advocate, Inc. v. California Legislature*, No. 324211 (Sacramento Superior Court, December 11, 1984), holding that Proposition 24 conflicts with CAL. CONST. art. IV, sec. 7(a); affirmed by *People's Advocate, Inc. v. Superior Court*, 181 Cal.App.3d 316, 325, 327 (1986). By comparison, see *Cole v. State of Colorado*, 673 P.2d 345 (Colo. 1983). In that case, the Colorado Supreme Court upheld Amendment 9 of 1972, a statutory initiative that, among other provisions, subjected legislative caucus meetings to the state's open meetings laws. An important distinction between the two measures is that the California initiative imposed a wider range of procedural rules on the state legislature.

[99] James E. Castello, "Comment: The Limits of Popular Sovereignty: Using the Initiative Power to Control Legislative Procedure," 74 CAL. L. REV. 491, 493 (1986).

[100] James Wilson (July 21, 1787), quoted in Elliot, ed., *Debates on the Federal Constitution, Vol. V*, 344. See also James B. Thayer, "The Origins and Scope of the American Doctrine of Constitutional Law," 7 HARV. L. REV 129, 140–41.

sentiments.[101] A number of them concluded that new interpretations of state constitutional law were needed to constrain citizen lawmaking. They explored several options, including the "no-revision rule," the "single-subject rule," and the "separate-vote requirement."

No-Revision Rule

One option was for courts to expand the definition of "revision." As we have seen, if a court characterizes a state constitutional change as a revision rather than an amendment, it bars citizens from making the change unilaterally through the initiative process. Instead, the change requires the participation and consent of both the legislature and the people.[102] The amendment-revision distinction is a matter of judicial interpretation and courts could choose to enforce the no-revision rule more aggressively.[103] In California, initiative opponents have repeatedly urged the state supreme court to give teeth to the rule, but it has rarely done so. In important tests, the court declined to hold that initiatives restoring capital punishment, restricting state taxing power, or limiting the terms of state legislators so fundamentally changed the state constitutional design that they were revisory rather than amendatory.[104] The court did invoke the no-revision rule in 1948, to remove a 21,000-word omnibus initiative from the statewide ballot and again, in 1990, to invalidate an initiative provision that stripped the courts of the power to interpret state constitutional rights beyond federal minimums.[105] But, these two decisions long remained isolated examples.

Nevertheless, proponents of same-sex marriage based their challenge to Proposition 8 on the no-revision rule. The petitioners argued that Proposition 8 "would constitute a revision of the California Constitution because it alters underlying principles on which the California Constitution is based and makes far-reaching changes to the basic governmental plan by severely compromising the core constitutional principle of equal protection of the laws,

---

[101] *Legislature v. Eu*, 54 Cal.3d 492, 536 (1991) Mosk, J., dissenting, citing "Note: Putting the 'Single' Back in the Single Subject Rule: A Proposal for Initiative Reform in California," 24 U.C. DAVIS L. REV. 879, 929 (1991).

[102] CAL. CONST art. XVIII, secs. 1–3.

[103] See Legislature v. Eu, 542–544, Mosk, J. dissenting.

[104] See *People v. Frierson*, 25 Cal.3d 142 (1979), upholding Proposition 17 of 1972; *Amador Valley*, 22 Cal.3d 208 (1978), upholding Proposition 13 of 1978; *Legislature v. Eu*, 54 Cal. 3d 492 (1991), upholding Proposition 140 of 1990.

[105] See *McFadden v. Jordan*, 32 Cal.2d 330, 331–51 (1948), invalidating before the election a measure known as "Ham and Eggs" on the basis that it would have revised rather than amended the California Constitution. This measure sought to add dozens of new provisions to the state constitution, including provisions regarding election law, regulation of surface mining, the provision of retirement pensions, and the sale of oleomargarine. The measure prompted California to adopt a single-subject rule for initiatives in 1948. See also *Raven v. Deukmejian*, 52 Cal.3d 336 (1990), invalidating in part Proposition 115 of 1990 as an unconstitutional revision.

depriving a vulnerable minority of fundamental rights, inscribing discrimination based on a suspect classification into the Constitution, and destroying the courts' quintessential power and role of protecting minorities and enforcing the guarantee of equal protection under the law."[106]

The parties defending Proposition 8 countered that the California initiative power is broad and includes the power "to establish California's fundamental public policy in every area of the law. That power includes the authority to define – and thus expand or contract – the fundamental constitutional rights of particular classes of people."[107] They further noted that courts in Oregon and Alaska had recently rejected challenges to marriage amendments based on those states' no-revision rules.[108]

In *Strauss v. Horton*, (2009), the California Supreme Court declined to invoke the rule. The court concluded that "the constitutional change embodied in proposition 8 – although without question of great importance to the affected individuals – by no means makes such a far-reaching change in the California constitution as to amount to a constitutional revision."[109].

Single-Subject Rule

By contrast, courts in several states have increasingly used the single-subject rule to constrain citizen lawmaking. As the Florida example demonstrates, strict judicial enforcement of the single-subject rule can severely constrain the initiative power. Three-fourths of the initiative states have a version of the single-subject rule.[110] Many are similar to the Colorado version, which states:

---

[106] *Strauss v. Horton*, Case No. S168047, "Amended Petition for Extraordinary Relief, Including Writ of Mandate and Request for Immediate Injunctive Relief; Memorandum of Points and Authorities," November 5, 2008, 8, http://www.courtinfo.ca.gov/courts/supreme/highprofile/documents/s168078-amendedpetitionforextraordinaryrelief.pdf.

[107] *Strauss v. Horton*, Case No. S168047, "Preliminary Opposition of Proposed Intervenor Real Parties in Interest to Amended Petition for Extraordinary Relief Including Writ of Mandate and Request for Immediate Injunctive Relief," November 17, 2008, 9, http://www.courtinfo.ca.gov/courts/supreme/highprofile/documents/s168078-preliminary-opposition.pdf. See Maura Dolan and Tami Abdollah, "Gay Rights Backers File 3 Suits Challenging Prop. 8," *Los Angeles Times*, November 6, 2008.

[108] *Martinez v. Kulongoski*, 220 Ore.App. 142 (2008), *Bess v. Ulmer*, 985 P.2d 979 (Alaska, 1999).

[109] *Strauss v. Horton*, California Supreme Court Case No. 5168047 (2009).

[110] Anne G. Campbell, "In the Eye of the Beholder: The Single Subject Rule for Ballot Initiatives," in M. Dane Waters, ed., *The Battle Over Citizen Lawmaking: An In-Depth Review of the Growing Trend to Regulate the People's Tool of Self-Government: The Initiative and Referendum Process*. (Durham: Carolina Academic Press, 2001), 137–38. Campbell lists eighteen initiative states as either imposing a single-subject rule for initiatives or "probably" doing so. In six states – Idaho, Illinois, Montana, Nevada, Oklahoma, and Washington – the state constitution does not explicitly impose a single-subject requirement for initiatives, but either the state supreme court or the attorney general has determined that the rule is implied. Ibid., 138.

"If a measure contains more than one subject, . . . [it] shall not be submitted to the people for adoption or rejection at the polls."[111]

A standard explanation for the single-subject rule is that it limits "logrolling," which the Washington Supreme Court defined as "pushing legislation through by attaching it to other legislation."[112] The rule is also said to prevent deceptive measures and reduce voter confusion.[113] But, as UCLA law professor Daniel H. Lowenstein noted over two decades ago, the malleability of the term "subject" also makes the rule a potentially severe constraint on the initiative power. "The language of the single-subject rule . . . permits an interpretation that would abolish the initiative process altogether," Lowenstein warned. "That is, it is impossible to conceive of a measure that could not be broken down into parts, which could in turn be regarded as separate subjects."[114]

As a consequence of the rule's "malleability," courts possess wide discretion in interpreting and enforcing it. For most of the initiative era, courts generally opted for a liberal interpretation of the rule, rarely, if ever, using it to invalidate an initiative. The California Supreme Court provided a model. In *Perry v. Jordan* (1949), the court reversed a lower court ruling that struck an initiative from the ballot on the grounds that it violated the state's newly enacted single-subject rule for initiatives. The court announced that the test was whether the provisions of the initiative were "reasonably germane" to one another and to the general object of the initiative, the same standard the court had applied to interpreting the single-subject rule for legislative acts.[115]

Many initiative opponents have argued that courts should adopt a more exacting standard. In the 1980s, a vocal minority of the California Supreme Court, including Justice Mosk and Chief Justice Rose Bird, urged their colleagues to require all provisions of an initiative be "functionally related in furtherance of a common underlying purpose."[116] But, the court's majority never wavered from the more liberal germaneness test. Indeed, until 1999, the California Supreme Court never struck down a statewide initiative on single-subject grounds.[117] To the contrary, it rejected single-subject attacks against

---

[111] Colo. Const. art. V, sec. 1 (5.5).

[112] *Amalgamated Transit Union Local 587 v. State of Washington*, 142 Wash.2d 183, 207 (2000).

[113] For further discussion of the purposes other state courts have assigned to single-subject provisions, see Campbell, "In the Eye of the Beholder," 133–36.

[114] Daniel H. Lowenstein, "California Initiatives and the Single-Subject Rule," 30 U.C.L.A. L. Rev. 936, 942 (1983).

[115] *Perry v. Jordan*, 34 Cal.2d 87, 92 (1949).

[116] The "functional relationship" test was first advanced by Justice Wiley W. Manuel in *Schmitz v. Younger*, 21 Cal.3d 90, 97 (1978) (Manuel, J., dissenting).

[117] See *Senate of the State of California v. Jones*, 21 Cal.4th 1142, 1170 (1999), striking down, before the election, Proposition 24 on the grounds that its provisions were not reasonably germane. In addition, California appellate courts invalidated other initiatives on single-subject grounds. See *Chemical Specialties Manufacturers Association, Inc. v. Deukmejian*, 278 Cal.Rptr. 128 (1991) (invalidating California Proposition 105 of 1988, "The Public's Right to Know Act") and *California Trial Lawyers Association v. Eu*, 245 Cal.Rptr. 916 (1988),

numerous initiatives that contained multiple, loosely related elements. In one case, the court declared that "[a]lthough the initiative measure before us is wordy and complex, there is little reason to expect that claimed voter confusion could be eliminated or substantially reduced by dividing the measure into four or ten separate propositions. Our society being complex, the rules governing... [the] initiative will necessarily be complex. Unless we are to repudiate or cripple use of the initiative, risk of confusion must be borne."[118]

Courts in several other states, however, have used the single-subject rule to invalidate many initiatives, either before or after the election. The Florida Supreme Court is the leading example, but courts in other states have also aggressively enforced the rule. The Colorado Supreme Court has strictly enforced that state's single-subject rule ever since its adoption in 1994. The Colorado court has determined it will review initiatives for compliance with the rule prior to the election and require the subject matter of the initiative to be "necessarily or properly connected" and have a "unifying or common objective."[119] In practice, the court has used this strict standard to prevent many initiatives from reaching the Colorado ballot, much to the frustration of initiative activists in that state.[120]

The Washington Supreme Court invoked the state's single-subject rule to invalidate an initiative for the first time in 2000 when it struck down Initiative 695, a controversial tax limitation measure. I-695 sought to reduce vehicle license fees to thirty dollars and to require voter approval for future increases in taxes and fees. When opponents of the initiative challenged it after the election, its sponsors argued that all the provisions of I-695 were rationally related to the general subject of limiting taxation. But, the court rejected that view and invalidated the initiative.[121] In dissent, Justice Richard Sanders argued that the court's new strict enforcement of the rule placed a new and excessive constraint on citizens' power to enact law.[122]

Separate-Vote Requirement

Finally, some state courts have started strictly enforcing the separate-vote requirement to restrict the power of ICAs. The Oregon version of the separate-vote requirement (also known as the "one amendment rule") states that

striking down prior to the election a tort reform initiative). For further discussion, see Gerald F. Uelmen, "Handling Hot Potatoes: Judicial Review of California Initiatives After *Senate v. Jones*," 41 SANTA CLARA L. REV. 999 (2001).

[118] *Fair Political Practices Commission v. Superior Court*, 25 Cal.3d 33, 41–2 (1979).

[119] The Colorado Supreme Court announced this standard in *In re Title "Public Rights in Waters II*," 898 P.2d 1076, 1079–80 (Colo. 1995).

[120] Campbell, "In the Eye of the Beholder," 158–59. Some initiative proponents in Colorado were convinced that the state applied the single-subject rule in a manner that discriminated on the basis of the content of the initiative. They raised this claim in federal court, but the Tenth Circuit was not persuaded. *Campbell v. Buckley*, 203 F.3d 738, 746–747 (10th Cir. 2000).

[121] *Amalgamated Transit Union Local 587 v. State of Washington*, 142 Wn. 2d 83 (2000).

[122] Ibid, 264–65 (Sanders, J., dissenting).

"[w]hen two or more amendments shall be submitted . . . to the voters of this state at the same election, they shall be so submitted that each amendment shall be voted on separately."[123] The Oregon Supreme Court sparked intense controversy when, in *Armatta v. Kitzhaber* (1998), it invoked the state's separate-vote requirement to invalidate a victims' rights initiative, Measure 40 of 1996.[124] Measure 40's multiple provisions were all related to the criminal justice system and thus appeared to satisfy the court's interpretation of the state's single-subject rule. But, when opponents challenged the measure after the election, the court held that it failed to satisfy the separate-vote requirement. The court announced that the separate-vote requirement is a "narrower restriction than the requirement that a proposed amendment embrace only one subject."[125]

Through *Armatta*, the Oregon Supreme Court raised a significant new barrier to ICAs in that state and thus sharpened the distinction between ICAs and initiative statutes. As Professor Richard Ellis has observed, *Armatta* "creates an incentive for initiative sponsors to craft initiatives as statutory changes, where the hurdle will be a lenient single subject rule, rather than as constitutional amendments, where they will face a more exacting 'separate vote' requirement."[126] The Oregon court quickly reinforced the new doctrine by striking down on separate-vote grounds Measure 62 of 1998 (campaign finance reform); Measure 7 of 2000 (compensation for regulatory takings); and, perhaps most consequentially, Measure 3 of 1992 (term limits on elected officials).[127]

Shortly after *Armatta*, the Montana Supreme Court followed Oregon's lead. In *Marshall v. State ex rel. Cooney* (1999), the Montana court invalidated Constitutional Initiative 75 of 1998, a voter-approved initiative requiring voter approval for tax increases, on the basis that the measure violated the Montana Constitution's separate-vote requirement.[128] This ruling marked a sharp departure from the court's former liberal interpretation of the separate-vote requirement originally set forth in 1914.[129]

---

[123] ORE. CONST. art. XVII, sec. 1.

[124] *Armatta v. Kitzhaber*, 327 Ore. 250 (1998).

[125] Ibid., 277. For a defense of the court's rationale in *Armatta*, see Richard J. Ellis, *Democratic Delusions: The Initiative Process in America* (Lawrence: University Press of Kansas, 2002), 145–147.

[126] Ibid., 146.

[127] See *Swett v. Bradbury*, 333 Ore. 597 (2002) (invalidating Measure 62 of 1998, a campaign finance ICA); *League of Oregon Cities v. Oregon; McCall v. Kitzhaber*, 334 Ore. 645 (2002) (invalidating Measure 7 of 2000, an ICA requiring government payment to landowners for regulatory takings); and *Lehman v. Bradbury*, 333 Ore. 231 (2002) (invalidating the surviving provisions of Measure 3 of 1992, an ICA that imposed term limits on members of Congress and state elected officials).

[128] *Marshall v. State ex rel. Cooney*, 293 Mont. 274 (1999) (invalidating CI-75 of 1998 on the basis that it violated the separate-vote requirement of MONT. CONST. art. XIV, sec. 1).

[129] See *State ex rel. Hay v. Alderson*, 142 P. 210, 213 (Mont. 1914). In rejecting the former standard, the *Marshall* court held that "the unity of subject rule that the court applied in *Hay* and *Cooney* is unworkable. Under the courts' rationale in *Hay*, for example, a constitutional

An Arrogation of Power?

By the early 2000s, the trend was clear: Courts in several initiative states were more strictly enforcing two technical rules, the single-subject rule and the separate-vote requirement, as a constraint on the initiative power. In 2002, Professor Lowenstein observed that "[t]he recent change in judicial application of the single subject-rule has been dramatic. For better or worse, critics who have called for more aggressive application of the rule are getting their way."[130] The 2006 election cycle provided further examples of this trend. In that year alone, courts invoked single-subject and separate-vote requirements to invalidate a redistricting reform initiative in Florida, eminent domain initiatives in Oklahoma and Nevada, a budget cap initiative in Montana, and an initiative restricting state benefits to illegal immigrants in Colorado.[131] Notably, in these cases, courts were invalidating citizen initiatives not because they violated fundamental rights, nor because they expressly conflicted with powers of representative government, but because they failed to satisfy a court's strict enforcement of a technical rule.

Critics have attacked this trend. Lowenstein, in particular, has argued that the aggressive single-subject review exceeds the courts' legitimate power of judicial review, and instead amounts a subjective, standardless judicial veto over citizen-enacted laws. In his view, courts have "arrogated to themselves a nullification power comparable to the discretionary power proposed and rejected at Philadelphia for the Council of Revision."[132]

CONCLUSION

Especially in recent decades, citizen lawmakers have adopted many initiatives that threaten the institutional powers of representative government. The judicial power has countered these threats with varying degrees of success.

---

initiative to 'improve Montana's government' could amend virtually every part of Montana's constitution but have one single subject. The unity of subject rule set forth in *Hay* and *Cooney* is so elastic that it could swallow Montana's entire constitution. We decline to affirm such a rule." *Marshall v. State ex rel. Cooney,* 293 Mont. 274, 282 (1999).

[130] Daniel H. Lowenstein, "Initiatives and the New Single Subject Rule," 1 *Election Law Journal* 35 (2002).

[131] See *Advisory Opinion to the Attorney Gen. Re: Indep. Nonpartisan Comm'n To Apportion Legislative and Cong. Dists. Which Replaces Apportionment by the Legislature,* 926 So.2d 1218 (Fla. 2006); *Nevadans for the Protection of Property Rights v. Heller,* 141 P.3d 1235, 1245–46 (Nev. 2006); *In re Initiative Petition No. 382, State Question No. 729,* 142 P.3d 400 (Okla. 2006); and *Title and Ballot Title and Submission Clause for 2005–2006 #55 v. Lamm,* 138 P.3d 273 (Colo. 2006). For discussion, see Richard L. Hasen, "Ending Court Protection of Voters from the Initiative Process," 116 YALE L.J. POCKET PART 117, 119, 120–21 (2006); John Fund, "Taking the Initiative: How Judges Threaten Direct Democracy," *The Wall Street Journal* (October 16, 2006).

[132] Lowenstein, "Initiatives and the New Single Subject Rule," 35. Meanwhile, Professor Richard Hasen agreed that single-subject rules are comparatively "standardless" and that the best solution is for the people to repeal them. Hasen, "Ending Court Protection," 119, 120–21.

Courts have consistently prevented citizen lawmakers from undermining powers defined by the federal Constitution, but they have been less effective at countering initiatives that erode state-level government powers. This latter difficulty can be attributed to a number of factors, including the weak federal constitutional protection of state institutions, the constitutional status of some initiatives, and the non-justiciable nature of others. In recent years, courts in several states have expanded their check on initiatives by strictly enforcing the single-subject rule and the separate-vote requirement, but this shift has sparked allegations that courts have exceeded their legitimate powers.

The allegations of judicial tyranny invite us to examine the relationship between the people and the courts from the other side. Having analyzed the judicial power's check on direct democracy, we now ask: When judges overreach, can the people counter the courts?

PART III

THE MAJORITY STRIKES BACK

7

The People's Check on the Courts

Fear of judicial tyranny can be traced back to the founding when the Anti-Federalist Brutus warned that the Constitution made federal judges "independent in the fullest sense of the word...independent of the people, of the legislature, and of every power under heaven." Unaccountable judges, Brutus predicted, would exercise power "to the oppression of the people."[1] This prophecy remained largely unfulfilled until the *Lochner* era when the rising judicial power more aggressively asserted its will, often at the expense of popular majorities. A long series of conflicts caused many reformers to conclude that courts were out of control and needed to be constrained.

This chapter analyzes various attempts to counter the courts, especially at the state level, over the past century. The Progressives had limited success placing explicit constraints on judicial power, but some democratic devices, including initiative constitutional amendment (ICA) and judicial elections, have provided the people at least a partial check on activist judges.

THE PROGRESSIVE ERA COURT CRISIS

The Progressive Era conflict over judicial power is less well known than the later New Deal crisis, but it produced intense political controversy and was at the heart of the debate over the adoption of direct democracy. It was during the Progressive Era that the U.S. Supreme Court decided *Lochner v. New York* (1905), the case that came to symbolize the first wave of judicial activism.[2] *Lochner* was a challenge to an 1895 New York statute known as the "bake-shop law." The statute sought to improve the conditions of bakery workers by limiting their maximum hours of employment to sixty hours per week. When a

---

[1] Brutus, XV (20 March 1788) and XVI (10 April 1788), in Herbert J. Storing, ed., *The Anti-Federalist: Writings By the Opponents of the Constitution* (Chicago: University of Chicago Press, 1985), 183, 187.

[2] *Lochner v. New York*, 198 U.S. 45 (1905).

New York court convicted bakery owner Joseph Lochner for employing workers longer hours than the law allowed, he appealed his conviction on the theory
that the statute infringed on a "liberty of contract" implicit in the due process
clause of the Fourteenth Amendment. The U.S. Supreme Court embraced this
view, reversed Lochner's conviction, and invalidated the New York law.[3]

Lochner was part of a broader fight between Progressive reformers and conservative judges in both state and federal courts. As legislatures began enacting
a range of economic regulations, courts often invalidated these laws on the
basis that they exceeded the proper scope of government power or violated
state and federal constitutional rights of property and contract. Reformers, in
turn, alleged that these decisions were an abuse of the judicial function. University of Illinois Professor Walter F. Dodd expressed a widely held Progressive
view when he wrote that courts had usurped an "absolute power of veto"
and become "political organs of the government." Judicial activism upset the
constitutional balance, Dodd argued, because "courts exercise definite political power without a corresponding political responsibility."[4] Other reformers
joined the attack through speeches, articles, and books, such as *Our Judicial
Oligarchy* (1911), and began to explore ways to make courts more accountable
to the people.[5] In considering constraints on judicial power, reformers had to
distinguish between federal courts, which are highly insulated from democratic
accountability, and state courts, which are less so.

Federal judges, of course, enjoy life tenure "during good behavior" and
the people have no direct role in either their selection or removal.[6] Alexander
Hamilton argued in *Federalist* 78 that this provision was needed to preserve
judicial independence. "Periodical appointments [of judges], however regulated, or by whomsoever made, would, in some way or other, be fatal to their
necessary independence," Hamilton argued. "If the power of making [judicial
appointments] was committed to . . . the people . . . there would be too great a
disposition to consult popularity, to justify a reliance that nothing would be
consulted but the Constitution and the laws."[7] Following this theory, the federal Constitution prioritized judicial independence over judicial accountability,
and the barriers of the Article V process made it difficult for later reformers to
alter this design.

---

[3] Ibid., 64–5. Although *Lochner* was not the first case to use the due process clause to enforce a
"liberty of contract," it became the symbol of this doctrine.

[4] Walter F. Dodd, "The Recall and the Political Responsibility of Judges," 10 MICH. L. REV. 79,
85–6 (1911).

[5] Gilbert E. Roe, *Our Judicial Oligarchy* (New York: B.W. Huebsch, 1912), 30. Meanwhile, the
Socialist platform of 1912 was more radical in its attack on the courts, calling for the abolition
of the U.S. Supreme Court's power to invalidate federal laws, the abolition of federal district
courts and courts of appeal, the popular election of all judges for short terms and the power of
recall over state and federal judges. See Kirk H. Porter and Donald Bruce Johnson, eds., *National
Party Platforms, 1840–1964* (Urbana: University of Illinois Press, 1966), 190.

[6] U.S. CONST. art. III, sec. 1.

[7] Alexander Hamilton, *Federalist* 78, 469–70.

At the time of the founding, most state judges were also appointed for life, but states soon made their courts more accountable to the people.[8] Although most states introduced judicial elections during the nineteenth century, many Progressive reformers believed citizens still had too little control over judges. As their conflict with courts intensified, reformers promoted two distinct ways to shorten the leash: the recall of judges and the recall of judicial decisions.

The Recall of Judges

During the Progressive Era, reformers in several states advocated the adoption of judicial recall, a device that empowers citizens to call a special election to remove a judge from the bench. After Oregon adopted the first provision for recall of state judges in 1908, citizens in California and Arizona devised similar proposals and, by 1911, recall and its implications for judicial independence generated national debate.[9]

Leading political figures had a range of views on the question. William Jennings Bryan embraced this power, arguing that "recall is an evolution, rather than a revolution... society can better afford to risk such occasional injustice than to put the judge beyond the reach of the people."[10] Theodore Roosevelt was more ambivalent. He declared, "I do not believe in adopting the recall [of judges] save as a last resort," but added, "my purpose is to get justice, and if justice is resolutely denied by the courts, I would adopt the recall or any other expedient which was found necessary for the achievement of the purpose."[11] Woodrow Wilson opposed judicial recall, arguing the judiciary should be improved through the selection process rather than through threat of removal. Wilson observed that "[t]he recall can secure immediate results on a bad judge, but I fear in getting quick results the fundamental good of a true judiciary would be sacrificed. The judiciary must have stability and this the

---

[8] At the founding, judges in eight states were selected by either one or both houses of the legislature; in five states, the governor selected judges, subject to legislative approval. A majority of states provided judges with life tenure subject to good behavior. See Joseph R. Grodin, *In Pursuit of Justice: Reflections of a State Supreme Court Justice* (Berkeley: University of California Press, 1989), 164.

[9] William G. Ross, *A Muted Fury: Populists, Progressives, and Labor Unions Confront the Courts, 1890–1937* (Princeton: Princeton University Press, 1994), 111, 114. For discussion of the 1908 initiative adopting the recall, see James D. Barnett, *The Operation of the Initiative, Referendum, and Recall in Oregon* (New York: The Macmillan Company, 1915), 191.

[10] William Jennings Bryan, "The People's Law," repr. S. Doc. 523, 63rd Cong., 2nd sess., June 24, 1914.

[11] Theodore Roosevelt, "'A Charter of Democracy': Address before the Ohio Constitutional Convention at Columbus, Ohio, February 21, 1912," reprinted in Theodore Roosevelt, *Progressive Principles: Selections form Addresses Made During the Presidential Campaign of 1912* (New York: Progressive National Service, 1913), 65; Theodore Roosevelt, "Introduction," in William L. Ransom, *Majority Rule and the Judiciary: An Examination of Current Proposals for Constitutional Change Affecting the Relation of Courts to Legislation* (New York: Charles Scribner's Sons, 1912), 13. See also Theodore Roosevelt, "Workmen's Compensation," *The Outlook* (March 13, 1911), 53 (offering a qualified endorsement of the people's power to recall judges).

recall might endanger."[12] President William Howard Taft was the staunchest opponent, denouncing the recall of judges as "legalized terrorism."[13]

Arizona. The issue of judicial recall moved to the center of national politics in 1911 when the territory of Arizona sought admission to the Union under a proposed state constitution that provided for recall of public officials, including judges. Congress adopted an Arizona statehood resolution, but President Taft refused to sign it so long as the proposed constitution allowed for judicial recall. In his veto message, Taft wrote that "[t]his provision of the Arizona constitution, in its application to county and state judges, seems to me to be so pernicious in its effect, so destructive of independence in the judiciary, so likely to subject the rights of the individual to the possible tyranny of popular majority, and, therefore, to be so injurious to the cause of free government, that I must disapprove a constitution containing it."[14]

To mollify the president, Arizona yielded. But, a newspaper editor named Colonel Thomas F. Weedin expressed the sentiments of many in the state when he wrote:

> We will tolerate your gall
> And surrender our recall
> Till safe within the statehood stall,
> Billy Taft, Billy Taft
> Then we'll fairly drive you daft
> With the ring of our horse laugh
> Billy Taft, Billy Taft
> As we joyously re-install
> By the vote of one and all,
> That ever-glorious recall,
> Billy Taft, Billy Taft.[15]

And, indeed, shortly after securing admission in February 1912, Arizonans readopted the power to recall judges.

---

[12] Frederick L. Bird and Frances M. Ryan, *The Recall of Public Officers: A Study of the Operation of the Recall in California* (New York: The Macmillan Co., 1930), 52, citing *Los Angeles Record* (May 12, 1911).

[13] George E. Mowry, *Theodore Roosevelt and the Progressive Movement* (Madison: University of Wisconsin Press, 1946), 171, citing *New York Times* (August 16, 1911). According to Taft, "[t]he People at the polls, no more than kings upon the throne, are fit to pass upon questions involving the judicial interpretation of the law." Ibid.

[14] William H. Taft, "Veto Message [Returning without approval a joint resolution for the admission of the Territories of New Mexico and Arizona into the Union as States] August 22, 1911" in Burton, ed., *The Collected Works of William Howard Taft, Vol. IV* (Athens: Ohio University Press, 2002), 149. See also, William Howard Taft, "The Selection and Tenure of Judges," 38 Rep. Am Bar Ass'n 418, 422–23 (1913). For a further discussion of the application of the Arizona and California recall laws to judges see Dodd, "The Recall and the Political Responsibility of Judges," 79.

[15] Jay J. Wagoner, *Arizona Territory 1863–1912: A Political History* (Tucson: University of Arizona Press, 1970), 475–82. In the November 1912 election, Taft was outpolled in Arizona by Wilson, Roosevelt, and even Debs. Ibid., 481.

California. Meanwhile, in California's historic 1911 campaign for initiative, referendum, and recall, opponents of direct democracy leveled their strongest attacks against the recall of judges. In response, Governor Hiram Johnson asserted that a political check on courts was appropriate because judges made political decisions. A court exercising judicial review may say "anything it pleases with reference to the law," Johnson argued. "The power is there and it is nonsense to deny it."[16] Johnson further contended that California courts were too often biased in favor of corporate interests, especially the railroads. When confronted with the charge that the threat of recall would make judges beholden to public opinion, Johnson replied that "[w]e would rather that the judges keep their ears to the ground than to the railroad tracks in California."[17] California voters adopted the recall by a 3-to-1 margin.

During this period, however, only five western states – Oregon (1908), California (1911), Arizona (1912), Colorado (1912), and Nevada (1912) – adopted provisions for judicial recall and no judges were removed through the procedure.[18] The device failed to spread further during these years because even many Progressives who supported other forms of direct democracy feared that recalling judges would dangerously undermine judicial independence.

Theodore Roosevelt's Plan for "Recall of Judicial Decisions"

Although Theodore Roosevelt harbored doubts about the wisdom of judicial recall, he detested conservative judicial activism and sought alternative ways to curb the courts. Roosevelt's critique of judicial power dated back to the mid-1880s. As a state lawmaker during that period, he had helped enact public health legislation banning the manufacture of cigars in tenement houses, but the New York Court of Appeal struck down the law on the grounds that it exceeded the scope of the state's police power.[19]

During his presidency, Roosevelt continued to believe that courts were too autocratic and that comprehensive social and economic reforms could not be achieved unless judges were made to yield.[20]

Roosevelt's critique of the judicial power hardened after he left office. In an August 1910 speech before the Colorado legislature, Roosevelt railed against

---

[16] Bird and Ryan, *The Recall of Public Officers*, 52–3.

[17] Ibid. When it was suggested that judges would be intimidated by the threat of recall, Governor Johnson responded, "Cowards! My friends, you can't make a coward of a man by holding a pistol at his head; you can only demonstrate whether he is one." Ibid. See also George E. Mowry, *The California Progressives* (Berkeley: University of California Press, 1951), 148–49.

[18] Later, North Dakota (1920), Wisconsin (1926), Montana (1976), and Georgia (1978) adopted statewide recall of public officials, including judges. In total, nine states allow for recall of judges. Thomas E. Cronin, *Direct Democracy: The Politics of Initiative, Referendum, and Recall* (Cambridge, MA: Harvard University Press, 1989), 126. See also Joseph F. Zimmerman, *The Recall: Tribunal of the People* (Westport, CT: Praeger, 1997), 25–7, 46–9.

[19] *In the Matter of Jacobs*, 98 N.Y. 98, 99 (1885). Edward Hartnett, "Why is the Supreme Court of the United States Protecting State Judges from Popular Democracy?" 75 TEX. L. REV. 907, 933–49 (1997).

[20] Mowry, *Theodore Roosevelt and the Progressive Movement*, 214.

the Supreme Court's decision in *Lochner*.[21] The bakery regulation, he argued, perfectly reflected the will of the public. But, the Court had "declared the action of the State of New York unconstitutional, because, forsooth, men must not be deprived of their 'liberty' to work under unhealthy conditions." In Roosevelt's view, conservative judges were "fossilized" because they refused to allow reformers to "work for the betterment of conditions among the wage-earners on the ground that we must not interfere with the 'liberty' of a girl to work under conditions which jeopardize life and limb, or the 'liberty' of a man to work under conditions which ruin his health over a limited number of years."[22]

In March 1911, the New York Court of Appeals further provoked Roosevelt when it struck down the state's newly enacted workers' compensation statute, the first of its kind in the nation.[23] In *Ives v. South Buffalo Railway Company* (1911), the court held that legislation requiring employers to compensate their workers for on-the-job injuries regardless of fault was "plainly revolutionary" and constituted a taking of the employer's property without due process of law.[24] Roosevelt attacked *Ives* as a dangerous extension of Lochnerism. "[T]his decision of the Court of Appeals of the State of New York is a case, not really of interpretation of the law, but of the enactment of judge-made law in defiance of the legislative enactment.... Whatever the form, the substance of the action is not the interpretation of law but the making of law."[25]

Largely in response to *Ives*, Roosevelt began promoting a new form of direct democracy he called "recall of judicial decisions." He floated the idea in magazine articles in 1911 then formally presented it in his February 1912 Charter of Democracy address before the Ohio constitutional convention. Declaring that "it is both absurd and degrading to make a fetish of a judge or of any one else," Roosevelt urged the immediate adoption of his plan to allow voters to reverse state court decisions.[26]

Roosevelt explained his plan as follows:

When the supreme court of a State declares a given statute unconstitutional, because in conflict with the State or the National Constitution, its opinion should be subject to revision by the people themselves.... If any considerable number of the people feel that

[21] Ibid, 142; Ross, *Muted Fury*, 131.

[22] Roosevelt published this portion of his address to the Colorado legislature in Theodore Roosevelt, "Criticism of the Courts," *The Outlook* (September 24, 1910), 149.

[23] *Ives v. South Buffalo Railway Company*, 201 N.Y. 271 (1911), invalidating *New York Labor Law Article 14-a*. See Theodore Roosevelt, "Workmen's Compensation," *The Outlook* (May 13, 1911). Professor Gerald Gunther discusses the importance of the *Ives* case in TR's decision to confront the judicial power in *Learned Hand: The Man and the Judge* (New York: Knopf, 1994), 209–26.

[24] *Ives*, 285, 298–300.

[25] Roosevelt, "Workmen's Compensation," 49. See also, Roosevelt, "Introduction," in Ransom, *Majority Rule and the Judiciary*, 19.

[26] Roosevelt, "A Charter of Democracy;" 72. For a discussion, see Bickel and Schmidt, *The Judiciary and Responsible Government*, 1910–21, 13–16.

the decision is in defiance of justice, they should be given the right by petition to bring before the voters at some subsequent election, special or otherwise, as might be decided, and after the fullest opportunity for deliberation and debate, the question whether or not the judges' interpretation of the Constitution is to be sustained. If it is sustained, well and good. If not, then the popular verdict is to be accepted as final, the decision is to be treated as reversed, and the construction of the Constitution definitely decided – subject only to action by the Supreme Court of the United States.[27]

To illustrate how his plan would work, Roosevelt pointed to *Ives*. If the recall device were in place, he said, once the New York Court of Appeals struck down the state's worker's compensation law, "the people of the State of New York, after due deliberation, would have had an opportunity to decide for themselves whether the constitution which they themselves made should or should not be so construed as to prevent them from doing elementary justice in these matters."[28]

Roosevelt's concept was greeted by intense opposition from the organized bar and much of the Republican Party, including former members of his administration and other Eastern Progressives. In February and March 1912, the *New York Times* ran a series of six hostile editorials with headlines including "No Longer a Republican," "Reversing John Marshall," and "The Road to Despotism."[29] Meanwhile, Elihu Root warned that if "the decisions of our courts are to be considered in the same way and upon the same presumptions and with no greater respect for authority than in the case of political opinions, the authority of the courts will inevitably decline, the independence of the judicial branch will cease, [and] judicial decision will interpret the law always to suit the majority of the moment."[30] And, again, President Taft most strenuously objected. In a speech in Toledo in March 1912, Taft called Roosevelt's plan a "grotesque proposition" and argued that "[t]his proposed method of reversing judicial decisions ... lays the axe to the root of the tree of well-ordered freedom and subjects the guarantees of life, liberty, and property without remedy to the fitful impulses of a temporary majority of the electorate."[31]

Although Roosevelt's proposal deepened his estrangement from Taft and hardened the Old Guard's resolve to deny him the 1912 Republican presidential nomination, he refused to abandon it. When the Republican National

---

[27] Ibid., 188. For further elaboration of Roosevelt's plan, see Ransom, *Majority Rule and the Judiciary*, 98–125.

[28] Roosevelt, "Introduction," in Ransom, *Majority Rule and the Judiciary*, 19–20.

[29] See "No Longer a Republican," *The New York Times* (February 22, 1912), 8; "Reversing John Marshall," ibid., (February 27, 1912), 10; "Progressing Backward," ibid., (February 27, 1912), 8; "The Lawyers to the Defense," ibid., (March 5, 1912), 10; "The Road to Despotism," ibid., (March 9, 1912), 12; "To Make Cowards of Judges," ibid., (March 12, 1912), 12.

[30] Elihu Root, "Judicial Decisions and Public Feeling: Presidential Address at the Annual Meeting of the New York State Bar Association in New York City, January 19, 1912," in Robert Bacon and James Brown Scott, eds., *Addresses on Government and Citizenship* (Cambridge, MA: Harvard University Press, 1916), 452.

[31] William Howard Taft, "The Judiciary and Progress," address delivered at Toledo, Ohio, March 8, 1912, repr. S. Doc. 408, 62nd Cong., 2nd sess., March 13, 1912, 9.

Convention nominated Taft for president in August 1912, Roosevelt immediately accepted the nomination of the newly formed Progressive Party. In his famed "Armageddon" acceptance speech at the Progressive Party convention, Roosevelt renewed his assault on the courts and again advocated his plan to constrain them. "We in America have peculiar need thus to make the acts of the courts subject to the people," he declared, "because . . . the courts have here grown to occupy a position unknown in any other country, a position of superiority over both the legislature and the Executive." Roosevelt argued that "the American people, and not the courts, are to determine their own fundamental policies. . . . The people themselves must be the ultimate makers of their own Constitution, and where their agents differ in their interpretations of the Constitution, the people themselves should be given the chance, after full and deliberate judgment, authoritatively to settle what interpretation it is that their representatives shall therefore adopt as binding."[32]

In response to these provocations, Taft devoted much effort in the 1912 campaign defending the independence of the courts. For his part, Woodrow Wilson largely avoided the court issue and benefited from the schism on the Republican side.

Colorado Amendment 16 (1912). In 1912, citizens in Colorado seized the opportunity to adopt Roosevelt's proposal.[33] This was the first year that Coloradans possessed the initiative power and they used it to place a long slate of measures on the ballot. One of these measures provided for "recall" of judicial decisions. According to the initiative, the procedure would work as follows: If citizens objected to a decision by the Colorado Supreme Court to invalidate a law on either state or federal constitutional grounds, they had sixty days to submit a referendum petition to the secretary of state that had been signed by at least five percent of the voters of the state. The secretary of state would publish the text of the invalidated law and the voters would have the opportunity to override the court's decision at the next election. If the voters approved the law, it would "be and become the law of this state notwithstanding the decision of the Supreme Court."[34]

---

[32] Theodore Roosevelt, "A Confession of Faith," in Hagedorn, ed., *The Works of Theodore Roosevelt*, Vol. XIX, 367–8. Roosevelt continued this theme to the end of the 1912 campaign. In his last speech of the campaign, before 16,000 at Madison Square Garden, Roosevelt took one parting shot: "We recognize in neither court, nor Congress, nor president any divine right to override the will of the people." Mowry, *Theodore Roosevelt and the Progressive Movement*, 278.

[33] Colorado was the only state to adopt Roosevelt's plan. Ross, *Muted Fury*, 152–4. In 1913, legislators in Oregon proposed a state constitutional amendment to institute a slightly modified version of the plan, but the measure died without reaching the ballot. Some reformers in Oregon viewed the recall of judicial decisions as unnecessary because the people could use the power of initiative constitutional amendment to override state constitutional interpretations that conflicted with majority will. See Barnett, *The Operation of the Initiative, Referendum, and Recall in Oregon*, 174–6.

[34] Ibid.

The Direct Legislation League organized support for the initiative by tapping into popular anger at conservative judicial activism. Corporate interests and leaders of the Colorado bar formed the main opposition.[35] On Election Day, voters adopted the measure by a 57-to-43-percent margin. Theodore Roosevelt was gratified by the result. After the election, he wrote to the initiative's leading proponent, "I am extremely pleased to hear how many of the acts for which we stand were adopted in Colorado. Will you let me know as soon as you see the definite information about them, especially the Recall of Decision matter."[36]

As it turned out, no judicial decision ever faced a "recall." Before the people invoked the device, the Colorado Supreme Court invalidated it through its decisions in *People v. Western Union* (1921) and *People v. Max* (1921).[37] Insisting that judges, not the people, had final authority to interpret constitutions, the court declared that Western Union and Max had valid constitutional claims that the people had no power to overturn.[38] More specifically, in *Western Union*, the court declared that the people cannot override judicial enforcement of federal constitutional rights. "There is no sovereignty in a state to set at naught the Constitution of the Union and no power in its people to command their courts to do so," the court wrote. "That issue was finally settled at Appomattox."[39] And, in *Max*, the court dealt a final blow to Roosevelt's plan by holding that allowing the people to "recall" judicial enforcement of state constitutional rights would violate due process. Again, the court held that it is the judiciary's duty to interpret constitutional rights and if the people are dissatisfied with the interpretation, their remedy is to change the text itself through the process of constitutional amendment.[40] The judicial invalidation

---

[35] Duane A. Smith, "Colorado and the Judicial Recall," *The American Journal of Legal History* 7, no. 3 (July 1963): 198–209; Jesse G. Northcutt, "The Recall in Colorado," THE GREEN BAG 25, no. 9 (September 1913).

[36] Theodore Roosevelt, "To Benjamin Barr Lindsey" (November 16, 1912), in Elting E. Morison, ed., *The Letters of Theodore Roosevelt*, Vol. 7 (Cambridge, MA: Harvard University Press, 1954), 650.

[37] *People v. Western Union Telegraph Company*, 70 Colo. 90 (1921); *People v. Max*, 70 Colo. 100 (1921). In 1920, prior to the decisions in these cases, a brief movement arose to recall a Colorado Supreme Court decision involving public utilities, but the issue never reached the ballot. Smith, "Colorado and Judicial Recall," 209.

[38] The *Western Union* case arose when the company violated the state's *Anti-Coercion Act* by demanding an employee sever his connection from the Commercial Telegraphers' Union. Western Union argued that enforcement of the act deprived the company of liberty and property without due process, in violation of the state and federal constitutions. A district court judge in Denver sided with Western Union on the constitutional claim. *People v. Western Union Telegraph Company*, 91–3. In *Max*, an unlicensed physician violated the state's licensing law, but argued that the retroactive application of the law deprived him of his constitutional rights. Again, a lower court in Denver agreed with this constitutional challenge. *People v. Max*, 101.

[39] *People v. Western Union*, 97.

[40] *People v. Max*, 104, 110–114. See also, "Recall of Judicial Decision Held to be Unconstitutional," 92 CENTRAL LAW JOURNAL 425 (1921).

of Roosevelt's plan produced almost no public reaction – by 1921, citizens had lost interest in the device.[41]

More generally, after 1912, the movement for direct popular control of courts dissipated. Late in the decade, the American Bar Association reported that no further states had adopted the power to recall judges and that the process had never been successfully invoked.[42] Moreover, no other states had adopted Roosevelt's proposal for recall of judicial decisions, and Congress failed to enact a federal version of the plan introduced in Congress in late 1912.[43] As Alexander Bickel observed, "These and other specific proposals for curbing the judiciary as an institution were bruited about for some little time, [but] they cannot be said ever to have gathered widespread responsible support, even from Progressives, or to have come anywhere near to general adoption by the states, let alone the federal system."[44]

Of course, controversy over the judicial power reemerged with new intensity during the New Deal crisis. But, in that conflict, critics of the courts did not seek to apply direct popular checks on them. Instead, Franklin D. Roosevelt and other Depression Era reformers sought to change the courts' direction by other means, including FDR's famous Judiciary Reorganization Bill of 1937, better known as the "court packing plan."[45]

STATE COURT JUDICIAL ACTIVISM AND POPULAR OVERRIDE

In 1937, the judicial tables turned. Conservatives abandoned the judicial power as a check on economic regulation, but as they yielded, a new generation

---

[41] Smith, "Colorado and the Judicial Recall," 209.

[42] Ross, *Muted Fury*, 127. After the Progressive Era, a number of states adopted the statewide recall power, sometimes including judicial recall, but use of the power remained rare. Cronin, *Direct Democracy*, 132, 143.

[43] Congress failed to act on a proposed constitutional amendment introduced in December 1912 by Senator Joseph L. Bristow (R-KS) that would have allowed Congress to refer to the people for approval or disapproval any federal law declared invalid by the U.S. Supreme Court. S. J. Res 142, 62nd Cong., 3rd sess., December 5, 1912. See Ross, *Muted Fury*, 153. In 1914, Congress did place an important check on state court judicial activism by granting federal courts jurisdiction to review state court decisions, which invalidated state laws on federal constitutional grounds. This change, enacted in response to *Ives*, allowed federal courts to overturn activist state court judicial review based on federal constitutional principles, but did not affect state court decisions based on independent state grounds. See *Act of Dec. 23, 1914*, ch. 2, 38 Stat. 790 (codified as amended at 28 U.S.C. 1257). For discussion, see Hartnett, "Why is the Supreme Court," 949–71.

[44] Bickel and Schmidt, *The Judiciary and Responsible Government, 1910–1921*, 14. William G. Ross has similarly argued that "[t]he proposal for both forms of recall were peculiarly part of the clamor for direct popular democracy that reached its zenith during the height of the Progressive Era." Ross, *Muted Fury*, 154.

[45] *Judiciary Reorganization Bill*, S. 1392, 62d Cong. (1937). The Senate famously rejected FDR's proposal to pack the Court by nominating an additional justice for every sitting justice aged seventy years, six months. For an account, see Leonard Baker, *Back to Back: The Duel Between FDR and the Supreme Court* (New York: Macmillan, 1968).

of liberal judges sought to promote social change through aggressive judicial enforcement of civil rights and liberties.[46] The new judicial activism had a broader scope than the old. Judges now dictated outcomes in a wider range of policy areas, including race- and gender-specific legislation, apportionment, church-state relations, abortion, and criminal procedure. And, whereas its ends had changed, judicial activism remained as controversial as ever, with courts often thwarting majority preferences and facing the charge that they were usurping legislative power.

During the Warren Era (1953–1969), courts engaged in judicial activism almost exclusively through expansive reading of the federal Constitution. But, beginning in the 1970s, as the Burger Court began limiting the scope of some federal constitutional rights, many liberals looked to state constitutions to pick up the slack.[47] Supreme Court Justice William H. Brennan, Jr., was a leading advocate of this movement. In an influential 1977 *Harvard Law Review* article, Justice Brennan argued that "state courts cannot rest when they have afforded their citizens the full protections of the federal Constitution. State constitutions, too, are a font of individual liberties, their protections often extending beyond those required by the Supreme Court's interpretation of federal law. The legal revolution which has brought federal law to the fore must not be allowed to inhibit the independent protective force of state law – for without it, the full realization of our liberties cannot be guaranteed."[48] A number of state justices, including Oregon's Hans A. Linde and California's Stanley Mosk, shared this view and urged state supreme courts to find independent state constitutional grounds for their rulings.[49] As state courts embraced this "new judicial federalism," they became attractive arenas for liberal activists seeking to expand constitutional rights.

New judicial federalism was based on the understanding that state courts, like federal courts, can expand constitutional rights. This is certainly true,

---

[46] Important decisions marking the shift included *West Coast Hotel v. Parrish*, 300 U.S. 379 (1937) and *United States v. Carolene Products Co.*, 304 U.S. 144 (1938).

[47] For analysis of the rise of "new judicial federalism," see G. Alan Tarr, *Understanding State Constitutions* (Princeton: Princeton University Press, 1998), 161–70. See also Mary Cornelia Porter and G. Alan Tarr, eds., *State Supreme Courts: Policymakers in the Federal System* (Westport, CT: Greenwood Press, 1982) and Stanley H. Friedelbaum, ed., *Human Rights in the States: New Directions in Constitutional Policymaking* (New York: Greenwood Press, 1988).

[48] William H. Brennan, Jr., "State Constitutions and the Protection of Individual Rights," 90 Harv. L. Rev. 489-504, 491 (1977). Brennan suggested that the trend toward liberal state constitutionalism was a response to the Burger Court's retreat from the Warren Era's aggressive enforcement of rights. Ibid., 495–502.

[49] See, e.g., Hans A. Linde, "First Things First: Rediscovering the States' Bill of Rights," 9 U. Balt. L. Rev. 379 (1980); Stanley Mosk, "State Constitutionalism: Both Liberal and Conservative," 63 Tex. L. Rev. 1081 (1985). A number of institutional factors allowed state courts to become more active policymakers during this period. For example, the creation of intermediate appellate courts allowed state supreme courts to reduce their caseloads and focus on more significant and controversial state constitutional questions. See Robert A. Kagan, Bliss Cartwright, Lawrence M. Friedman, Stanton Wheeler, "The Business of State Supreme Courts, 1870–1970," 30 Stan. L. Rev. 121, 123–32 (1977).

but it is also true that expansions of state constitutional rights are more vulnerable to popular override than expansions of federal constitutional rights.[50] State supreme courts that move too far from the will of the people can be reversed by what political scientist John Dinan has called "court-constraining amendments."[51] These amendments can be proposed by the legislature and adopted by the people – or, in states where citizens have the power of initiative constitutional amendment, can be proposed and adopted by the people themselves.[52] The following controversies demonstrate how, the people have sometimes reversed the judicial expansion of state constitutional rights.

THE DEATH PENALTY

In the ferment of the 1960s, the death penalty produced intense debate. Proposals to abolish or restrict capital punishment competed with calls to expand its use. Notably, the existence of the death penalty was still widely viewed as a matter of legislative discretion. The U.S. Supreme Court avoided ruling squarely on the constitutionality of the death penalty and most state and lower federal courts reviewing capital appeals dispensed with Eighth Amendment claims in two or three sentences.[53] Few believed that either the U.S. Constitution or state constitutions prohibited capital punishment.

But, legal mobilization converted the death penalty debate into a constitutional question. An influential 1970 law review article by former Supreme Court Justice Arthur Goldberg and Harvard law professor Alan Dershowitz argued that the death penalty was *per se* unconstitutional, and courts began to analyze the question in these terms.[54] In its October 1971 term, the U.S. Supreme Court granted certiorari in four cases – *Furman v. Georgia, Aikens v. California, Schneble v. Florida,* and *McKenzie v. Texas* – to consider the question of whether the death penalty constituted cruel and unusual punishment in violation of the Eighth and Fourteenth Amendments.[55] Although these cases

---

[50] Douglas S. Reed, "Popular Constitutionalism: Toward a Theory of State Constitutional Meanings," 30 RUTGERS L. J. 871 (1999).

[51] John J. Dinan, "Court-Constraining Amendments and the State Constitutional Tradition," 38 RUTGERS L. J. 983 (2007).

[52] States with direct forms of ICA are Arizona, Arkansas, California, Colorado, Florida, Illinois, Michigan, Missouri, Montana, Nebraska, Nevada, North Dakota, Ohio, Oklahoma, Oregon, and South Dakota. In Illinois, however, the power of ICA can be used only for amendments to Article IV of the state constitution, which pertains to the legislature. In two states, Massachusetts and Mississippi, citizens possess a limited, indirect ICA power that the legislature may obstruct. The Council of State Governments, *The Book of the States* (2007), 13–15.

[53] Arthur J. Goldberg and Alan M. Dershowitz, "Declaring the Death Penalty Unconstitutional," 83 HARV. L. REV. 1773, 1774–5 (1970). Goldberg and Dershowitz reported that within the large body of commentary on the death penalty, they could find only four articles arguing that capital punishment is unconstitutional. Ibid., 1774.

[54] Ibid., 1775.

[55] The orders granting certiorari in the four cases were reported at 403 U.S. 952 (1971). In *Furman*, a fragmented Court concluded that the death penalty as then practiced in the United

provided an opportunity for the Supreme Court to abolish capital punishment throughout the nation, many liberals feared that the reconstituted Court – which now included Nixon appointees Warren E. Burger, Harry A. Blackmun, Lewis F. Powell, and William H. Rehnquist – would reject the constitutional challenge. At this crucial moment, the California Supreme Court entered the fray.

People v. Anderson *(1972)*. In late 1971, the California Supreme Court ordered argument in *People v. Anderson* to determine whether the California Constitution prohibited capital punishment. Robert Page Anderson had already made a long journey through the California courts. In 1965, a San Diego jury found him guilty of robbing a pawnshop, murdering a clerk, and attempting to murder three other men. The jury sentenced Anderson to death for these crimes. By 1971, Anderson's appeals had already twice reached the state supreme court. In 1966, the court affirmed his conviction and sentence.[56] But, in 1968, responding to new federal rules for jury selection in capital cases, the court ordered a retrial on the issue of penalty.[57]

In the 1968 ruling, the court squarely rejected Anderson's constitutional challenge to the death penalty, declaring that "retention or abolition [of capital punishment] raises a question of legislative policy which under our system of division of powers falls within the competence of the Legislature or the electorate."[58] Concurring in this judgment, Justice Stanley Mosk observed that during his tenure as California's attorney general (1959–1964) he had "frequently repeated a personal belief in the social invalidity of the death penalty" and conceded that he was "tempted by the invitation of petitioners to join in judicially terminating this anachronistic penalty." Nevertheless, quoting U.S. Supreme Court Justice Felix Frankfurter, Justice Mosk wrote that "to yield to my predilections would be to act willfully 'in the sense of enforcing individual views instead of speaking humbly as the voice of law by which society presumably consents to be ruled....' As a judge, I am bound by the law as I find it to be and not as I might fervently wish it to be."[59]

However, when Anderson's case was again ready for review, the process of legal mobilization had taken effect. By late 1971, Justice Mosk and a number

States violated the Eighth Amendment because states lacked rational standards for determining when it would be imposed. After *Furman*, states were forced to revise their death penalty laws. In *Gregg v. Georgia*, 428 U.S. 153 (1976), the Court held that capital punishment was not *per se* unconstitutional.

[56] *People v. Anderson*, 64 Cal.2d 633 (1966).

[57] *In re Anderson*, 69 Cal.2d 613, 616 (1968), responding to new *voir dire* requirements in capital cases set forth in *Witherspoon v. Illinois*, 391 U.S. 510 (1968).

[58] *In re Anderson*, 616.

[59] Ibid., 634–5, Mosk, J. concurring, quoting Felix Frankfurter, "The Supreme Court in the Mirror of Justices," 105 U. PENN. L. REV. 781, 784 (1957). In several cases after *In re Anderson*, the court either explicitly or implicitly rejected the argument that capital punishment was cruel and unusual punishment. See Edward L. Barrett, Jr., "*Anderson* and the Judicial Function," 45 S. CAL. L. REV. 739, 739 (1972).

of his colleagues had changed their views on the constitutionality of the death penalty and, indeed, approached the matter with a sense of urgency. Although the federal constitutional challenge to capital punishment was scheduled for argument on January 17, 1972, and all California executions were stayed pending that litigation's outcome, the court was unwilling to wait for the U.S. Supreme Court's expected ruling in June. Instead, it scheduled oral argument in *Anderson* on January 6, and issued its decision in the case only six weeks later.[60]

On February 18, 1972, by a 6-to-1 vote, the California Supreme Court declared in *People v. Anderson* that capital punishment violated the state constitution's prohibition on cruel or unusual punishment.[61] The court's ruling had sweeping impact. It overturned Anderson's death sentence as well as those of over 100 other inmates, including notorious killers Sirhan Sirhan and Charles Manson, and prevented the state from imposing the death penalty in any future cases.[62]

In its opinion, the court sought to explain why it was now abolishing the state's death penalty when it had repeatedly upheld it in the past, and when the question of the punishment's federal constitutional validity was still pending before the U.S. Supreme Court. Writing for the majority, Chief Justice Donald R. Wright emphasized that this was the first time the court had examined the independent scope of the California Constitution's prohibition on cruel or unusual punishment. According to Wright, the text and history of the state constitution suggested that its drafters had intended the protection to be broader than the Eighth Amendment.[63]

Moreover, Chief Justice Wright asserted that the state constitution's protections must expand as society evolves. "We must construe [the 'cruel or unusual punishment' clause] in accordance with contemporary standards," Wright declared. "We have recognized before that our Constitution is a progressive document and . . . have accepted the . . . formulation of 'evolving standards of decency that mark the progress of a maturing society' as an appropriate expression of the applicable standard."[64]

Finally, Wright set aside substantial evidence from polling data and other sources that that capital punishment did not in fact offend "contemporary standards of decency," and instead argued that a number of trends, including a decrease in the frequency of executions, demonstrated that society had evolved to the point where capital punishment was "unacceptable."[65]

By resting its decision to abolish the death penalty on the state constitution, the California Supreme Court insulated the ruling from review by the U.S. Supreme Court under the well-settled doctrine that federal courts generally do

---

[60] See Barrett, "*Anderson* and the Judicial Function," 739–40.
[61] *People v. Anderson*, 6 Cal.3d 628, 633–34 (1972).
[62] See *People v. Sirhan*, 7 Cal.3d 710, 717 (1972), *People v. Manson*, 61 Cal.App.3d 102, 217 (1976).
[63] *People v. Anderson*, 641.
[64] Ibid., 647–48, citing *Trop v. Dulles*, 356 U.S. 86, 101 (1958).
[65] Ibid., 649.

not have the power to review a state court's interpretation of state law.[66] But, this move also made the decision vulnerable to attack from the people themselves.

Counter-mobilization: Proposition 17 (1972)

The *Anderson* decision met a swift and largely hostile reaction, with many viewing it as a judicial usurpation of the legislative power. Governor Ronald Reagan declared that the court had placed itself "above the will of the people."[67] The decision made "a mockery of the constitutional processes involved in establishing the laws of California," Reagan argued, and reinforced "the widespread concern of our people that some members of the judiciary inject their own philosophy into their decision rather than carry out their constitutional duty to interpret and enforce the law."[68] Law enforcement officials also denounced the ruling and *The San Francisco Examiner* expressed a widely held view that capital punishment is "an issue of such overriding importance that it should never be abolished except by a vote of the people or their chosen legislative representatives."[69]

The public outrage quickly turned to popular counter-mobilization. A coalition of law-and-order groups prepared an ICA to reverse *Anderson* and restore the state constitutional validity of capital punishment. Citizens had no difficulty collecting enough signatures to qualify the measure for the November ballot as Proposition 17. The initiative proposed to amend the state constitution to provide that the death penalty "shall not be deemed to be, or to constitute, infliction of cruel or unusual punishments... nor shall such punishment for such offenses be deemed to contravene any other provision of this constitution."[70]

---

[66] California's attorney general sought U.S. Supreme Court review of the *Anderson* decision, but the Court denied certiorari. *California v. Anderson*, 406 U.S. 958 (1972). In addition, the U.S. Supreme Court reversed its decision to grant certiorari in *Aikens v. California*, the pending federal constitutional challenge to the California death penalty, on the grounds that the challenge had been mooted by the California court's ruling in *Anderson*. *Aikens v. California*, 406 U.S. 813 (1972). For discussion, see Scott H. Bice, "*Anderson* and the Adequate State Ground," 45 S. Cal. L. Rev. 750 (1972).

[67] Ed Meagher, "Reagan Says Court Puts Itself 'Above the Will of the People,'" *The Los Angeles Times* (February 18, 1972), A-3.

[68] *The San Francisco Chronicle* (February 19, 1972), cited in Barrett, "*Anderson*," 743. See also Lou Cannon, *Governor Reagan: His Rise to Power* (New York: Public Affairs, 2003), 223–5. The day after the decision, the *Los Angeles Times* ran a provocative front-page picture of Mary Sirhan, the mother of Sirhan Sirhan, over the caption "A Happy Mother." Ed Meagher, "Court Setting Itself Above the People, Governor Charges," *The Los Angeles Times* (February 19, 1972), A-1.

[69] "Death Penalty and the Court," *The San Francisco Examiner* (February 20, 1972); Cannon, *Governor Reagan*, 224.

[70] See California Secretary of State, *Proposed Amendments to the Constitution, Propositions and Proposed Laws Together with Arguments: General Election, Tuesday, November 7, 1972*, 42. http://traynor.uchastings.edu/ballot_pdf/1972g.pdf.

The ballot statement supporting the proposition defended the merits of capital punishment and reminded voters:

This proposition qualified for a place on this ballot because over one million Californians signed petitions in one of the most successful initiative drives in the history of California. They did this so that the people of this state would have the opportunity to vote on this critical issue.

We are faced with a question of the utmost gravity. The people of this state, rather than the Court, now have the opportunity to decide whether or not they need the death penalty for the protection of innocent citizens. Accept that responsibility and vote YES on Proposition 17.[71]

In November 1972, less than nine months after *Anderson*, Californians approved Proposition 17 by a decisive 2-to-1 vote.[72] Through the ICA process, the citizens of California had reversed an activist state court decision and enforced the popular will regarding the constitutional validity of capital punishment.

After the election, opponents challenged Proposition 17. They argued that eliminating the state constitutional right against capital punishment was such a fundamental change to the state constitution that it could be achieved only through constitutional revision, not directly by the people through an initiative. But, in *People v. Frierson* (1979), the California Supreme Court yielded to the voters and upheld the death penalty initiative. Writing for the court, Justice Frank Richardson concluded that in circumventing *Anderson* and restoring the death penalty, the voters had enacted a change "not so broad as to constitute a fundamental constitutional revision." To rule otherwise, the court reasoned, "might effectively bar the people from ever directly reinstating the death penalty, despite the apparent belief of a very substantial majority of our citizens in the necessity and appropriateness of the ultimate punishment."[73]

Similar patterns of state constitutional conflict emerged in other states. In 1980, the Massachusetts Supreme Judicial Court held in *District Attorney for Suffolk District v. Watson* that the death penalty violated the Massachusetts Constitution; two years later, Massachusetts voters approved a legislative constitutional amendment which provided that "[n]o provision of the Constitution . . . shall be construed as prohibiting the imposition of the punishment of

---

[71] George Deukmejian, S. C. Masterson, and John W. Holmdahl, "Argument in Favor of Proposition 17," ibid., 42–3. In response, opponents of the measure asked, "Would you kill in cold blood? If not, don't ask others to do it for you." Edmund G. ("Pat") Brown, Erwin Loretz, and Bill Cosby, "Rebuttal to Argument in Favor of Proposition 17," ibid., 43–4.

[72] The vote on California Proposition 17 (1972) was Yes 5,447,165 (67.5%); No 2,617,514 (32.5%). California Secretary of State, *Statement of Vote, November 7, 1972 General Election*.

[73] *People v. Frierson*, 25 Cal.3d 142, 187 (1979).

death."[74] Similarly, in 1981, the Oregon Supreme Court declared in *State v. Quinn* that the procedures for imposing the death penalty violated the state constitution's right to jury trial, but voters quickly adopted an ICA to respond to *Quinn* and to prevent the courts from invalidating the death penalty on other state constitutional grounds.[75]

Meanwhile, citizens reversed judicial expansion of state constitutional rights in other areas of the criminal law. During the 1970s and 1980s, several state supreme courts expanded the state constitutional rights of criminal defendants beyond what the U.S. Supreme Court required. Citizens in California, Oregon, and Arizona responded by drafting and adopting a series of ICAs to scale back these rights and thus strengthen the prosecutor's hand.[76] Finally, as we have noted, citizens in California enacted an initiative that attempted to abolish altogether the state supreme court's power to expand rights in the area of criminal procedure and punishment. Proposition 115 of 1990 sought to add a clause to Article I, section 24 of the California Constitution to read: "In criminal cases, the rights of a defendant... shall be construed by the courts of this state in a manner consistent with the Constitution of the United States. This Constitution shall not be construed by the courts to afford greater rights to criminal defendants than those afforded by the Constitution of the United States."[77] This comprehensive constraint was too much for the court to accept. In *Raven v. Deukmejian* (1990), the court determined that this provision "not only unduly restricts the judicial power, but it does so in a way which severely limits the independent force and effect of the California Constitution."[78] Invoking the no-revision rule, the court struck down this broad constraint on the judicial power, but, it let stand the initiative's other, more specific restrictions on the state constitutional rights of criminal defendants.[79] Thus, through Proposition 115 and other initiatives, the people were able to reverse judicial decisions and impose the majority will in many important areas of the criminal justice system.

---

[74] *District Attorney for the Suffolk District v. Watson*, 381 Mass. 648, 671 (1980) was effectively overturned by new Article 116 of the Massachusetts Constitution. However, after the legislature adopted a new capital statute (ch. 554, *Acts of 1982*), the court declared it invalid on other state constitutional grounds in *Commonwealth v. Colon-Cruz* 393 Mass. 150 (1984). Following the *Colon-Cruz* decision, the Massachusetts legislature did not reenact the death penalty.

[75] *State v. Quinn*, 290 Ore. 383 (1981). Oregon voters responded with Measure 7 (1984).

[76] These measures included California Proposition 8 (1982); California Proposition 115 (1990); Oregon Measure 40 (1996); and Arizona Proposition 104 (1990).

[77] California Secretary of State, *California Ballot Pamphlet, Primary Election, June 5, 1990*, 33. http://traynor.uchastings.edu/ballot_pdf/1990p.pdf. See Dinan, "Court-Constraining Amendments," 1011–16.

[78] *Raven v. Deukmejian*, 52 Cal. 3d 336, 353 (1990).

[79] Ibid., 341.

SAME-SEX MARRIAGE

Most recently, citizens have sought to prevent courts from expanding the definition of marriage and granting marriage rights to same-sex couples. The controversy has taken different forms in different states and has demonstrated how a state's rules for constitutional amendment can determine whether the people or the courts will have the last word on a contested issue.

The right of same-sex couples to marry first emerged as a prominent constitutional question in the 1990s.[80] In 1993, proponents of same-sex marriage achieved their first breakthrough in the courts. In *Baehr v. Lewin* (1993), the Hawaii Supreme Court ruled that the state's denial of marriage licenses to same-sex couples created a constitutionally suspect gender classification.[81] Opponents quickly launched a counter-mobilization to reverse the decision. Since Hawaii has no initiative process, defenders of traditional marriage had to persuade the legislature to refer to the voters an amendment to override *Baehr*. Although polls indicated a majority of the public supported a marriage amendment, the legislature resisted. After further pressure, and over the objections of gay rights activists, legislators negotiated a compromise. In exchange for approving a marriage amendment, the legislature enacted new laws allowing same-sex couples to register with the state and become "reciprocal beneficiaries." In 1998, the citizens of Hawaii approved the amendment by a 69 percent vote.[82]

Fearing that other courts would establish rights of same-sex marriage, conservatives sought to preempt the issue at the national level. Conservatives in Congress introduced several amendments to the U.S. Constitution seeking to protect the traditional definition of marriage, but none of them came close to winning the necessary two-thirds vote of both houses of Congress required by Article V. In 1996, as an alternative, Congress passed, and President Clinton signed, a statute called the federal Defense of Marriage Act (DOMA).[83] This act defined marriage as a "legal union between one man and one woman as husband and wife," denied federal benefits to same-sex couples, and attempted to protect each state's power to deny recognition of same-sex marriages performed in other states.[84] However, the federal DOMA did not prevent state supreme courts from declaring same-sex marriage a state constitutional right, and the struggle thus continued on a state-by-state basis. Advocates of

---

[80] For discussion of strategies used in the same-sex marriage controversy, see Reed, "Popular Constitutionalism," 920–32; Daniel R. Pinello, *America's Struggle for Same-Sex Marriage* (New York: Cambridge University Press, 2006).

[81] *Baehr v. Lewin*, 74 Haw. 530 (1993).

[82] HAW. CONST. art. I, sec. 23: "The legislature shall have the power to reserve marriage to opposite-sex couples." Robert Arakaki (legislative assistant, Hawaii legislature) interview with the author, May 17, 2005. Reed, "Popular Constitutionalism," 924–32.

[83] See S.J. Res. 56 (2003); S.J. Res. 40 (2004); S.J. Res. 1 (2005); H.J. Res. 88 (2006).

[84] *Defense of Marriage Act*, Pub. L. No. 104–99, 110 Stat. 2419 (Sept. 21, 1996), codified at 1 U.S.C. §7 and 28 U.S.C. §1738.

same-sex marriage mobilized in state courts to seek judicial expansion of the right to marry, whereas conservatives counter-mobilized to constrain courts through constitutional amendment.

Massachusetts: Goodridge *and the Triumph of Judicial Power.*

The next major battle between citizens and a court came in Massachusetts when the Massachusetts Supreme Judicial Court issued its landmark decision in *Goodridge v. Department of Public Health* (2003). In this case, the court struck down the state's existing marriage laws and ordered the legislature to enact new laws allowing same-sex couples to marry.[85]

The *Goodridge* litigation commenced in April 2001 when Hillary Goodridge, her partner Julie Goodridge, and six other same-sex couples filed an action in the Suffolk County superior court asserting that the Massachusetts Constitution guaranteed their right to marry. The superior court rejected their claim, but the Supreme Judicial Court granted review and, in November 2003, issued its decision.

In a plurality opinion, Chief Justice Margaret Marshall framed the issue as "whether, consistent with Massachusetts Constitution, the Commonwealth may deny the protections, benefits, and obligations conferred by civil marriage to two individuals of the same sex who wish to marry."[86] The court began by emphasizing that it was interpreting state constitutional rights. "The Massachusetts Constitution is, if anything, more protective of individual liberty and equality than the Federal Constitution," the court declared. "[I]t may demand broader protection for fundamental rights; and it is less tolerant of government intrusion into the protected spheres of life."[87]

The court then analyzed the state's existing marriage laws and found that they were "rooted in persistent prejudices against persons who are (or who are believed to be) homosexual," and "work[ed] a deep and scarring hardship on a very real segment of the community for no rational reason." The court found that these restrictions "violate[d] the basic premises of individual liberty and equality under law protected by the Massachusetts Constitution."[88]

After declaring the state's existing marriage laws unconstitutional, the court established a new definition of marriage. Henceforth, in Massachusetts, civil marriage would mean "the voluntary union of two persons as spouses, to the exclusion of all others."[89]

Governor Mitt Romney denounced the court's decision and called for a state constitutional amendment to override it.[90] Public opinion in the state was divided on the substantive issue of same-sex marriage. In the week after the

---

[85] *Goodridge v. Dept. of Public Health*, 440 Mass. 309 (2003).
[86] Ibid., 312.
[87] Ibid., 313.
[88] Ibid., 341–2, internal quotations and citations omitted.
[89] Ibid, 343.
[90] Frank Phillips and Rick Kline, "Lawmakers are Divided on Response." *The Boston Globe* (November 19, 2003), A1.

ruling, *The Boston Herald* published a poll indicating that 76 percent of respondents in Massachusetts supported granting full legal benefits to same-sex couples, whereas far fewer, 49 percent, supported same-sex marriage.[91] Over the next several months, as the governor, leaders of the Roman Catholic Church, and other opponents of same-sex marriage spoke out strongly against the decision, resistance to *Goodridge* grew. A February 22, 2004, poll by *The Boston Globe* showed declining public support for the court's ruling: 53 percent of respondents in Massachusetts now opposed same-sex marriage, whereas 60 percent backed creation of civil unions.[92] Significantly, on the question of who should decide the matter, 71 percent of the respondents said the issue should be decided by the voters in a referendum. One respondent summed up this widely held sentiment: "It doesn't belong in the courts. It's too important and the people should decide."[93]

During this period, the Massachusetts legislature was split on whether to place an amendment on the ballot to reverse the court. After a long debate, the legislature refused to do so.[94] When the legislative constitutional amendment (LCA) process collapsed, conservative activists were forced to turn to the state's initiative constitutional amendment process. In 2005, petitioners gathered sufficient signatures to qualify an ICA banning same-sex marriage. But, the Massachusetts process for an ICA is different from most other states' ICA procedures because it is *indirect*. Unlike in states where citizens can place a constitutional amendment directly on the ballot, proponents of ICAs in Massachusetts must first submit the proposed amendment to the legislature. To reach the ballot, the amendment must win the support of at least 50 (of 200) lawmakers in two consecutive sessions.[95]

As it turned out, the citizens' marriage amendment won sufficient legislative support in one session of the Massachusetts legislature, but fell short in the

[91] David R. Guarino, "Poll Finds Mass.-ive Backing for Gay Unions; Narrow Marriage Support," *The Boston Herald* (November 23, 2003), 7.

[92] Between November 2003 and February 2004, the percentage of Catholic respondents in Massachusetts who opposed same sex marriage increased from 47 to 66 percent. See Frank Phillips, "Majority in Mass Poll Oppose Gay Marriage; Survey Also Finds Civil Union Support," *The Boston Globe* (February 22, 2004), A-1.

[93] Ibid.

[94] In February 2004, the legislature held a constitutional convention to consider various options for constitutional amendments, but none of the proposals could win sufficient support. In March 2004, the legislature reconvened a constitutional convention and narrowly adopted a compromise amendment. This proposal would restrict the definition of marriage to a man and a woman, but would also establish civil unions "to provide same-sex persons with entirely the same benefits, protections, rights, privileges, and obligations as are afforded to married persons." This amendment failed, 105-to-92, because some conservative legislators opposed granting same-sex couples the right to civil unions, which they considered marriage in all but name, while many liberals argued that the arrangement would create a second-class status for same-sex couples. Mass. H. 3190 (2004).

[95] Mass. Const. art. 48.

second. The state's restrictive form of direct democracy, combined with legislative resistance, prevented Massachusetts citizens from directly deciding the marriage question.[96]

California: Proposition 22, In re Marriage Cases, *Proposition 8, and the People's Rule.* In California, the dynamics were in many ways similar to Massachusetts, but the state's stronger form of direct democracy gave the people the opportunity to vote on the state's definition of marriage.

As we have seen, in 2000, citizens in California adopted Proposition 22, an initiative amending the Family Code to read: "Only marriage between a man and a woman is valid or recognized in California." But, because the initiative was a statute rather than a constitutional amendment, it was vulnerable to judicial override. And, indeed, in May 2008, the California Supreme Court struck down the initiative and declared in *In re Marriage Cases* that the California Constitution protected the right of same-sex couples to marry.[97]

As in Massachusetts, the California legislature opposed a constitutional amendment to override the court. Thus, if Californians had no power of ICA – or a weak form like in Massachusetts – the court's decision in *Marriage Cases* would have been the last word on the issue. But, under California's strong form of direct democracy, citizens were able to bypass the legislature and adopt an ICA that reversed the court's ruling and reinstated the traditional definition of marriage.

The Shape of the Controversy in Other States

As the marriage controversy has developed, many states have adopted state constitutional amendments designed to constrain the judicial power to redefine marriage rights – but others have not. A state's rules for constitutional amendment have sometimes determined whether the people have been able to vote on the question. In many states, legislatures have been eager to submit "defense of marriage amendments" to citizens for their approval. But, in other states, including Massachusetts, Connecticut, and California – legislatures oppose DOMAs and the people can vote on the marriage question only if they have a strong form of the initiative constitutional amendment process.

In all, between 1998 and 2008, thirty states held statewide elections on state constitutional amendments defining marriage as a union between a man and a woman. Legislatures placed nineteen of these measures on the ballot for voter approval; citizens initiated twelve amendments. (In Arizona, voters rejected a 2006 ICA on the issue, but approved a 2008 legislative constitutional amendment.) Including Arizona, voters approved marriage amendments in all

---

[96] See Frank Phillips and Andrea Estes, "Right of Gays to Marry set for Years to Come: Vote Keeps Proposed Ban Off 2008 State Ballot," *The Boston Globe* (June 15, 2007), A1.

[97] *In re Marriage Cases*, 43 Cal.4th 757 (2008).

TABLE 7.1. *State DOMAs Placed on Ballot by Legislatures, 1998–2006*

State	Year	Amendment Procedure	% Yes
Baehr (Hawaii) 1993			
Hawaii	1998	LCA	69
Alaska	1998	LCA	68
Goodridge (Mass.) 2003			
Missouri	2004	LCA	71
Louisiana	2004	LCA	78
Georgia	2004	LCA	76
Kentucky	2004	LCA	75
Mississippi	2004	LCA	86
Oklahoma	2004	LCA	76
Utah	2004	LCA	66
Kansas	2005	LCA	70
Texas	2005	LCA	76
Alabama	2006	LCA	81
South Carolina	2006	LCA	78
South Dakota	2006	LCA	52
Tennessee	2006	LCA	81
Virginia	2006	LCA	57
Idaho	2006	LCA	63
Wisconsin	2006	LCA	59
Marriage Cases (Calif.)/Kerrigan (Conn.) 2008			
Arizona	2008	LCA	56

thirty states where they were able to vote on the question, usually by large margins.

By November 2008, voters in fifteen of sixteen states that have a direct power of initiative constitutional amendment were able to vote on the marriage question, either by ICA or by amendments placed on the ballot by the legislature. The only exception was Illinois, where the question fell outside the subject-matter limitations of the state's initiative process.[98] Meanwhile, in some parts of the country, especially the South and parts of the Midwest, legislatures have placed the matter before voters. But, in states where citizens lack the power of ICA and legislatures resist putting the matter to a popular vote, the courts, not the people, can have the last word.

The marriage controversy thus demonstrates that under certain circumstances the state-specific rules for constitutional amendment will determine whether the people can exercise a meaningful check on judicial power. The

---

[98] In Illinois, initiated amendments are limited to "structural and procedural subjects" contained in the legislative article. ILL. CONST OF 1970, art. XIV, sec. 3.

TABLE 7.2. *State DOMAs Placed on Ballot by Citizen Initiatives, 2000–2008*

State	Year	Amendment Procedure	% Yes
Baehr (Hawaii) 1993			
Nebraska	2000	Initiative	70
Nevada	2000/2002	Initiative	70/67
Goodridge (Mass.) 2003			
Arkansas	2004	Initiative	75
Michigan	2004	Initiative	58
Montana	2004	Initiative	67
North Dakota	2004	Initiative	73
Ohio	2004	Initiative	62
Oregon	2004	Initiative	57
Colorado	2006	Initiative	55
Arizona	2006	Initiative	48
Marriage Cases (Calif.)/Kerrigan (Conn.) 2008			
California	2008	Initiative	52
Florida	2008	Initiative	62

states with the strongest forms of ICA can exercise the most effective constraint on courts. These institutional differences have had consequences for the state constitutional status of the death penalty and same-sex marriage, and will shape other state-level conflicts between the people and the courts over the definition of rights.

REMOVING JUDGES FROM OFFICE

When the people have deep conflict with the courts, their last resort is to try to remove judges from the bench. By constitutional design and long-standing practice, federal judges are protected against this threat. For example, when federal district judge Thelton Henderson declared California's anti-affirmative action initiative unconstitutional in 1996, conservatives called for his impeachment. Representative Tom Delay (R-TX) said, "We've had judges impeached for public drunkenness. Why can't we impeach judges that are drunk with power?"[99] But, the effort was quickly abandoned because Congress never removes judges merely for issuing unpopular decisions. A few states similarly protect judges from voters. Notably, Massachusetts is one of three states where judges never have to face election and can issue counter-majoritarian decisions without fear of voter reprisal.[100]

---

[99] Harriet Chiang, "Film Captures Trials of Judge Henderson," *The San Francisco Chronicle*, (October 7, 2005), F-1.

[100] The other states without judicial elections are Rhode Island and New Hampshire. Council of State Governments, *The Book of the States* (2007), 263–5.

In 47 states, however, judges must face voters. Although political scientist G. Alan Tarr has observed that removal of judges in those states remains "episodic rather than endemic," the trend is toward greater exercise of popular control over courts.[101] In 1986, voters in California contributed to that trend by removing three justices from the state supreme court.

Backlash Against the Bird Court

The California Constitution authorizes the governor to fill vacancies on the state supreme court, subject to confirmation by the three-member Commission on Judicial Appointments and approval by the voters. Justices appear on the ballot at the first gubernatorial election following appointment, again at the end of the predecessor's twelve-year term, and again every twelve years thereafter. In each confirmation election, the justice's name appears alone on the ballot and voters can opt to support or oppose the justice's continued tenure on the court. Justices who receive less than a majority of the vote are dismissed.[102] California voters have almost always approved supreme court justices without controversy.[103] But, during the 1970s and early 1980s, increasing conflict between the people and the court exposed justices to political attack.

After the court issued its 1971 *Anderson* decision abolishing the death penalty, voters issued a sharp rebuke by amending the state constitution to override the decision. But, despite this strong message, the court continued to resist the popular will by routinely overturning death sentences it reviewed on appeal.[104] This record of reversals, combined with a line of activist decisions in other cases, prompted a coalition of conservative groups to mobilize against the court. The effort culminated in 1986 when four liberal members of the seven-member court – Chief Justice Rose Bird and Associate Justices Stanley Mosk, Cruz Reynoso, and Joseph Grodin – all appeared on the ballot.

---

[101] G. Alan Tarr, "Politicizing the Process: The New Politics of State Judicial Elections," in Keith J. Bybee, ed., *Bench Press: The Collision of Courts, Politics, and the Media* (Stanford: Stanford University Press, 2007), 57–8.

[102] CAL. CONST. art. VI, sec. 16.

[103] A notable exception was the retention election for Chief Justice Roger Traynor in 1966, which became controversial after the court's ruling in *Mulkey v. Reitman*, 64 Cal.2d 529 (1966). Traynor received 65 percent of the vote, down 20 percent from his prior election. See Grodin, *In Pursuit of Justice*, 105.

[104] In 1980, the California court formally upheld the constitutional validity of the state's new death penalty statute in *People v. Frierson*, 25 Cal.3d 142 (1979), but between 1977 (when Rose Bird joined the court) and May 1986, the court overturned death sentences in all but three of the 56 capital cases it had reviewed, and no one was executed in the state. See John H. Culver and John T. Wold, "Rose Bird and the Politics of Judicial Accountability in California," 70 *Judicature* 86 (1986). See also Barry Latzer, "California's Constitutional Counterrevolution," in G. Alan Tarr, ed., *Constitutional Politics in the States: Contemporary Controversies and Historical Patterns* (Westport, CT: Greenwood Press, 1996), 158; Gerald F. Uelmen, "Review of Death Penalty Judgments by the Supreme Courts of California: A Tale of Two Courts," 23 LOY. L.A. L.REV. 237 (1989).

District attorneys, victims' rights groups, business interests, and initiative entrepreneurs Howard Jarvis and Paul Gann mobilized the anticourt campaign and received influential support from Republican Governor George Deukmejian. As the campaign heated up, the movement dropped its opposition to Justice Mosk and focused its attack on Bird, Reynoso, and Grodin. The justices' opponents raised funds through direct mail, including a mailer that invited contributors to choose one of the targeted justices and donate a specified amount to ensure his or her defeat. They spent over $7 million on the campaign, whereas Bird, Grodin, and Reynoso collectively spent approximately $4.5 million – figures that were unprecedented for a judicial election.[105] Both sides allocated most of their money to thirty-second television ads that either attacked or defended the justices. One prominent ad explained that if viewers wanted to keep the death penalty in California, they should vote no on Bird, Reynoso, and Grodin.[106] On Election Day, voters soundly defeated the three justices – Chief Justice Bird received only 34 percent of the vote, whereas Justices Reynoso and Grodin received 40 and 43 percent, respectively.[107]

This outcome fundamentally reoriented the court. Governor Deukmejian appointed three new justices who helped form a new center-right majority. The court quickly began affirming a much higher percentage of capital sentences and, at least for a time, abandoned activism in the interpretation of state constitutional rights.

Trends in Judicial Elections

The popular overthrow of the Bird Court did not generate many similar incidents. For over a generation, no other California justice faced a serious threat of removal and in other states judicial removal remained "episodic."[108] One such episode occurred in 1996 when an organization called "Citizens for Responsible Government" targeted Nebraska Supreme Court Justice David Lanphier for defeat in a judicial retention election. Whereas Judge Lanphier's opponents objected to his rulings in a series of criminal cases (which were perceived as soft on crime), they also focused on his opinion in *Duggan v. Beermann* (1994), the case that invalidated Nebraska's 1992 term limits initiative.[109] In 1996, voters removed Lanphier from the court by nearly a 2-to-1 vote. Tennessee

---

[105] Grodin, *In Pursuit of Justice*, 169–78.

[106] Ibid., 179.

[107] The votes in the retention elections were: Bird (33.8% Yes, 66.2% No); Reynoso (39.8% Yes, 60.2% No); Grodin (43.4% Yes, 56.6% No). California Secretary of State, *Statement of Vote, November 4, 1986 General Election*, 36–7. For a discussion, see John H. Culver, "The Transformation of the California Supreme Court: 1987–1997," 61 ALB. L. REV. 1461 (1998).

[108] Tarr, "Politicizing the Process," 57.

[109] The case was *Duggan v. Beermann*, 245 Neb. 907 (1994). For a discussion, see B. Michael Dann and Randall M. Hansen, "National Summit on Improving Judicial Selection: Judicial Retention Elections," 34 LOY. L.A. L. REV. 1429 (2001).

Justice Penny White (1996), and Pennsylvania Justice Russell Nigro (2005) were also defeated in retention elections, and, in recent years, several other justices been voted off the bench in contentious partisan or nonpartisan judicial elections.[110]

Although removal of sitting state supreme court justices remains the exception, judicial elections have become more highly politicized, as evidenced by the number of contested elections, the money spent in the contests, and the use of television attack ads.[111] A number of factors help explain this change. First, partisan shifts in some states created tensions between new popular majorities and holdover judges. Second, state court activism fostered the perception that courts had become "political organs of the government" and thus fair game for political reprisal.[112] And third, in some cases (like Lanphier's), the heavy judicial check on citizen initiatives contributed to popular resentments and antagonized the same initiative entrepreneurs who have the capacity to organize an attack on judges.[113]

Indeed, frustrated initiative sponsors promoted measures to place new constraints on courts, including judicial recall, term limits on judges, and new rules for judicial elections.[114] It is important to note, however, that these court-constraining measures have enjoyed little success. Despite occasional frustration with the courts, voters seem to remain committed to the norm of judicial independence.

Impact on Judicial Decisions

Does the increase in politicization of the courts affect the outcomes of judicial decisions? Some state judges have candidly acknowledged that the threat of voter retribution weighs on them as they decide high-profile, controversial

---

[110] In 2008, six sitting state supreme court justices were defeated in judicial elections in four states (Michigan, Mississippi, West Virginia, and Wisconsin). Charles W. Hall, "Down, Dirty Judicial Races: Elections Reshape Supreme Court," *The Clarion-Ledger*, November 16, 2008.

[111] Tarr, "Politicizing the Process," 54–61.

[112] Ibid., 59–65. The quoted reference comes from Dodd, "The Recall and the Political Responsibility of Judges," (1911), 85–6.

[113] Gerald F. Uelmen, "Handling Hot Potatoes: Judicial Review of California Initiatives After *Senate v. Jones*," 41 SANTA CLARA L. REV. 999, 1000–1; Tarr, "Politicizing the Process," 63.

[114] See, e.g., Colorado Amendment 40 (1996), imposing retroactive term limits on Colorado appellate judges (defeated 57-to-43 percent); Oregon Measure 40 (1996), requiring district elections for members of state supreme court (defeated 56-to-44 percent); and South Dakota Amendment E (2006), known as the "J.A.I.L." Amendment, which sought to allow convicted criminals or disappointed civil litigants to bring personal actions against judges that could result in fines or imprisonment for the judge (defeated 89-to-11 percent). In addition, in 1996, activists in Montana sought to qualify an initiative adopting judicial recall, but the Montana Supreme Court struck the measure from the ballot for signature gathering violations. For a discussion, see David Rottman, "The State Courts in 2006: Surviving Anti-Court Initiatives and Demonstrating High Performance," The Council of State Governments, *The Book of the States*, Vol. 38 (Lexington, KY: The Council of State Governments, 2006), 249–53.

cases.[115] However, judges also insist that they cannot yield to fear of voter reprisal when rendering decisions. The initiative litigation record indicates that state judges have had sufficient fortitude to exercise a strong check on voter-approved initiatives, which is surely a high-profile, counter-majoritarian act. But, the California Supreme Court's cautious behavior in the immediate aftermath of the removal of three sitting justices also shows that popular checks can have a constraining effect on state court activism.

CONCLUSION

Over the past century, the rising judicial power has sometimes produced intense popular resentments. Judicial decisions as varied as *Lochner* and *In re Marriage Cases* have given rise to charges that courts are out of control. When federal courts have issued counter-majoritarian decisions, citizens have had little recourse. But, at the state level, citizens in some states have been able to hold courts to account when they stray too far from the majority will. Although Theodore Roosevelt's plan for recall of judicial decisions never took hold, citizens have been able to use other state-level devices such as judicial elections and ICAs to check the judicial power and reassert the sovereignty of the people.

---

[115] Former California Supreme Court Justice Otto Kaus described the pressures he faced in ruling on an initiative challenge when a retention election was pending. Acknowledging that his vote to uphold the initiative may subconsciously have been influenced by thoughts of his upcoming election, Kaus noted that trying to ignore the political implications of his decision in the case was like "ignoring a crocodile in your bathtub." Paul Reidinger, "The Politics of Judging," *A.B.A. Journal* 73 (April 1987): 52–58. See also Gerald F. Uelmen, "Crocodiles in the Bathtub: Maintaining the Independence of State Supreme Courts in an Era of Judicial Politicization," 72 Notre Dame L. Rev. 1133 (May 1997). Former California Supreme Court Justice Joseph Grodin similarly noted that his votes in some cases may have been subconsciously affected by his upcoming retention election and argued that "the potential that the pendency or threat of a judicial election is likely to have for distorting the proper exercise of the judicial function is substantial, and palpable." Joseph R. Grodin, "Developing a Consensus of Constraint: A Judge's Perspective on Judicial Retention Elections," 61 S. Cal. L. Rev. 1969, 1980 (1988).

Conclusion: A New Constitutional Equilibrium

First introduced as an "experiment in government" long ago, direct democracy has made a dramatic resurgence in recent decades. But, despite its expanding power and impact, direct citizen lawmaking has been largely contained by the constitutional system in which it operates. The people's rule has been limited by state and federal constitutional boundaries which, in turn, are enforced by courts.

Most importantly, the U.S. Constitution strictly confines direct democracy to the states. The Founders absolutely rejected direct popular rule and the Constitution prohibits direct citizen votes on questions of federal policy or constitutional design. Indeed, the United States is one of only five established democracies that have never held a national referendum – one of the enduring legacies of the founding.[1] The Constitution also excludes citizens from directly exercising a state's federal constitutional powers. Citizens cannot directly trigger a call for a federal constitutional convention, nor ratify or reject federal constitutional amendments, nor instruct their representatives in Congress, nor, presumably, determine a state's rules for allocating electoral votes for President of the United States. The U.S. Supreme Court has determined that these decisions may be made, if at all, by legislatures, not by the people directly. Reformers from William Jennings Bryan to Ralph Nader have tried to introduce direct democracy at the national level.[2] But, the exacting requirements for federal constitutional amendment make it unlikely that the United States will soon adopt any form of national direct democracy.

---

[1] The five established democracies that have never held a national referendum are India, Israel, Japan, the Netherlands, and the United States. See David Butler and Austin Ranney, eds., *Referendums Around the World: The Growing Use of Direct Democracy* (Washington, D.C.: AEI Press, 1994), 4.

[2] Thomas E. Cronin, *Direct Democracy: The Politics of Initiative, Referendum, and Recall* (Cambridge, MA: Harvard University Press, 1989), 157–95.

Although direct democracy cannot invade the national sphere, it has developed vigorously in the states. A defining characteristic of America's dual constitutional system is that the states are able to pursue distinctive policies and constitutional arrangements within the boundaries set by the federal Constitution. Supreme Court Justice Louis Brandeis observed that "[i]t is one of the happy incidents of the federal system that a single courageous State may, if its citizens choose, serve as a laboratory; and try novel social and economic experiments without risk to the rest of the country."[3] Brandeis was referring to policy experimentation, but federalism also allows states to experiment with institutional design, within the loosely defined limits of the Article IV guarantee clause. Progressive Era reformers exploited this opportunity by introducing direct democracy into many state constitutions.

Nearly half of the states now allow some form of the statewide initiative process, and each applies different rules for the exercise of this power. The twenty-four initiative states have created an array of hybrid state constitutional systems, with different mixtures of representative and direct democracy. In some initiative states, such as Illinois and Mississippi, the initiative process is so weak that the hybrid system is virtually indistinguishable from neighboring, noninitiative states. But, in other states, such as California, Oregon, Washington, Colorado, and Arizona, the initiative process has become so strong that consequential public decisions are often made directly by citizens, without the mediation of legislatures.

EXPECTATIONS AND EXPERIENCE

During the Progressive Era debate, both supporters and opponents of the initiative process accurately predicted many of its effects. Advocates like Bryan, Woodrow Wilson, and Theodore Roosevelt believed that the initiative process would increase citizen participation, promote public education on policy issues, increase accountability of elected officials, and make government more responsive to the popular will. Although it has done so imperfectly, the initiative process has, in fact, achieved these goals. Initiatives have increased voter participation and policy knowledge and have made government more responsive to the people, especially when malapportionment, gerrymandering, or extreme incumbency advantages have otherwise insulated representatives from shifts in public opinion.

At the same time, however, the early critics of the initiative process, including William Howard Taft and Elihu Root, accurately predicted many of the system's troublesome effects. As they expected, initiatives are too often poorly drafted, poorly understood, and immoderate. Moreover, as they predicted, the system has eroded the legislature's authority on fiscal and other important policy matters. And, as they feared, direct democracy has, at times, deepened

---

[3] *New State Ice Co. v. Liebmann*, 285 U.S. 262, 311 (1932), Brandeis, J. dissenting. See also, Felix Frankfurter, *The Public and Its Government* (New Haven: Yale University Press), 1930, 49–51.

factional divides and threatened minority and individual rights by putting those rights to a direct popular vote.

But, neither side of the Progressive Era debate envisioned how strongly courts would counter the initiative power. Elihu Root did predict that the Fourteenth Amendment would place a constraint on the initiative process, but he could not have foreseen how robust that constraint would be.[4] At the time, the U.S. Supreme Court had not incorporated most of the Bill of Rights into the Fourteenth Amendment, nor aggressively enforced the Amendment's equal protection clause to prevent state discrimination against minorities or women, nor expanded its due process clause to protect various forms of non-economic liberty and privacy against state interference. Similarly, state courts had not expansively interpreted state constitutional provisions to protect non-economic individual and minority rights. But in ways that were not easily foreseeable a century ago, the judicial power has expanded in all of these areas and has thus become a formidable check on direct democracy.

THE JUDICIAL CHECK

Federal Constitutionalism and Judicial Supremacy

The judicial check on initiatives has operated in two primary ways. When an initiative has raised a justiciable question of *federal* constitutional powers or rights, the courts have had the last word on the measure's validity. Courts have consistently struck down initiatives that imposed term limits on members of Congress, instructed representatives to support federal term limits, modified the rules for ratifying federal constitutional amendments, or established policies in areas preempted by federal law. When courts have invalidated these initiatives, citizens have had no practical way to reverse the decision. Similarly, when a court has determined that an initiative violated a federal constitutional right, the court's ruling was effectively final.

State Constitutionalism and the Fight for the Last Word

When conflicts between the people and the courts moved to the arena of state constitutional law, power shifted to the point where courts sometimes lost the upper hand. In some states, when the people disagreed with a judicial decision, they could, by petition and simple majority vote, override it. Courts and citizens engaged in pitched battles over the scope of state constitutional rights, especially in the areas of criminal procedure and punishment, privacy, and marriage.

---

[4] Elihu Root, "Experiments in Government and the Essentials of the Constitution," in Robert Bacon and James Brown Scott, eds., *Addresses on Government and Citizenship* (Cambridge, MA: Harvard University Press, 1916), 90.

Battles between citizens and state courts followed different patterns in different states. Much depended on the specific rules governing a state's initiative process and the judicial enforcement of these rules. A crucial factor was whether citizens had access to initiative constitutional amendment (ICA). In states with no ICA, courts could determine state constitutional questions without fear of quick reversal at the polls. But, in most ICA states, citizens were able to override judicial rulings that countered the majority will. Once adopted by the people, initiated amendments were also insulated from attacks by the legislature. The ICA option was thus highly attractive to initiative activists and many framed initiatives as constitutional amendments rather than statutes.

By the 1990s, many state supreme court justices had come to believe that the initiative process was out of control. In particular, they believed that it was too easy for citizens to use the ICA process to make frequent, fundamental changes to state constitutions. Courts began to explore ways to use technical rules to counteract this power. The Oregon Supreme Court took the lead by reinterpreting the state's separate-vote requirement for constitutional amendments. Through strict new enforcement of this rule, the court struck down, in quick succession, a criminal justice initiative, the state's term limit initiative, an initiative establishing new rules for campaign finance, and a property rights initiative.[5] Courts in other states looked for similar ways to limit the initiative power. Several state courts more aggressively enforced other technical rules, such as the single-subject rule, subject matter restrictions, and title rules, in order to void initiatives, either before or after the election, on those grounds.

The stakes in these disputes were high. The California Supreme Court acknowledged that if it strictly enforced the rules governing citizen lawmaking, it could "repudiate or cripple" the initiative process.[6] For the most part, the court has avoided doing so. However, courts in Florida and some other states have been less accommodating. Although they may not have crippled the initiative process through strict application of these rules, they have substantially limited its power. This judicial check has limited citizen lawmaking, but critics argue that the check is arbitrary, standardless, and beyond the legitimate scope of judicial review.

AN IMPERFECT EXPERIMENT

The Progressives hoped that direct democracy would redeem and strengthen representative government. But, in recent years, in at least some states, direct democracy has instead marginalized and weakened legislatures. The development of an aggressive, populist form of direct democracy, coupled with the rise of an activist judicial power, has shifted policy making from legislatures to the

---

[5] *Armatta v. Kitzhaber*, 327 Ore. 250 (1998); *Lehman v. Bradbury*, 333 Ore. 231 (2002); *Swett v. Bradbury*, 333 Ore. 597 (2002); and *League of Oregon Cities v. Oregon; McCall v. Kitzhaber*, 334 Ore. 645 (2002).

[6] *Fair Political Practices Commission v. Superior Court*, 25 Cal.3d 33, 41–2 (1979).

competing arenas of the initiative system and the courts. Whereas reasonable people can disagree whether a state is better off with direct democracy and a strong judicial power as part of its constitutional mix, it is easy to see that problems arise when a state's most important policy decisions are resolved through combat between direct democracy and courts.

The Polarization of Politics

First, battles between these two forces deepen rather than moderate factional divisions in the society. All liberal democracies struggle to reconcile the claims of majority and minority factions. The genius of the Madisonian design is that majority will and minority rights are expressed only *indirectly*, and are harmonized through the medium of the representative system. The legislature, the central institution of the Madisonian system, is constructed so that neither majorities nor minorities hold a "trump" on major policy issues. Instead, divisive questions are resolved through the complex, moderating processes of deliberation, persuasion, coalition-building, and compromise. Although legislatures certainly struggle to resolve divisive issues, their institutional dynamics generally require both sides to moderate their claims and seek broad consensus. Neither side may be fully satisfied with legislative outcomes, but even losing factions are often able to win concessions through the course of the process.

By contrast, the constitutional systems in the strong initiative states balance the claims of majority and minority factions in a very different way. In these systems, majority power and minority rights are expressed *directly*, through the competing forces of direct democracy and rights litigation. Unlike in a legislature, contestants in these arenas have the opportunity to seek total victory, and there is little incentive or opportunity for compromise.

The availability of the initiative process tempts majority factions to impose their will without having to accommodate even intense minorities. Initiative proponents can draft a measure in the strongest possible terms, and, if it has the support of a bare majority of the electorate, it becomes law. Conversely, an activist judiciary tempts minority groups to try to establish new rights or settle other hard questions without having to win broad-based support through normal political mobilization.[7]

The conflict over same-sex marriage in California again illustrates these dynamics. As the issue emerged, the state had a range of ways to address it. The classical, Madisonian option would have been for advocates and opponents of same-sex marriage to resolve the issue in the legislature. The likely

---

[7] See Alan Brinkley, "The Challenge to Deliberative Democracy," in Alan Brinkley, Nelson W. Polsby, and Kathleen M. Sullivan, eds., *New Federalist Papers: Essays in Defense of the Constitution* (New York: W.W. Norton & Co., 1997), 24–5; Rainer Knopff, "Populism and the Politics of Rights: The Dual Attack on Representative Democracy," *Canadian Journal of Political Science* 31, no. 4 (Dec. 1998): 683, 684–5.

outcome, at least for the short term, would have been a compromise that preserved the traditional definition of marriage as between a man and a woman, but secured to same-sex couples most or all of the legal rights and responsibilities of marriage through a civil union or domestic partner arrangement.[8] This outcome would not have fully satisfied either side, but it would have harmonized majority preferences and minority rights in a way that was broadly acceptable to most Californians.

But, because California has a hybrid constitutional system with a strong form of direct democracy and an activist judicial power, the legislature lost its authority to resolve the controversy as the issue shifted to the courts, through rights-based litigation, and to the electorate, through the initiative process. These competing arenas promised one side or the other a more definitive victory than the legislature could offer. But, pursuing the issue in these venues marginalized the legislature and polarized the debate.

Justice Marvin Baxter, in his dissenting opinion in *Marriage Cases*, lamented that the issue had shifted from the democratic process to the courts, and that the California Supreme Court, "not satisfied with the pace of democratic change," had substituted, "by judicial fiat, its own social policy views for those expressed by the People themselves."[9]

The court's decision in *Marriage Cases* was, indeed, a fiat, or a decree, or the playing of a trump. But so, too, were Propositions 22 and 8, which stripped the legislature of the authority to recognize same-sex marriage. Indeed, in this hybrid constitutional system, the initiative system and the judicial power have fed off each other as they have competed in a high-stakes fight for the last word.

This pattern of polarized conflict between citizens and the courts is well worth noting, because it will likely repeat in California and other states as various groups seek total victory on contested state constitutional issues.

The Politicization of the Courts

The hybrid constitutional system presents a second, related problem: the politicization of the courts. If a court invalidates an initiative, it exposes itself to the charge that it is thwarting the will of the people. And, if it does so frequently, especially on issues of major public concern, it risks losing its institutional legitimacy. If the people come to see judges as political actors rather than as neutral

---

[8] In fact, in 2003, the California legislature adopted the nation's most comprehensive domestic partnership law. See *California Domestic Partner Rights and Responsibilities Act of 2003* (Stats. 2003, ch. 421.) and subsequent amendments. The legislature sought to ensure that registered domestic partners would have "the same rights, protections, and benefits, and...be subject to the same responsibilities, obligations, and duties under law...as are granted to and imposed upon spouses." *California Family Code* sec. 297.5 (a). See *In re Marriage Cases*, 43 Cal.4th 757, 803 (2008).

[9] *In re Marriage Cases*, 43 Cal.4th at 863–4, Baxter, J. dissenting.

interpreters of the law, they are more likely to treat judges like politicians and hold them politically accountable for their decisions.

This danger, although real, should not be overstated. Federal judges, with their lifetime tenures, are wholly protected from popular accountability. State court judges are more accountable to voters through various systems of judicial elections, but they, too, are protected by the public's broad support for judicial independence. In 2005, a poll by researchers at Syracuse University found that nearly three-quarters of respondents agreed with the proposition that "judges should be shielded from outside pressure and allowed to make their decisions based on their own independent reading of the law."[10] The respondents' attitude was consistent across party and ideological lines. This survey confirmed that, in the United States, there is a large reservoir of public support for judicial independence. And, indeed, in most states, citizens have rarely voted to remove appellate judges from the bench.

Nevertheless, judges risk depleting this reservoir of public support if they engage in frequent conflict with the electorate over the validity of citizen-enacted law. If citizens believe that a state judge has given too little deference to initiatives, they may decide to try to shorten the judge's career. And, the same political operatives who promote ballot initiatives can employ their arts to unseat the judge in a judicial election. Whereas the people generally defer to judges, their restraint has limits and the increasing conflict between the people and the courts poses real threats to the independence of state judges.[11]

Potential Remedies

In the hybrid constitution states, the forces driving policy debates into the initiative arena and the courts are formidable, and may be irreversible. But, it is worth considering ways to restore the authority of representative institutions in these states. Meaningful progress toward this goal would require changes in both the initiative system and the courts.

The Initiative System. The great appeal – as well as the danger – of the initiative process is that it allows citizens to bypass representative government and enact

---

[10] Campbell Public Affairs Institute, Syracuse University. *The Maxwell Poll on Civic Engagement and Inequality* (October 2005), 5, http://www.maxwell.syr.edu/campbell/Poll/CitizenshipPoll.htm. See also Keith J. Bybee, "Introduction: The Two Faces of Judicial Power," in Keith J. Bybee, ed., *Bench Press: The Collision of Courts, Politics, and the Media* (Stanford: Stanford University Press, 2007), 1–17.

[11] Notably, some have argued that where citizens are able to override a judge's decision by popular vote (that is, through the ICA process), they may be less motivated to remove the judge. In making his case for "recall" of judicial decisions, Theodore Roosevelt argued that it would "obviate the need for such a drastic measure as the recall." See Theodore Roosevelt, "Introduction," in William L. Ransom, *Majority Rule and the Judiciary* (New York: Charles Scribner's Sons, 1912), 13. Similarly, the initiative constitutional amendment allows voters to reverse the court on a contested area of state constitutional law, such as criminal procedure or the scope of marriage rights, rather than targeting the judges themselves.

laws directly. In most initiative states, this bypass occurs most dramatically through initiative constitutional amendment. Initiative activists zealously guard the ICA power because they distrust both legislatures and courts and want to prevent them from thwarting citizen-enacted laws. Citizens have loaded up many state constitutions with a string of initiated amendments, in part because the task of qualifying and adopting a constitutional initiative is very similar to adopting a statutory initiative. In recent years, judges have sought to limit the power of the ICA, but these efforts have only reinforced citizen distrust of judges. A more constructive approach would be for states to make some modest adjustments to their initiative systems, particularly to strengthen the distinction between statutory and constitutional initiatives.[12] There are various ways to do this. One approach would be to require a supermajority vote for adoption of state constitutional amendments. Another approach, used with success in Nevada, would require affirmative votes in two consecutive elections for adoption of initiative constitutional amendments.[13] The Nevada rule preserves the people's power to amend the constitution directly, but affords them an opportunity for longer deliberation and a "sober second thought" on these important decisions.

The Courts. Courts can also help restore the authority of representative government by allowing legislatures to resolve most difficult policy issues. In particular, courts should exercise restraint when interpreting and expanding rights. Adhering to the norm of restraint would not mean renouncing the power of judicial review nor would it mean refraining from ever making a counter-majoritarian decision. But, it would mean avoiding activist decisions like those in *People v. Anderson* and *In re Marriage Cases*. In these cases, judges established new rights through the stroke of a pen rather than allowing legislatures to do the hard work of harmonizing majority will with emerging rights claims.

NEW EQUILIBRIUM

Finally, although the hybrid constitutional systems in the initiative states can certainly benefit from internal adjustments, it must be said that they work surprisingly well – largely because the remarkable institutional design developed by the Founders has adapted to state-level direct democracy. To be more

---

[12] For further analyses of potential initiative reforms, see, e.g., Elisabeth R. Gerber, "Reforming the California Initiative Process: A Proposal to Increase Flexibility and Legislative Accountability," in Bruce E. Cain and Roger G. Noll, eds., *Constitutional Reform in California: Making State Government More Effective and Responsive* (Berkeley: Institute of Governmental Studies Press, 1995), 291; Philip L. Dubois and Floyd Feeney, "Improving the California Initiative Process: Options for Change," (California Policy Seminar 1992); California Commission on Campaign Financing, *Democracy by Initiative: Shaping California's Fourth Branch of Government* (Los Angeles: Center for Responsive Government, 1992), 263–91.
[13] NEV. CONST. art. 19, sec. 2(4).

precise, the Madisonian system has controlled direct democracy and its potential excesses, largely through the power of judicial review.

Judicial enforcement of the federal Constitution has protected against the greatest potential abuses of pure majority rule, and allowed state-level constitutional dynamics to operate in a robust way. Citizens in the strong initiative states exercise power more directly than the Founders intended, but the checks and balances relationship between the people and the courts has conformed to the basic Madisonian principle that power should never be concentrated in the hands of any individual or group – even a majority of the people themselves. Through the conflict between direct democracy and the courts, power has countered power, and the hybrid constitutional systems have established a new equilibrium.

Appendix: Post-Election Initiative Invalidations

Year State #	Initiative Summary	Post-election Challenge	Outcome	Basis for Invalidation
CA 1914 22	Establishes procedures for certification of land titles	Follette v. Pacific Light and Power Corp., 189 Cal. 193 (1922)	IP	14th A DPC (depriving property without due process)
CA 1918 3	Restricts interest and fees that may be charged on loans ("usury law")	Wallace v. Zinman, 200 Cal. 585 (1927)	IP	14th A EPC, Cal. Const. art. I, sec. 11 uniform operation rule; art. I, sec. 21 privileges and immunities clause; art. IV, sec. 24 subject and title rules
CA 1920 1	Restricts acquisition or transfer of real property in the state by aliens not eligible for U.S. citizenship and not covered by treaty ("alien land law")	Oyama v. California, 332 U.S. 633 (1948)	IP	14th A EPC (citizens who are children of aliens)
		Sei Fujii v. State, 38 Cal.2d 718 (1952)	IE	14th A EPC, DPC

(continued)

(continued)

Year State #	Initiative Summary	Post-election Challenge	Outcome	Basis for Invalidation
CA 1926 28	Requires legislature to reapportion the state after each federal census into 40 senate and 80 assembly districts; establishes "federal plan" whereby assembly has equal population districts, but no county gets more than one senate district and small-population counties are grouped no more than three to a senate district; provides for redistricting commission in event legislature fails to enact plan	Jordan v. Silver, 381 U.S. 415 (1965)	IP	14th A EPC (unequal population senate districts)
		Legislature v. Reinecke, 6 Cal.3d 595 (1972) See also Baker v. Carr, 369 U.S. 186 (1962)	IP	Severability (redistricting commission non-severable from invalid redistricting process)
CA 1934 5	Establishes rules for criminal trials, including allowing court and counsel to comment on defendant's refusal to testify	Griffin v. California, 380 U.S. 609 (1965), reversing Adamson v. California, 332 U.S. 46 (1947)	IP	5th A (comment on defendant's failure to testify)
CA 1964 14	Repeals Rumford Fair Housing Act; prohibits state from imposing housing anti-discrimination laws; creates exceptions	Reitman v. Mulkey, 387 U.S. 369 (1967)	IE	14th A EPC (state authorization of private discrimination)
CA 1964 15	Prohibits fee-based television; creates limited exceptions	Weaver v. Jordan, 64 Cal.2d 235 (1966)	IE	1st A; Cal. Const. Art. I rights of free speech, press

Year State #	Initiative Summary	Post-election Challenge	Outcome	Basis for Invalidation
CA 1972 21	Repeals existing public school desegregation laws; bans racial assignments in public schools	Santa Barbara School Dist. v. Superior Court, 13 Cal.3d 315 (1975)	IP	14th A EPC (prohibition on racial assignments in public schools)
CA 1974 9	Establishes Political Reform Act, imposing new restrictions and disclosure rules on campaign contributions, expenditures, and lobbying activities; establishes Fair Political Practices Commission to implement and enforce rules	Citizens for Jobs and Energy v. Fair Political Practices Commission, 16 Cal.3d 671 (1976)	IP	1st A (expenditure limits on initiatives, lobbyist contribution ban, some reporting requirements)
		Hardie v. Eu, 18 Cal.3d 371 (1976)	IP	1st A (limitations on expenditures for initiative petition gathering)
		California Pro-Life Council v. Randolph, 507 F.3d 1172 (9th Cir. 2007)	IP	1st A (recipient committee requirements)
CA 1978 7	Increases penalties for persons convicted of first degree murder; expands categories of special circumstances; revises rules regarding assessment of aggravating and mitigating circumstances	People v. Ramos, 37 Cal.3d 136 (1984) [on remand from California v. Ramos, 463 U.S. 992 (1983)]	IP	Cal. Const. art. I, sec. 7 DPC (rules for jury instructions at penalty stage)
CA 1982 5	Repeals gift and inheritance taxes	Estate of Gibson v. Bird, 139 Cal. App. 3d 733 (1983)	IE	Cal. Const. art. II, sec. 10(b) two-in-conflict rule (conflicts with Proposition 6)

(continued)

(continued)

Year State #	Initiative Summary	Post-election Challenge	Outcome	Basis for Invalidation
CA 1982 8	Enacts new rules regarding criminal procedure, sentencing, bail, and release; establishes right to restitution	Brosnahan v. Brown, 32 Cal.3d 236 (1982)	IP	Cal. Const. art. XVIII, sec. 4 two-in-conflict rule (bail provisions conflict with Proposition 4)
CA 1984 24	Enacts rules for legislature regarding partisan composition of committees, voting, and other procedural, operational, staffing, and funding requirements	People's Advocate, Inc. v. Superior Court, 181 Cal. App. 3d 316 (1986)	IP	Cal. Const. art. IV legislative powers
CA 1988 68	Enacts new regulations on campaign finance; provides for public funding of campaigns	Taxpayers to Limit Campaign Spending v. Fair Political Practices Commission, 51 Cal. 3d 744 (1990)	IE	Cal. Const. art. II, sec. 10(b) two-in-conflict rule (conflicts with Proposition 73)
CA 1988 73	Enacts new regulations on campaign finance, without public funding of campaigns	Service Employees International Union vs. Fair Political Practices Commission, 955 F.2d 1312 (9th Cir. 1992)	IP	1st A, 14th A EPC (limits on contributions based on fiscal year and restrictions on transfers)
CA 1988 103	Rolls back automobile insurance rates; creates new insurance regulations; creates elected office of insurance commissioner to implement and enforce	Calfarm Insurance Co. v. Deukmejian, 48 Cal.3d 805 (1989)	IP	14th A DPC, Cal. Const. art. I, sec. 7 DPC (restricting opportunity for regulated companies to redress "confiscatory rates"); rule against naming private corporation to perform function

Year State #	Initiative Summary	Post-election Challenge	Outcome	Basis for Invalidation
CA 1988 105	Requires disclosure regarding household toxics, insurance policies, nursing homes, contributions to ballot initiative campaigns, investments in South Africa	Chemical Specialties Manufacturers Assn., Inc. v. Deukmejian, 227 Cal. App. 3d 663 (1991)	IE	Cal. Const. art. II, sec. 8(d) single subject rule
CA 1990 115	Imposes new criminal penalties; restricts defendants' state constitutional rights to a level no greater than federal constitutional requirements; enacts other rules of criminal procedure	Raven v. Deukmejian, 52 Cal.3d 336 (1990)	IP	Cal. Const. art. XVIII, secs. 1, 2 no revision rule (limitation on state constitutional rights)
CA 1990 140	Imposes term limits on members of the legislature (three 2-year terms in Assembly; and two 4-year terms in Senate) and state-wide elected officials (two 4-year terms); reduces legislature's budget; bans legislative pensions	Legislature v. Eu, 54 Cal.3d 492 (1991)	IP	Art. I, sec. 10 contracts clause (restriction on pensions for incumbent legislators)
CA 1992 164	Imposes term limits on California's representatives in Congress (6 years for U.S. representatives; 12 years for U.S. Senators)	U.S. Term Limits, Inc. v. Thornton, 514 U.S. 779 (1995)	IE	Art. I, secs. 2, 3 qualifications clauses (state-imposed term limits on federal representatives)

(continued)

(continued)

Year State #	Initiative Summary	Post-election Challenge	Outcome	Basis for Invalidation
CA 1994 187	Restricts illegal immigrants' eligibility for public services, including social services, health care, public education; requires specified public employees to report suspected illegal aliens; increases penalties for making, using, or selling false citizenship or residency documents	League of United Latin American Citizens v. Wilson, 1998 U.S. Dist. LEXIS 3372 (C.D. Cal. 1998)	IP	Art. VI supremacy clause (all provisions except imposition of new penalties for false IDs) 14th A EPC (education restrictions)
CA 1996 198	Establishes blanket primary, providing single primary ballot to all voters, except for separate partisan ballots for selection of party committee members	California Democratic Party v. Jones, 530 U.S. 567 (2000)	IE	1st A right of association
CA 1996 208	Regulates campaign finance by limiting contributions, limiting fundraising to a specified period before the election, restricting contributions by lobbyists, increasing disclosure requirements	California Pro-Life Council Political Action Committee v. Scully, 164 F.3d 1189 (9th Cir. 1999)	IP	1st A (contribution limits) (litigation superseded by passage of subsequent proposition)
		California Republican Party v. Fair Political Practices Commission, 2004 U.S. Dist. LEXIS 22160 (E.D. Cal. 2004)	IP	1st A (disclosure laws for political advertisements)
CA 1998 225	Requires disclosure on ballot regarding candidate's position on congressional term limits	Bramberg v. Jones, 20 Cal.4th 1045 (1999)	IE	Art. V amendment rules

Year State #	Initiative Summary	Post-election Challenge	Outcome	Basis for Invalidation
CA 1998 4	Bans use of specified animal traps and poisons	National Audubon Society, Inc. v. Davis, 307 F.3d 835 (9th Cir. 2002)	IP	Art. VI supremacy clause (preempted by federal Migratory Bird Treaty Act, Endangered Species Act, and Wildlife Refuge System Improvement Act)
CA 1998 5	Mandates governor enter into compacts with tribes to authorize casinos on tribal lands; establishes related regulations	Hotel Employees and Restaurant Employees International Union v. Davis, 21 Cal.4th 585 (1999)	IE	Cal. Const. art. IV, sec. 19(e) prohibition on Nevada-style gambling
CA 2000 22	Adopts statute that "Only marriage between a man and a woman is valid or recognized in California"	In re Marriage Cases, 43 Cal.4th 757 (2008)	IE	Cal. Const. art. I, sec. 1 privacy; art. I, sec. 7 EPC, DPC
OR 1908 16 – 330	Limits campaign contributions and expenditures; enacts penalties for corrupt and illegal practices in nominations and elections; provides for information for voters; prohibits electioneering on election day; allows for post-election contests; establishes related regulations ("Corrupt Practices Act")	Combs v. Groener, 256 Ore. 336 (1970)	IP	Ore. Const. art. IV, sec. 11 power of legislature to judge elections

(continued)

(continued)

Year State #	Initiative Summary	Post-election Challenge	Outcome	Basis for Invalidation
OR 1910 16 – 330	Creates rules to protect laborers in hazardous employment; enacts safety regulations; provides incentives for employers to provide insurance; establishes employers' liability for injuries; restricts use of certain tort defenses	Birrer v. Flota Mercante Grancolombiana, 386 F. Supp. 1105 (D. Ore. 1974)	IP	Art. VI supremacy clause (state standard that is stricter than the national standard)
OR 1912 29 – 358	Regulates railroad freight rates; sets minimum carload weights; authorizes railroad commission to implement	Southern Pacific Company v. Railroad Commission of Oregon, 208 F. 926 (D. Ore. 1913)	IE	14th A DPC, EPC (rate regulations)
OR 1922 6 – 314	Requires parents and guardians to send children 8–16 years old to public schools; eliminates private school exemption; creates limited exceptions; establishes penalties for violations	Pierce v. Society of Sisters of the Holy Names of Jesus and Mary, 268 U.S. 510 (1925)	IE	14th A DPC
OR 1938 9 – 316	Defines labor disputes; restricts picketing and boycotting by labor unions	American Federation of Labor v. Bain, 165 Ore. 183 (1940)	IE	1st A
OR 1978 8	Authorizes death penalty for murder under specified conditions; provides for other criminal punishments where death sentence not imposed; establishes sentencing procedures	State v. Quinn, 290 Ore. 383 (1981)	IP	Ore. Const. art. I, sec. 11 right to jury trial of all facts constituting the crime
		State v. Shumway, 291 Ore. 153 (1981)	IP	Ore. Const. art I, sec. 16 restrictions on punishments

Year State #	Initiative Summary	Post-election Challenge	Outcome	Basis for Invalidation
OR 1984 3	Creates citizens' utility board to represent interests of electric, telephone, gas, and heating utility consumers	Oregon Independent Telephone Association. v. Citizens' Utility Board of Oregon, 1985 U.S. Dist. LEXIS 16128 (D. Ore. 1985)	IP	1st A (requirement that utilities disseminate certain materials in billing envelopes)
OR 1988 8	Revokes state executive branch ban on discrimination based on sexual orientation; provides that no state official shall forbid taking personnel action against a state employee because of employee's sexual orientation	Merrick v. Board of Higher Education, 116 Ore. App. 258 (1992)	IE	Ore. Const. art. I, sec. 8 rights of free speech
OR 1992 3	Establishes lifetime term limits for state legislators (6 years in state house of representatives and 8 years in state senate); for statewide elected officials (8 years); and for Oregon's representatives in Congress (6 years for U.S. Representatives and 12 years for U.S. Senators)	U.S. Term Limits, Inc. v. Thornton, 514 U.S. 779 (1995)	IP	Art. I, secs. 2, 3 qualifications clauses (state-imposed term limits on federal representatives)
		Lehman v. Bradbury, 333 Ore. 231 (2002)	IE	Ore. Const. art. XVII, sec. 1 separate vote requirement
OR 1994 6	Restricts use of political contributions from out-of-district residents	VanNatta v. Keisling, 151 F.3d 1215 (9th Cir. 1998)	IE	1st A

(continued)

(continued)

Year State #	Initiative Summary	Post-election Challenge	Outcome	Basis for Invalidation
OR 1994 8	Requires state employees to contribute percentage of salary to retirement benefits	Oregon State Police Officers' Association. v. State of Oregon, 323 Ore. 356 (1996)	IE	Art. I, sec. 10 contracts clause
OR 1994 9	Establishes mandatory political contribution limits, voluntary expenditure limits, other campaign finance regulations	VanNatta v. Keisling, 324 Ore. 514 (1997)	IP	Ore. Const. art. I, sec. 8 rights of free speech (certain contribution and expenditure provisions); other related provisions void as incomplete, incapable of being executed
OR 1996 40	Increases rights of crime victims; expands admissible evidence in criminal proceedings; limits pretrial release	Armatta v. Kitzhaber, 327 Ore. 250 (1998)	IE	Ore. Const. art. XVII, sec. 1 separate vote requirement
OR 1998 62	Requires campaign finance disclosure; regulates signature gathering by making signature gatherers be registered Oregon voters; allows regulation or prohibition of payments for signatures	Swett v. Bradbury, 333 Ore. 597 (2002)	IE	Ore. Const. art. XVII, sec. 1 separate vote requirement
OR 2000 7	Requires government payment to landowners for regulatory takings	League of Oregon Cities v. Oregon; McCall v. Kitzhaber, 334 Ore. 645 (2002)	IE	Ore. Const. art. XVII, sec. 1 separate vote requirement

Year State #	Initiative Summary	Post-election Challenge	Outcome	Basis for Invalidation
WA 1914 8	Forbids employment agents from collecting fees in exchange for providing workers employment or employment information	Adams v. Tanner, 244 U.S. 590 (1917)	IE	14th A DPC (restriction on liberty to engage in a useful business)
WA 1932 69	Establishes graduated state income tax	Culliton v. Chase; McKale's, Inc. v. Chase, 174 Wash. 363 (1933)	IE	WA Const. art. VII, sec. 1 restriction on unequal taxation of property (income is "intangible property")
WA 1948 169	Provides payment of additional compensation to World War II veterans; authorizes state bonds to support compensation fund; imposes tobacco tax to finance bonds	Gilman v. State Tax Commission, 32 Wn.2d 480 (1949)	IE	WA Const. art. VIII, sec. 3 limits on state debt
WA 1960 25*	Prohibits construction or operation of any dam over 25 feet on specified rivers and streams; conserves state fishery resources	City of Tacoma v. Taxpayers of Tacoma, 60 Wn.2d 66 (1962)	IP	Art. I, sec. 8 commerce clause authority over navigable waters
WA 1972 276	Establishes new requirements for disclosure of campaign contributions and expenditures; limits campaign expenditures; regulates activities of lobbyists; requires reporting of lobbyist	Bare v. Gorton, 84 Wn.2d 380 (1974)	IP	1st A (expenditure limits)
		State of Washington, ex rel. Public Disclosure Commission v. Rains, 87 Wn.2d 626 (1976)	IP	1st A (expenditure disclosure rules)

(continued)

(continued)

Year State #	Initiative Summary	Post-election Challenge	Outcome	Basis for Invalidation
	activities; strengthens public access to records of government agencies; provides for civil penalties; establishes a public disclosure commission to administer the act			
WA 1975 316	Requires mandatory death penalty for aggravated murder in the first degree; imposes life sentence without parole if governor commutes sentence or if death penalty held unconstitutional	State of Washington v. Green, 91 Wn.2d 431 (1979)	IE	8th A (mandatory death penalty)
WA 1977 355	Defines moral nuisances; places prohibitions on lewd or pornographic theaters and publications; creates private right of action to abate nuisance; establishes penalties for violations	State of Washington ex rel. Jones v. Charboneau's, 27 Wn. App. 5 (1980)	IE	WA Const. art. II, sec. 19 ballot title rules
		Spokane Arcades, Inc. v. Brockett, 631 F.2d 135 (9th Cir. 1980)	IP	1st A (prior restraint)
WA 1978 350	Prohibits assigning students to other than the nearest or next-nearest school; creates limited exceptions	Washington v. Seattle School District No. 1, 458 U.S. 457 (1982)	IE	14th A EPC

Year State #	Initiative Summary	Post-election Challenge	Outcome	Basis for Invalidation
WA 1980 383	Bans the importation and storage of nonmedical radioactive wastes generated outside Washington unless otherwise permitted by interstate compact	Washington State Building and Construction Trades Council, AFL-CIO v. Spellman, 684 F.2d 627 (9th Cir. 1982)	IE	Art. VI supremacy clause, Art. I sec. 8 commerce clause
WA 1981 394	Requires public agencies to obtain voter approval before issuing bonds for construction or acquisition of major public energy projects	Continental Illinois National Bank and Trust Company of Chicago v. State of Washington, 696 F.2d 692 (9th Cir. 1983)	IP	Art. I, sec. 10 contracts clause (pre-existing bond issues)
WA 1992 134	Limits campaign contributions; establishes new disclosure rules; imposes related regulations and penalties for violations	Washington State Republican Party v. Public Disclosure Commission, 141 Wn.2d 245 (2000)	IP	1st A (restrictions on use of exempt funds for issue advocacy)
WA 1992 573	Establishes term limits for governor and lieutenant governor (no more than 8 of 14 years); members of state legislature (no more than 6 of 12 years in lower house, 8 of 14 years in state senate, and 14 of 20 years in legislature); establishes term limits for Washington representatives in Congress (no more than 6 of 12 years in House; 12 of 18 years	U.S. Term Limits Inc. v. Thornton, 514 U.S. 779 (1995) See also Thorsted v. Gregoire, 841 F. Supp. 1068 (W.D. Wash. 1994)	IP	Art. I, secs. 2, 3 qualifications clauses (state-imposed term limits on federal representatives)
		Gerberding v. Munro, 134 Wn.2d 188 (1998)	IE	WA Const. art. II, sec. 1 initiative power (WA initiatives cannot amend or revise state constitution)

(continued)

(continued)

Year State #	Initiative Summary	Post-election Challenge	Outcome	Basis for Invalidation
	in Senate); stipulates that limits on federal representatives will go into effect only if 9 or more other states other adopt term limits on their members of Congress			
WA 1999 695	Repeals existing vehicle tab fees; sets fees at $30 per year; requires voter approval for all subsequent tax increases	Amalgamated Transit Union Local 587 v. State of Washington, 142 Wn.2d 183 (2000)	IE	WA Const. art. II, sec. 19 single subject rule; art. II, sec. 19 title rules; art. II, sec. 37 requirement that initiatives record all laws that they will amend or revise; art. II, sec. 1 scope of initiative power
WA 2000 722	Nullifies all tax and fee increases adopted without voter approval between July 2 and December 31, 1999; exempts vehicles from property tax; limits property tax increases to 2% annually	City of Burien v. Kiga, 144 Wn.2d 819 (2001)	IE	WA Const. art. II, sec. 19 single subject rule
WA 2000 732	Provides annual cost-of-living salary adjustments to public school teachers, other school employees, and certain employees of state community colleges and technical colleges	McGowan v. State of Washington, 148 Wn.2d 278 (2002)	IP	WA Const. art. II, sec. 1 scope of initiative power (exceeds constitutional definition of basic education)

Year State #	Initiative Summary	Post-election Challenge	Outcome	Basis for Invalidation
WA 2001 747	Requires state and local governments to limit property tax increases to 1% per year without voter approval for a larger increase	Washington Citizens Action of Washington v. State of Washington, 162 Wn.2d 142 (2007)	IE	WA Const. art. II, sec. 37 rule that initiatives record all laws that they will amend or revise
WA 2002 776	Limits tab fees to $30 per year for motor vehicles, including light trucks; repeals certain local-option excise taxes and fees for roads and public transit	Pierce County v. State of Washington, 159 Wn.2d 16 (2006)	IP	WA Const. art. I, sec. 23 contracts clause (impairs contractual obligations to bondholders)
CO 1912 16	Prohibits any state court except the supreme court from declaring a law unconstitutional; gives the people the right to overrule or "recall" decisions of the state supreme court declaring laws or charter amendments unconstitutional; creates procedures for such "recall" of judicial decisions; establishes juvenile courts	People v. Western Union Telegraph Co., 70 Colo. 90 (1921)	IP	Art. VI supremacy clause; Colo. Const. art. VI, sec. 2, art. XII, sec. 8 (restriction on state court determination of federal constitutional questions)
		People v. Max, 70 Colo. 100 (1921) (companion case to 70 Colo. 90)	IP	14th A DPC (restrictions on review of state constitutional questions; recall of judicial decisions); severability
CO 1962 7	Enacts "federal model" redistricting plan for state legislature, with lower house districts based on population, senate districts based on other factors	Lucas v. Forty-Fourth General Assembly of Colorado, 377 U.S. 713 (1964)	IE	14th A EPC (senate apportionment)

(continued)

(continued)

Year State #	Initiative Summary	Post-election Challenge	Outcome	Basis for Invalidation
CO 1984 3	Prohibits public funding for abortions; allows legislature to create exception to appropriate funds for medical services to prevent death of pregnant woman or her unborn child	Hern v. Beye, 57 F.3d 906 (10th Cir. 1995)	IP	Art. VI supremacy clause (restrictions on funding abortions where required by federal law)
CO 1992 2	Prohibits state or local governments from enacting laws providing that homosexual, lesbian, or bisexual orientation, conduct, or relationships entitle a person to claim any minority or protected status, quota preferences, or discrimination	Romer v. Evans, 517 U.S. 620 (1996)	IE	14th A EPC
CO 1994 17	Imposes shorter term limits on Colorado's representatives in Congress (6 years for U.S. House Members and 12 years for U.S. Senators); extends term limits to local nonjudicial elected officials	U.S. Term Limits, Inc. v. Thornton, 514 U.S. 779 (1995)	IP	Art. I, secs. 2, 3 qualifications clauses (state-imposed term limits on federal representatives)
CO 1996 12	Places "scarlet letter" on ballot for candidates who fail to endorse federal constitutional amendment establishing congressional term limits	Morrissey v. State, 951 P.2d 911 (Colo. 1998)	IE	Art. V amendment rules

Year State #	Initiative Summary	Post-election Challenge	Outcome	Basis for Invalidation
CO 1996 15	Limits campaign contributions; establishes voluntary expenditure limits; increases disclosure requirements, including for independent expenditures; requires statement in ballot pamphlet regarding adherence to limits; enacts related regulations	Citizens for Responsible Government State Political Action Committee v. Davidson, 236 F.3d 1174 (10th Cir. 2000)	IP	1st A (rules for independent expenditures)
CO 1998 12	Requires parental notification, 48-hour waiting period for unemancipated minor seeking abortion; provides for exceptions and judicial bypass	Planned Parenthood of the Rocky Mountains Services Corporation v. Owens, 287 F.3d 910 (10th Cir. 2002)	IE	14th A DPC (failure to provide health exception)
CO 2002 27	Restricts campaign contributions; limits contributions and expenditures by corporations or labor organizations; creates voluntary expenditure limits; increases disclosure requirements; transfers some existing election law into constitution ("Fair Campaign Practices Act")	Colorado Right to Life Committee, Inc. v. Coffman, 498 F.3d 1137 (10th Cir. 2007)	IP	1st A (definition of political committee; restriction on corporation funding electioneering communication)

(continued)

(continued)

Year State #	Initiative Summary	Post-election Challenge	Outcome	Basis for Invalidation
AZ 1914 314	Establishes and provides appropriation for old age and mothers pension system; abolishes "almshouses"	Board of Control of the State of Arizona v. Buckstegge, 18 Ariz. 277 (1916)	IE	Ariz. Const. art. IV, sec. 13 ballot titles rules; contains incomplete, unenforceable statutory language
AZ 1914 318	Restricts employment of non-citizens (80 percent of employees must be U.S. citizens)	Truax v. Raich, 239 U.S. 33 (1915)	IE	14th A EPC
AZ 1914 322	Regulates the placement, erection, and maintenance of electric poles, wires, cables, and appliances	Pacific Gas and Electric Co. v. State, 23 Ariz. 81 (1921)	IE	Ariz. Const. art. XV, sec. 3 powers of corporation commission
AZ 1914 324	Authorizes state board of control to develop state resources and to establish state printing plant and banking system; changes contract system for state construction	Tillotson v. Frohmiller, 34 Ariz. 394 (1928)	IE	Ariz. Const. art. III distribution of powers
AZ 1916 306	Imposes restrictions on hunting and fishing	U.S. v. Hunt, 19 F.2d 634 (1927)	IP	Art. VI supremacy clause (as applied to federal lands)
AZ 1918 306	Reinstates death penalty; establishes rules for implementation	State of Arizona v. Endreson, 109 Ariz. 117 (1973) See also Furman v. Georgia, 408 U.S. 238 (1972)	IE	8th A (unlimited jury discretion)

Year State #	Initiative Summary	Post-election Challenge	Outcome	Basis for Invalidation
AZ 1948 306	Creates state civil service system; establishes civil service board to implement; requires specified counties to establish civil service system for county employees and authorizes others to do so	Hernandez v. Frohmiller, 68 Ariz. 242 (1949)	IE	Ariz. Const. art. III distribution of powers (improper delegation of legislative power); art. IV title rules; art. IV, part 2, sec. 19 prohibition on special laws; art. XI, sec. 2 powers of existing boards
AZ 1952 312	Prescribes conditions for legal picketing; prohibits secondary boycotts; establishes penalties for violations	Baldwin v. Arizona Flame Restaurant, Inc., 82 Ariz. 385 (1957)	IE	1st A, 14th A DPC
AZ 1988 106	Designates English as the state's official language; requires the state and its political subdivisions to "act" only in English	Ruiz v. Hull, 191 Ariz. 441 (1998)	IE	1st A, 14th A EPC
AZ 1992 107	Establishes term limits for state legislators (8 years in each house) and for Arizona's representatives in Congress (6 years for U.S. Representatives; 12 years for U.S. Senators)	U.S. Term Limits, Inc. v. Thornton, 514 U.S. 779 (1995)	IP	Art. I, secs. 2, 3 qualifications clauses (state-imposed term limits on federal representatives)
AZ 1996 102	Requires juveniles ages 15 and older to be tried as adults when accused of murder, aggravated sexual assault, armed robbery, other designated violent offenses, or when chronic felony offenders	State of Arizona v. Davolt, 207 Ariz. 191 (2004)	IP	8th A (juvenile death penalty requires greater protections)
		Roper v. Simmons, 543 U.S. 551 (2005)	IP	8th A (juvenile death penalty per se unconstitutional)

(continued)

(continued)

Year State #	Initiative Summary	Post-election Challenge	Outcome	Basis for Invalidation
AZ 1998 200	Creates a voluntary alternative campaign finance system with public funding and restrictions on contributions to and expenditures by participating candidates; establishes related regulations and an appointed commission to administer system	Citizens Clean Elections Commission v. Myers, 196 Ariz. 516 (2000)	IP	Ariz. Const. art. VI, secs. 36, 37 (powers of commission on appellate court appointments) (improper expansion of commission's powers)

IE = Invalidated in entivety; IP = Invalidated in part. DPC = due process clause; EPC = equal protection clause.

For additional information on initiatives and post-initiative letigation, see Miller-Rose Initiative Database at www.cmc.edu/rose.

References

Abraham, Henry J. and Barbara A. Perry. *Freedom and the Court: Civil Rights and Liberties in the United States*, Eighth Edition. Lawrence: University Press of Kansas, 2003.

Allswang, John M. *The Initiative and Referendum in California, 1898–1998*. Stanford: Stanford University Press, 2000.

Amar, Akhil Reed and Vikram David Amar. "How to Achieve Direct National Election of the President without Amending the Constitution." Findlaw, December 28, 2001.

Arakaki, Robert, legislative assistant, Hawaii legislature. Interview, May 17, 2005.

Arkansas Secretary of State, "Amendment 73. Arkansas Term Limitation Amendment." http://www.sos.arkansas.gov/ar-constitution/arcamend73/arcamend73.htm.

———. "Elections." http://www.sos.arkansas.gov/elections_election_results.html.

Axelrad, Jacob. *Patrick Henry: The Voice of Freedom*. New York: Random House, 1947.

Bailyn, Bernard. *The Ideological Origins of the American Revolution*. Cambridge, MA: Harvard University Press, 1967.

Baker, Gordon E. *The Reapportionment Revolution: Representation, Political Power, and the Supreme Court*. New York: Random House, 1966.

Baker, Leonard. *Back to Back: The Duel Between FDR and the Supreme Court*. New York: Macmillan, 1968.

Baker, Lynn. "Direct Democracy and Discrimination: A Public Choice Perspective." 67 CHI-KENT L. REV. 707 (1991).

Bangs, Elizabeth T. "Who Should Decide What is Best for California's LEP Students? Proposition 227, Structural Equal Protection, and Local Decision-Making Power." 11 LA RAZA L. J. 113 (2000).

Barker, Ernest, ed. *Social Contract: Locke, Hume and Rousseau*. New York: Oxford University Press, 1962.

Barnett, James D. *The Operation of the Initiative, Referendum, and Recall in Oregon*. New York: Macmillan, 1915.

Barrett, Edward L., Jr. "*Anderson* and the Judicial Function." 45 S. CAL. L. REV. 739 (1972).

Beard, Charles A. *The Supreme Court and the Constitution*. New York: Macmillan, 1912.

_____. *An Economic Interpretation of the Constitution of the United States.* New York: Macmillan, 1913.

Beard, Charles A. and Birl E. Shultz. *Documents on the Statewide Initiative, Referendum and Recall.* New York: Macmillan, 1912.

Beckner, Gary, Thomas Fong, and Jeanne Murray. "Argument in Favor of Proposition 22." *California Voter Information Guide, Primary Election, March 7,* 2000, 52. http://traynor.uchastings.edu/ballot_pdf/2000p.pdf.

Bell, Derrick A., Jr. "The Referendum: Democracy's Barrier to Racial Equality." 54 WASH. L. REV. 1 (1978).

Benjamin, Gerald and Michael J. Malbin, eds. *Limiting Legislative Terms.* Washington, D.C.: CQ Press, 1992.

Bennett, Robert W. "Popular Election of the President without Constitutional Amendment." 4 GREEN BAG 2d. 241 (2001).

Bessette, Joseph. *The Mild Voice of Reason: Deliberative Democracy and American National Government.* Chicago: University of Chicago Press, 1994.

Bice, Scott H. "*Anderson* and the Adequate State Ground." 45 S. CAL. L. REV. 750 (1972).

Bickel, Alexander M. *The Least Dangerous Branch: The Supreme Court at the Bar of Politics.* Indianapolis: Bobbs-Merrill, 1962.

Bickel, Alexander M. and Benno C. Schmidt, Jr. *The Judiciary and Responsible Government, 1910–1921.* New York: Macmillan, 1984.

Bird, Frederick L. and Frances M. Ryan. *The Recall of Public Officers: A Study of the Operation of Recall in California.* New York: Macmillan, 1930.

Boehmke, Frederick J. *The Indirect Effect of Direct Legislation: How Institutions Shape Interest Group Systems.* Columbus: The Ohio State University Press, 2005.

Boehmke, Frederick J. and R. Michael Alvarez, "The Influence of Initiative Signature Gathering Campaigns on Political Participation." Caltech/MIT Voting Technology Project Working Paper #27 (March 2005).

Bolt, Ernest C., Jr. *Ballots Before Bullets: The War Referendum Approach to Peace in America, 1914–1941.* Charlottesville: University Press of Virginia, 1977.

Bork, Robert H. *Slouching Towards Gomorrah: Modern Liberalism and American Decline.* New York: ReganBooks, 1996.

Botelho, Bruce M. and Christine O. Gregoire. "Brief of the States of Washington and Alaska as Amici Curiae in Support of Respondents, *California Democratic Party v. Jones,* No. 99–401." 2000 U.S. S. Ct. Briefs Lexis 240 (March 30, 2000).

Bowler, Shaun and Todd Donovan. *Demanding Choices: Opinion, Voting, and Direct Democracy.* Ann Arbor: University of Michigan Press, 1998.

_____. "Institutions and Attitudes about Citizen Influence on Government." *British Journal of Political Science* 32 (2002): 371–390.

_____. "Measuring the Effect of Direct Democracy on State Policy: Not All Initiatives are Created Equal." *State Politics and Policy Quarterly* 4, (Fall 2004): 345–363.

Bowler, Shaun, Todd Donovan, and Caroline J. Tolbert, eds. *Citizens as Legislators: Direct Democracy in the United States.* Columbus: The Ohio State University Press, 1998.

Bowler, Shaun and Amihai Glazer. "Hybrid Democracy and Its Consequences." Shaun Bowler and Amihai Glazer, eds. *Direct Democracy's Impact on American Political Institutions.* New York: Palgrave Macmillan, 2008.

Brennan, William H., Jr. "State Constitutions and the Protection of Individual Rights." 90 HARV. L. REV. 489 (Jan. 1977).

Briffault, Richard. "Distrust of Democracy." 63 U. TEX. L. REV. 1347 (1985).

Briggs, John V. "Arguments in Favor of Proposition 13." California Secretary of State, *California Voters Pamphlet, Primary Election, June 6, 1978*, 58. http://traynor .uchastings.edu/ballot_pdf/1978p.pdf.

Brinkley, Alan. "The Challenge to Deliberative Democracy." Alan Brinkley, Nelson W. Polsby, and Kathleen M. Sullivan, eds. *New Federalist Papers: Essays in Defense of the Constitution*. New York: W.W. Norton & Co., 1997.

Brinkley, Alan, Nelson W. Polsby, and Kathleen Sullivan. *The New Federalist Papers: Essays in Defense of the Constitution*. New York: W.W. Norton & Co., 1997.

Broder, David S. *Democracy Derailed: Initiative Campaigns and the Power of Money*. New York: Harcourt, Inc., 2000.

Brown, Edmund G. ("Pat") Brown, Erwin Loretz, and Bill Cosby. "Rebuttal to Argument in Favor of Proposition 17." California Secretary of State, *Proposed Amendments to the Constitution, Propositions and Proposed Laws Together with Arguments: General Election, Tuesday, November 7, 1972*, 43–44. http://traynor. uchastings.edu/ballot_pdf/1972g.pdf.

Bryan, William Jennings. "The People's Law." Repr. *S. Doc.* 523, 63rd Cong., 2nd sess., 1914.

Bryce, James. *The American Commonwealth*, Vol. I (Indianapolis: Liberty Fund 1995) (first published 1914).

Burton, David H., ed. *The Collected Works of William Howard Taft, Vol. IV: Presidential Messages to Congress*. Athens: Ohio University Press, 2002.

———, ed. *The Collected Works of William Howard Taft, Vol. V: Popular Government and The Anti-trust Act and the Supreme Court*. Athens: Ohio University Press, 2003.

Burns, John and The Citizens' Conference on State Legislatures. *The Sometime Governments: A Critical Study of the 50 American Legislatures by the Citizens Conference on State Legislatures*. New York: Bantam, 1971.

Butler, David and Austin Ranney, eds. *Referendums: A Comparative Study of Practice and Theory*. Washington, D.C.: American Enterprise Institute for Public Policy Research, 1978.

———. *Referendums Around the World: The Growing Use of Direct Democracy*. Washington, D.C.: American Enterprise Institute for Public Policy Research, 1994.

Bybee, Jay S. "Substantive Due Process and the Free Exercise of Religion: *Meyer, Pierce*, and the Origins of *Wisconsin v. Yoder*." 25 CAP. U. L. REV. 887 (1996).

Bybee, Keith J. "Introduction: The Two Faces of Judicial Power." Keith J. Bybee, ed. *Bench Press: The Collision of Courts, Politics, and the Media*. Stanford: Stanford University Press, 2007.

———, ed. *Bench Press: The Collision of Courts, Politics, and the Media*. Stanford: Stanford University Press, 2007.

Cain, Bruce E. "Epilogue: Seeking Consensus Among Conflicting Electorates." Gerald C. Lubenow and Bruce E. Cain, eds. *Governing California: Politics, Government, and Public Policy in the Golden State*. Berkeley: Institute of Governmental Studies Press, 1997.

Cain, Bruce E. and Elisabeth R. Gerber, eds. *Voting at the Political Fault Line: California's Experiment with the Blanket Primary*. Berkeley: University of California Press, 2002.

Cain, Bruce E., Sara Ferejohn, Margarita Najar, and Mary Walther. "Constitutional Change: Is It Too Easy to Amend our State Constitution?" Bruce E. Cain and Roger G. Noll, eds. *Constitutional Reform in California: Making State Government More Effective and Responsive*. Berkeley: Institute of Governmental Studies Press, 1995.

Cain, Bruce E. and Thad Kousser. *Adapting to Term Limits: Recent Experiences and New Directions*. San Francisco: Public Policy Institute of California, 2004.

Cain, Bruce E. and Kenneth P. Miller. "The Populist Legacy: Initiatives and the Undermining of Representative Government." Larry J. Sabato, Howard R. Ernst, and Bruce A. Larson, eds. *Dangerous Democracy?: The Battle Over Initiatives in America*. Lanham, MD: Roman & Littlefield, 2001.

Cain, Bruce E. and Roger G. Noll. "Principles of State Constitutional Design." Bruce E. Cain and Roger G. Noll, eds. *Constitutional Reform in California Making State Government More Effective and Responsive*. Berkeley: Institute of Governmental Studies Press, 1995.

California Commission on Campaign Financing. *Democracy by Initiative: Shaping California's Fourth Branch of Government*. Los Angeles: Center for Responsive Government, 1992.

California Secretary of State. *Proposed Amendments to the Constitution, Propositions and Proposed Laws Together with Arguments to be Submitted to the Electors of the State of California at the General Election, Tuesday, Nov. 3, 1964*, http://traynor.uchastings.edu/ballot_pdf/1964g.pdf.

_____. *Proposed Amendments to the Constitution, Propositions and Proposed Laws Together with Arguments to be Submitted to the Electors of the State of California at the General Election, Tuesday, Nov. 8, 1966*, http://traynor.uchastings.edu/ballot_pdf/1966g.pdf.

_____. *California Statement of Vote and Supplement, November 8, 1966 General Election*.

_____. *Proposed Amendments to the Constitution, Propositions and Proposed Laws Together with Arguments: General Election, Tuesday, November 7, 1972*, http://traynor.uchastings.edu/ballot_pdf/1972g.pdf.

_____. *Statement of Vote, November 7, 1972 General Election*.

_____. *California Voters Pamphlet, Primary Election, June 6, 1978*, 55–60. http://traynor.uchastings.edu/ballot_pdf/1978p.pdf.

_____. *Statement of Vote, November 4, 1986 General Election*.

_____. *California Ballot Pamphlet, Primary Election, June 5, 1990*, http://traynor.uchastings.edu/ballot_pdf/1990p.pdf.

_____. *California Ballot Pamphlet, General Election, November 8, 1994*, 50–55. http://traynor.uchastings.edu/ballot_pdf/1994g.pdf.

_____. *Statement of Vote, November 8, 1994 General Election*.

_____. *California Voter Information Guide, Primary Election, June 2, 1998*, http://traynor.uchastings.edu/ballot_pdf/1998p.pdf.

_____. *California Voter Information Guide, Primary Election, March 7, 2000*, http://traynor.uchastings.edu/ballot_pdf/2000p.pdf.

_____. *Statement of Vote, March 7, 2000 Primary Election*. http://www.sos.ca.gov/elections/sov/2000_primary/measures.pdf.

_____. *California General Election, Tuesday, November 4, 2008 Official Voter Information Guide*, http://traynor.uchastings.edu/ballot_pdf/2008g.pdf.

_____. *Statement of Vote, November 4, 2008 General Election*.

Campbell, Anne G. "In the Eye of the Beholder: The Single Subject Rule for Ballot Initiatives." M. Dane Waters, ed. *The Battle Over Citizen Lawmaking*. Durham, N.C.: Carolina Academic Press, 2001.

Cannon, Lou. *Governor Reagan: His Rise to Power*. New York: Public Affairs, 2003.

Casstevens, Thomas W. *Politics, Housing, and Race Relations: California's Rumford Act and Proposition 14*. Berkeley: Institute of Governmental Studies, 1967.

Castello, James E. "Comment: The Limits of Popular Sovereignty: Using the Initiative Power to Control Legislative Procedure." 74 CAL. L. REV. 491 (1986).

Chang, Stanley. "Updating the Electoral College: The National Popular Vote Legislation." 44 HARV. J. ON LEGIS. 205 (2007).

Charlow, Robin. "Judicial Review, Equal Protection, and the Problem with Plebiscites." 79 CORNELL L. REV. 527 (1994).

Chávez, Lydia. *The Color Bind: California's Battle to End Affirmative Action*. Berkeley: University of California Press, 1998.

Chiang, Harriet. "Film Captures Trials of Judge Henderson." *The San Francisco Chronicle* (October 7, 2005), F-1.

Choper, Jesse H. *Judicial Review and the National Political Process: A Functional Reconsideration of the Role of the Supreme Court*. Chicago: University of Chicago Press, 1980.

_____. "Observations on the Guarantee Clause – As Thoughtfully Addressed by Justice Linde and Professor Eule." 65 U. COLO. L. REV. 741 (1994).

Citrin, Jack. "Who's The Boss? Direct Democracy and Popular Control of Government." Stephen C. Craig, ed. *Broken Contract? Changing Relationships Between Americans and Their Government*. Boulder, CO: Westview Press, 1996.

_____. "Introduction: The Legacy of Proposition 13." Terry Schwadron, ed., *California and the American Tax Revolt: Proposition 13 Five Years Later*. Berkeley: University of California Press, 1984.

Citrin, Jack, Beth Reingold, Evelyn Walters, and Donald P. Green. "The 'Official English' Movement and the Symbolic Politics of Language in the States." *Western Political Quarterly* 43, no. 3 (Sept. 1990): 535–59.

Clark, Sherman J. "A Populist Critique of Direct Democracy." 112 HARV. L. REV. 434 (1998).

Collins, Richard B. and Dale Oesterle. "Governing By Initiative: Structuring the Ballot Initiative: Procedures that Do and Don't Work." 66 U. COLO. L. REV. 47 (1995).

Copeland, Gary W. "Term Limitations and Political Careers in Oklahoma: In, Out, Up, or Down." Gerald Benjamin and Michael J. Malbin, eds. *Limiting Legislative Terms*. Washington, D.C.: CQ Press, 1992.

Corwin, Edward S. *The Doctrine of Judicial Review: Its Legal and Historical Basis and Other Essays*. Princeton: Princeton University Press, 1914.

Cottrell, Edwin A. "Twenty-five Years of Direct Legislation in California." *Public Opinion Quarterly* 3 (Jan. 1939): 30–45.

The Council of State Governments. *The Book of the States* Vol. 38. Lexington, KY: The Council of State Governments, 2006.

_____. *The Book of the States* Vol. 39. Lexington, KY: The Council of State Governments, 2007.

Craig, Stephen C., ed. *Broken Contract: Changing Relationships Between Americans and Their Government*. Boulder, CO: Westview, 1996: 282.

Croly, Herbert. *Progressive Democracy*. New York: Macmillan, 1914.

Cronin, Thomas E. *Direct Democracy: The Politics of Initiative, Referendum and Recall*. Cambridge, MA: Harvard University Press, 1989.

Culver, John H. "The Transformation of the California Supreme Court: 1987–1997." 61 ALB. L. REV. 1461 (1998).

Culver, John H. and John T. Wold. "Rose Bird and the Politics of Judicial Accountability in California," 70 *Judicature* 86 (1986): 81–9.

Currie, David P. "The Constitution in the Supreme Court: The Powers of the Federal Courts, 1801–1835." 49 U. CHI. L. REV. 646 (1982).

Dahl, Robert A. *A Preface to Democratic Theory*, expanded edition. Chicago: University of Chicago Press, 2006.

Dann, B. Michael and Randall M. Hansen. "National Summit on Improving Judicial Selection: Judicial Retention Elections." 34 LOY. L.A. L. REV. 1429 (2001).

"Death Penalty and the Court." *The San Francisco Examiner* (February 20, 1972).

De Tocqueville, Alexis. *Democracy in America*. Translated by George Lawrence. Edited by J. P. Mayer. New York: HarperCollins 2000.

Deukmejian, George, S. C. Masterson, and John W. Holmdahl. "Argument in Favor of Proposition 17." California Secretary of State, *Proposed Amendments to the Constitution, Propositions and Proposed Laws Together with Arguments: General Election, Tuesday, November 7, 1972*, 42. http://library.uchastings.edu/ballot_pdf/1972g.pdf.

Dolan, Maura and Tami Abdollah. "Gay Rights Backers File 3 Suits Challenging Prop. 8." *The Los Angeles Times*, November 6, 2008.

DiCamillo, Mark and Mervin Field. "55% of Voters Oppose Proposition 8, the Initiative to Ban Same-Sex Marriages in California." The Field Poll, Release #2287, September 18, 2008.

DiMassa, Cara Mia and Jessica Garrison. "Why Gays, Blacks are Divided on Proposition 8: For Many African Americans, it's not a Civil Rights Issue." *The Los Angeles Times* (November 8, 2008), A-1.

Dinan, John J. *Keeping the People's Liberties: Legislators, Citizens, and Judges as Guardians of Rights*. Lawrence: University Press of Kansas, 1998.

_____. "Court-constraining Amendments and the State Constitutional Tradition." 38 RUTGERS L. J. 983 (2007).

Dodd, Walter F. "The Recall and Political Responsibility of Judges." 10 MICH. L. REV. 79 (1911).

Domanick, Joe. *Cruel Justice: Three Strikes and the Politics of Crime in America's Golden State*. Berkeley: University of California Press, 2004.

Donovan, Todd. "Direct Democracy as 'Super-Precedent'? Political Constraints of Citizen-Initiated Laws." 43 WILLAMETTE L. REV. 191 (2007).

Donovan, Todd and Shaun Bowler. "Direct Democracy and Minority Rights: An Extension." *American Journal of Political Science* 42, no. 3 (1998): 1020–4.

Drage, Jennie. "State Efforts to Regulate the Initiative Process." M. Dane Waters, ed. *The Battle Over Citizen Lawmaking: An In-Depth Review of the Growing Trend to Regulate the People's Tool of Self-Government: The Initiative and Referendum Process*. Durham: Carolina Academic Press, 2001.

Dubois, Philip L. and Floyd Feeney. "Improving the California Initiative Process: Options for Change." 3 *CPS Brief* (California Policy Seminar, Nov. 1991): 1–5.

_____. *Lawmaking by Initiative: Issues, Options, and Comparisons*. New York: Agathon Press, 1998.

Duncan, Christopher M. *The Anti-Federalists and Early American Political Thought*. DeKalb, IL: Northern Illinois University Press, 1995.

DuVivier, K. K. "State Ballot Initiatives in the Federal Preemption Equation: A Medical Marijuana Case Study." 40 WAKE FOREST L. REV. 221 (2005).

Egan, Patrick J. and Kenneth Sherrill. "California's Proposition 8: What Happened, and What Does the Future Hold?" National Gay and Lesbian Task Force, January 2009, http://www.thetaskforce.org/downloads/issues/egan_sherrill_prop8_1_6_09.pdf.

Ehlers, Scott. "Drug Policy Reform Initiatives and Referenda." M. Dane Waters, ed. *Initiative and Referendum Almanac*. Durham: Carolina Academic Press, 2003.

Elliot, Jonathan, ed. *The Debates on the Federal Constitution in the Convention Held at Philadelphia in 1787*, Vol. V. New York: Burt Franklin, 1888.

_____. *The Debates of the Several State Conventions on the Adoption of the Constitution*, Vols. 1–4. New York: Burt Franklin, 1888.

Ellis, Richard J. *Democratic Delusions: The Initiative Process in America*. Lawrence: University Press of Kansas, 2002.

_____. "Signature Gathering in the Initiative Process: How Democratic is It?" 64 Mont. L. Rev. 35 (2003).

Ely, John Hart. *Democracy and Distrust: A Theory of Judicial Review*. Cambridge, MA: Harvard University Press, 1980.

Emmert, Craig F. "Judicial Review in State Supreme Courts: Opportunity and Activism." Paper Presented at the 1988 Annual Meeting of the Midwest Political Science Association, Chicago IL (1988).

Epstein, David F. *The Political Theory of* The Federalist. Chicago: University of Chicago Press, 1984.

Eule, Julian N. "Judicial Review of Direct Democracy." 99 Yale L. J. 1503 (1990).

_____. "Representative Government: The People's Choice." 67 Chi.-Kent L. Rev. 777 (1991).

_____. "Crocodiles in the Bathtub: State Courts, Voter Initiatives, and the Threat of Electoral Reprisal." 65 U. Colo. L. Rev. 733 (1994).

Even, Jeffrey T. "Direct Democracy in Washington: A Discourse on the Peoples' Powers of Initiative and Referendum." 32 Gonz. L. Rev. 247 (1996–7).

"Federal Judge Issues Final Ruling on Immigrant Initiative." Associated Press State and Local Wire (September 13, 1999).

The Field Institute. "A Digest Describing the Public's Confidence in Institutions." *California Opinion Index*, vol. 6 (October 1981).

_____. The Field Poll, (August 1994).

_____. The Field Poll #1909 (October 31, 1998).

Flournoy, Houston I., Tom Bradley, and Gary Sirbu. "Argument Against Proposition 13." California Secretary of State, *California Voters Pamphlet, Primary Election, June 6, 1978*, 59. http://traynor.uchastings.edu/ballot_pdf/1978p.pdf.

Frankfurter, Felix. *The Public and Its Government*. New Haven: Yale University Press, 1930.

_____. "The Supreme Court in the Mirror of Justices." 105 U. Penn. L. Rev. 781 (1957).

Frey, Bruno S. and Lorenz Goette. "Does the Popular Vote Destroy Civil Rights?" *American Journal of Political Science* 42, no. 4 (1998): 1343–8.

Frickey, Philip P. "Interpretation on the Borderline: Constitution, Canons, Direct Democracy." 1 N.Y.U. J. Legis. & Pub. Pol'y 105 (1997).

Friedelbaum, Stanley H., ed. *Human Rights in the States: New Directions in Constitutional Policymaking*. New York: Greenwood Press, 1988.

Frohnmeyer, David B. and Hans A. Linde. "Initiating 'Laws' in the form of 'Constitutional Amendments': An Amicus Brief." 34 Willamette L. Rev. 749 (1998).

Fund, John H. "Term Limitation: An Idea Whose Time Has Come." Gerald Benjamin and Michael J. Malbin, eds. *Limiting Legislative Terms*. Washington, D.C.: CQ Press, 1992.

_____. "Taking the Initiative: How Judges Threaten Direct Democracy." *The Wall Street Journal* (October 16, 2006).

Gamble, Barbara S. "Putting Civil Rights to a Popular Vote." *American Journal of Political Science* 41, no. 1 (1997): 245–269.

Garrett, Elizabeth. "Hybrid Democracy." 73 Geo. Wash. L. Rev. 1096 (2005).

Garrett, Elizabeth, Elizabeth Graddy, and Howell Jackson, eds. *Fiscal Challenges: An Inter-Disciplinary Approach to Budget Policy*. New York: Cambridge University Press, 2008.

Gerber, Elisabeth R. "Reforming the California Initiative Process: A Proposal to Increase Flexibility and Legislative Accountability." Bruce E. Cain and Roger G. Noll, eds. *Constitutional Reform in California: Making State Government More Effective and Responsive*. Berkeley: Institute of Governmental Studies Press, 1995.

———. "Legislative Response to the Threat of Popular Initiatives." *American Journal of Political Science* 40, no. 1 (1996): 99–128.

———. *The Populist Paradox: Interest Group Influence and the Promise of Direct Legislation*. Princeton: Princeton University Press, 1999.

———. "Prospects for Reforming the Initiative Process." Larry J. Sabato, Howard R. Ernst, and Bruce A. Larson, eds. *Dangerous Democracy?: The Battle Over Initiatives in America*. Lanham, MD: Roman & Littlefield, 2001.

Gerber, Elisabeth R., Arthur Lupia, Mathew D. McCubbins, and D. Roderick Kiewiet. *Stealing the Initiative: How State Government Responds to Direct Democracy*. Upper Saddle River, New Jersey: Prentice Hall, 2001.

Glendon, Mary Ann. *Rights Talk: The Impoverishment of Political Discourse*. New York: The Free Press, 1991.

Goebel, Thomas. *A Government by the People: Direct Democracy in America, 1890–1940*. Chapel Hill: University of North Carolina Press, 2002.

Goldberg, Arthur J. and Alan M. Dershowitz. "Declaring the Death Penalty Unconstitutional." 83 Harv. L. Rev. 1773 (1970).

Gordon, James D. III and David B. Magleby. "Pre-election Judicial Review of Initiatives and Referendums." 64 Notre Dame L. Rev. 298 (1989).

Green, Ashbel S. and Lisa Grace Lednicer. "State High Court Strikes Term Limits." *The Oregonian* (January 17, 2002), A-1.

Grodin, Joseph R. "Developing a Consensus of Constraint: A Judge's Perspective on Judicial Retention Elections." 61 S. Cal. L. Rev. 1969 (1988).

———. *In Pursuit of Justice: Reflections of a State Supreme Court Justice*. Berkeley: University of California Press, 1989.

Guarino, David R. "Poll Finds Mass.-ive Backing for Gay Unions; Narrow Marriage Support." *The Boston Herald* (November 23, 2003), 7.

Gunn, P. F. "Initiatives and Referenda: Direct Democracy and Minority Interests." *Urban Law Annual* 22 (1981): 135–59.

Gunther, Gerald. *Learned Hand: The Man and the Judge*. New York: Knopf, 1994.

Hajnal, Zoltan L., Elisabeth R. Gerber, and Hugh Louch. "Minorities and Direct Legislation: Evidence from California Ballot Proposition Elections." *Journal of Politics* 64, no. 1 (2002): 154–77.

Hall, Charles W. "Down, Dirty Judicial Races: Elections Reshape Supreme Court." *The Clarion-Ledger* (November 16, 2008).

Hamilton, Alexander, James Madison, and John Jay. *The Federalist Papers*. Clinton Rossiter, ed. New York: Signet Classic, 2003.

Hamilton, Howard D. "Direct Legislation: Some Implications of Open Housing Referenda." *American Political Science Review* 64, no. 1 (Mar. 1970): 124–37.

Hartnett, Edward. "Why is the Supreme Court of the United States Protecting State Judges from Popular Democracy?" 75 TEX. L. REV. 907 (1997).

Hasen, Richard L. "Judging the Judges of Initiatives: A Comment on Holman and Stern." 31 LOY. L.A. L. REV. 1267 (1998).

———. "Ending Court Protection of Voters from the Initiative Process." 116 YALE L. J. POCKET PART 117 (2006).

Haskell, John. *Direct Democracy or Representative Government? Dispelling the Populist Myth.* Boulder, CO: Westview Press, 2001.

Haynes, George H. "'People's Rule' in Oregon, 1910." *Political Science Quarterly* 26, no. 1 (March 1911): 32–62.

Hendrick, Burton J. "The Initiative and Referendum and How Oregon Got Them." *McClure's Magazine* (July 1911), 235.

Hero, Rodney E., Caroline J. Tolbert, and Robert Lopez. "Race/Ethnicity and Direct Democracy: Reexamining Official English and Its Implications." Paper presented at the Annual Meeting of the American Political Science Association, August 26–September 1, 1996, San Francisco, CA.

Hicks, John D. *The Populist Revolt: A History of the Farmers' Alliance and the People's Party.* Minneapolis: University of Minnesota Press, 1931.

Higham, John. *Strangers in the Land: Patterns of American Nativism, 1860–1925.* New Brunswick: Rutgers University Press, 1955.

Hill, Elizabeth G. *Ballot Box Budgeting.* Menlo Park, CA: EdSource Publications, 1990.

Hofstadter, Richard. *The Age of Reform: From Bryan to F.D.R.* New York: Vintage Books, 1955.

Holman, Craig B. and Robert Stern. "Judicial Review of Ballot Initiatives: The Changing Role of the State and Federal Courts." 31 LOY. L.A. L. REV. 1239 (1998).

Holsinger, M. Paul. "The Oregon School Bill Controversy, 1922–1925." *The Pacific Historical Review* 37, no. 3 (Aug. 1968): 327–41.

Hook, Janet. "House Votes Down Term Limits, Deals Setback to GOP Congress." *The Los Angeles Times* (March 30, 1995), A-1.

Howard, Thomas W., ed. *The North Dakota Political Tradition.* Ames, Iowa: Iowa State University Press, 1981.

Hunt, Gaillard and James B. Scott, eds. *Debates in the Federal Convention of 1787 Reported by James Madison.* Buffalo, New York: Prometheus Books, 1920.

Hyink, Bernard L. "California Revises Its Constitution." *Western Political Quarterly,* 22, no. 3 (Sept. 1969): 637–654.

Initiative and Referendum Institute. Historical Database. http://www.iandrinstitute.org/.

Jacob, Paul. "Term Limits and the I & R Process." M. Dane Waters, ed., *Initiative and Referendum Almanac.* Durham: Carolina Academic Press, 2003.

———. "Silence Isn't Golden: The Legislative Assault on Citizen Initiatives." M. Dane Waters, ed. *The Battle Over Citizen Lawmaking: An In-Depth Review of the Growing Trend to Regulate the People's Tool of Self-Government: The Initiative and Referendum Process.* Durham: Carolina Academic Press, 2001.

Jarvis, Howard with Robert Pack. *I'm Mad as Hell.* New York: Times Books, 1979.

Johnson, Claudius. "The Adoption of the Initiative and Referendum in Washington." *Pacific Northwest Quarterly* 35 (1944): 291–304.

Johnson, Donald Bruce and Kirk H. Porter, eds. *National Party Platforms, 1840–1972.* Urbana: University of Illinois Press, 1973.

Johnson, Kirk. "Coloradans to Consider Splitting Electoral College Votes." *The New York Times* (September 19, 2004), A-22.

Jones, Bill, Secretary of State. "A History of the California Initiative Process." Sacramento: California State Printing Office, 1996.

Jordan, Frank C., Secretary of State. "Summary of Amendments to the Constitution of California (1883–1920)." Sacramento: California State Printing Office, 1921.

Kagan, Robert A., Bliss Cartwright, Lawrence M. Friedman and Stanton Wheeler, "The Business of State Supreme Courts, 1870–1970." 30 STAN. L. REV. 121 (1977).

Kesler, Charles R. "Bad Housekeeping: The Case Against Congressional Term Limits." Gerald Benjamin and Michael J. Malbin, eds. *Limiting Legislative Terms*. Washington, D.C.: CQ Press, 1992.

_____. "The Founders' Views of Direct Democracy and Representation." Elliott Abrams, ed., *Democracy: How Direct?* Lanham, MD: Rowman and Littlefield, 2002.

_____. "Introduction." Alexander Hamilton, James Madison, and John Jay, *The Federalist Papers*, Clinton Rossiter, ed. New York: Signet Classic, 2003.

Key, V. O., Jr. and Winston W. Crouch. *The Initiative and the Referendum in California*. Berkeley: The University of California Press, 1939.

Klarman, Michael J. "Majoritarian Judicial Review: The Entrenchment Problem." 85 GEO. L. J. 491 (1997).

Knopff, Rainer. "Populism and the Politics of Rights: The Dual Attack on Representative Democracy." *Canadian Journal of Political Science* 31, no. 4 (Dec. 1998): 683–705.

Koppelman, Andrew. "*Romer v. Evans* and Invidious Intent." 6 WM & MARY BILL OF RTS J. 89 (1997).

Kousser, Thad. *Term Limits and the Dismantling of Legislative Professionalism*. New York: Cambridge University Press, 2005.

Kousser, Thad, Mathew D. McCubbins, and Kaj Rozga. "When Does the Ballot Box Limit the Budget? Politics and Spending Limits in California, Colorado, Utah, and Washington." Elizabeth Garrett, Elizabeth Graddy, and Howell Jackson, eds. *Fiscal Challenges: An Inter-Disciplinary Approach to Budget Policy*. New York: Cambridge University Press, 2008.

Koza, John R., Barry Fadem, Mark Grueskin, Michael Mandell, Robert Richie, and Joseph Zimmerman. *Every Vote Equal: A State-Based Plan for Electing the President by National Popular Vote*. Los Altos, CA: National Popular Vote Press, 2006.

Kurland, Philip B. and Gerhard Casper, eds. *Landmark Briefs and Arguments of the Supreme Court of the United States*. Arlington, VA: University Publications, 1975.

Lacey, Michael J. and Knud Haakonssen. "History, Historicism, and the Culture of Rights." Michael J. Lacey and Knud Haakonssen, eds. *A Culture of Rights: The Bill of Rights in Philosophy, Politics, and Law – 1791 and 1991*. New York: Cambridge University Press, 1991.

Langer, Laura. *Judicial Review in State Supreme Courts: A Comparative Study*. Albany: State University of New York Press, 2002.

LaPalombara, Joseph G. *The Initiative and Referendum in Oregon: 1938–1948*. Corvallis: Oregon State College Press, 1950.

LaPalombara, Joseph G. and Charles Hagan. "Direct Legislation: An Appraisal and a Suggestion." *American Political Science Review*, 45, no. 2 (June 1951): 400–421.

Latzer, Barry. " California's Constitutional Counterrevolution." G. Alan Tarr, ed. *Constitutional Politics in the States: Contemporary Controversies and Historical Patterns*. Westport, CT: Greenwood Press, 1996.

"The Lawyers to the Defense." *The New York Times* (March 5, 1912), 10.

LaVally, Rebecca and Russell Snyder. "Proposition 13 Paved the Way for Tax Revolts Across U.S." *The Los Angeles Times* (February 14, 1988), A-3.

Lawrence, Jill. "Favorable Conditions Make Amendments Moot: Public Approves of GOP Goals, but 'Intensity is Gone.'" *USA Today* (February 25, 1997).

"The Lawyers to the Defense." *The New York Times* (March 5, 1912), 10.

Lee, Eugene C. "The Revision of California's Constitution." 3 *CPS Brief* (California Policy Seminar, April 1991): 1–8.

Leip, Dave. "1892 Presidential General Election Results." *Dave Leip's Atlas of U.S. Presidential Elections.* http://www.uselectionatlas.org/RESULTS/national.php?f=0&year=1892.

Lerche, Charles O., Jr. "The Guarantee Clause in Constitutional Law." *The Western Political Quarterly* 2, no. 3, (Sept. 1949): 358–374.

Lincoln, Abraham. *First Inaugural Address*, March 4, 1861.

Linde, Hans A. "First Things First: Rediscovering the States' Bill of Rights." 9 U. Balt. L. Rev. 379 (1980).

_____. "When is Initiative Lawmaking Not 'Republican Government'?" 17 Hastings Const. L. Q. 159 (1989).

_____. "When Initiative Lawmaking Is Not 'Republican Government'": The Campaign Against Homosexuality." 72 Ore. L. Rev. 19 (1993).

_____. "Who is Responsible for Republican Government?" 65 U. Colo. L. Rev. 709 (1994).

Lipscomb, Andrew A. and Albert E. Bergh, eds. *The Writings of Thomas Jefferson*, Vol. 15. Washington, D.C.: Thomas Jefferson Memorial Association, 1904.

Lobingier, Charles Sumner. *The People's Law or Popular Participation in Law-making.* New York: Macmillan, 1909.

Lodge, Henry Cabot. *The Democracy of the Constitution and Other Addresses and Essays*. New York: Charles Scribner's Sons, 1915.

Lowenstein, Daniel Hays. "California Initiatives and the Single-Subject Rule." 30 U.C.L.A. L. Rev. 936 (1983).

_____. "Initiatives and the New Single Subject Rule." 1 *Election Law Journal* 35 (2002).

Lowenstein, Daniel Hays and Richard L. Hasen, eds. *Election Law: Cases and Materials*, Third Edition. Durham: Carolina Academic Press, 2004.

Lubenow, Gerald C., ed. *California Votes: The 1994 Governor's Race: An Inside Look at the Candidates and Their Campaigns by the People Who Managed Them.* Berkeley: Institute of Governmental Studies Press, 1995.

Lutz, Donald S. "The Electoral College in Historical and Philosophical Perspective." Paul D. Schumaker and Burdett A Loomis, eds. *Choosing a President: The Electoral College and Beyond*. New York: Chatham House Publishers/Seven Bridges Press, 2002.

_____. "Patterns in Amending of American State Constitutions." G. Alan Tarr, ed. *Constitutional Politics in the States: Contemporary Controversies and Historical Patterns.* Westport, CT: Greenwood Press, 1996.

Maass, Dave. "The Mark of a Clean Election." *Tucson Weekly* (May 30, 2002).

Madison, James. *Papers of Madison*, Vol. 12. Robert Allen Rutland, ed. Charlottesville: University Press of Virginia, 1979.

Magleby, David B. *Direct Legislation: Voting on Ballot Propositions in the United States.* Baltimore: Johns Hopkins University Press, 1984.

Manweller, Mathew. *The People vs. The Courts: Judicial Review and Direct Democracy in the American Legal System*. Bethesda, MD: Academica Press, 2005.

Mathews, Joe. *The People's Machine: Arnold Schwarzenegger and the Rise of Blockbuster Democracy*. New York: Public Affairs, 2006.

Matsusaka, John G. *For the Many or the Few: The Initiative, Public Policy, and American Democracy*. Chicago: University of Chicago Press, 2004.

———. "Direct Democracy and Fiscal Gridlock: Have Voter Initiatives Paralyzed the California Budget? *State Politics and Policy Quarterly*, 5, no. 3 (2005): 248–264.

McCuan, David, Shaun Bowler, Todd Donovan, and Ken Fernandez. "California's Political Warriors: Campaign Professionals and the Initiative Process." Shaun Bowler, Todd Donovan and Caroline J. Tolbert, eds. *Citizens as Legislators: Direct Democracy in the United States*. Columbus: The Ohio State University Press, 1998.

McKay, Robert B. *Reapportionment: The Law of Politics and Equal Representation*. New York: Twentieth Century Fund, 1965.

McWilliams, Carey. "Government by Whitaker and Baxter." *The Nation* (April 14, April 21, May 5, 1951).

Meagher, Ed. "Reagan Says Court Puts Itself 'Above the Will of the People,'" *The Los Angeles Times* (February 18, 1972), A-3.

———. "Court Setting Itself Above the People, Governor Charges." *The Los Angeles Times* (February 19, 1972), A-1.

Michael, Douglas C. "Judicial Review of Initiative Constitutional Amendments." 14 U.C. DAVIS L. REV. 461 (1980).

Miller, John Chester. *Crisis in Freedom: The Alien and Sedition Acts*. Boston: Little Brown, 1951.

Miller, Kenneth P. "Constraining Populism: The Real Agenda of Initiative Reform." 41 SANTA CLARA L. REV. 1037 (2001).

———. "The Davis Recall and the Courts." *American Politics Research* 33 (March 2005): 135–62.

Mosk, Stanley. "State Constitutionalism: Both Liberal and Conservative." 63 TEX. L. REV. 1081 (1985).

Mountjoy, Dick, Ronald Prince, and Barbara Kiley. "Argument in Favor of Proposition 187." California Secretary of State, *California Ballot Pamphlet, General Election, November 8, 1994*, 54. http://traynor.uchastings.edu/ballot_pdf/1994g.pdf.

Mowry, George E. *The California Progressives*. Berkeley: University of California Press, 1951.

———. *Theodore Roosevelt and the Progressive Movement*. Madison: University of Wisconsin Press, 1946.

Muir, William K., Jr. *Legislature: California's School for Politics*. Chicago: The University of Chicago Press, 1982.

Munro, William B., ed. *The Initiative, Referendum, and Recall*. New York: Appleton, 1912.

Murphy, Paul L. *World War I and the Origin of Civil Liberties in the United States*. New York: W.W. Norton & Co. 1979.

Musselman, Lloyd K.. "Governor John F. Shafroth and the Colorado Progressives: Their Fight for Direct Legislation, 1909–1910." MA thesis, University of Denver, 1961.

Myers, Hardy. "The Guarantee Clause and Direct Democracy." 34 WILLAMETTE L. REV. 659 (1998).

"National and California Exit Poll Results." *The Los Angeles Times* (November 6, 2008), A1.

National Conference of State Legislatures. "Legislative Term Limits: An Overview." http://www.ncsl.org/programs/legismgt/ABOUT/termlimit.htm.

New, Michael J. "Limiting Government Through Direct Democracy." *Policy Analysis*, No. 420. Washington, D.C.: Cato Institute, Dec. 13, 2001.

"No Longer a Republican." *The New York Times* (February 22, 1912), 8.

Northcutt, Jesse G. "The Recall in Colorado." THE GREEN BAG (September 1913).

Note. "Putting the 'Single' Back in the Single Subject-Rule: A Proposal for Initiative Reform in California." 24 U.C. DAVIS L. REV. 879 (1991).

Oberholtzer, Ellis Paxson. *The Referendum in America, Together with Some Chapters on the History of the Initiative and Other Phases of Popular Government in the United States*. New York: Charles Scribner's Sons, 1900.

O'Connell, Sue. "The Money Behind the 2004 Marriage Amendments." Helena, MT: Institute on Money in State Politics, 2006. Available from http://www.followthemoney.org/press/Reports/200601271.pdf.

"Odds Stacked Against Passage of Amendments." *Seattle Post Intelligencer* (February 25, 1997). http://www.seattlepi.com/national/161933_amend25.html.

Odegard, Peter H. *Pressure Politics: A Story of the Anti-Saloon League*. New York: Columbia University Press, 1928.

Olson, David J. "Term Limits Fail in Washington: The 1991 Battleground." Gerald Benjamin and Michael J. Malbin, eds. *Limiting Legislative Terms*. Washington, D.C.: CQ Press, 1992.

Oregon Blue Book. "Initiative, Referendum, and Recall: 1922–1928." http://bluebook.state.or.us/state/elections/elections14.htm.

Oregon State Library. "Walter Marcus Pierce." http://www.osl.state.or.us/home/lib/governors/wmp.htm.

State of Oregon, *Proposed Constitutional Amendments and Measures (with Arguments) to be Submitted to the Voters of Oregon at the General Election, Tuesday, November 7, 1922*.

Pacelle, Wayne. "The Animal Protection Movement: A Modern-Day Model Use of the Initiative Process." M. Dane Waters, ed. *The Battle Over Citizen Lawmaking: An In-Depth Review of the Growing Trend to Regulate the People's Tool of Self-Government: The Initiative and Referendum Process*. Durham: Carolina Academic Press, 2001.

Persily, Nathaniel A. "The Peculiar Geography of Direct Democracy: Why the Initiative, Referendum, and Recall Developed in the American West." 2 MICH. L. & POL'Y REV. 11 (1997).

Petracca, Mark P. "Rotation in Office: The History of an Idea." Gerald Benjamin and Michael J. Malbin, eds. *Limiting Legislative Terms*. Washington, D.C.: CQ Press, 1992.

Phillips, Frank. "Majority in Mass. Poll Oppose Gay Marriage; Survey Also Finds Civil Union Support." *The Boston Globe* (February 22, 2004), A-1.

Phillips, Frank and Andrea Estes. "Right of Gays to Marry set for Years to Come: Vote Keeps Proposed Ban Off 2008 State Ballot," *The Boston Globe* (June 15, 2007), A-1.

Phillips, Frank and Rick Kline. "Lawmakers are Divided on Response." *The Boston Globe* (November 19, 2003): A-1.

Pildes, Richard. H. "Foreword: The Constitutionalization of Democratic Politics." 118 HARV. L. REV. 28 (2004).

Pillsbury. E. S. and Oscar Sutro, "Brief of Pacific States Telephone and Telegraph Company in *Pacific States Telephone and Telegraph Company v. State of Oregon*," summarized in *Pacific States Telephone and Telegraph v. Oregon*, 223 U.S. 118 (1912).

Pinello, Daniel R. *America's Struggle for Same-Sex Marriage.* New York: Cambridge University Press, 2006.

Piott, Steven L. *Giving Voters a Voice: The Origins of the Initiative and Referendum in America.* Columbia: University of Missouri Press, 2003.

Polsby, Daniel D. "*Buckley v. Valeo*: The Special Nature of Political Speech." *Supreme Court Review* 1976 (1976): 1–43.

Polsby, Nelson W. "The Institutionalization of the U.S. House of Representatives." *The American Political Science Review* 62, no. 1 (March 1968): 144–68.

———. "Some Arguments Against Congressional Term Limits." 16 HARV. J. L. & PUB. POL'Y 101 (1993).

———. "Term Limits." Alan Brinkley, Nelson W. Polsby, and Kathleen M. Sullivan, eds. *New Federalist Papers: Essays in Defense of the Constitution.* New York: Norton & Co. 1997.

———. "Legislatures." Fred L. Greenstein and Nelson W. Polsby, eds. *Handbook of Political Science*, Vol. 3. Reading, MA: Addison-Wesley, 1975.

Porter, Kirk H. and Donald Bruce Johnson, eds. *National Party Platforms, 1840–1964.* Urbana: University of Illinois Press, 1966.

Porter, Mary Cornelia and G. Alan Tarr, eds. *State Supreme Courts: Policymakers in the Federal System.* Westport, CT: Greenwood Press, 1988.

Postman, David. "I-695 Ruling Fuels Debate Over Role of Courts." *The Seattle Times* (April 11, 2000), B-1.

Prentice, Ron, Rosemary "Rosie" Avila, and Bishop George McKinney. "Argument in Favor of Proposition 8" in California Secretary of State, *California General Election, Tuesday, November 4, 2008 Official Voter Information Guide*, 56. http://traynor.uchastings.edu/ballot_pdf/2008g.pdf.

Price, Charles M. "The Initiative: A Comparative State Analysis and Reassessment of a Western Phenomenon." *Western Political Quarterly* 28, no. 2 (June 1975): 243–262.

———. "The Guillotine Comes to California: Term-Limit Politics in the Golden State." Gerald Benjamin and Michael J. Malbin, eds. *Limiting Legislative Terms.* Washington, D.C.: CQ Press, 1992.

Pritchard, Amy. "A Brief History of Abortion Related Initiatives and Referendums." M. Dane Waters, ed. *Initiative and Referendum Almanac.* Durham: Carolina Academic Press, 2003.

"Progressing Backward." *The New York Times* (February 27, 1912), 8.

Public Policy Institute of California. *Just the Facts: Californians and the Initiative Process.* San Francisco: Public Policy Institute of California, 2006.

Pugno, Andrew, attorney for Proposition 22 Legal Defense and Education Fund. Interview. August 22, 2008.

Rakove, Jack N. "Parchment Barriers and the Politics of Rights." Michael J. Lacey and Knud Haakonssen, eds. *A Culture of Rights: The Bill of Rights in Philosophy, Politics, and Law – 1791 and 1991.* New York: Cambridge University Press, 1991.

Ransom, William L. *Majority Rule and the Judiciary: An Examination of Current Proposals for Constitutional Change Affecting the Relation of Courts to Legislation.* New York: Charles Scribner's Sons, 1912.

"Recall of Judicial Decision Held to be Unconstitutional." 92 CENTRAL LAW JOURNAL. 425 (1921).

Reed, Douglas S. "Popular Constitutionalism: Toward a Theory of State Constitutional Meanings." 30 Rutgers L. J. 871 (2001).

Reidinger, Paul. "The Politics of Judging." *A.B.A. Journal 73*, (April 1987): 52–58.

"Republican Contract with America." http://www.house.gov/house/Contract/CONTRACT.html.

"Reversing John Marshall." *The New York Times* (February 27, 1912), 10.

Reynolds, Mike and Bill Jones with Dan Evans. *Three Strikes and You're Out! A Promise to Kimber: The Chronicle of America's Toughest Anti-Crime Law*. Fresno, CA. Quill Driver Books, 1996.

"The Road to Despotism." *The New York Times* (March 9, 1912), 12.

Roe, Gilbert E. *Our Judicial Oligarchy*. New York: B.W. Huebsch, 1912.

Rojas, Aurelio. "Ruling on Ballot Title is Setback for Proposition 8 Backers." *The Sacramento Bee* (August 9, 2008), 3A.

Roosevelt, Theodore. "Criticism of the Courts." *The Outlook* (September 24, 1910).

———. "Nationalism and Popular Rule." *The Outlook* (January 21, 1911).

———. "Workmen's Compensation." *The Outlook* (March 13, 1911).

———. "A Charter of Democracy: Address Before the Ohio Constitutional Convention." Theodore Roosevelt. *Progressive Principles: Selections form Addresses Made During the Presidential Campaign of 1912*. New York: Progressive National Service, 1913.

———. "The Right of the People to Rule." Address at Carnegie Hall, New York, March 20, 1912. Theodore Roosevelt, *Progressive Principles: Selections form Addresses Made During the Presidential Campaign of 1912*. New York: Progressive National Service, 1913.

———. "A Confession of Faith" [1912]. Hermann Hagedorn, ed. *The Works of Theodore Roosevelt, Vol. XI: Social Justice and Popular Rule*. New York: Charles Scribner's Sons, 1925.

———. "Progressive Democracy: The People and the Courts." *The Outlook* (August 17, 1912).

———. "Introduction." William L. Ransom, *Majority Rule and the Judiciary: An Examination of Current Proposals for Constitutional Change Affecting the Relation of Courts to Legislation*. New York: Charles Scribner's Sons, 1912.

———. "To Benjamin Barr Lindsey" (November 16, 1912). Elting E. Morison, ed. *The Letters of Theodore Roosevelt*, Vol. 7. Cambridge. MA: Harvard University Press, 1954.

———. "The Right of the People to Review Judge-Made Law." *The Outlook* (August 8, 1914).

Roosevelt, Theodore and Henry Cabot Lodge. *Selections from the Correspondence of Theodore Roosevelt and Henry Cabot Lodge, 1884–1918*, Vol. II. New York: Charles Scribner's Sons, 1925.

Root, Elihu. "The Perils of the Judicial Recall." *Case and Comment*, Vol. 18, 308–313 (1911).

———. "Experiments in Government and the Essentials of the Constitution." Robert Bacon and James Brown Scott, eds., *Addresses on Government and Citizenship* (Cambridge, MA: Harvard University Press, 1916).

———. "Judicial Decisions and Public Feeling: Presidential Address at the Annual Meeting of the New York State Bar Association in New York City, January 19, 1912." Robert Bacon and James Brown Scott, eds., *Addresses on Government and Citizenship* (Cambridge, MA: Harvard University Press, 1916).

Ross, William G. *A Muted Fury: Populists, Progressives, and Labor Unions Confront the Courts, 1890–1937*. Princeton: Princeton University Press, 1994.

_____. *Forging New Freedoms: Nativism, Education, and the Constitution, 1917–1927*. Lincoln: University of Nebraska Press, 1994.

Rothenberg, Stuart. "Transplanting Term Limits: Political Mobilization and Grass-Roots Politics." Gerald Benjamin and Michael J. Malbin, eds. *Limiting Legislative Terms*. Washington, D.C.: CQ Press, 1992.

Rottman, David. "The State Courts in 2006: Surviving Anti-Court Initiatives and Demonstrating High Performance." *The Book of the States*, Vol. 38. Lexington, KY: The Council of State Governments, 2006.

Schaller, Thomas F. "Democracy at Rest: Strategic Ratification of the Twenty-First Amendment." *Publius* 28, no. 2 (Spring 1998): 81–97.

Schmidt, David D. *Citizen Lawmakers: The Ballot Initiative Revolution*. Philadelphia: Temple University Press, 1989.

Schrag, Peter. *Paradise Lost: California's Experience, America's Future*. New York: The New Press, 1998.

_____. "The Fourth Branch of Government: You Bet." 41 SANTA CLARA L. REV. 937 (2001).

_____. *California: America's High-Stakes Experiment*. Berkeley: University of California Press, 2006.

Schumacher, Waldo. "Thirty Years of the People's Rule in Oregon: An Analysis." *Political Science Quarterly*. 47 (June 1932): 243–58.

Sears, David O. and Jack Citrin. *Tax Revolt: Something for Nothing in California*, enlarged edition. Cambridge, MA: Harvard University Press, 1985.

Seelye, Katherine Q. "House Turns Back Measures to Limit Terms in Congress." *The New York Times* (March 30, 1995), A-1.

Seidman, Louis Michael. "*Romer's* Radicalism: The Unexpected Revival of Warren Court Activism." 1996 SUP. CT. REV. 203 (1996).

Sepp, Pete. "A Brief History of I & R and the Tax Revolt." M. Dane Waters, ed. *Initiative and Referendum Almanac*. Durham: Carolina Academic Press, 2003.

Shultz, Jim. *The Initiative Cookbook: Recipes and Stories from California's Ballot Wars*. San Francisco: Democracy Center, 1996.

Smith, Daniel A. *Tax Crusaders and the Politics of Direct Democracy*. New York: Routledge, 1998.

_____. "Overturning Term Limits: The Legislature's Own Private Idaho?" *PS: Political Science and Politics* 36 (2003): 215–20.

_____. "Homeward Bound?: Micro-Level Legislative Response to Ballot Initiatives." *State Politics and Policy Quarterly* 1, no. 1 (Spring 2001): 50–61.

Smith, Daniel A. and Dustin Fridkin "Delegating Direct Democracy: Interparty Legislative Competition and the Adoption of Direct Democracy in the American States." *American Political Science Review* 102, no. 3 (Aug. 2008): 333–50.

Smith, Daniel A. and Joseph Lubinski. "Direct Democracy During the Progressive Era: A Crack in the Populist Veneer?" *The Journal of Policy History* 14, no. 4 (2002): 350–83.

Smith, Daniel A. and Caroline J. Tolbert. *Educated by Initiative: The Effects of Direct Democracy on Citizens and Political Organizations in the American States*. Ann Arbor: The University of Michigan Press, 2004.

Smith, Duane A. "Colorado and the Judicial Recall." *The American Journal of Legal History* 7, no. 3 (1963): 198–209.

Smith, J. Allen. "Recent Institutional Legislation." *Proceedings of the American Political Science Association*. 4 (1907): 141–51.

Schwadron, Terry, ed. *California and the American Tax Revolt*. Proposition 13 Five Years Later. Berkeley: University of California Press, 1984.

Steyer, Tom. Letter to Patricia Galvan, Initiative Coordinator, Office of the Attorney General of the State of California, August 20, 2007. Available at http://ag.ca.gov/cms_attachments/initiatives/pdfs/2007-08-21_07-0048_Initiative.pdf.

Storing, Herbert J. *What the Anti-Federalists Were* For. Chicago: University of Chicago Press, 1981.

———, ed. *The Complete Anti-Federalist*. Chicago: University of Chicago Press, 1981.

———. *The Anti-Federalist: Writings by the Opponents of the Constitution*. Chicago: University of Chicago Press, 1985.

Sullivan, James W. *Direct Legislation by the Citizenship through the Initiative and Referendum*. New York: Twentieth Century Publishing Co., 1892.

Sullivan, Kathleen M. "Political Money and Freedom of Speech." 30 U.C. DAVIS L. REV. 663 (1997).

Taft, William Howard. "Veto Message [Returning without approval a joint resolution for the admission of the Territories of New Mexico and Arizona into the Union as States], August 22, 1911." David H. Burton, ed., *The Collected Works of William Howard Taft*, Vol. IV (Athens: Ohio University Press, 2002).

———. "The Judiciary and Progress." Address delivered at Toledo, Ohio, March 8, 1912, repr. *S. Doc*. 408, 62nd Cong., 2d. sess., 1912, 9.

———. "The Selection and Tenure of Judges." 38 REP. AM. BAR ASS'N 418 (1913).

———. "The Initiative and the Referendum." David H. Burton, ed. *The Collected Works of William Howard Taft*, Vol. V. Athens: Ohio University Press, 2003.

———. "The Initiative, the Referendum, the Recall." David H. Burton, ed. *The Collected Works of William Howard Taft*, Vol. V. Athens: Ohio University Press, 2003.

———. "The Representative System." David H. Burton, ed. *The Collected Works of William Howard Taft*, Vol. V. Athens: Ohio University Press, 2003.

Takaki, Ronald. *Strangers from a Different Shore: A History of Asian Americans*. New York: Little Brown, 1989.

Tallian, Laura. *Direct Democracy: An Historical Analysis of the Initiative, Referendum, and Recall Process*. Los Angeles: People's Lobby, 1977.

Tarr, G. Alan, ed., *Constitutional Politics in the States: Contemporary Controversies and Historical Patterns*. Westport, CT: Greenwood Press, 1996.

———. *Understanding State Constitutions*. Princeton: Princeton University Press, 1998.

———. "For the People: Direct Democracy in the State Constitutional Tradition." Elliott Abrams, ed. *Democracy: How Direct? Views from the Founding Era and the Polling Era*. Lanham, MD: Rowman and Littlefield, 2002.

———. "Politicizing the Process: The New Politics of State Judicial Elections," in Keith J. Bybee, ed., *Bench Press: The Collision of Courts, Politics, and the Media* (Stanford: Stanford University Press, 2007).

Tarr, G., Alan and Mary Cornelia Aldis Porter. *State Supreme Courts in State and Nation*. New Haven: Yale University Press, 1988.

"Term Limits: Full Scope of Defeat May Wait Until '96." *The Hotline* (March 30, 1995).

Thayer, James Bradley. "The Origin and Scope of the American Doctrine of Constitutional Law." 7 HARV. L. REV. 129 (1893).

Thomas, David Y. "Direct Legislation in Arkansas." *Political Science Quarterly* 29 (March 1914): 84–110.

_____. "Initiative and Referendum in Arkansas Come of Age." *American Political Science Review* 27, no. 1 (February, 1933): 66–75.

Thoron, Samuel and Julia Miller Thoron. "Argument Against Proposition 8" in California Secretary of State, *California General Election, Tuesday, November 4, 2008 Official Voter Information Guide,* 56. http://traynor.uchastings.edu/ballot_pdf/2008g.pdf.

"To Make Cowards of Judges." *The New York Times* (March 12, 1912), 12.

Tolbert, Caroline J. "Changing Rules for State Legislatures: Direct Democracy and Governance Policies." Shaun Bowler, Todd Donovan, and Caroline J. Tolbert, eds. *Citizens as Legislators: Direct Democracy in the United States.* Columbus: The Ohio State University Press, 1998.

_____. "Public Policymaking and Direct Democracy in the Twentieth Century: The More Things Change, the More They Stay the Same." M. Dane Waters, ed. *The Battle Over Citizen Lawmaking: An In-Depth Review of the Growing Trend to Regulate the People's Tool of Self-Government: The Initiative and Referendum Process.* Durham: Carolina Academic Press, 2001.

Tushnet, Mark. "Fear of Voting: Differential Standards of Judicial Review of Direct Legislation." 1 N.Y.U. J. LEGIS & PUB. POL'Y 1 (1997).

Tyack, David B. "The Perils of Pluralism: The Background of the *Pierce* Case." *The American Historical Review* 74, no. 1 (Oct. 1968): 74–98.

Uelmen, Gerald F. "Review of Death Penalty Judgments by the Supreme Courts of California: A Tale of Two Courts." 23 LOY. L.A. L. REV. 237 (1989).

_____. "Crocodiles in the Bathtub: Maintaining the Independence of State Supreme Courts in an Era of Judicial Politicization." 72 NOTRE DAME L. REV. 1133 (1997).

_____. "Handling Hot Potatoes: Judicial Review of California Initiatives After *Senate v. Jones.*" 41 SANTA CLARA L. REV. 999 (2001).

Villaraigosa, Antonio R., the Right Reverend William E. Swing, and Krys Wulff. "Argument Against Proposition 22," California Secretary of State, *California Voter Information Guide, Primary Election, March 7, 2000,* 53. http://traynor.uchastings.edu/ballot_pdf/2000p.pdf.

Vitiello, Michael and Andrew J. Glendon. "Article III Judges and the Initiative Process: Are Article III Judges Hopelessly Elitist?" 31 LOY. L.A. L. REV. 1275 (1998).

Wagoner, Jay J. *Arizona Territory 1863–1912: A Political History.* Tucson: University of Arizona Press, 1970.

Walsh, Edward. "Voters Say No but Sizemore Fights On." *The Sunday Oregonian,* September. 7, 2008, B-1.

Waters, M. Dane, ed. *The Battle Over Citizen Lawmaking: An In-Depth Review of the Growing Trend to Regulate the People's Tool of Self-Government: The Initiative and Referendum Process.* Durham: Carolina Academic Press, 2001.

_____, ed., *Initiative and Referendum Almanac.* Durham: Carolina Academic Press, 2003.

Wilson, Woodrow. *Congressional Government: A Study in American Politics,* Ninth Edition. Cambridge, MA: The Riverside Press, 1892.

_____. *Constitutional Government in the United States.* New York: Columbia University Press, 1908.

_____. "The Issues of Reform." William Bennett Munro, ed. *The Initiative, Referendum, and Recall.* New York: D. Appleton and Co., 1912.

Wolfinger, Raymond E. and Fred I. Greenstein. "The Repeal of Fair Housing in California: An Analysis of Referendum Voting." *American Political Science Review* 62, no. 3 (Sep. 1968): 753–769.

Wood, Gordon. *The Creation of the American Republic, 1776–1787*. Chapel Hill: University of North Carolina Press, 1969.

Yardley, William. "Drive to Alter Race Rules Advances." *St. Petersburg Times* (October 27, 1999) 1B.

Zimmerman, Joseph F. *The Recall: Tribunal of the People*. Westport, CT: Prager, 1997.

———. *The Initiative: Citizen Law-making*. Westport, CT: Prager, 1999.

Zimring, Franklin E., Gordon Hawkins, and Sam Kamin. *Punishment and Democracy: Three Strikes and You're Out in California*. New York: Oxford University Press, 2001.

Index